Insolvency in Commercial Arbitration

Insolvency in Commercial Arbitration

A German and International Perspective

Fabian van de Ven

Wolters Kluwer

Published by:
Kluwer Law International B.V.
PO Box 316
2400 AH Alphen aan den Rijn
The Netherlands
E-mail: lrs-sales@wolterskluwer.com
Website: www.wolterskluwer.com/en/solutions/kluwerlawinternational

Sold and distributed by:
Wolters Kluwer Legal & Regulatory U.S.
920 Links Avenue
Landisville, PA 17538
United States of America
E-mail: customer.service@wolterskluwer.com

ISBN 978-94-035-0067-6

e-Book: ISBN 978-94-035-0077-5
web-PDF: ISBN 978-94-035-0087-4

Submitted as PhD thesis at the Law Faculty of the University of Marburg

Table of Contents

List of Abbreviations xv

Preface xxi

Introduction 1
1 Topic 1
2 Objective, Scope and Method 3
3 Terminology 4

CHAPTER 1
Theoretical Background and Legal Framework 7
1 Insolvency in Germany 8
1.1 National Insolvency Framework 8
1.2 International Insolvencies 10
1.2.1 European Insolvencies: The EIR 10
1.2.2 Other International Insolvencies 12
1.2.3 The UNCITRAL Model Law on Cross-Border Insolvency 13
1.2.4 The UNCITRAL Model Law on Insolvency-Related Judgments 14
2 International Insolvency Theory 15
2.1 The Position of Insolvency Within a Legal Order 15
2.2 Territorialism 17
2.3 Universalism 17
2.4 The Practical Middle Ground 18
2.5 The German Approach 19
3 Arbitration in Germany 20
3.1 The Legal Framework 23
3.1.1 UNCITRAL Model Law on International Commercial Arbitration 24
3.1.2 The New York Convention 24

3.2 The Arbitration Agreement: The Basis for Arbitration 26
4 Arbitration Theory 28
4.1 The Jurisdictional Theory 29
4.2 The Contractual Theory and Delocalisation 30
4.3 The Hybrid Theory 31
4.4 The Autonomous Theory 32
5 Final Remark on the Theoretical Background and Framework 32

CHAPTER 2
Insolvency and Arbitration in the National Context: Germany 35
1 Arbitrability 36
1.1 Arbitrability and Public Policy 37
1.2 Objective and Subjective Arbitrability 38
1.3 Arbitrability in Germany 38
1.4 Arbitrability of Insolvency Disputes Generally 40
1.5 Arbitration of Insolvency Disputes in Germany 42
2 The Effect of Insolvency Proceedings on Arbitration 45
2.1 The Binding Power of Insolvency in the Seat Jurisdiction 46
2.1.1 The Relationship Between the Seat Jurisdiction and the Arbitration 47
2.1.2 Position and Analysis 50
i Localised or Delocalised Arbitration 50
ii Arbitration as the Performance of a Contract or Part of the Judicial Order 51
2.2 Standing and Representation: The Administrator 53
2.2.1 Standing in the Arbitration Proceedings 55
2.2.2 The Administrator's Power to Enter into Arbitration Agreements 57
2.3 The Effect on the Proceedings 58
2.3.1 Stay of Proceedings 59
i The Functioning of § 240 ZPO 60
ii Applicability to Arbitration 60
iii A Factual Stay of Proceedings 61
iv Analogous Application 63
2.3.2 Resumption of Proceedings 65
i Application of § 180(2) InsO to Arbitration 65
ii The Functioning of § 180(1) and (2) InsO: Continuation or New Proceedings 67
iii § 180(1) and (2) InsO and Arbitration 69
2.3.3 Claim Registration and Object of the Proceedings 72
2.3.4 The Special Case of Liabilities of the Estate 74
2.3.5 The Scope of the Proceedings: Preliminary Questions 75
2.3.6 The Choice of Arbitrator 77
2.4 The Effect of the Dissolution of the Insolvent 78
2.5 Conclusion and Position 84

3 The Effect of Insolvency Proceedings on the Arbitration Agreement 85
3.1 The Nature of the Arbitration Agreement 86
3.2 The Validity of the Arbitration Agreement 88
3.3 Binding Power of the Arbitration Agreement 89
3.4 Incapability to Perform the Arbitration Agreement 91
3.5 Possibilities to Dissolve, Defunct or Challenge an Existing Arbitration Agreement 94
3.5.1 § 103 InsO: The Right to Choose 94
3.5.2 § 115 InsO: Expiration of Mandates 96
3.5.3 §§ 129–133 InsO: Contesting Pre-insolvency Transactions 96
3.5.4 § 314 BGB: Terminating Continuing Contracts for Compelling Reasons 99
3.6 The Effective Scope of the Arbitration Agreement in Insolvency 101
3.6.1 Rights of Separation and Separate Satisfaction 103
3.6.2 § 103 InsO: The Right to Choose 103
3.6.3 §§ 129–133 InsO: Insolvency Contestation 106
3.6.4 Insolvency Verification: §§ 174 Et Seq. InsO 107
3.6.5 Insolvency Verification and Objecting Creditors 108
3.7 Conclusion on the Arbitration Agreement in Insolvency 109
4 The Effect of the Insolvency Proceedings on the Arbitrator's Contract 110
4.1 The Nature of the Arbitrator's Contract 111
4.2 Possibilities to Dissolve, Defunct or Challenge an Existing Arbitrator's Agreement 114
4.2.1 § 103 InsO: The Administrator's Right to Choose 114
4.2.2 § 113 InsO: Dissolution of Service and Employment Contracts 115
4.2.3 §§ 115, 116, 117 InsO: Dissolution of Mandates, Agencies and Proxies 116
4.2.4 §§ 129–133 InsO: Insolvency Contestation 117
4.2.5 §§ 314, 626 et seq. BGB: Termination for Compelling Reason 119
4.3 Conclusion: Effect of the Insolvency on the Arbitrator's Contract 120
5 Effect of the Insolvency Proceedings on Post-award Proceedings and Awards 120
5.1 Awards Rendered Post-insolvency 121
5.2 Awards Rendered During the Insolvency Proceedings 123
5.2.1 Insolvency Claims 123
5.2.2 Claims Regarding Exception Rights and Debts Incumbent on the Estate 124
5.3 Non-enforced Pre-insolvency Awards 125
5.3.1 The Status of the Award 125
5.3.2 Disputing the Claim 127
5.4 Awards in Enforcement Proceedings 130
5.4.1 Suspension of the Proceedings 130

5.4.2 Resumption of the Proceedings 132
5.5 Awards in Annulment Proceedings 136
5.6 The Grounds for Annulment and Non-enforcement in Insolvency 137
5.7 Correction, Interpretation and Additional Award Proceedings 138
5.7.1 Suspension of Ongoing Proceedings 138
5.7.2 Resumption of Proceedings and the Original Award 140
5.7.3 The Status of Additional Awards in Insolvency 140
5.8 Enforced Awards 141
5.9 Awards and Execution Proceedings 142
5.10 Enforced and Performed or Executed Awards 142
5.11 Award in Favour of the Insolvency Debtor 144
5.12 Conclusion and Summary: Effects of the Insolvency on Post-arbitration Proceedings 145
6 Conclusory Remarks to Chapter 2 146

CHAPTER 3
Insolvency in Arbitration: International Aspects 149
1 Recognition of Insolvencies 150
1.1 Relevant Concepts of Recognition 151
1.1.1 Recognition of Insolvency Rulings and Decisions 152
1.1.2 Recognition of the Substantive Effects of Insolvency 154
1.1.3 Recognition of Insolvency as a Fact 155
1.2 Recognition under the UNCITRAL Model Law on Cross-Border Insolvency 156
1.3 The European Insolvency Regulation 157
1.3.1 'Any judgment opening insolvency proceedings' 158
1.3.2 'handed down by a court of a Member State which has jurisdiction pursuant to Article 3' 160
1.3.3 'from the moment that it becomes effective in the State of the opening of proceedings' 160
1.3.4 Interim Conclusion: Recognition Based on the EIR 161
1.4 Recognition Based on the German Insolvency Code 161
1.4.1 'The Opening of a Foreign Insolvency Proceeding' 162
1.4.2 Unless the Court of Opening Is Not Competent under German Law 164
1.4.3 Unless It Constitutes a Violation of Public Order or Constitutional Rights 164
1.4.4 Interim Conclusion: Recognition Based on the German Insolvency Code 165
1.5 Recognition of Insolvency in Arbitration in General 166
1.5.1 Arbitration and Recognised 'Foreign' Insolvencies 167
1.5.2 Arbitration and Non-recognised 'Foreign' Insolvencies 169
i The Need for Recognition 169
ii The Ability to Recognise Foreign Insolvencies: Arbitrability and Scope 171

iii Applicable Law 173
iv Analysis 176
1.6 Recognition of Insolvency by Tribunals in Germany 176
1.6.1 Recognition in the Context of the InsO 177
1.6.2 Recognition in the Context of the EIR 178
1.7 Conclusion on the Recognition of Insolvencies in Arbitration 182
2 Conflict-of-Laws and Applicable Law in the Courts 182
2.1 The EIR 183
2.1.1 Conflict-of-Laws Rules 183
2.1.2 Coordination and Material Norms 186
2.1.3 The EIR and the Applicable Law to Insolvencies Effects on Arbitration and Related Issues 186
i Reference to National or International Insolvency Law 187
ii Preliminary Issues Regarding Article 18 EIR 189
iii The Scope of Article 7(2)(e) and Its Relationship to 18 EIR 192
iv Law Applicable to Objective Arbitrability 194
v Law Applicable to the Arbitrator's Agreement 195
vi Law Applicable to the Award: Status in Insolvency, Annulment and Enforcement 197
vii Interim Conclusion: Arbitration and the EIR 198
2.2 German Autonomous International Insolvency Law 198
2.2.1 Conflict-of-Laws Rules 199
2.2.2 Coordination and Material Norms 201
2.2.3 German Autonomous International Insolvency Law and the Applicable Law to the Effects of the Insolvency 201
i Applicability of § 335 InsO to Arbitration Agreements 202
ii Applicability of § 352 InsO to Arbitration Proceedings 203
iii §§ 335 and 352 InsO: The Syska v. Vivendi Question or Lack Thereof 205
iv Law Applicable to Objective Arbitrability 207
v Law Applicable to the Arbitrator's Agreement 207
vi The Law Applicable to Award: Status in the Insolvency and Annulment and Enforcement 208
vii Interim Conclusion: Arbitration and the German Autonomous International Insolvency Law 210
2.3 Conclusion on the Conflicts-of-Rules and Applicable Law in the Court 210
3 Conflict-of-Laws Rules Before the Tribunal 211
3.1 The Traditional Approach: Law of the Seat 212
3.2 The Autonomous Approach 214
3.3 Building an Autonomous Conflict-of-Laws Approach 218

3.3.1 Relevant Interests. 219
i Enforceability and Non-annulment 219
ii Legal Certainty, Predictability and Legitimate Expectations 221
iii Uniformity of Decisions 223
iv Neutrality 224
v Efficiency and Effectiveness 225
vi Final Remarks on Relevant Interests 225
3.3.2 Ex Nunc *or* Ex Tunc *Interests: Changing Interests* 226
3.3.3 Characterisation and Categorisation 226
3.4 Conclusion on the Conflict-of-Laws Rules Before a Tribunal 228
4 Applicable Law in the Arbitration 228
4.1 Applicable Law Within the Scope of the EIR 229
4.2 The Validity and Binding Power of the Arbitration Agreement 229
4.3 The Competence to Enter into Arbitration Agreements 233
4.4 Standing, Representation and Competencies of the Administrator and Insolvent 234
4.5 The Regulation of the Proceedings, Including the Staying of Proceedings 237
4.6 Objective Arbitrability 240
4.7 The Insolvent Estate 243
4.8 The Substantive Dispute 244
4.9 The Arbitrator's Contract 246
4.10 Conclusion on the Applicable Law in the Arbitration 247
5 Conclusory Remarks to Chapter 3 248

CHAPTER 4
Conclusion 249
1 Proposal for a List of Considerations for Insolvency in International Arbitration 249
1.1 Considerations for Insolvency in Arbitration 250
1.1.1 Relevance and Application 250
1.1.2 Definitions 251
1.1.3 General Principle 251
i Consideration No. 1 Concerning the Role of Insolvency in Arbitration 252
ii Consideration No. 2 Concerning Arbitrability 253
iii Consideration No. 3 The Arbitration Agreement 254
iv Consideration No. 4 The Role and Position of the Insolvency Practitioner 255
v Consideration No. 5 The Suspension of Proceedings 257
vi Consideration No. 6 Resumption of Proceedings 258
vii Consideration No. 7 The Object of the Proceedings 259
viii Consideration No. 8 Dissolution 260

ix Consideration No. 9 Impecuniosity and Costs 261
x Consideration No. 10 Arbitrator's Contract 262
xi Consideration No. 11 Applicable Law to Insolvency-Related Issues 262
2 Conclusory Remarks and Reflection 264

References 269

Index 287

List of Abbreviations

a.M. (Frankfurt)	*am Main* (German: on the Main); *Frankfurt am Main*
aF	*Alte Fassung* (German: old edition)
AktG	*Aktiengesetz* (German: Stock Corporation Act): German Stock Corporation Act of 6 September 1965
Annals FLB	Annals of the Faculty of Law in Belgrade
Arb.ML	Model Law on International Commercial Arbitration; UNCITRAL Model Law on International Commercial Arbitration of 21 June 1985, with amendments as adopted on 7 July 2006.
ASA Bull.	*Association Suisse de L'Arbitrage Bulletin*; Swiss Arbitration Association Bulletin
BAG	*Bundesarbeitsgericht* (German: Federal Labour Court); German Federal Supreme Court for Labour Law
BeckOK-*law*	*Beck'sche Online-Kommentar* (German: Beck's Online Commentary)
BGB	*Bürgerliches Gesetzbuch* (German: Civil Code); German Civil Code of 18 August 1896
BGE	*Bundesgericht* (German: Federal Tribunal); Federal Tribunal of Switzerland
BGH	*Bundesgerichtshof* (German: Federal Supreme Court); German Federal Supreme Court
Brook. J. Int'l L.	Brooklyn Journal of International Law
BSG	*Bundessozialgericht* (German: Federal Social Court); German Federal Supreme Court for Social Law
c.q.	*Casu quo* (Latin: in which case)
Cf.	Confer
Ch.	Chapter
CJEU	Court of Justice of the European Union

COMI	Centre of Main Interests
Contemp. Asia Arb. J.	Contemporary Asia Arbitration Journal
DIS	*Deutsche Institution für Schiedsgerichtsbarkeit* (German Arbitration Institute)
Diss.	*Dissertation* (German: Dissertation)
Disp. Resol. Int'l	Dispute Resolution International
e.g.	*Exemplum gratia* (Latin: for example)
EC	European Commission
ECT	Treaty Establishing the European Community
ed(s).	editor(s)
EGBGB	*Einführungsgesetz zum Bürgerlichen Gesetzbuche* (German: Introductory Law to the Civil Code); German Introductory Law to the Civil Code of 18 August 1896
EGInsO	*Einführungsgesetz zur Insolvenzordnung* (German: Introductory Law to the Insolvency Code) German Introductory Law to the Insolvency Code of 5 October 1994
EIR	European Insolvency Regulation; Regulation (EU) 2015/848 of the European Parliament and of the Council of 20 May 2015 on insolvency proceedings
EIR-old	European Insolvency Regulation; Council Regulation (EC) No 1346/2000 of 2 May 2000 on insolvency proceedings
et al.	*et alii* (Latin: and others)
et seq.	*et sequens* (Latin: and the following)
EU	European Union
EuInsVO	German abbreviation for EIR; *see* EIR
EuR	*Europarecht* (German: European Law)
EWiR	*Entscheidungen zum Wirtschaftsrecht* (German: Decisions on Business Law)
FamFG	*Gesetz über das Verfahren in Familiensachen und in den Angelegenheiten der freiwilligen Gerichtsbarkeit* (German: Act on Proceedings in Family Matters and Matters of Non-contentious Jurisdiction); German Act on Proceedings in Family Matters and in Matters of Non-contentious Jurisdiction of 17 December 2008
FK-*law*	*Frankfurter Kommentar* (German: Frankfurter Commentary)
fn.	Footnote
GG	*Grundgesetz* (German: Basic Law, often translated as Constitution); Basic Law for the German Federal Republic of 23 May 1949

GmbHG	*Gesetz betreffend die Gesellschaften mit beschränkter Haftung* (German: Law regarding Companies with limited liability); German Limited Liability Company Law of 20 April 1892.
GRUR	*Gewerblicher Rechtsschutz und Urheberrecht* (German: Intellectual Property and Copyright International)
GWR	*Gesellschafts- und Wirtschaftsrecht* (German: Company and Business Law)
HambKomm-*law*	*Hamburger Kommentar* (German: Hamburger Commentary)
i.a.	*inter alia* (Latin: amongst others)
i.e.	*id est* (Latin: it is)
ICC	International Chamber of Commerce
ICC Rules	Rules of Arbitration of the International Chamber of Commerce; https://iccwbo.org/dispute-resolution-services/arbitration/rules-of-arbitration/
ICSID	International Centre of the Settlement of Investment Disputes
IfM (Bonn)	Institut für Mittelstandsforschung (Bonn) (German: Institute for small business research)
IJLSR	International Journal of Legal Studies and Research
ILA	International Law Association
Ins.ML	Model Law on Cross-Border Insolvency Proceedings; UNCITRAL Model Law on Cross-Border Insolvency of 30 May 1997
InsO	*Insolvenzordnung* (German; Insolvency Code); German Insolvency Code of 5 October 1994
InsOBekV	*Verordnung zu öffentlichen Bekanntmachungen in Insolvenzverfahren im Internet* (German: Regulation on the publication of insolvency proceedings on the internet); German regulation for the online publication of insolvencies of 12 February 2002
InsVV	*Insolvenzrechtliche Vergütungsverordnung* (German: Insolvency Reimbursement Law) German Law for reimbursement in insolvency of 19 August 1998.
Int'l Trade & Bus. L. Rev.	International Trade and Business Law Review
InVO	*Insolvenz & Vollstreckung* (German: Insolvency and Execution)
JIBLR	Journal of International Banking Law and Regulation
JSDLP	Journal of Sustainable Development Law and Policy
KG	*Kammergericht* (German, literally; Chamber Court); Highest Regional Court of Berlin
KPB-*InsO*	*Kübler/Prütting/Bork* Commentary on the InsO
LCIA	London Court of International Arbitration
MJIL	Melbourne Journal of International Law

MüKo	*Münchener Kommentar* (German; Munich Commentary)
NCPC	*Code de procédure civile* (French: Civil Procedure Code); French Code of Civil Procedure of 14 May 1981 (book IV on Arbitration)
NJOZ	*Neue Juristische Online-Zeitschrift* (German: New Online Legal Journal)
NJW	*Die Neue Juristische Wochenschrift* (German: The new legal weekly magazine)
No(s).	*Numero(s)* (Latin: Number(s)); used to refer to margin numbers
Nr.	Number
Nw. J. Int'l L. & Bus.	Northwestern Journal of International Law & Business
NY	State of New York (U.S.)
NYC	New York Convention; The Convention on the Recognition and Enforcement of Foreign Arbitral Awards of 10 June 1958
NYJL	New York Law Journal
NZBau	*Neue Zeitschrift für Baurecht und Vergaberecht* (German: New Journal for Construction and Public Procurement Law)
NZG	*Neue Zeitschrift für Gesellschaftsrecht* (German: New Journal for Company Law)
NZI	*Neue Zeitschrift für Insolvenz- und Sanierungsrecht* (German; New Journal for Insolvency and Reorganisation Law)
NZM	*Neue Zeitschrift für Miet- und Wohnungsrecht* (German: New Journal for Rent and Housing Law)
OLG	*Oberlandesgericht* (German; Higher Regional Court); Higher Regional Court in Germany – Court of second instance
p(p).	Page(s)
P.R.C.	People's Republic of China
PILA	Private International Law Act
Rec.	Recital
Rev. Arb.	*Revue de l'Arbitrage* (French: Arbitration Review)
RIW	*Recht der Internationalen Wirtschaft* (German: Law of International Economy)
s.d.	*Sine dato* (Latin: without a date)
s.l.	*Sine loco* (Latin: without a place)
SA	*Société Anonyme* (French: anonymous company); Public Limited Liability Company in French language jurisdictions
SAcLJ	The Singapore Academy of Law Journal
SchiedsVZ	*Zeitschrift für Schiedsverfahrens* or German Arbitration Journal

Sic	*Sic erat scriptum* (Latin: So it was written); used to mark errors in source texts.
TFEU	Treaty on the Functioning of the European Union
US	United States (of America)
U.S.C.A.	United States Code Annotated
Univ.	*Universität* (German: University) or University; used in title supplement to German dissertations.
USBC	United States Bankruptcy Code; Title 11 U.S. Code 'Bankruptcy'
UK	United Kingdom
UNCITRAL	United Nations Commission on International Trade Law
v.	versus
VbrInsVV	*Verordnung zur Einführung von Formularen für das Verbraucherinsolvenzverfahren und das Restschuldbefreiungsverfahren* (German: Regulation on the introduction of forms for private insolvency and the discharge of residual debt); German form regulation for private insolvency and residual debts discharge of 17 February 2002
vol.	volume
Y.B. Com. Arb.	Yearbook Commercial Arbitration
Yale L.J.	Yale Law Journal
ZaöRV	*Zeitschrift für ausländisches öffentliches Recht und Völkerrecht* (German: Journal for foreign public law and international law)
ZinsO	*Zeitschrift für das gesamte Insolvenzrecht* (German: Journal for all of Insolvency Law)
ZIP	*Zeitschrift für Wirtschaftsrecht* (German: Journal for Business Law)
ZPO	*Zivilprozessordnung* (German: Civil Procedural Code) German Code of Civil Procedure of 12 September 1950
Zugl.	*Zugelassen* (German: Admitted); used in title supplements of German dissertations.

Preface

The writing of this book has been a journey, a journey with highs and lows, and a journey that would not have been possible without the help and advice of many friends, family members and colleagues.

I want to thank Prof. Dr Voit for his patience in his support of a doctoral candidate who, at the beginning of the journey, had not mastered the German language or the German legal system. Of course, I also want to thank Prof. Dr Wertenbruch for his efforts as my second corrector. Similar thanks goes to my wife Sonya and my parents for their endless support and understanding. My good friend Tim deserves mention for going above and beyond in his support. Finally, I also thank all the professionals that were so kind as to provide me with feedback and food for thought on the list of considerations.

Introduction

1 TOPIC

This book discusses how insolvency-related issues are (to be) dealt with in arbitral proceedings. When the fields of insolvency and arbitration clash resulting in many legal questions. Insofar as a dissertation allows, this book's purpose is to approach this clash and the resulting legal questions holistically.

There are three points that, in varying ways and compositions, are often made to introduce the subject discussed in this book. The first one is the growing importance of commercial arbitration. The second one is the increasing risk of international insolvency and importance of its regulation with reference to the financial crisis and the last is the seeming diagonal opposition between the fields of arbitration and insolvency. Running the risk of being wholly unoriginal, this introduction will also use these three points to introduce the topic and relevance of this work.

It can be seen in the statistics of nearly every major arbitration institution that the importance of arbitration is growing and has been growing for a while. For example, the International Chamber of Commerce (ICC) has more than doubled its caseload between 1993 and 2013, and the London Court of International Arbitration (LCIA) has multiplied its caseload by a multiple of ten in the same period.[1] In some fields, arbitration has become the primary and preferred method of dispute settlement. This is to a point where the 'alternative' in alternative dispute resolution almost seems inappropriate if it was not clear that the word alternative in this term has a more systematic meaning. The settling of disputes in the international commodity trade or large or international and often technical construction projects can hardly be imaged without the institution that is arbitration. The last decades of growth of the field have also come with a substantial professionalisation and specialisation of the field. The field mentioned above of construction arbitration is a good example thereof.

The trend towards more and more arbitration described above is clear and hardly disputed in practice. This brings us to the second point: the persisting and evolving

1. *Born*, International Commercial Arbitration, p. 16.

importance of insolvency regulation and the growing importance of international insolvency regulation. Insolvency has a long history. Its regulation, c.q. the regulation of the clash of opposing private interests and societal interests, has long been a subject in legal systems. However, the financial crisis that started a little over a decade ago and the preceding crisis in the early 2000s did indeed shine a fresh light on a need for more international coordination and cooperation in the field of insolvency. It also made the failures of current domestic insolvency regimes in many jurisdictions painfully clear. The field has responded. We have seen what could be called a 'turnaround' towards turnaround organisation and facilitation. Whereas classically insolvency regimes organised the 'death' of a company, the last decade has seen many jurisdictions introduce laws to promote the economic survival of companies through reorganisation and turnaround laws. These laws are meant to ensure that when the next financial bubble pops, it does not lead to the massive rise in corporate insolvencies, as seen at the financial crisis's height. During the previous crisis, this was the case in Germany. In Germany in the last two financial crises, the highest years in the crisis of the early 2000s saw rises in corporate insolvencies of 14.3% in 2001 and 16.4% in 2002 and the highest year in the financial crisis that started in 2008 was 2009, which saw a rise of 11.6%.[2] While corporate insolvencies have been steadily declining since 2009, October 2018 registered 3.5% more corporate insolvencies than that same month in 2017, with the Federal Statistic Office registering 1.694 corporate insolvencies for the month alone.[3] The (at the time of writing) ongoing Corona crisis has also yet to be reflected in the number of insolvencies,[4] although this is linked to measures such as the temporary suspension of the duty for companies to file for insolvency taken in April 2020.[5] A rise linked to the crisis is, however, to be expected.[6] Although the current situation is still a far cry from the numbers at the height of the crises, insolvency will remain a part of the lifecycle of corporations within the currently existing economic system. As such, their proper organisation is of enduring interest. The crises of the last two decades have shown that on the preventative front and the international scale, efficiency and effectiveness gains can be made in the insolvency legislation and framework. The prime example of the complexities that the insolvency frameworks must learn to handle appropriately is the Lehmann Brothers insolvency which led to insolvency

2. *Statistisches Bundesamt*, Insolvenzverfahren, p. 3.
3. *Statistisches Bundesamt*, Oktober 2018: 3.5% mehr Unternehmensinsolvenzen als im Oktober 2017.
4. *Uttamchandani/Muro/Bertens*, The Calm Before the Storm: Early Evidence on Business Insolvency amid COVID-19, https://blogs.worldbank.org/psd/calm-storm-early-evidence-business-insolvency-amid-covid-19.
5. *Statistisches Bundesamt*, Juli 2020: 16.7% weniger Unternehmensinsolvenzen als im Juli 2019 durch ausgesetzte Antragspflicht; *Uttamchandani/Muro/Bertens*, The Calm Before the Storm: Early Evidence on Business Insolvency amid COVID-, https://blogs.worldbank.org/psd/calm-storm-early-evidence-business-insolvency-amid-covid-19.
6. *Vizepräsidentin Prof. Dr Claudia Buch*, Finanzstabilitätsbericht 2020 der Deutschen Bundesbank, under 'Phase 2'; *Uttamchandani/Muro/Bertens*, The Calm Before the Storm: Early Evidence on Business Insolvency amid COVID-19, https://blogs.worldbank.org/psd/calm-storm-early-evidence-business-insolvency-amid-covid-19.

proceedings or related proceedings in at least fifteen different jurisdictions, showing us the insufficiencies in the insolvency organisation of many of them.[7]

The third point is the reason for this entire book: the clash between these two fields. Arbitration and insolvency represent two vastly different approaches to proceedings. A quote by a US court that has often served as an illustration hereto states: 'The statutory interaction inherent in the current dispute presents a conflict of near polar [sic] extremes: bankruptcy policy exerts an inexorable pull towards centralization while arbitration policy advocates a decentralized approach towards dispute resolution.'[8] This opposition is also clearly visible in the legal organisation of these two proceedings; the insolvency proceedings are very heavily regulated with little autonomy left for the parties involved, whereas the autonomy of the parties is the central tenet of arbitration. Regardless of what theoretical or doctrinal perspective one has, the potential for conflict is foreseeable. Add to this an international dimension, and the potential issues seem to multiply by several factors.

2 OBJECTIVE, SCOPE AND METHOD

Therefore, the objective of this book is to holistically investigate the issues that can occur when the fields of insolvency and arbitration interact. However, even a holistic approach needs boundaries and a perspective.

The perspective taken in this book is primarily that of the arbitral tribunal or the arbitration proceedings broadly. This perspective is primarily responsible for the ordering of the subjects in this book. An attempt has been made to order them in the order in which the tribunal and parties might be confronted with them. As such, issues that concern jurisdiction and preliminary issues in arbitration are talked about first, e.g., arbitrability. The perspective of the arbitral tribunal and proceedings also further specifies the goal of this book in the sense that not only does it mean to provide a holistic discussion of the subject interaction, but it also aims simultaneously to point in the right direction for tribunals that have to deal with such issues. Whereas this goal underlies much of the discussion in this book, it is most plainly visible in the shape chosen for the conclusion of this book. Aside from a more traditional conclusion, further conclusions will primarily take the shape of a list of substantiated considerations for tribunals dealing with insolvency in arbitration informed by the findings in this research. The author hopes that these might, in the future, help tribunals navigate the treacherous waters of insolvency in arbitration.

To further facilitate a better understanding and to prevent having to deal with a plethora of issues simultaneously, the interaction of insolvency and arbitration is first discussed in a purely domestic situation, only afterwards the complicating factor of internationality will be discussed. However, even the national discussion requires a good understanding of the legal framework and fundamental theories and doctrines underlying arbitration and insolvency. Therefore, the book is split into four main parts:

7. *Van de Ven*, The Cross-Border Insolvency Protocol: What Is It and What Is in It?, p. 6.
8. *U.S. District Court, D. Massachusetts*, 17 March 1987 – 80 B.R. 606, p. 610.

the first part (Chapter 1) is the theoretical and legal background, the second part (Chapter 2) is insolvency in arbitration in Germany, part three (Chapter 3) is insolvency in international arbitration, and the final part (Chapter 4) is the conclusion including the considerations. As a background and legal framework, the first part will be highly descriptive and serve an introductory purpose. It is the author's aim that someone who is not versed in arbitration and insolvency can, by reading this part, receive the necessary theory and background to follow the discussion in Parts II and III. For this reason, conclusions and positions by the author on these theories have been purposely left primarily for Chapters 2 and 3. In those parts, the author will directly relate these conclusions and positions to the discussion on the relevant interaction between insolvency and arbitration. This also enables the well-informed reader to skip ahead to parts relevant to him or her directly.

To prevent too many theoretical discussions which do not support the above goals, the term 'insolvency proceedings' in this book excludes reorganisation and turnaround proceedings and will generally be meant only to refer to proceedings that involve the complete divestment of the insolvent and the satisfaction or attempt thereto, of all creditors. At a few points, reference will be made to these excluded proceedings to contrast the discussion. Arbitration will refer to commercial arbitration, excluding investment arbitration from the discussions. Furthermore, this also excludes the other methods of alternative dispute resolution, such as mediation and conciliation. The primary domestic perspective taken in this book is the German one, although at points reference will be made to the regulation in other jurisdictions to provide an interesting contrast to the rules that apply in Germany and to internationalise and raise the relevance of the discussion on the domestic interaction between insolvency and arbitration.

An inherent and persistent issue of research in the field of arbitration is that academia is hamstrung by the confidentiality of arbitral awards, which leaves only a fraction of awards available for research. Nonetheless, in the literature and case law review made to write this book, much effort has been made to provide as many arbitration case law examples and discussions as possible. Due to the nature of arbitration, there is no hierarchy in the cited awards. An award's relative value and authority can only be established by its reasoning. Furthermore, a reasoning that frequently returns can, to a degree, be afforded more weight.

A further purpose of this book is to distil some practical guidance, which can perhaps make up for the sometimes lacking and sometimes confusing guidance of existing case law and literature as it can be used to fill in the gaps left there or provide a more international frame of reference. This practical guidance will take the form of a proposal for considerations for tribunals confronted with insolvency in arbitration. Specifically, the author has sought discussion with and feedback from practitioners on the draft of these considerations to bolster their usefulness in practice.

3 TERMINOLOGY

As a final issue to be discussed in this introduction, the terminology used herein must be mentioned. Above, specific terms were already discussed insofar as they limit or specify the scope of this research. The terms introduced here do not have such methodical significance and are mainly choices of convenience that need not be read into.

The first such semantic choice is the usage of the term insolvency over the term bankruptcy. Whereas insolvency is often also used to refer to the state of insolvency, in this book it is used to refer to insolvency proceedings. This term must mostly be understood also to cover bankruptcy proceedings, as they are called primarily in Anglo-American systems, as an overarching term needed to be chosen for use in this research. The term bankruptcy is still used to refer to specific procedures at some points in this book or citations from and references to case law and other sources from jurisdictions using this nomenclature.

Similarly, the term insolvency administrator, sometimes shortened to administrator, has been chosen as a neutral reference to the office or person holding the office created by insolvency regulations to administer the insolvent estate. Insolvency administrator, therefore, covers such titles as trustee, official receiver, curator and the German '*Insolvenzverwalter*'. In the singular, the insolvency administrator and the arbitrator will be referred to as 'he', as 'it' is not fitting. However, such a reference should, of course, be always understood to include all genders.

Furthermore, the French *ordre public* in international arbitration is widely used interchangeably with the English 'public policy'. *Ordre public* seems to be the preferred term in many civil law jurisdictions.[9] § 1059(2)(2)(b) ZPO (German Code of Civil Procedure) uses this term next to the German '*öffentlichen Ordnung*'. In this book, these terms will also be used interchangeably. However, this usage here is not meant to comment on the nature and definition of public policy and *ordre public* and existing discussion on how they do or do not differ.[10] Finally, the terms setting-aside or set-aside and annulment are similarly used interchangeably.[11]

9. *Born*, International Commercial Arbitration, 253, 333, 407.
10. Cf. *Schwarz/Ortner*, 'Chapter III: The Arbitration Procedure – Procedural Ordre Public and the Internationalization of Public Policy in Arbitration', 133, pp. 135–136.
11. *Born*, International Commercial Arbitration, p. 3164.

Chapter 1
Theoretical Background and Legal Framework

This part provides an elementary introduction to insolvency and arbitration's theoretical background and legal framework. Dealing with insolvency issues in international commercial arbitration is a very complex topic, as it has many aspects. For example, an international arbitral tribunal will have to contend with the question of which law to apply to questions that arise when a party goes insolvent. However, to build up to these questions and their possible answers, one first needs to understand and examine the fundamentals. As such, in this first part, the fundamentals will be discussed. The fundamentals are also necessary to form a well-founded opinion about the discussed opinions and solutions, as they form the starting point of any proposed solution, albeit often an implicit starting point. As an expose on the relevant background and legal framework – especially for readers not familiar with the German legal framework – this part is limited in scope to the necessary fundamentals and will *not* present the in-depth scientific discussion as found in the further parts of the book. If a reader is interested in learning more about the discussed topics in this part, discussions can be found in more general arbitration or insolvency literature.[12] Consequently, those readers who are experienced with insolvency and arbitration may prefer to skip to sections of interest in Chapters 2 and 3.

To facilitate an understanding of the issues in Chapters 2 and 3, the theoretical background introduced below goes slightly beyond the German context. The second part of this book focuses on the national context in Germany. This focus is to study the interaction of insolvency with arbitration in the relative isolation of a single jurisdiction without the complicating factor of internationality. Moving forward, the third part focuses on those complicating factors and the specific questions raised in an international context. Consequently, Chapter 1 must be slightly broader than the

12. For the topic of international insolvency the author highly recommends the works of Dutch professor emeritus *Wessels* and for international arbitration the works of *Born*. *Wessels*, International Insolvency Law; *Born*, International Commercial Arbitration.

German context to also provide an essential background for the larger whole of this study.

1 INSOLVENCY IN GERMANY

This section will introduce some of the fundamentals of insolvency in Germany, primarily the relevant frameworks. First, the national insolvency framework is introduced (§ 1.1) and then the framework for international insolvencies (§ 1.2).

1.1 National Insolvency Framework

German insolvency law is primarily found in the Insolvency Code and the introductory act to the Insolvency Code. In 1999, shortly after the reunification of Germany, a unified insolvency code was created in the shape of the *Insolvenzordnung*, i.e., the Insolvency Code (InsO).[13] This code replaced several West-German codes, i.e., the *Konkursordnung* of 1877 and the *Vergleichsordnung* of 1935, and the main East-German code on the subject, the *Gesamtvollstreckungsordnung* of 1975.[14]

In contrast to the previous systems, the InsO knows only one insolvency procedure (German: *Einheitsverfahren*). Nonetheless, this proceeding can have several different results, such as regular liquidation or confirmation of an insolvency arrangement, i.e., a plan for debt sanitation of the company confirmed by the insolvency judge, *see* § 1 InsO.[15] Like most modern insolvency codes, German law also allows for the restructuring of the insolvent company. In 2011, in line with the current international trend in this direction, the legislator tried to further accommodate and promote restructuring over liquidation with the law for the further facilitation of the restructuring of companies (German: *Gesetz zur weiteren Erleichterung der Sanierung von Unternehmen*). Further facilitation of that trend came on 1 January 2021, when the German transposition of the EU Restructuring Directive, Directive (EU) 2019/1023, came into force in the form of the law on the stabilisation and restructuring framework for companies (German: *Gesetz über den Stabilisierungs- und Restrukurierungsrahmen für Unternehmen (StaRUG)*).

Aside from the Insolvency Code itself, Germany has what can be translated as an introductory act to the Insolvency Code, the *Einführungsgesetz zur Insolvenzordnung* (EGInsO).[16] Introductory acts are not uncommon in German law and are usually enacted as corollaries to significant legal acts or amendments to legal acts. Usually, they include ancillary information on the main acts, such as effective dates. Some, however, actually include important annexes to the main legal acts. The prime example of such an Introductory Act is the *Einführungsgesetz zum Bürgerlichen Gesetzbuch* (EGBGB), the introductory act to the civil code that contains an important regulation of

13. Insolvenzordnung of 1.1.1999, BGBl. I 1994, 2866.
14. *Lazić*, Insolvency Proceedings and Commercial Arbitration, p. 25; *Fenger*, Insolvenzrecht, p. 2; *Becker*, Insolvenzrecht, pp. 17–19.
15. *Becker*, Insolvenzrecht, p. 19; *Kramer/F.K. Peter*, Insolvenzrecht, p. 18.
16. Einführungsgesetz zur Insolvenzordnung of 5.10.1994, BGBl. I 1994, 2991.

international private law (Articles 2 et seq. EGBGB). Such an introductory act, the EGInsO, was also used to introduce the European Insolvency Regulation (EIR) into the German insolvency framework, *see* Articles 102 and 102c EGInsO.

Insolvency law generally reflects three procedural elements: (i) it starts with the finding by a judge or other administrative body of the state; (ii) it provides a collective procedure covering all the assets of the insolvent and the divestment of the insolvent; and (iii) it involves a change of control to an administrator.[17] German insolvency includes all these elements and is, in general, very similar to that of many other jurisdictions, especially in Europe. It centres around the creditors, their rights and the aim to satisfy as large a part of their claims as possible. It follows the common insolvency principle of equality of creditors or *paritas creditorum*.[18] Although prima facie, this concept can be a somewhat deceiving principle as, in actuality, 'not all debts are born equal'; only creditors of equal rank are treated equally, and creditors who, for example, hold a security will by virtue of that security be treated preferentially. Hence comes the term 'preferential creditors'. Without such a preference, a creditor is unlikely to see much of his or her money anytime soon.

As a system to satisfy debtors, as referred to under element (ii) above, insolvency proceedings are arguably relatively ineffective. The percentage of a claim paid out in insolvency is marginal, and years can pass before any payment is received. For corporate insolvencies finalised in Germany between 2011 and 2015, the coverage ratio lay at a scant 3.9% of the claim. For personal insolvencies, the coverage ratio was even lower at a measly 1.5% of the claim.[19] After the opening of the insolvency, which in itself takes two or three months, corporate insolvency takes on average four years and a personal insolvency two years.[20] Numbers have been slightly more optimistic in more recent years, with the coverage ratio for corporate insolvencies starting after 2010 and finalised before the end of 2017 standing at 6.2%, with a coverage ratio of 2% in private insolvencies. Encouraging is also that 23.8% of large insolvencies, with claims of EUR 5 million or more, could be sanitised, i.e., the company was not liquidated.[21] This is partially due to the development of tools and changes of laws to facilitate the sanitation of debts without liquidation, e.g., the restructuring laws mentioned earlier in this section, stimulation of self-administration procedures before an actual inability to pay debts when due and the debtor-in procession arrangement of the so-called *Schutzschirmverfahren* of §§ 270–285 InsO, a change in the definition of overindebtedness (German: *Überschuldungsbegriff*) of § 19 InsO that averts insolvency when there is positive continuation prognosis.[22] Further development of instruments such as debt-equity swaps also aids in the avoidance of unnecessary liquidations.

17. *Berset/Lévy*, ASA Bull. 16 (1998), pp. 664–665.
18. In Germany, this adage is often cited as *par conditio creditorum*; equal situation of creditors, others know it as the *pari pasu* principle; equal step principle. However, essentially, they all refer to the general equality of creditors; *see, e.g.*, MüKoInsO/*Ganter/Bruns* § 1 InsO, No. 52.
19. *Statistisches Bundesamt*, Bis 2015 beendete Insolvenz-verfahren: Gläubiger erhielten durchschnittlich 2.2% ihrer Forderungen zurück.
20. *Icks/K. Peter*, Sanierungen in Insolvenzverfahren, IX, 11.
21. *Statistisches Bundesamt*, Bis 2017 beendete Insolvenzverfahren: Gläubiger müssen auf 96.1% ihrer Forderungen verzichten.
22. BeckOK InsO/*Wolfer* § 19 InsO, No. 1.

The creditors are the main 'beneficiaries' of insolvency proceedings, but they should also theoretically be the primary directors of the insolvency proceedings. As the creditors, at least theoretically, to a substantial extent control how the insolvency proceeds, e.g., if all assets should be liquidated or if the company will continue to operate in some capacity. This principle is enshrined in § 157 InsO.

To a large degree, the above could describe many continental insolvency systems. The last aspect to be mentioned here is also no stranger to many continental systems and concerns the transitional period and the appointment of a preliminary administrator.[23] After the request for insolvency and before the decision on the opening thereof, the court can appoint a preliminary insolvency administrator, *see* § 21(2)(1) InsO. This insolvency administrator can be 'weak' or 'strong'. This 'weakness' or 'strength' refers to the extent of the administrator's power in the proceeding and the powers the debtor retains at this stage or (pre-)insolvency.[24] In case the insolvency court removes the debtor's general dispositive power regarding the pre-insolvent mass, the administrator alone will have this authority and will, therefore, be called a 'strong' preliminary insolvency administrator § 22(1) InsO. A *contrario*, if the administrator is put in a more supervisory role and the debtor retains primary dispositive power, the administrator is 'weak', *see* § 22(2) InsO. However, whether weak or strong, upon the opening of the insolvency proceedings proper, the dispositive and administrative power concerning the estate is finally and fully transferred to the insolvency administrator.

1.2 International Insolvencies

For national insolvencies, most rules are found in the German insolvency code. This is necessarily different when one speaks about the effect of foreign insolvencies on local arbitration proceedings. In such circumstances, the relevant two legal orders interact. While questioning the effect of foreign insolvencies in Germany, a difference must be made between intra-EU Insolvencies and extra-EU insolvencies. Intra-EU insolvencies are governed by the EIR, whereas insolvencies from 'third countries' are governed by a special part of the Insolvency Code, §§ 335 et seq. InsO. First, the EIR is introduced (§ 1.2.1), and then insolvency outside the context of the EIR is discussed (§ 1.2.2). After this, two model laws are introduced: the model on cross-border insolvency (§ 1.2.3) and the model law on insolvency-related judgments (§ 1.2.4).

1.2.1 European Insolvencies: The EIR

The latest EIR[25] is an interesting instrument regardless of the fact that it is also highly significant from a practical standpoint, as it arguably constitutes the only successful,

23. *Final Award in ICC Case No. 16369*, Y.B. Com. Arb. XXXIX, 2014, 169, No. 6262.
24. MüKoInsO/*Haarmeyer/Schildt* § 22 InsO, Nos 23, 28.
25. Regulation (EU) 2015/848 on insolvency proceedings of 20.5.2015, OJ L 141/19.

'multilateral'[26] and fully binding international set of rules on international insolvency. The second iteration of the regulation replaces the from 2000[27] and is similarly applicable in the Member States, as per the Treaty on the Functioning of the European Union (TFEU), except Denmark. As stated above, Germany introduced this regulation into its legal system via the EGInsO.

The Regulation does not prescribe a material insolvency procedure but mainly facilitates recognition and coordination.[28] The regulation aims to create an effective and efficient framework for insolvencies that involve multiple EU states and put a stop to internal forum shopping.[29] As stated, it is important to note that it does not attempt to regulate insolvency between EU states and extra-EU states but merely within the EU.[30]

The EIR operates as an overarching framework functioning mainly as a set of conflict-of-laws rules.[31] However, it introduces some very fascinating tools that go beyond that role. Most importantly, the idea of main and secondary insolvency procedures and rules provides the basis for further inter-court cooperation and communication.

The main proceedings can be opened in the country where the Centre of Main Interests (COMI) is located, as stated in Article 3(1) EIR.[32] As follows from Article 3(2) EIR, if there is a presence that does not amount to the COMI but is merely an establishment, only so-called territorial proceedings can be opened. Finally, Article 3(3) EIR states that territorial proceedings are referred to as secondary proceedings in case of an existing main proceeding.[33] In terms of the application within one jurisdiction, there is little distinction between main and secondary proceedings. However, within the EU and the EIR framework, it has several different consequences as to what effects the proceedings have outside the borders of the opening jurisdiction.

The presumption under EU law is the general and direct recognition of the main proceeding. Initially, the law of the opening state is applicable EU-wide. All debtors and assets are to be included in this main proceeding.[34] This can be described as a form of internal universalism. Article 7(1) EIR embodies this fundamental principle and Article 7(2) EIR provides a non-limited list of issues that are governed by the law of the opening state. For example, Article 7(2)(b) EIR provides that the insolvency law of the opening state determines which assets, EU-wide, are part of the insolvent estate. For

26. The regulation itself is in the literal sense of the word not multilateral, the framework in which it functions, the EU, c.q. the TFEU is.
27. Council Regulation (EC) No 1346/2000 on insolvency proceedings of 29.5.2000, Official Journal of the European Communities L 160.
28. *Wessels*, International Insolvency Law, pp. 347–349.
29. *Wessels*, International Insolvency Law, pp. 346–347.
30. *Wessels*, International Insolvency Law, p. 356; *Wessels*, International Insolvency Law Part II: European Insolvency Law, p. 26.
31. *Wessels*, International Insolvency Law, pp. 348–349.
32. Cf. *Wessels*, International Insolvency Law, p. 365.
33. *Wessels*, International Insolvency Law, p. 365; Beyond this basic description, the practical meaning of COMI and establishment have been the subject of much discussion, *see CJEU*, 2.5.2006 - C-341/04; Judgment of 20.10.2011 - C-396/09; MüKoInsO/*Thole* Art. 3 EuInsVO, Nos 23–37.
34. *Wessels*, International Insolvency Law, pp. 366–368.

example, if a primary insolvency proceeding is opened in Germany, German insolvency law determines which assets in the Netherlands are part of the insolvent estate. Similarly, the law of the opening state determines, EU-wide, the law applicable to ongoing contracts, *see* Article 7(2)(e) EIR, which will be discussed in great detail in Chapter 3. There is, however, a series of exceptions to this general rule of Article 7(1) EIR. The 'local' law remains applicable to so-called rights in rem, *see* Article 8 EIR, or the law applicable to contracts concerning immovable property, *see* Article 11 EIR.

Territorial proceedings are also recognised in the other Member States, but they do not have any cross-border effect and merely open a local insolvency proceeding involving local assets and debtors.[35] Although that could be described as a cross-border effect when looked upon from the perspective of a main proceeding, as it removes the local assets and debtors from the grasp of the foreign main proceeding. Within the secondary or territorial proceedings, the insolvency law of the relevant country applies to all questions regarding local assets and debtors, *see* Article 3(2) EIR. In this sense, it can be stated that territorial proceedings within the meaning of the EIR have an absolute territorial effect, meaning that it only portends to and factually has local effects.

When a main proceeding is opened, all running territorial proceedings, which involve the same debtor, will henceforth be seen as secondary proceedings, *see* Article 3(3) EIR. This creates certain obligations towards the main proceedings, mostly centred on the sharing of information but also notably involving asset location and allocation. Territorial proceedings can still be opened after the opening of a main proceeding but only in the form of secondary proceedings.[36] The EIR will be further discussed and analysed in the context of its effect on arbitration in Chapter 3.

1.2.2 Other International Insolvencies

International insolvencies can also fall outside of the scope of the EIR in Germany. The last parts of the German Insolvency Code organise international, third-country insolvencies and their relationship to the German legal order. This organisation starts in § 335 InsO, which incorporates the main policy point that the material effect of the proceedings shall be determined by the law of the place of the insolvency proceedings or the '*lex fori concursus*'.

Therefore, the Insolvency Code, not unlike the EIR, provides mainly conflict-of-law rules. This is embodied in the above principle of applying the *lex fori concursus* and a series of exceptions thereto, *see* §§ 336–442. InsO. Another primary function of the autonomous German international insolvency law is the provision of the rules for recognition of insolvencies opened in third countries, *see* § 343 InsO. The recognition of foreign insolvencies, in § 343 InsO, in its requirements mirrors mostly those of the EIR, i.e., the insolvency order must merely have come into effect in the relevant country. Somewhat uncommon in international insolvency and a testament to the

35. *Wessels,* International Insolvency Law, p. 368.
36. *Wessels,* International Insolvency Law, pp. 370–371.

German universalist approach is that these third-country insolvencies also do not require a separate recognition proceeding as they are also recognised automatically.[37]

The regulations provided by the autonomous German International Insolvency Law, in many ways, follow the EIR. For example, both frameworks require an insolvency proceeding that emulates the local understanding of an insolvency proceeding in its goal and purpose. As such, the EIR's Annex A can be used as a guideline.[38]

However, it is important to note that the German Federal Supreme Court seems to take a very light approach to this test. It ruled that Chapter 11 US Bankruptcy proceedings, which materially can be described as reorganisation proceedings, were to be recognised under § 343 InsO.[39] This leads to the conclusion that reorganisation proceedings can fall under the recognition rules of § 343 InsO as long as they are defined as insolvency proceedings within the home jurisdiction. § 1 InsO does not list the goal of insolvency proceeding to be the dissolution of the insolvent company. Instead, this is merely an effect that is ascribed to insolvency proceedings in the relevant corporate laws, e.g., § 60(1)(4) GmbHG or § 262(1)(3) AktG. § 1 InsO posits the collective satisfaction of creditors as the goal of the insolvency proceedings. As such, proceedings can, independent of how different they are from German insolvency proceedings, when they are nominally insolvency proceedings in their home jurisdiction and at least serve collective satisfaction, be recognised under § 343 InsO.[40]

1.2.3 The UNCITRAL Model Law on Cross-Border Insolvency

In the context of international insolvency mechanisms, the UNCITRAL Model Law on Cross-Border Insolvency (Ins.ML) is worth mentioning. It provides valuable insight into the international consensus or lack thereof on specific topics.

The Model Law on Cross-Border Insolvency was adopted on 30 May 1997 by the United Nations Commission on International Trade Law (UNCITRAL). The model aims to function as a template for jurisdictions to use in the creation of national legislation regarding cross-border insolvencies.[41] The Model Law has not been adopted in Germany and will not be dealt with in significant detail at this point. References will be made to this Model Law in specific sections throughout this book. However, it has been a relative success, as legislation based on the Model Law for Cross-Border Insolvency has been adopted or used as a basis in forty-four countries, including the United States and the United Kingdom, several of them adopting relevant legislation in the last years, e.g., Singapore in 2017 and Israel in 2018.[42] Besides this, the Model Law is likely as close as one can get to international common ground on the relevant subjects, including recognition.

---

37. More on recognition and recognition Germany in § 1; Uhlenbruck/*Lüer/Knof* § 343 InsO, 2 et seq.
38. Regulation (EU) 2015/848 on insolvency proceedings of 20.5.2015, OJ L 141/19, Annex A.
39. *BGH*, NZI 2009, 859–862.
40. *BGH*, NZI 2009, 859, pp. 860–861.
41. *Wessels*, International Insolvency Law, p. 143.
42. *UNCITRAL*, Status, http://www.uncitral.org/uncitral/en/uncitral_texts/insolvency/1997Model_status.html; *Vorburger*, International Arbitration and Cross-Border Insolvency, p. 11.

The Model Law is intended to smoothen out cross-border insolvency relations.[43] The core principles employed therefor are access, recognition, relief and cooperation.[44] However, it specifically does not create substantive unification of national insolvency laws. It merely aims to reconcile and respect national differences.[45] It does not replace national insolvency regulations but merely supplements and operates as a part of existing national laws.[46]

Access means that representatives of, and creditors in, insolvency procedures should have access to procedures in other jurisdictions. Recognition means that foreign insolvency proceedings should be recognised. The Model Law provides a framework for this and provides for recognition as either main or non-main proceedings, like in the EIR. Main proceedings are proceedings where the debtor has its centre of main interest (COMI). Non-main proceedings are there where the debtor merely has an establishment. Further definitions of those terms can be found in case law and can slightly differ between adopting jurisdictions. The Mode law achieves this relief in the form of the possibility to request and receive relief for foreign insolvency proceedings. Cooperation and Communication point to the express possibility and authority created by the Model Law for courts to cooperate and communicate with foreign courts to fulfil the goals of the Model Law.[47]

1.2.4 The UNCITRAL Model Law on Insolvency-Related Judgments

In its 2018 session, UNCITRAL agreed on what can be called an additional cross-border insolvency model law, a 'model law on cross-border recognition and enforcement of insolvency-related judgments'.[48] While this Model Law is relevant in the context of insolvency, it is of supplementary nature to the Model Law described in the previous paragraph.

This Model Law does not apply to the decisions opening the insolvency proceeding but to other judgments surrounding insolvency proceedings.[49] The working group lists as examples of judgments it does deem within the scope of this model law: verification and disposal decisions, decisions regarding avoidable actions, decisions regarding director liability, decisions confirming insolvency plans, decisions on the

43. *UNCITRAL,* UNCITRAL Model Law on Cross-Border Insolvency (1997), http://www.uncitral.org/uncitral/en/uncitral_texts/insolvency/1997Model.html.
44. *UNCITRAL,* UNCITRAL Model Law on Cross-Border Insolvency (1997), http://www.uncitral.org/uncitral/en/uncitral_texts/insolvency/1997Model.html; *Wessels,* International Insolvency Law, p. 148.
45. *Wessels,* International Insolvency Law, p. 143.
46. *UNCITRAL,* UNCITRAL Model Law on Cross-Border Insolvency with Guide to Enactment and Interpretation, http://www.uncitral.org/pdf/english/texts/insolven/1997-Model-Law-Insol-2013-Guide-Enactment-e.pdf.
47. *UNCITRAL,* UNCITRAL Model Law on Cross-Border Insolvency (1997), http://www.uncitral.org/uncitral/en/uncitral_texts/insolvency/1997Model.html.
48. *UNCITRAL,* Report of the United Nations Commission on International Trade Law, Agenda Point 12.A.
49. *UNCITRAL Working Group V,* Recognition and Enforcement of Insolvency-Related Judgments: Draft Guide to Enactment of the Model Law, pp. 56–61.

discharge of residual debt and several further examples.[50] This does not diminish but instead reinforces the relevance of this model law, as one can imagine the relevance of a decision to discharge a debtor of his or her residual debt to any ongoing proceeding, including arbitration.

Recognition is subject to several criteria; the decision being a decision 'related to insolvency' as described above is only the first. The decision must have legal effect, and the person requesting recognition must be competent to do so. Furthermore, a public policy exception is adopted in the 7th article of the model law.

Interestingly the model law in its 14th article gives enacting states the choice of giving a successfully recognised insolvency-related judgment the same effect as it has in its home jurisdiction, in its *lex fori concursus* or the effect that a similar judgment would have in the recognising jurisdiction.

However, this Model Law is still in its infancy and consequently has, at the moment of the writing of this book, not yet been adopted in any jurisdiction, making further discussion of its workings relatively speculative and unnecessary here.

2 INTERNATIONAL INSOLVENCY THEORY

Behind international insolvency laws stand international insolvency theories. In the third part of this book, the legal questions regarding international aspects of insolvency in arbitration will be discussed. To facilitate understanding of that discussion, this paragraph introduces international insolvency theory.

The challenge arises from the fact that many companies have assets in various countries while, in principle, each of these countries only has authority within its own borders. Large companies nowadays seldom have assets in only one country. Even if there is just one foreign bank account, one can speak of international insolvency. Most jurisdictions view insolvency law as an integral part of their administrative sovereignty and, in so doing, often claim jurisdiction over assets of an insolvent foreign company situated in their country. Other countries claim global jurisdiction over assets of companies that bear their 'nationality' according to their law. Combine the two, and one can easily see the potential collisions. The sections below will shortly discuss the leading theories in international insolvency.

The introduction in this section includes the position of insolvency within a legal order (§ 2.1), territorialism (§ 2.2), universalism (§ 2.3), the practical middle ground (§ 2.4), and the German approach (§ 2.5).

2.1 The Position of Insolvency Within a Legal Order

There are multiple relevant theories that describe the position of insolvency in a legal order. Insolvency law, unlike arbitration law, is still heavily dominated by local law

50. *UNCITRAL Working Group V*, Recognition and Enforcement of Insolvency-Related Judgments: Draft Guide to Enactment of the Model Law, p. 59.

and principles.[51] Many states view both the procedural and material aspects of insolvency as core matters of national jurisdiction and sovereignty. This view is also reflected in the sparsity of effective and binding international treaties on the subject and the lack of a systematic legal framework.[52] In contrast, many international and professional organisations have tried to fill this gap with conventions, best practices and other, mostly non-binding, instruments.[53] Most notable are the UNCITRAL Model Laws, which were shortly discussed above.[54]

As previously mentioned, insolvency proceedings might seem ineffective from the perspective of time and money recovered. However, this is perhaps not the foremost goal of insolvency law. The primary purpose of insolvency law is to provide a functional legal framework for the situation in which companies can no longer pay their debts or meet their obligations.[55] It also sees to the prevention, regulation and administration of the discontinuation of that company's legal relationships. However, its core remains the streamlining and handling of the situation of the inability to make good on payment obligations.[56] Aside from this regulatory purpose, it also aims to distribute what money is left fairly, to prevent a free-for-all amongst the creditors and any preferential treatment from the debtor's side, hence the common insolvency principle of *paritas creditorum*.[57]

As insolvency law is viewed as a core part of national sovereignty, adding a cross-border element to the insolvency creates a situation of possible competition between two or more jurisdictions. Legally this presents questions regarding jurisdiction, the law applicable and the effects of the procedure on foreign creditors, which will be dealt with in the other parts of this book.[58] However, any explanation of cross-border insolvency often begins with an explanation of the two main competing theories: territorialism and universalism.[59] Most legal systems are then put somewhere in between these two extremes and are described with terms such as modified universalism[60] or limited cooperation.[61]

51. *Vorburger*, International Arbitration and Cross-Border Insolvency, p. 6.
52. *Nadeau-Séguin*, Disp. Resol. Int'l 5 (2011), 79, pp. 80–81; *Wessels*, International Insolvency Law, p. 3.
53. *Wessels/Boon*, Cross-Border Insolvency Law, annexes.
54. For more information, *see* United Nations Commission for International Trade Law, www.uncitral.org.
55. *Siehr*, Das internationale Privatrecht der Schweiz, p. 688; *Fenger*, Insolvenzrecht, p. 6; *Wessels*, International Insolvency Law, p. 1; *Vorburger*, International Arbitration and Cross-Border Insolvency, p. 6; *Draguiev*, Journal of International Arbitration 32 (2015), 511, pp. 512–513.
56. *Wessels*, International Insolvency Law, p. 1.
57. Braun/*Kießner* § 1 InsO, No. 2; BeckOK InsO/*Madaus* § 1 InsO, Nos 2.1–3.
58. *Wessels*, International Insolvency Law, pp. 6–7.
59. *Kamalnath*, International Journal of Legal Studies and Research (IJLSR) 2 (2013), 172, p. 175; *Raykin/Wouters*, Emory Bankruptcy Developments Journal 29 (2013), 387, I.A; *van de Ven*, The Cross-Border Insolvency Protocol: What Is It and What Is in It?, p. 15; *Wessels*, International Insolvency Law, pp. 7–18.
60. *Zumbro*, Business Law International 11 (2010), 157, p. 160.
61. *Westbrook*, Brook. J.Int'l L 17 (1991), p. 499.

2.2 Territorialism

Territorialism is the idea that insolvency is a national creature, interwoven intrinsically with the national sovereignty of the relevant country or jurisdiction.[62] In this philosophy, insolvency cannot naturally reach across borders.[63] The effect of a principled application of such a view is that the assets of an insolvent in a foreign country are not affected by the insolvency in the local jurisdiction.[64] Any form of international effect is solely achieved by cooperation, parallel proceedings or a form of secondary proceedings. Following this theory, every jurisdiction solely applies the local insolvency system. That includes when questions about the applicable material law regarding such internationally relevant issues as denying or recognising foreign insolvency measures are raised.[65]

A presumptive advantage of territorialism is the simple and consistent application of local insolvency law within the local jurisdiction. This approach obviates the need for additional legislation on foreign insolvencies as the local law will always apply. Local creditors can thus rely on their local insolvency law and the rights and expectations enshrined therein.[66]

Disadvantages include that local insolvency does not prevent a debtor from disposing of foreign assets due to the purely local effects of insolvency. It risks a run on foreign assets described as the 'grab rule'[67] or a 'Raubsystem', literally a 'robbery system' in German.[68] Insolvency of an international company will lead to multiple insolvency proceedings across several jurisdictions adhering to different principles and rules. International reorganisation procedures are virtually impossible within such a system. These are just some of the legal issues, but there are also many practical issues regarding the location of assets and, for example, in the international banking practice regarding securities for credit.[69]

2.3 Universalism

Universalism can be described as the opposite of territorialism.[70] It assumes a universal effect of the insolvency of a debtor. Universal means global, as the fundamental concept of universalism is to have the insolvency of a debtor automatically apply and reach into every jurisdiction around the globe without separation or differentiation.

62. *Berends,* Insolventie in het internationaal privaatrecht, p. 12; *van de Ven,* The Cross-Border Insolvency Protocol: What Is It and What Is in It?, p. 15.
63. *Wessels,* International Insolvency Law, p. 11.
64. *Paulus,* Insolvenzrecht, p. 122; *Wessels,* International Insolvency Law, p. 11; *Kamalnath,* International Journal of Legal Studies and Research (IJLSR) 2 (2013), 172, p. 175; *Vorburger,* International Arbitration and Cross-Border Insolvency, p. 99.
65. *Wessels,* International Insolvency Law, pp. 11–12.
66. *Wessels,* International Insolvency Law, p. 12.
67. *Westbrook,* Brook. J.Int'l L 17 (1991), 499–538, p. 501.
68. *Wessels,* International Insolvency Law, p. 12.
69. *Wessels,* International Insolvency Law, pp. 12–14.
70. *Kamalnath,* International Journal of Legal Studies and Research (IJLSR) 2 (2013), 172, p. 175; *Raykin/Wouters,* Emory Bankruptcy Developments Journal 29 (2013), 387, I.A.

The concept prescribes the application of the same rules universally. Practically speaking, that means applying the insolvency rules from the jurisdiction where the debtor is initially found insolvent in every other jurisdiction. In effect, there would be one single insolvency proceeding governed by one legal system, including all assets and creditors regardless of their location.[71]

The advantages of such a system include a single administration of insolvency and equal treatment of all creditors and assets. This, primarily from the perspective of the opening jurisdictions, creates a predictable and orderly outcome. A more practical but equally important point is the cost efficiency of this system. Cost efficiency is a major goal of insolvency proceedings as these costs are generally borne by the estate, i.e., the creditors, and a primary goal of insolvency proceedings is estate maximisation.[72]

Drawbacks are that local creditors can be confronted by foreign and unfamiliar insolvency regimes and, to a certain extent, the sheer challenge of creating a truly functional and globally accepted universalistic insolvency system.

2.4 The Practical Middle Ground

Practice neither fully embraces universalism nor territorialism, and a middle-ground approach is often preferred. Legal literature is most often opposed to territorialism and in favour of universalism, while in reality practice still sees a lot of territorialism.[73] A primary concern about territorialism in literature is that it breaches the *pari passu* or *paritas creditorum* principle, the equal treatment of creditors, as it discriminates between creditors based on nationality, c.q. their jurisdiction.[74]

The primary concern against universalism seems to be the reservations of states regarding accepting and applying foreign insolvencies and insolvency law. Although this is often voiced as concerns about procedural fairness and the application of basic legal principles in foreign jurisdictions and proceedings, these arguments can be considered sovereignty-based arguments. This concern can be exemplified by the *ordre public* or other basic principles of law exceptions to recognition rules in cross-border insolvency treaties and regulations. *See, e.g.*, Article 33 EIR.

Over the years, several alternative theories have been proposed.[75] The author *LoPucki* proposed the concept of 'Cooperative Territorialism', which is essentially an application of territorialism and a dismissal of universalism. Roughly it describes a system wherein all states control the assets within their borders, applying a territorial approach. However, it stipulates that cooperation should be allowed and facilitated when necessary.[76] In the 1990s, a concept was developed under the moniker

71. *Van Buchem-Spapens/Pouw*, Faillissement, surseance van betaling en schuldsanering, p. 115; *Vorburger*, International Arbitration and Cross-Border Insolvency, p. 10.
72. BeckOK InsO/*Madaus* § 1 InsO, No. 5.
73. *Wessels*, International Insolvency Law, p. 15.
74. *Wessels*, International Insolvency Law, p. 15.
75. *Wessels*, International Insolvency Law, pp. 17–18.
76. *Wessels*, International Insolvency Law, pp. 14–15; *LoPucki*, The American Bankruptcy Law Journal 79 (2005), 143, 143, 163.

'Contractualism'.[77] This concept is closely related to universalism as it advocates the uniform application of a singular insolvency regime. Within this approach, the applicable insolvency regime could be 'contractually' decided upon at the start of the company's legal life.[78] Within certain boundaries, this choice should then be uniformly accepted and applied. Besides those theories, some argue that neither universalism nor territorialism should be universally applied to all legal questions in insolvency, and a new and separate theoretical orientation should be made. *Von Wilmowsky* proposes such a theory under the title '*Neuorientierung*'.[79] He broadly argues that some questions should be answered by the *lex concursus* of the state of initial opening and others by the local law.

In reality, the systems applied by most jurisdictions fall somewhere in between the two extremes described above.[80] These systems are often described as mixed or modified models.[81] In practice, these systems as signified by, for example, allowing foreign creditors into local insolvency proceedings, modifying conditions for opening insolvency proceedings and moving them away from a pure territorial approach or by creating intra-jurisdictions cooperation systems and mechanisms.[82] For incoming foreign insolvencies, subordinated secondary proceedings can be allowed as a move away from pure universalism, and exemptions can be granted against the complete application of the law of the opening state, as proposed by Von Wilmowsky and as seen, for example, in the EIR.[83]

2.5 The German Approach

The German approach is often described as universalism.[84] Although it cannot be said that Germany follows a purely universalistic approach, as it leaves several checks and balances on foreign law, it comes relatively close. The turn away from a more territorial approach to the current state of affairs was a process of years. However, if one point in time should be identified as the turning point, this is probably the German Federal Supreme Court decision of 17 July 1985.[85] In this case, the court essentially accepted that the Belgian insolvency proceedings included the debtor's assets in Germany. After this, foreign insolvencies were recognised and accepted as including assets located in Germany upon meeting some basic criteria.[86] As seen in the previous section, this approach has since been incorporated into the relevant German laws.

77. *Goode,* Principles of Corporate Insolvency Law, pp. 2-20; *A. Schwartz,* Yale L.J. 71 (1998), 1807, Ch. II; *Wessels,* International Insolvency Law, p. 18.
78. *A. Schwartz,* Yale L.J. 71 (1998), 1807, p. 1811.
79. *Wessels,* International Insolvency Law, p. 21; *Wilmowsky,* Choice of Law in International Insolvencies - A Proposal for Reform, pp. 197-212.
80. *Vorburger,* International Arbitration and Cross-Border Insolvency, p. 14.
81. *Wessels,* International Insolvency Law, p. 23.
82. *Wessels,* International Insolvency Law, p. 23.
83. *Wessels,* International Insolvency Law, p. 23.
84. *Kindler,* § 1. Grundlagen, Nos 1-3.
85. *BGHZ* 95, 256-273, 35-41.
86. *Schack,* Internationales Zivilverfahrensrecht, No. 1145.

Nowadays, the EIR would apply to the relationship described in that 1985 case. This regulation plays a major role in contemporary cross-border insolvencies in Germany as it applies to all intra-EU insolvencies. The approach embodied in the EIR can be described as modified universalism. This can be primarily concluded from its implementation of the concept of primary and secondary insolvency proceedings and the general rule of applicability of the law of the opening state with some important exceptions.[87] The framework provided seems to lead to further, not legally required, although encouraged, cooperation.[88] An example of such cooperation can be found in the concept of the international cross-border insolvency protocol, which played a prominent role in the largest private insolvency in history, that of the Lehmann Brothers bank, and is essentially a procedural and practical agreement between insolvency professionals on how to handle and coordinate multiple proceedings.[89]

3 ARBITRATION IN GERMANY

In this section, a selection of subjects is discussed: key pieces of legislation (§ 3.1) and the arbitration agreement (§ 3.2) that the author finds necessary to introduce to provide a basic understanding of the framework in which arbitration operates in Germany.

Arbitration is an old concept. The standard introduction to many texts on arbitration, similar to the one used here, mentions that arbitration has become more and more popular. Arbitration has become the norm in several industries in Germany. Prime examples are the construction industry and large parts of the commodities trade and industry.[90] While it is true that arbitration is indeed still gaining popularity in several branches and markets, one should not think that arbitration is something new.[91] In fact, within the definition of a procedure of submitting a conflict to a neutral third person for binding resolution by consent of the parties, arbitration is ancient, almost certainly older than the public court system.[92] The actual origin of arbitration is lost in history, but there are many early examples. Examples can be found in the writings of Aristotle but also in the well-known biblical story of the Judgment of Solomon, although one could argue there if the king was not part of the regular judicial system.[93]

There is no official unified definition of the concept of arbitration, but the constituent elements are quite broadly accepted and can be found throughout

87. *Vorburger*, International Arbitration and Cross-Border Insolvency, pp. 11–12.
88. *Wessels*, International Insolvency Law, pp. 24–25.
89. *Van de Ven*, The Cross-Border Insolvency Protocol: What Is It and What Is in It?, p. 16.
90. Cf. *Böckstiegel/S.M. Kröll/Nacimiento*, Part I: Germany as a Place for International and Domestic Arbitrations – General Overview, 1, p. 5.
91. National Judicial systems are also hard at work with trying to regain territory with new initiatives that incorporate some of the perceived advantages of arbitration, *see*, *e.g.*, the Netherlands Commercial Court (https://www.rechtspraak.nl/English/NCC) or the 'Justizinitiative Frankfurt' which introduce English speaking litigation (http://conflictoflaws.net/2017/the-justice-initiative-frankfurt-am-main-2017-law-made-in-frankfurt/).
92. *Bell*, Treatise on the Law of Arbitration in Scotland, p. 1.
93. *Wolaver*, University of Pennsylvania Law Review 1934, p. 132; *Emmerson*, Cleveland State Law Review 19 (1970), p. 155.

legislation and literature. It might be surprising at first that many laws, including the ZPO, do not provide a legal definition of arbitration as a procedure. This lack of a definition becomes slightly less surprising when one realises that one of the primary ideas of arbitration is the autonomy of the parties and that defining arbitration might mean confining this autonomy. However, a few core characteristics of arbitration are generally agreed upon in literature and practice. These characteristics also provide boundaries, albeit sometimes vague ones, between arbitration, court proceedings and other alternative dispute resolution mechanisms, such as mediation or expert determination. *Born* summarises these generally agreed-upon aspects by describing arbitration as the consensual submission of a dispute (1) to a non-governmental adjudicator (2), chosen by or for the parties (3), providing for a binding resolution of the dispute (4) based on a procedure following neutral rules, which permit the parties an opportunity to present their case (5).[94] However, many of these aspects can be found in the definition of the arbitration agreement itself and rules concerning the procedure and choosing of arbitrators. One can find them in: § 1029 ZPO, which defines the arbitration contract; § 1035 ZPO, which provides for the parties' right to determine the selection of arbitrators; § 1036 ZPO, which provides for neutral arbiters; and § 1042 ZPO, which provides for equal treatment and the right to be heard. Therefore, the elements of the definition, as provided by *Born*, can be found in the ZPO. However, as stated, the ZPO does not itself provides a complete and explicit definition of the concept of arbitration.

A short discussion of the mentioned constituent elements provided by *Born* follows. This discussion shows that arbitration can be clearly differentiated from court proceedings and other alternative dispute resolution methods based on these elements.

The first (1) element, the fact that arbitration is a consensual proceeding, sets it firmly apart from state court proceedings, although not from other alternative dispute resolution mechanisms. While there are many controversial discussions about binding third parties to arbitration agreements and awards, the underlying principle is still that only the parties to an arbitration agreement can be bound to the arbitration process. This core concept can be found in most arbitration laws. Arguably, German law does not make this explicit. However, it does follow from many of the relevant articles. *See, e.g.*, the definition of the arbitration agreement in § 1029 ZPO.[95] The need for a valid arbitration agreement is also posited negatively by way of sanctions if one is lacking. *See* therefor, for example, § 1059(2) ZPO, which states that a non-functional arbitration agreement, or the excess of the authority provided in one, can lead to setting aside of the award.[96] An arbitration agreement is also a necessary prerequisite to be bound to arbitration in the context of the access to justice principle. Germany, just like most countries, adheres to the fundamental legal principle guarantying its citizens access to justice, contained in the European context in Article 6 of the European Convention on Human Rights. In practice, this principle is often translated into the right of access to the courts. A derogation from this right needs to be explicit. An arbitration agreement

94. *Born*, International Arbitration, p. 2; *see also Law*, Oxford Dictionary of Law, Arbitration.
95. MüKoZPO/*Münch* § 1029 ZPO, No. 48; Musielak/Voit/*Voit* § 1029 ZPO, No. 2.
96. MüKoZPO/*Münch* § 1059 ZPO, No. 15.

is generally viewed as an explicit derogation from the right of access to the courts in favour of final dispute resolution by the tribunal.[97]

For successful arbitration and successful enforcement of the subsequent award, it is essential to clearly define the relevant disputes that can be submitted to arbitration by the party. The derogation from access to state court is limited only to those disputes actively taken away from court jurisdiction by the parties' agreement.[98] This limitation is reflected positively in § 1029 ZPO, the definition of the arbitration agreement, which states that an arbitration agreement encompasses a defined (set of) dispute(s). However, it is perhaps more clearly defined in the negative sense in the rules of annulment of awards and the recognition of foreign awards, i.e., an award can be annulled and cannot be enforced if it goes beyond the maters subjected to arbitration by the parties. Under § 1059(2)(1)(c) ZPO, a German award can be annulled by the German court in case the arbiters have acted in excess of their jurisdiction *ratione materiae.* Similarly, the German courts can refuse the enforcement of both domestic and foreign awards in Germany based on the same excess of jurisdiction *ratione materiae, see* §§ 1060–1061 ZPO and *see* Article V(1)(c) of the New York Convention on the Recognition and Enforcement of Foreign Arbitral Awards (also New York Convention (NYC)).[99] In a reflection of the importance of material jurisdiction of the arbitrators, parties regularly choose to subject a wide range of potential disputes to arbitration with blanket statements such as 'all disputes connected to this contractual relationship'. Inversely they can also clearly demarcate the limited nature of the arbitration agreement or reserve arbitration for one particular dispute or sort of dispute.

The second (2) and third (3) elements, the derogation from the right to go to court and submission of the dispute to a non-governmental adjudicator chosen by the parties, is also a key differentiation between arbitration and court proceedings. This 'adjudicator' is a reference to the arbitrator or arbitrators. Although some governments might offer services similar to arbitration, choosing a governmental forum essentially translates the arbitration agreement into a choice of forum agreement, as it is no longer an agreement for private dispute resolution. The fact that, in general, arbitrators are chosen by the parties is also a major difference from state court proceedings, where a judge is typically assigned to the case by the state.[100]

The fourth element (4), the principle that decisions rendered should be final and binding, sets arbitration apart from such instruments as mediation and conciliation. Because parties agree to final and binding dispute resolution, arbitral awards can be enforced against those parties. So-called optional clauses, i.e., arbitration clauses stating that a party may choose to go to arbitration or state court, are often controversial. Under some circumstances, courts can consider such clauses to be mandatory arbitration clauses, which can be enforced. However, if the arbitration is optional, it

97. As recently reconfirmed in *European Court of Human Rights*, 1.3.2016 – 41069/12 *Tabbane v. Switzerland*; MüKoZPO/*Münch* § 1029 ZPO, No. 6; Musielak/Voit/*Voit* § 1029 ZPO, Nos 2, 20.
98. MüKoZPO/*Münch* § 1029 ZPO, No. 90; Musielak/Voit/*Voit* § 1029 ZPO, No. 16.
99. Cf. *BGH*, NJW 2002, 3031, p. 3032.
100. *Born*, International Arbitration, 3 et seq.

cannot be enforced upon a party.[101] Clauses stating that a party may still resort to state court after the award is rendered are often not considered arbitration clauses as the prescribed procedure lacks the final and binding effect. Whereas in the US, the Supreme Court in 2008 did not allow for an extensive review of an award by the court,[102] the German Federal Supreme Court in 2007 did give effect to an arbitration agreement that allowed for de novo review by a state court and in 2018 confirmed the suspensive effect of an appeal period in a two-tiered arbitration clause.[103]

The fifth (5) and final element mentioned by *Born* is the specific procedural rules that provide both parties with a chance to present their case. This aspect is necessary to set arbitration apart from such procedures in which the third-party adjudicator makes an independent investigation without necessarily providing the parties with an opportunity for input, e.g., certain expert determinations and valuations.[104] This aspect also embodies the right to be heard, a core aspect of arbitration. A violation of the right to be heard can lead to the annulment and non-enforcement of awards, *see* Article V(1)(b) NYC and § 1059(2)(1)(c) ZPO for setting aside and §§ 1060(2), 1061(1) ZPO for recognition.[105]

3.1 The Legal Framework

This subsection shortly introduces the legal framework for arbitration in Germany. In Germany, arbitration is regulated in the 10th book of the Code of Civil Procedure (ZPO), §§ 1025–1066 ZPO. The ZPO does not make a difference between national and international arbitration. This means that arbitration in Germany between or including a non-German party concerning foreign assets or claims is not treated differently from a purely German arbitration. This lack of distinction should not be confused with another differentiation that is made in Germany between foreign and domestic arbitration and awards, which concerns the seat of arbitration, i.e., it being in Germany or in another jurisdiction.

The 10th book of the ZPO is primarily an adaptation of the Model Law on International Commercial Arbitration (Arb.ML).[106] While it should be noted that they have chosen to diverge on some issues, this is not relevant to the discussion here. Aside from this, Germany is also a Member State of the NYC, making Germany, in general, a very arbitration-friendly jurisdiction. These last two rulesets are introduced more fully in the following paragraphs §§ 3.1.1–3.1.2.

101. *Born*, International commercial arbitration, p. 327; *U.S. District Court for the Southern District of New York*, 3.5.1994 - 93 Civ. 3859; *U.S. Court of Appeals, 4th Circuit*, 5.9.1991 - 944 F.2d 190.
102. *U.S. Supreme Court*, 25.3.2008 - 552 U.S. 576.
103. *BGH*, NJW-RR 2018, 1334, p. 1335; SchiedsVZ 2007, 160, p. 162 the case concerns a condition that the award only becomes binding when a party does not go to court within a certain time period after the award is rendered; *see also Wolff*, ASA Bull. 26 (2008), 626–641.
104. *Born*, International Arbitration, 3 et seq.
105. MüKoZPO/*Münch* § 1059 ZPO, No. 27.
106. *Böckstiegel/S.M. Kröll/Nacimiento*, Part I: Germany as a Place for International and Domestic Arbitrations - General Overview, 1, p. 8.

3.1.1 *UNCITRAL Model Law on International Commercial Arbitration*

The German arbitration law closely follows the UNCITRAL Model Law on International Commercial Arbitration. For this reason, the UNCITRAL Model Law is introduced in this introduction to the legal framework. The UNCITRAL Model Law on International Commercial Arbitration is a model law made by UNCITRAL. Its full name is mostly shortened to UNCITRAL Model Law or just the Model Law within an arbitration context. However, the commission has made several model laws, including, for example, the UNCITRAL Model Law on Cross-Border Insolvency discussed earlier.

First adopted on 21 June 1985 by UNCITRAL, the Model Law represents the most relevant 'statute' in international commercial arbitration. Of course, it does not have legislative power by itself, but many jurisdictions have adopted the Model Law, and in other jurisdictions, it has served as a basis or inspiration for the local arbitration law. According to UNCITRAL, seventy-three states have currently adopted legislation based on the Model Law.[107] Thus, it has achieved a significant level of success given its goal of the harmonisation of arbitration law.

Germany transposed the Model Law into the tenth book of the Civil Procedural Code, with few, but not unimportant, changes. The German legislator has decided to apply its adaptation to both national and international arbitration, as it only requires the arbitration to be seated in Germany for it to be applicable. By their nature, the applicability of the rules on the enforcement of foreign awards is based on the seized forum.

In keeping with the Model Law, the German arbitration law is quite arbitration-friendly. § 1032(1) ZPO states, for example, that upon request, a court must deny the admissibility of and jurisdiction over a claim subject to an arbitration agreement. The exceptions stated are the arbitration agreement being null and void, inoperable or incapable of being performed. This makes both international and domestic arbitration agreements relatively easily enforceable.

3.1.2 *The New York Convention*

Aside from the German national legislation, when talking about the legal framework of arbitration in Germany, the 1958 – New York Convention on the Recognition and Enforcement of Foreign Arbitral Awards, commonly known as the New York Convention (NYC), must be mentioned as this Convention plays a prominent role in international arbitration.

Although it can already be gleaned from the title that this convention is only directly relevant to foreign arbitral awards, it has also profoundly influenced national/domestic arbitration legislation. Most of its rules have into the UNCITRAL Model Law on International Commercial Arbitration, which, as mentioned, in turn largely forms the basis for German arbitration legislation. The previously mentioned

107. UNCITRAL, 'Status: UNCITRAL Model Law on International Commercial Arbitration (1985), with amendments as adopted in 2006' (2017) http://www.uncitral.org/uncitral/en/uncitral_texts/arbitration/1985Model_arbitration_status.html accessed 11 January 2017.

grounds for a refusal to deny jurisdiction, as mentioned in § 1032(1) ZPO, are the same as those mentioned in Article II(3) NYC. There are several other examples to be made, but perhaps the most strikingly is the straightforward reference to the NYC made in § 1061(1) ZPO concerning the grounds to refuse the recognition of a foreign arbitral award.

In terms of the number of stipulations, the convention is a relatively short international treaty that forms the bases of international commercial arbitration in its 156 Member States and counting. Of course, the NYC is not a fully-fledged piece of arbitration legislation. However, it is the framework in which international commercial arbitration operates, and it is safe to say that without the NYC international arbitration as it is known today would not exist or function.[108] Anyone wanting to have an international award or arbitration agreement recognised or enforced in any of the 156 Member States will base such a request on the NYC. Recognition and enforcement are also the nominal goals of the NYC.[109] More widely, the NYC was intended to promote international arbitration. Both goals seem to have been achieved with a large number of Member States and the constant growth in the number of arbitration proceedings.

The NYC functions on what can be described as a higher level than the national legislation, as treaties and conventions are often described as higher or above national legislation, i.e., supranational rules. Thus, the NYC forms a hierarchical framework together with the national arbitration legislation. These two parts of the framework, which are determined by the chosen jurisdiction, are supplemented by the arbitration agreement itself and the institutional rules often incorporated therein. Together they form the four-tier framework in which international commercial arbitration operates.[110]

The convention was adopted in 1958 and entered into force the following year. As stated in Article VII(2) NYC, the NYC replaced the Geneva Protocol of 1923 and Convention of 1927, which respectively provided for referral to arbitration and recognition and enforcement of arbitral awards.[111]

In most signatory states, the convention has been implemented via national law.[112] The danger inherent in this approach is that national courts can interpret their local implementation of the convention differently than the courts in other jurisdictions. A body of case law on the implementation acts has arisen. However, in practice, diverging case law has, for the most part, not become a significant problem as courts increasingly often cite international sources and make their decisions more widely accessible than in the past.[113]

The convention has a mere sixteen articles, of which only a hand full is relevant in practice. Article I NYC identifies the scope of application as applying to arbitral

108. *Born*, 16, 19; *Lazić*, Insolvency Proceedings and Commercial Arbitration, p. 58.
109. *Born*, International Arbitration, p. 20.
110. *Born*, International Arbitration, p. 17.
111. *Born*, International Arbitration, pp. 17–18.
112. This relates to jurisdictions either having a monist or dualist system regarding international law c.q. treaties.
113. *Born*, International Arbitration; *Lazić*, Insolvency Proceedings and Commercial Arbitration, p. 61.

awards of an international nature. Sometimes this is interpreted as meaning outside of the relevant jurisdiction, but more often and correctly, it is viewed as referring to awards that have international aspects.[114] Article II NYC provides the legal requirements for the recognition of an arbitration agreement. The convention goes on to provide an extensive duty (Article III NYC) to enforce the aforementioned awards. A description of what needs to be submitted for a request of enforcement can be found in Article IV NYC. The relatively narrow grounds on which awards can be declared unenforceable are found in Article V NYC. It is important to note the use of the word 'can' as opposed to 'must'. Article V NYC does not create a duty to find the award unenforceable; it merely provides the possibility. Article VI NYC contains the last substantial rule, providing for the possibility of security or adjournment in case of an ongoing setting aside procedure. Article VII NYC states that the convention does not prejudge the applicability of other treaties or conventions. The remaining articles are filled with treaty technical arrangements.

Aside from the NYC, Germany is also party to the European Convention on International Commercial Arbitration of 1961. However, it is of minor relevance and mainly a product of the Cold War era. It might, however, come into play under very specific circumstances as its Article IX, for example, offers an option to recognise awards that were annulled in the seat country, something that, in general, is not done in Germany.[115]

3.2 The Arbitration Agreement: The Basis for Arbitration

Arbitration is based on an arbitration agreement, *see* § 1029 ZPO, the parties' agreement to derogate from their right to go to court in favour of settling certain disputes by arbitration. Above, in Chapter 1 § 3, it has been discussed what the hallmarks of arbitration are. However, the arbitration agreement itself is the fundament of any arbitration.[116] Thus, in addition to these general aspects of arbitration, it is vital to understand the basics of arbitration agreements and a few key concepts that are relevant in the further discussion of arbitration and insolvency.

In terms of content, it is often mentioned that theoretically a functional arbitration agreement could be limited to nothing more than the word 'arbitration', which would then, by interpretation of the context, mean, 'all disputes shall be finally resolved by arbitration'.[117] It is true that the absolute indispensable core of an arbitration agreement is only that: the agreement to arbitrate. Therefore, a clause containing only the agreement to arbitrate attached to a contract should theoretically suffice in a pro-arbitration environment. All the other relevant aspects, e.g., the seat of

114. *Born*, International Arbitration, p. 51.
115. *Böckstiegel/S.M. Kröll/Nacimiento*, Part I: Germany as a Place for International and Domestic Arbitrations - General Overview, 1, pp. 10-11; *OLG Dresden*, SchiedsVZ 2007, 327-330 the decision was subsequently upheld by the German Supreme Court, *see*; *BGH*, SchiedsVZ 2008, 195-196.
116. *Born*, International Arbitration, p. 45.
117. *See* similarly in German commentary MüKoZPO/*Münch* § 1029 ZPO, Nos 112-113.

the arbitration, could be found by interpretation or fall-back options through the application of a *lex arbitri*.[118]

However, arbitration clauses usually contain several other important terms regarding several aspects of the arbitration. *Born* lists as primary examples of such incidental terms: the scope of the arbitration, i.e., the material jurisdiction of the tribunal, the seat, the applicable institutional rules, the number of arbitrators, their qualifications and selection method, the language of the proceedings, and choice-of-law clauses.[119]

In Germany, the definition of the arbitration agreement is organised in § 1029(1) ZPO, a relatively straightforward adoption of Article 7 Arb.ML. It states that an arbitration agreement is: '[...] an agreement by the parties that they subject themselves to the decision passed by an arbitral tribunal on all or individual disputes that have arisen between them or may arise in future as regards a specific legal relationship that is contractual or non-contractual in nature'. Again, this description primarily posits the 'agreement to arbitrate' as the primary substantive requirement and adds that the agreement must relate to a specific legal relationship.

From this description, it can be concluded that, under German law, the bare minimum agreement, as mentioned by *Born*, 'all disputes shall be finally resolved by arbitration' added to a contractual agreement, could indeed suffice.[120] Beyond the agreement to arbitrate, which is the only substantive requirement, the determination of material jurisdiction – the issues which the parties resolved to settle by arbitration – is one of certainty and specificity. However, to avoid having to rely heavily on fall-back options in national law and leaving important aspects of the arbitration up to the discretion of the tribunal, adding the aforementioned incidental terms is highly advisable.[121] The scope of the arbitration agreement is a relevant topic in the further discussion on arbitration and insolvency. This primarily concerns the questions: Can and did the parties agree to arbitrate insolvency matters? These topics are discussed in Chapter 2.

§ 1031 ZPO adds a form requirement to these relatively minimal requirements, stating that arbitration agreements must be written agreements: *see* § 1031(1) ZPO. However, that same paragraph provides a host of alternatives, from exchanged letters, faxes, and telegrams to other methods of communication that allow for evidence of the agreement, *see* § 1031(1) ZPO. This must be read to include e-mails.[122] Finally, § 1031(5) ZPO puts forward specific requirements for arbitration agreements involving a consumer. As follows from the first sentence of § 1031(5) ZPO, the arbitration agreement must be included in a document personally signed by both parties. However, further elaborations on this point fall beyond the scope of this book.

In an international context, more requirements can apply. An arbitration agreement being enacted in Germany but subject to the law of another state will have the

118. *Born*, International Arbitration, p. 75; Cf. *S.M. Kröll*, The 'Incapable of Being Performed' Exception in Article II(3) of the New York Convention, 323, pp. 330–332.
119. *Born*, International Arbitration, 35–39, 75.
120. MüKoZPO/*Münch* § 1029 ZPO, No. 113.
121. Cf. MüKoZPO/*Münch* § 1029 ZPO, No. 122.
122. MüKoZPO/*Münch* § 1031 ZPO, No. 3.

requirements applied cumulatively with that of § 1031 ZPO by a German court.[123] Within the context of the application of the NYC or the European Convention on International Commercial Arbitration, their respective rules also apply in conjunction with the ZPO. Both these conventions have their own written form requirements. However, the NYC includes a most-favourable law conflict-of-laws rule, meaning that if an award is being enforced in Germany and an agreement is valid under § 1031 ZPO, the NYC does not prevent a party from relying on it, *see* Article VII(1) NYC. Similarly, Article I(2)(a) European Convention on International Commercial Arbitration allows the application of lower standards if prescribed by one of the home jurisdictions of the parties.[124]

This last concept introduced here is 'separability'. Separability is one of the basic and crucially important characteristics of the arbitration agreement and is introduced here as it must also be considered relevant to the insolvency and arbitration context. Whereas the precise application and extent of the doctrine of separability is a matter of debate, the doctrine generally states that the arbitration agreement is to be considered a separate agreement from the underlying contract.[125] While an arbitration agreement can be physically incorporated into many sorts of contracts, the arbitration agreement is legally treated as separate from such contracts. Thus, arbitration agreements pertaining to agreements that have been dissolved are not automatically also dissolved.[126] This ensures that parties can still resort to arbitration if a dispute concerning this underlying agreement occurs, for example, regarding the dissolution thereof. However, this also means that the arbitration agreement is not per se covered by the same law as the underlying relationship or subjected to the same requirements.[127] In the context of insolvency, insolvency administrators often have insolvency-specific powers to choose to perform or not-perform mutual contracts. In Germany, this is regulated in § 103 InsO. If such a power is exercised on a material agreement including an arbitration agreement, the faith of the arbitration agreement remains separate from this material contract. This topic and the nature of the arbitration agreement are further explored in Chapter 2 § 3.5.1.

In conclusion, the basis for arbitration, i.e., the arbitration agreement is separable from the agreement or legal relationship to which it applies. In Germany, it is primarily organised in § 1029(1) ZPO.

4 ARBITRATION THEORY

In this section, the fundamental theories underlying arbitration are introduced. Together with the previous discussion of arbitration in Germany, insolvency in Germany

123. Musielak/Voit/*Voit* § 1031 ZPO, No. 17.
124. Musielak/Voit/*Voit* § 1031 ZPO, Nos 18–19.
125. *Born*, International Commercial Arbitration, pp. 350–353; *see* for its relevance in insolvency for example, *Strauch*, Schutz von Schiedsvereinbarung und vereinbarter Vertraulichkeit bei Insolvenzeröffnung, pp. 66–67.
126. *See, e.g.*, *Partial Award in ICC Case No. 6719*, Collection of ICC Awards III, 1997, 567, p. 571.
127. *Born*, International Arbitration, pp. 54–55.

and insolvency theory, arbitration theory forms the extent of the background and framework introduction part of this book.

When one compares insolvency to arbitration, one finds a public and collective proceeding on the one hand and a proceeding focused on the resolution of a single dispute between the parties only on the other hand.[128] The related theoretical debates reflect this difference. While the debate on insolvency is centred around a struggle for jurisdiction and the concept of state sovereignty, arbitration theory follows a more autonomy-orientated, internationalist trend. A different view on arbitration can lead to very different results regarding core issues of arbitration, including different qualifications of the arbitration agreement and arbitration proceedings. Depending on the doctrine one adheres to, the arbitration agreement can be viewed as a procedural agreement, a regular contract, or as part of the system of legal remedies.[129]

As in the German ZPO, it is not uncommon for legislation to not define arbitration. It is even harder to find an authoritative definition in an international context. However, as to what arbitration is in general, the description discussed above in Chapter 1 § 3 is an accurate description of international consensus: A consensual means by which parties submit disputes to a non-governmental decision-maker selected by the parties to receive binding dispute resolution using a neutral adjudicatory procedure affording both parties the opportunity to present their case.[130] However, there are competing theories when it comes to the relationship and role of arbitration in and to the national legal order.

Different theories about international arbitration lead to fundamentally different answers to questions on the intersection of the two legal fields.[131] It is, therefore, relevant to discuss the leading theories regarding international commercial arbitration. For this purpose, the jurisdictional theory (§ 4.1), the contractual theory (§ 4.2), the middle ground or so-called hybrid theory (§ 4.3), and finally, the autonomous theory (§ 4.4) will be discussed here.

4.1 The Jurisdictional Theory

The first theory introduced in this section is the jurisdictional theory. The jurisdictional theory is a classical theory that can be viewed as the arbitration equivalent of the territorial approach to insolvency in the sense that it also focuses on the sovereignty of jurisdictions. It views arbitration as part of the state's function to adjudicate legal disputes within its jurisdiction.[132] In this view, an arbitrator is a private judge,[133] and their authority can only reach as far as what is bestowed upon them by the local legal system. As a result, arbitrators are fully bound to local law, as far as it cannot be contracted out of.[134] As the arbitrators are integrated into the local adjudication system,

128. *Fouchard*, Rev. Arb. 1998, 471, p. 473.
129. *Born*, International Commercial Arbitration, p. 215.
130. *Born*, International Arbitration, p. 2.
131. *Vorburger*, International Arbitration and Cross-Border Insolvency, p. 4.
132. *Badel*, ASA Bull. 25 (2007), p. 36.
133. *Born*, International Commercial Arbitration, p. 214.
134. *Vorburger*, International Arbitration and Cross-Border Insolvency, p. 5.

their awards are as well. Those awards are *ipso iure* provided with a status similar to that of court judgments.[135]

Although this theory does not deny that the foundation of arbitration lies within the parties' contract, the focus is lain on the supervisory task of states, most importantly, that of the 'forum state'.[136] One of the crucial differences between this theory and the contractual theory is what one considers the primary source of the arbitrator's power and authority; the state's legal order or the arbitration agreement. Within the jurisdictional theory, that source is primarily the state's legal system, primarily its arbitration law and procedural laws. Thus, the *lex fori*, in many ways, plays a central role in this theory.[137] For example, following this theory, arbitrators will be bound to the choice-of-law and conflict-of-laws rules in the same way as local judges when it comes to finding the applicable substantive law.[138]

4.2 The Contractual Theory and Delocalisation

'Opposite' the jurisdictional theory stands the contractual theory and, related to its extremes, the concept of delocalisation. These are introduced here. The contractual theory focuses on the private and consensual nature of arbitration.[139] Its views arbitration as based purely on the private contract; established by the mutual consent of the parties.[140] The arbitrators, in this view, are not considered judges and do not perform a public role in the legal sense.[141] As such, the state is not thought to have any role in the arbitral process,[142] except in as far as the state has a role in the enforcement of any contractual obligation between the parties. That contractual enforcement can be sought at any stage in the arbitral process, including the enforcement of arbitral awards.[143] Complying with the awards is to be seen as complying with the contractual agreement to submit disputes to binding arbitration. Logically, within this theory, the arbitral award also enjoys no higher or lower status than that of a contract.[144]

The contractual theory, with its focus on the autonomy of the parties, is the basis for the idea that arbitration is without any home jurisdiction or 'location', hence the

135. *Yu*, Contemp. Asia Arb. J. 2008, 255, p. 262.
136. 'Forum state' is a problematic term in arbitration as it is often argued that arbitration, particularly international arbitration, does not have a forum but is detached from any jurisdiction. However, following the jurisdictional theory naturally leads to a denial of such a detachment.
137. *Yu*, Contemp. Asia Arb. J. 2008, 255, p. 258.
138. *Yu*, Contemp. Asia Arb. J. 2008, 255, p. 263.
139. *Yu*, Contemp. Asia Arb. J. 2008, 255, p. 265.
140. *Born*, International Commercial Arbitration, p. 213; *F.-E. Klein*, Considérations sur l'arbitrage en droit international privé, précédées d'une étude de législation, de doctrine et de jurisprudence comparées en la matière, § 106; *J.D.M. Lew/Mistelis/Kröll*, Comparative International Commercial Arbitration, §§ 5.18, 5.3.
141. *Final Award in ICC Case No. 6379*, Collection of ICC Awards III, 1997, No. 2121; *Bogdan*, Swedish and International Arbitration 1990, 70, p. 76; *Born*, International Commercial Arbitration, p. 213.
142. *J.D.M. Lew/Mistelis/Kröll*, Comparative International Commercial Arbitration, § 5.18.
143. *J.D.M. Lew*, Applicable Law in International Commercial Arbitration § 56.
144. *Yu*, Contemp. Asia Arb. J. 2008, 255, p. 271.

term delocalisation.[145] This means that arbitration should be viewed as separate from any specific jurisdiction.[146] The parties' intent and autonomy should be afforded the maximum weight. Only the restrictions of regular contractual validity and the restrictions of the chosen law or *lex contractus* should apply.[147]

Consequently, a tribunal confronted with insolvency should not be bothered with considerations of territoriality or universality but merely with the execution of the arbitration agreement and finding a solution in accordance with it.[148] Furthermore, in the German context, this means that the tribunal is not bound to German law by way of Article 20(3) GG (German Constitution) as German judge would be, but merely – in the extreme view – to the parties' will.[149]

4.3 The Hybrid Theory

Similar to the discussion on the insolvency theories above, there is also a hybrid theory within the discussion of arbitration theories. This theory generally reflects reality better than the two previously discussed theories.[150] The so-called hybrid theory contains aspects from both the contractual and jurisdictional theories.[151]

In line with the contractual theory, the arbitration agreement itself, including the choice of arbitrators, is wholly determined by the parties in the hybrid theory.[152] However, the framework in which arbitration operates is controlled by the state, which reflects an aspect of the jurisdictional theory. Some authors do not see a clear dominance of one of the aforementioned theories in the hybrid theory.[153] However, it appears that the contractual theory dominates. This follows from the observation that, in the hybrid theory, intervention is seen as an exception and serves only as a check on party autonomy. Whereas the party autonomy itself is considered the cornerstone of arbitration[154] and thus plays the dominant role in this theory.[155]

It has become clear that the hybrid theory, similar to the middle ground in the insolvency debate, has become the dominant approach. This is reflected in the legal framework provided in arbitration laws, the relevant court decisions and many available arbitral awards reflect hybrid approaches.[156]

145. *Bělohlávek*, ASA Bull. 31 (2013), 262, p. 269.
146. *Final Award in ICC Case No. 1512*, Collection of ICC Awards I, 1990, 3–5, p. 4.
147. *Vorburger*, International Arbitration and Cross-Border Insolvency, pp. 4–5; *Barraclough /Waincymer*, MJIL 2005, 205–245, § II.
148. *Berset/Lévy*, ASA Bull. 16 (1998), 664, p. 666.
149. *Schultze-Moderow*, Schiedsverfahren und Insolvenz, pp. 102–103.
150. *Yu*, Contemp. Asia Arb. J. 2008, 255, p. 274.
151. *Vorburger*, International Arbitration and Cross-Border Insolvency, p. 5.
152. *Yu*, Contemp. Asia Arb. J. 2008, 255, p. 277.
153. *Vorburger*, International Arbitration and Cross-Border Insolvency, p. 5; *Barraclough /Waincymer*, MJIL 2005, 205–245, § II.
154. *Redfern/Hunter, Martin, Blackaby, Nigel/Partasides*, Law and Practice of International Commercial Arbitration, p. 315; *Fagbemi*, JSDLP 6 (2016), 202, p. 245.
155. *Born*, International Commercial Arbitration, p. 214.
156. *J.D.M. Lew*, Applicable Law in International Commercial Arbitration, § 57; *J.D.M. Lew /Mistelis/Kröll*, Comparative International Commercial Arbitration, § 5.26.

4.4 The Autonomous Theory

The final theory introduced in this section and Chapter 1 is the autonomous theory of arbitration. Some authors place arbitration outside of the scope of any of the theories described in this section. *Rubellin-Devichi* argues that arbitration must be viewed as an autonomous system outside of the confines of other areas of law to achieve maximum effect.[157] In her opinion, both the contractual and jurisdictional theories fail to correspond with reality. She disregards the hybrid theory as the scope of its application is viewed as too undefined.[158] In reality, the supranational nature of arbitration should be recognised. Part of this view is that one should stop trying to recognise contractual and jurisdictional aspects within the arbitration practice, which within this view is a meritless exercise in any case.[159] Arbitration and arbitrators should be regarded as having an autonomous nature in which the necessary authority flows from its own purpose and necessity.[160] This autonomous system would be more flexible, closer to reality and more able to fulfil ever-changing needs.

Following this would be the conclusion that an arbitral award would neither carry the status of a judgment nor that of a contractual obligation but would be in a category of its own. The autonomous system follows a delocalised approach to arbitration, detaching the arbitration from any national legal system. In consequence, the supervisory role of the *lex fori* is denied. They argue that a new system must be founded to fulfil this supervisory role, free from contractual and jurisdictional ideas.[161]

5 FINAL REMARK ON THE THEORETICAL BACKGROUND AND FRAMEWORK

This concludes Chapter 1 of this book. In the above, the author introduced the relevant legal theories for insolvency and arbitration and the frameworks in which insolvency and arbitration operate in Germany. This broad stokes representation and introduction are meant as sufficient and necessary background for the discussions in Chapters 2 and 3. Further reference can be had to the sources cited in this part.

The above discussion and representation of the relevant theories and legal framework primarily show two facts. First, Germany has a relatively open and universalistic insolvency system and a similarly open pro-arbitration system. Second, and more important, both the insolvency theory debate and the arbitration theory debate bring opposing and competing views to the table, which play an important role in the discussions ahead.

157. *Rubellin-Devichi,* L'Arbitrage: Nature juridique, droit interne et droit international privé, p. 365.
158. *Yu,* Contemp. Asia Arb. J. 2008, 255, p. 278.
159. *Yu,* Contemp. Asia Arb. J. 2008, 255, p. 278.
160. *Samuel/Currat,* Jurisdictional Problems in International Commercial Arbitration, p. 59.
161. *Samuel/Currat,* Jurisdictional Problems in International Commercial Arbitration, p. 60; *Yu,* Contemp. Asia Arb. J. 2008, 255, pp. 279–280.

In consequence, in the following parts, the theories here described play a fundamental role, informing many of the conclusions. Likewise, the facts and discussions in practice and the conclusions that can be reached based thereon can further develop the discussion on these fundamental theories. *See*, *e.g.*, the discussion in Chapter 2 § 2.1.2.

CHAPTER 2

Insolvency and Arbitration in the National Context: Germany

Chapter 2 of this book discusses insolvency-related issues in arbitration within the national context of Germany. From the titles in this part, one can glean that the interaction between insolvency and arbitration is mostly a one-way street. The insolvency will have consequences for the arbitration proceedings and the related proceedings, but while the arbitration can feature in the insolvency process, it will typically not affect the proceedings per se.[162] The subject of this part is why this is the case and what the actual effects are.

The setup of this part is geared towards providing the reader with a readable and understandable order of subjects. Therefore, the procession of subjects will continue to build on conclusions and information provided in previous topics. However, readers with specific questions should still be able to skip to the relevant parts without too much cross-referencing. Further to the above, this part includes a discussion on arbitrability (1), both in general and specific to insolvency (§ 1.3). This includes a discussion on which insolvency issues are deemed arbitrable and why. The second section concerns the effect of insolvency on ongoing arbitration proceedings. This includes the role of the administrator (§ 2.2) and the possibility of a stay of proceedings (§ 2.3). Section 3 concerns the effect of insolvency on the arbitration agreement. This includes the fundamental question of the validity of this agreement in insolvency. Section 4 concerns the effect of insolvency on the arbitrators' agreement, and finally, section 5 concerns the effect of insolvency on awards. This includes the question of enforceability.

As stated in the introduction, to avoid discussing too many factors at once, this part will focus on insolvency in arbitration in the national context, i.e., primarily the German context. This will set up the discussion in the third part on the effect of international aspects as an extra factor.

162. *Fouchard*, Rev. Arb. 1998, 471, p. 473.

1 ARBITRABILITY

The first topic to be discussed in Chapter 2 is arbitrability. The concept of arbitrability provides the differentiation between topics that can be arbitrated and those that cannot be arbitrated. In this way, it plays a significant role in the discussion of insolvency in arbitration, as insolvency-related topics could potentially be considered non-arbitrable. This section builds toward the discussion of arbitrability of insolvency disputes in Germany in Chapter 2 § 1.5 by introducing the concept of arbitrability in this paragraph, demarking arbitrability from public policy (§ 1.1), discussing objective and subjective arbitrability (§ 1.2), general arbitrability in Germany (§ 1.3) and arbitrability of insolvency issues in general (§ 1.4).

While other views on the nature of arbitration and arbitrability can be held. It seems generally and internationally accepted that arbitrability is a state-imposed limitation on the autonomy of the parties.[163] It is essentially the boundary to arbitration that the state provides in the sense of who can agree to arbitration and, more importantly: what can be arbitrated.[164] In that last sense, the doctrine of arbitrability mirrors what the states considered too important for the public good to be privately handled or subjects in need of judicial protection through state adjudication. Thus, arbitrability can be considered a public policy limitation on arbitration.[165] For example, many jurisdictions find large swaths of insolvency issues non-arbitrable because so many third-party rights are affected by the outcome of the proceeding. As an example of people granted special judicial protection, EU law protects consumers from arbitration clauses incorporated in standard terms.[166]

Arbitration is controlled by the framework of the NYC, other treaties and arbitration legislation. Arbitrability functions on both the international and national levels. Articles II(1), V(2)(a) NYC provide jurisdictions with an exception to their general duty under the convention to recognise arbitration agreements and awards if it concerns issues that the jurisdiction considers not capable of being settled by arbitration.[167] This exception is mirrored in most national legislation, in Germany under § 1059(2)(2)(a) ZPO and also § 1030 ZPO.[168] Even though the arbitration agreement or award may otherwise be valid, it can be set aside or become unenforceable if it concerns an issue considered non-arbitrable.[169] In essence, the consequence of

163. *Born*, International Commercial Arbitration, § 6.1; *Lazić*, Insolvency Proceedings and Commercial Arbitration, p. 136; *BGH*, NJW 1996, 1753–1756, II.4.
164. *Born*, International Commercial Arbitration, § 6.1; *Schmitz*, Schiedsverfahren und Insolvenz, p. 38.
165. *Lazić*, Insolvency Proceedings and Commercial Arbitration, p. 137; referring to *Redfern/Hunter*, Law and Practice of International Commercial Arbitration, p. 137.
166. *Born*, International Arbitration, 87–89.
167. *Born*, International Commercial Arbitration, p. 87; *Sachs*, Collected Courses of the International Academy for Arbitration Law, year 2011 1 (2013), 1–48, p. 32. For the German approach refer to 2.1.1., as an extensive discussion falls outside of the scope of the background theory exposé in this part.
168. Musielak/Voit/*Voit* § 1030 ZPO, No. 2.
169. *Born*, International Arbitration, p. 87.

non-arbitrability is a limitation on the tribunal's jurisdiction that limits its competence.[170]

Interestingly the Model Law on International Commercial Arbitration remains silent on the definition of arbitrability. This is attributed to the lack of consensus on the subject.[171] As a result, countries, even those countries that adopt the Model Law, remain free to determine what they consider arbitrable.[172] Germany does this, for example, in § 1030 ZPO, which is discussed later in this section in Chapter 2 § 1.3.

Most states have limited their concept of non-arbitral claims considerably over recent years. The US, for example, now follows a relatively broad interpretation; only when there is clear legislative intent to have specific claims settled by courts is the claim deemed non-arbitrable.[173]

Areas (still or until recently) often defined as non-arbitrable are: competition and antitrust claims, securities claims, insolvency claims, labour and employment claims and consumer disputes.[174] This varies between jurisdictions, making the question of the applicable law of crucial importance.[175]

1.1 Arbitrability and Public Policy

Rules of arbitrability are often referred to as public policy rules. The terms arbitrability and public policy overlap but are separate terms.[176] They overlap because both arbitrability and public policy prevent recognition or enforcement of awards or agreements based on conflict with basic rules or public policies of the state in which enforcement or recognition is sought.[177] However, as the separation of arbitrability and public policy or *ordre public* in rules such as § 1059(2)(2)(a) and (b) ZPO and Article V(2)(a) and (b) NYC suggests the terms are not interchangeable:

> **Section 1059 ZPO:**
> (1) (...)
> (2) An arbitration award may be reversed only if:
>   1. (...)
>   2. The court determines that:
>   a) the subject matter of the dispute is *not eligible for arbitration* under German law; or
>   b) The recognition or enforcement of the arbitration award will lead to *a result contrary to public order*. [Emphasis added]

170. *Lazić*, Insolvency Proceedings and Commercial Arbitration, p. 139; *see, e.g.*, the phrasing of the arguments on arbitrability in ICC Case 6719, framing arguments of non-arbitrability as competence issues, *see Partial Award in ICC Case No. 6719*, Collection of ICC Awards III, 1997, 567, p. 568.
171. *Sachs*, Collected Courses of the International Academy for Arbitration Law, year 2011 1 (2013), 1-48, pp. 35-36; referring to *Mustill/Boyd*, Commercial Arbitration, p. 71.
172. *Jones*, Arbitration 78 (2012), 123, p. 124.
173. *U.S. Supreme Court*, Decision of 2.7.1985 - 473 U.S. 614, p. 628.
174. *Born*, International Arbitration, 87, 89.
175. *Sachs*, Collected Courses of the International Academy for Arbitration Law, year 2011 1 (2013), 1-48, p. 36; Cf. *Lazić*, Insolvency Proceedings and Commercial Arbitration, p. 139.
176. *Born*, International Commercial Arbitration, p. 950.
177. *Born*, International Commercial Arbitration, p. 950.

Art V NYC:

1. (...)
2. Recognition and enforcement of an arbitral award may also be refused if the competent authority in the country where recognition and enforcement is sought finds that:
   (a) The subject matter of the difference is *not capable of settlement by arbitration under the law of that country*; or
   (b) The recognition or enforcement of the award would be contrary *to the public policy of that country*. [Emphasis added]

Public policy is a broader concept than arbitrability. Rules of public policy are not necessarily rules that affect arbitrability.[178] For example, the right to be heard and the prohibition on individual enforcement do not render issues non-arbitrable per se. Public policy and mandatory law merely require that specific laws and rules are applied. In fact, the application of those rules is often itself arbitrable.[179]

1.2 Objective and Subjective Arbitrability

In discussions on arbitrability, the subject is typically divided into objective and subjective arbitrability.[180] Subjective arbitrability refers to arbitrability in regard to the entity submitting to arbitration or arbitrability *ratione personae*. In the past, state entities have argued that they cannot be a party to arbitration due to national regulations limiting their competence to enter into such contracts.[181]

In the context of this research, objective arbitrability will be the main focus of the arbitrability discussion. Objective arbitrability concerns the subject matter arbitrability and is therefore referred to as arbitrability *ratione materiae*.[182]

1.3 Arbitrability in Germany

To discuss the arbitrability of insolvency issues in Germany, a discussion of Germany's general rules of arbitrability is necessary. The first point of reference for the question of arbitrability in Germany is § 1030 ZPO, titled 'Arbitrability' (German: *Schiedsfähigkeit*). The state-provided translation of § 1030(1) ZPO provides that any claim under property law can be subject to arbitration:

(1) Any claim under property law may become the subject matter of an arbitration agreement. An arbitration agreement regarding non-pecuniary claims has legal effect insofar as the parties to the dispute are entitled to conclude a settlement regarding the subject matter of the dispute.

178. *Partial Award in ICC Case No. 6719*, Collection of ICC Awards III, 1997, 567, pp. 570–571.
179. *Born*, International Commercial Arbitration, p. 950.
180. *Fortier*, Arbitrability of Disputes, pp. 269–270.
181. *Fortier*, Arbitrability of Disputes, p. 270.
182. *Fortier*, Arbitrability of Disputes, p. 270; *Lazić*, Insolvency Proceedings and Commercial Arbitration, p. 135.

It has been established that the German *'Jeder vermögensrechtliche Anspruch'* (German: Any claim under property law) should be interpreted broadly,[183] leaving authors to often simply state that any claim with an 'economic interest' should be considered arbitrable.[184] The second sentence of § 1030(1) ZPO provides that non-pecuniary claims are also arbitrable to the extent that parties can privately settle such disputes, e.g., a party can request arbitration in order to gain a declaratory judgment unless it concerns, for example, criminal responsibility or something else that the parties cannot 'decide' amongst themselves.

§ 1030(2) ZPO provides a big exception concerning rental claims and disputes in the context of rental properties in Germany.

§ 1030(3) ZPO provides that rules in other laws that exclude arbitrability of issues remain unaffected by the general rule of arbitrability. In other words, if it is evident in other laws that there is a court monopoly on specific issues, this will exclude arbitrability.[185] This includes, for example, certain labour disputes, *see* §§ 101–102 of the German Labour Court Act. However, German and EU competition claims are, for example, no longer generally held as non-arbitrable.[186] Other issues that throughout history and in many jurisdictions were held non-arbitrable are now considered arbitrable in Germany, e.g., certain intellectual property law issues[187] and most corporate law matters.[188] The arbitrability of corporate law issues has been a source of much academic discussion in Germany.[189] The discussion primarily surrounds a series of judgments by the German Federal Supreme Court creatively named 'Arbitrability I, II, III'.[190] A full review of these cases goes beyond the scope of this book. However, an overarching view provides relevant insight into the fault lines surrounding the topic of arbitrability.

In the Arbitrability I case of 1996, the German Federal Supreme Court had to decide if an arbitral clause in the bylaws of a German GmbH (*Gesellschaft mit beschränkter Haftung*), a private limited liability company, also included disputes concerning deficiencies in corporate resolutions. Controversially, the Court decided that this could not be the case as this would provide an *erga omnes* effect in the sense that the decision would also affect other organs of the company and shareholders who had not participated in the arbitration, being settled by the parties.[191] As generally

183. MüKoZPO/*Münch* § 1030 ZPO, No. 13.
184. *Böckstiegel/S.M. Kröll/Nacimiento,* Part I: Germany as a Place for International and Domestic Arbitrations - General Overview, 1, p. 16.
185. Musielak/Voit/*Voit* § 1030 ZPO, No. 2.
186. *Böckstiegel/S.M. Kröll/Nacimiento,* Part I: Germany as a Place for International and Domestic Arbitrations - General Overview, 1, p. 17.
187. Although still disputed, mainly because of effect on third parties and the jurisdiction of patent courts, modern literature often concludes in favour of arbitrability but restricts the effect of the award to the parties *'inter partes'* effect. *See* for an analyses *E. Schäfer,* Part IV: Selected Areas and Issues of Arbitration in Germany, Arbitration of Intellectual Property Related Disputes in Germany, 907, pp. 913–917.
188. *Duve/Wimalasena,* Part IV: Selected Areas and Issues of Arbitration in Germany, Arbitration of Corporate Law Disputes in Germany, 927, p. 931.
189. *See, e.g., Borris,* NZG 2017, 761–767.
190. *BGH,* NJW 1996, 1753–1756; NJW 2009, 1962–1967; NJW-RR 2017, 876–878.
191. *BGH,* NJW 1996, 1753–1756, II.5.

arbitration requires consent, it cannot affect non-parties and cannot generally and directly have an erga omnes effect. So due to its *erga omnes* effect, the issue was deemed non-arbitrable. The German Federal Supreme Court identifies several issues, which go beyond the discussion here and refers these issues to the legislature.[192]

However, the legislator did not engage with the issues of Arbitrability I, i.e., it did not provide a legislative solution. Thus in 2009, in Arbitrability II, the German Federal Supreme Court reversed its position to a large degree. The Court concluded that, under several conditions, disputes about corporate decisions can be arbitrated. For this to happen, the arbitration agreement must be part of the bylaws or part of a shareholders' agreement to which all shareholders are parties, and the arbitral procedure must provide equal legal protection to the court.[193] Arbitrability III is less fundamental in nature than Arbitrability II, at least dogmatically. Whereas Arbitrability I and II concern a conflict in a GmbH (German Limited Liability Company), Arbitrability III clarifies that the same logic must apply to so-called *Personengesellschaften* or partnerships.

In general, it can be stated that German law provides a relatively broad scope of objective arbitrability, c.q. issues that can be arbitrated. When it comes to subjective arbitrability, there are no special rules in the ZPO regarding the capacity to enter into an arbitration agreement. In consequence, there are no requirements beyond the general ability to enter into a contract and associated legal personality and capacity, a discussion of which goes beyond the scope of this research.[194] This notwithstanding, insolvency affects these issues, e.g., the ability to enter into an arbitration agreement concerning the estate and representation (§ 2.2). These issues are discussed further in this book.

1.4 Arbitrability of Insolvency Disputes Generally

After discussing the concept of arbitrability and introducing the German concept of arbitrability, it is time for a closer look at the meaning of arbitrability in the context of insolvency. Insolvency, not entirely unlike the discussion in Arbitrability I and II, can give rise to many conflicts that have potential ergo omnes effects. The delimitation of what is and what is not arbitrable in such circumstances is essential when discussing the effects of insolvency on arbitration.

Generally, it is thought that in the situation wherein a party to an ongoing arbitration goes insolvent, the tribunal still has jurisdiction regarding issues stemming from non-performance or other contract-related claims covered by an arbitration agreement.[195] Insolvency does not take away the arbitrability of disputes.[196] This does not change that in many jurisdictions, e.g., France and Germany, a decision by the

192. *BGH*, NJW 1996, 1753-1756, II.6(b).
193. *BGH*, NJW 2009, 1962-1967, Leitsatz.
194. Vorwerk/Wolf/*Wolf/Eslami* § 1029 ZPO, No. 7; *See* §§ 2.2.2, 3.3 for a discussion on the insolvency administrator and arbitration agreements.
195. *Sachs*, Collected Courses of the International Academy for Arbitration Law, year 2011 1 (2013), 1-48, p. 54.
196. *Kreindler/J.K. Schäfer/Wolff*, Schiedsgerichtsbarkeit, No. 129; *Schmitz*, Schiedsverfahren und Insolvenz, p. 39.

tribunal will merely serve to prove a claim in insolvency proceedings and cannot be individually enforced. However, this is more due to the prohibition of individual enforcement in insolvency than a lack of objective arbitrability, *see* § 5 in this part.[197] The question thus remains; where does the concept of arbitrability intersect with insolvency?

The line of arbitrability is often drawn at claims that are based in insolvency law or are said to be of an insolvency law nature: claim verification, the collection of assets, payments out of the estate, and settlement of claims.[198] This becomes even clearer insofar as these claims concern the administration of the proceedings themselves, i.e., opening and closing and the previously mentioned appointment.[199]

The Arbitrator in an ICC Case in 2011 summarised the state of the debate as follows: 'There is a range of approaches and opinions as to how this tension has to be resolved. Generally speaking, "core insolvency" matters, such as the initiation of insolvency proceedings, the appointment of a receiver verifying claims, collecting assets, and the winding-up of a company, are thought to be non-arbitrable. Conversely, other disputes such as a contractual dispute where one party happens to be under insolvency proceedings, are considered arbitrable because the arbitral tribunal does not usurp public authority. Here, there is a general trend in favour of arbitration.'[200]

Therefore, it becomes key to consider the nature of a claim and ask the question if a claim is solely based on insolvency law. If insolvency occurs during an ongoing arbitration, it seems unlikely that the claim being arbitrated is based solely on the insolvency regulations governing that insolvency. This is for the simple reason that such a claim would likely not exist before insolvency is commenced. Therefore, the debtor pre-insolvency would not be able to dispose of such rights effectively.[201]

However, when insolvency occurs, all creditors and claims are affected. How to handle creditors in insolvency is an insolvency-specific issue. In most jurisdictions, individual actions against an insolvent debtor are not allowed, party autonomy is drastically restricted, and claims need to be put into a collective proceeding.[202] However, creditors with a preferential claim are often excluded from these rules.[203]

Does this automatically mean that any contractual, monetary claim against the debtor becomes non-arbitrable? This varies depending on the applicable law, but it is not the case in Germany. In practice, the arbitrability of claims surrounding insolvency mostly follows the extent to which the *vis attractiva concursus* principle is adopted in

197. *See* Chapter 2 § 2.3.3.
198. *Partial Award in ICC Case No. 6697*, Rev. Arb., 1992, 135–145; *Interim Award in ICC Case No. 6632*, unpublished, *see* Fouchard, Gaillard, Goldman, fn. 158; *Gaillard/Savage*, Fouchard, Gaillard, Goldman on International Commercial Arbitration, No. 587587; *Fouchard*, Rev. Arb. 1998, 471, pp. 477–478; *Lazić*, Insolvency Proceedings and Commercial Arbitration, p. 154.
199. Wolff/*Quinke* Article V(2)(a) NYC, No. 467.
200. *Final Award in ICC Case No. 16369*, Y.B. Com. Arb. XXXIX, 2014, 169, No. 5252; Cf. *Berset/Lévy*, ASA Bull. 16 (1998), 664, p. 672.
201. *See* § 3.6.
202. For a list of areas in which party autonomy is restricted in insolvency *see Kühn*, Disp. Resol. Int'l 5 (2011), 203, p. 207.
203. *P. Wagner*, Disp. Resol. Int'l 5 (2011), 189, p. 191.

a jurisdiction,[204] the principle that a single (insolvency) forum takes over all insolvency proceedings and claims and all the issues and disputes related to the insolvency.[205] Following that principle, issues given to the sole jurisdictions of the insolvency court are often deemed non-arbitrable.[206]

Since the qualification of the nature of claims is dependent on the applicable law, jurisdictions can and have developed their own doctrines on this point. While several EU Member States have followed a stringent *vis attractive concursus* rule, the EIR itself does not institute such a rule.[207] The US courts have dealt with this issue by separating so-called *core and non-core bankruptcy issues*.[208] That separation returns relatively often in international case law and doctrine.[209] Core insolvency issues are generally those issues based on insolvency law, which are mostly non-arbitrable. While mixed/non-core claims are issues pertaining to insolvency but not based on insolvency law, which can be arbitrable.[210]

As to the European approach, the arbitrator in the case mentioned above noted that: 'In Switzerland, as in other continental European countries, courts and arbitrators follow the more modern, or liberal, approach retaining jurisdiction to decide disputes relating even to insolvency issues, including claims brought on behalf of the estate itself.'[211]

In conclusion, in the discussion of the arbitrability of insolvency issues, several useful perspectives can be considered and are used in different jurisdictions, amongst others: the exclusive jurisdiction of insolvency courts, the nature of the claims, i.e., core or non-core bankruptcy issues, and the dispositive power of the insolvent.

1.5 Arbitration of Insolvency Disputes in Germany

This brings the discussion to the arbitrability of insolvency issues in Germany. As will be shown here, Germany has a liberal approach to the arbitrability of insolvency-related issues.

As discussed, § 1030(1) ZPO states that every economic interest can be arbitrated and every non-economic interest in as far as the parties are allowed to contract on the subject.[212] § 1030(2) ZPO only creates an exception for rent contracts. However, § 1030(3) ZPO refers to limitations that are imposed in other specific laws:

204. In other words the extent of the exclusive jurisdiction of the bankruptcy courts; *P. Wagner*, Disp. Resol. Int'l 5 (2011), 189, p. 196.
205. *Lazić*, Insolvency Proceedings and Commercial Arbitration, pp. 157–159.
206. Cf. *Badel*, ASA Bull. 25 (2007), 36, 39.
207. *Virgós/Garcimartín*, The European Insolvency Regulation, pp. 57–59.
208. *U.S. Court of Appeals, 3rd Circuit*, F.2d, 1149–1161; *U.S. Court of Appeals, 9th Circuit*, F. 3d, 1011–1026, p. 1021; *Vorburger*, International Arbitration and Cross-Border Insolvency, p. 64.
209. Even when the case has no relationship to U.S. doctrine, e.g., *Final Award in ICC Case No. 16369*, Y.B. Com. Arb. XXXIX, 2014, 169, p. 174.
210. *Jones*, Arbitration 78 (2012), 123, pp. 127–128.
211. *Final Award in ICC Case No. 16369*, Y.B. Com. Arb. XXXIX, 2014, 169, No. 5353.
212. *Ferrari/S. Kröll*, Conflict of laws in international arbitration, p. 366; *S.M. Kröll*, Part IV: Selected Areas and Issues of Arbitration in Germany, Insolvency and Arbitration – Effects of Party Insolvency on Arbitral Proceedings in Germany, 981, p. 988.

(3) Any stipulations of the law outside of the present Book, according to which disputes may not be subjected to arbitration proceedings, or only if specific prerequisites have been met, shall remain unaffected hereby.

As such, § 1030 ZPO by itself does not provide conclusive clarity but refers to potential restrictions in other laws. The insolvency code itself also makes no direct, explicit determinations on arbitrability. Consequently, for each insolvency-related subject, e.g., the opening of an insolvency procedure, one must consider if the relevant law or the nature of the issue provides evidence as to its arbitrability.

Regarding the arbitrability of insolvency issues, *Kröll* recognises three categories: (i) issues related to the insolvency proceeding; (ii) disputes based on facts or rights that predate the insolvency; and (iii) those that came after the insolvency was opened. The latter two are issues possibly related to insolvency as such.[213] *Kröll,* while considering these three categories of insolvency issues, concludes that issues concerning the insolvency proceeding per se (i), i.e., opening, appointing the administrator and closing the proceedings, are non-arbitrable due to their legal nature. He primarily bases this conclusion on the *erga omnes* effect of this insolvency proceedings issue, being its binding effect against everyone and not only the parties as is usual in arbitration.

However, the inferred intention of the legislator to exclude issues related to the proceedings per se from arbitration based on exclusive jurisdiction for insolvency courts and organisational considerations also supports the above conclusion of non-arbitrability.[214] This exclusive jurisdiction of the insolvency court and the inverse thereof - parties' ability to decide issues only amongst themselves - seems to be the guiding rule. As such, it is interesting to note that arbitrability of insolvency issues in Germany mostly seems to mirror the rule of the old German arbitration code: the question of if the parties, including here the administrator, could come to an agreement or '*Vergleich*' about the relevant issue, determined its arbitrability. *See* § 1025(1) ZPO aF (old edition).[215] To illustrate this, neither the insolvent nor the administrator could agree with the creditors to open or close insolvency proceedings as this is within the sole competence of the insolvency court. However, the administrator could come to an agreement with a creditor concerning the recognition of their claim. As a result, the opening and closing of the insolvency procedure are considered non-arbitrable, and the recognition of a claim is considered arbitrable. The German concept of arbitrability in insolvency issues, thus, seems to follow the old rule.

However, a further examination of the arbitrability of the process described in § 180 InsO shows that even this rule must be read liberally. The relevant rule in § 180(1) InsO provides sole jurisdiction to specific courts, which cannot be altered by a choice of forum by the parties:

(1) An action for the determination of a claim shall be brought under the provisions governing ordinary civil proceedings. *The local court where the*

213. *S.M. Kröll,* Part IV: Selected Areas and Issues of Arbitration in Germany, Insolvency and Arbitration - Effects of Party Insolvency on Arbitral Proceedings in Germany, 981, pp. 987-988.
214. *S.M. Kröll,* Part IV: Selected Areas and Issues of Arbitration in Germany, Insolvency and Arbitration - Effects of Party Insolvency on Arbitral Proceedings in Germany, 981, p. 990.
215. MüKoZPO/*Münch* § 1030 ZPO, No. 5.

> *insolvency proceedings are or were pending shall have exclusive jurisdiction for such action*. If the subject-matter of the action does not fall under the jurisdiction of the local courts, the regional court in whose district the insolvency court is located shall have exclusive jurisdiction. [Emphasis added]

However, this is not seen as excluding arbitration.[216] Germany does not follow the idea of *vis attractiva concursus* or the insolvency court having exclusive jurisdiction over all insolvency-related issues. Only the most core issues are subject to the exclusive jurisdiction of the court, e.g., the opening and closing of the proceedings.[217] Many important insolvency-related issues are, in fact, referred to regular courts. To name a few: the previously mentioned pre-existing claims that have been contested by the administrator, § 180(1) InsO, debts of the insolvency estate, §§ 53 et seq. InsO, separation rights, § 47 InsO, and separate satisfaction, § 49 InsO.[218] In this sense, the insolvency code does provide indirect guidance as to the arbitrability of insolvency-related claims. As these claims are not subject to the exclusive jurisdiction of the insolvency court, this implies that there is no court monopoly and thus no reason for these claims not to be deemed arbitrable. A relative competence, such as provided in § 180(1) InsO, for the court in a specific place, is viewed in German circles as having a limited scope, i.e., essentially stating that if a court is to be seized, it should be a specific one, which does not affect objective arbitrability.[219]

As a consequence of the above, issues that are not given over to the exclusive jurisdiction of the insolvency court and which can theoretically be settled by the parties – including the insolvency administrator – must be considered arbitrable in Germany. Reflecting on *Kröll*'s categories, topics which concern the insolvency proceedings per se (i) are thus non-arbitrable as they are not within the free determination of the parties and fall within the sole jurisdiction of the insolvency court. However, issues falling within *Kröll*'s remaining two categories must be deemed arbitrable. This pertains both to issues related to pre-existing facts and rights (ii) and those arising after the opening of the insolvency (iii). In general, both categories concern economic interests in the sense of § 1030(1) ZPO. Regarding debts of the estate, c.q. claims based on facts and rights after the start of insolvency, this is implicit in § 160(2)(3) InsO.[220] In line with this logic, even arbitrating the admission of a claim to the insolvency schedule is

---

216. *Riedel*, Insolvenz in nationalen und internationalen Schiedsverfahren, pp. 28–29.
217. *Lazić*, Insolvency Proceedings and Commercial Arbitration, p. 164; *S.M. Kröll*, Part IV: Selected Areas and Issues of Arbitration in Germany, Insolvency and Arbitration – Effects of Party Insolvency on Arbitral Proceedings in Germany, 981, p. 989; *Schultze-Moderow*, Schiedsverfahren und Insolvenz, p. 34; BeckOK InsO/*Zenker* § 180 InsO, No. 2.
218. Cf. *S.M. Kröll*, Part IV: Selected Areas and Issues of Arbitration in Germany, Insolvency and Arbitration – Effects of Party Insolvency on Arbitral Proceedings in Germany, 981, p. 989.
219. *BGH*, NJW 1996, 1753–1756, No. 7; *S.M. Kröll*, Part IV: Selected Areas and Issues of Arbitration in Germany, Insolvency and Arbitration – Effects of Party Insolvency on Arbitral Proceedings in Germany, 981, p. 989; *Schultze-Moderow*, Schiedsverfahren und Insolvenz, p. 34; *Riedel*, Insolvenz in nationalen und internationalen Schiedsverfahren, p. 29; *see* Badel for a discussion along similar lines regarding the arbitrability of Swiss insolvency provisions *Badel*, ASA Bull. 25 (2007), 36–47.
220. *Zöller*, in: *Zöller*, § 1030; *S.M. Kröll*, Part IV: Selected Areas and Issues of Arbitration in Germany, Insolvency and Arbitration – Effects of Party Insolvency on Arbitral Proceedings in Germany, 981, p. 988.

deemed possible.[221] After all, such a claim is possible of settlement between the creditor and the insolvency administrator and pertains to an economic interest.

In conclusion, Germany follows what can be considered a liberal approach to the arbitrability of insolvency issues. In this context, the primary discussion regarding the question of whether specific issues can be arbitrated in a specific insolvency will be more focused on the scope of the relevant arbitration agreement than on issues of objective arbitrability.[222] Due to the liberal approach taken to the arbitration of insolvency issues, the pre-insolvency arbitration agreement will provide a narrower jurisdiction than all insolvency-related issues considered theoretically arbitrable. This can either be found in the text of the specific agreement but also more generally in the dispositive power of the insolvent. For example, rights that are grounded in insolvency are deemed not at the disposal of the insolvent, as before insolvency these rights did not exist and thus, could not be disposed of and, after the opening of insolvency, are vested or conferred upon the administrator. Thus, such rights cannot fall under the scope of a pre-insolvency arbitration agreement.[223]

2 THE EFFECT OF INSOLVENCY PROCEEDINGS ON ARBITRATION

Aside from the arbitrability of insolvency matters, there are many important legal, practical and often urgent questions a tribunal, party or representative needs to answer when a party goes insolvent in arbitration. However, neither the ZPO nor InsO states anything about insolvency in arbitration. This section will deal with a set of these questions roughly in the order that they should – in the author's mind – be addressed by the arbitral tribunal.

First, the relation of the arbitration to the insolvency, i.e., the binding power of insolvency in the seat country on arbitration (§ 2.1), is discussed. The position one takes on this topic determines whether the insolvency will register in the arbitration or if it will not be taken into account. This topic is reserved mainly for discussion in an international context. However, it is perhaps equally important in the national context from a dogmatic point of view. How one views this interaction is indicative of the position of arbitration in the context of the legal order of the seat jurisdiction.

The section will continue with a short discussion on the standing and representation in the arbitration proceedings (§ 2.2). This choice is made because representation and standing become primary concerns when it is decided that insolvency will be taken into account. In most insolvency regimes the insolvent no longer has standing in cases concerning claims belonging to the insolvency estate. If this question is not promptly and adequately answered, issues of representation and the right to be heard can lead to the annulment of a subsequent award.

221. *BGH*, NJW 2009, 1747–1750; *Longrée/Gantenbrink*, SchiedsVZ 2014, 21, p. 23; *Riedel*, Insolvenz in nationalen und internationalen Schiedsverfahren, p. 29.
222. *S.M. Kröll*, Part IV: Selected Areas and Issues of Arbitration in Germany, Insolvency and Arbitration – Effects of Party Insolvency on Arbitral Proceedings in Germany, 981, pp. 990–991.
223. *S.M. Kröll*, Part IV: Selected Areas and Issues of Arbitration in Germany, Insolvency and Arbitration – Effects of Party Insolvency on Arbitral Proceedings in Germany, 981, p. 994; more on this in 3.6.

The issue that is most often the focus of these discussions is the effect of the opening of insolvency on the ongoing arbitration proceeding itself (§ 2.3). Many insolvency regimes require that ongoing claims concerning the claims belonging to the insolvent estate are suspended. Not properly taking this into account can be disastrous for the effectiveness of any subsequent arbitral award as such rules are often considered of a public policy nature.

As a final topic and arguably a small excursion, a discussion will be provided about the effect of the dissolution of a company (§ 2.4). Although dissolution is often not part of insolvency law, it is an effect intrinsically linked to insolvency. As such, an arbitrator dealing with an insolvent party has a good chance of being confronted with the dissolution of that party. As with the previous topics, it is necessary to properly deal with this issue to ensure the effectiveness of any award.

As stated, the chosen order is deliberate to deal with the issues broadly in the order a tribunal might confront them. Before a tribunal can look at the effects of an insolvency on the relevant arbitration, it must first discuss what role the insolvency plays or does not play in the proceedings. Having decided that it has to apply specific insolvency rules, effects on the arbitration agreement must be discussed, as this is an issue of jurisdiction. However, this discussion is due to its size and complexity reserved for the next section. If these questions are answered and the tribunal retains jurisdiction, the question arises if the insolvency affects the proceedings in any other way. The tribunal must determine if the insolvent is still the correct party and likely invite the administrator, as with the opening of the insolvency the right to dispose of the insolvent's assets will have shifted to the insolvency administrator. Partially, if not wholly, in parallel with this question, it must ask if proceedings need to be stayed, as a common aspect of insolvency law is the stay of any legal proceedings. Aside from the stay of proceedings, the insolvency might have other effects on the arbitration proceedings. Some of which will be discussed below.

2.1 The Binding Power of Insolvency in the Seat Jurisdiction

The first question to be discussed in this section is the binding power of an insolvency in the seat of arbitration. This topic is discussed first as a potential conclusion that an arbitration is not bound to take into account an insolvency in the seat jurisdiction might render any further discussion set out in this section unnecessary or partially unnecessary as an arbitrator would not be bound to apply the effects of insolvency to the arbitral proceedings. Aside from international situations wherein arbitration and insolvency could be governed by different laws, this question arises particularly if one views arbitration as not bound to the national jurisdiction of the seat and consequently not directly bound to apply rules of insolvency of the seat. Another issue is the nature of arbitration: a contractual view of arbitration leads to the conclusion that an arbitrator is not obliged – in the same way courts are – to apply insolvency rules. These topics are explored in the following paragraphs.

The question as to the relationship between the seat and the arbitration, more specifically the relationship between in-seat insolvencies and the arbitration is often ignored or left unanswered in practice and literature. Notably, the question is left unanswered as to why they need to be taken into account by the tribunal, as tribunals often do so without discussion.[224] If one follows a delocalised view of arbitration, one could call this a silent recognition of in-seat insolvencies. Whereas recognition is customarily used to describe the recognition of foreign legal acts,[225] some view every jurisdiction as foreign to the arbitration proceedings, as described above.

Ignoring the question of why a tribunal has to apply or take into account an insolvency order and insolvency rules of the seat is accepting by omission that these rules somehow apply to the tribunal. Whereas it can be stated a priori that it does not make any practical sense for a fully German arbitration to ignore German insolvency, such a conclusion must have a dogmatic legal foundation. Thus, this question merits scrutiny. The underlying theoretical discussion is one central to arbitration theory: what is the role of the law of seat? Is the arbitrator bound to apply the law of the chosen seat, or is the choice of seat merely an indirect choice for *lex arbitri* – does this choice extend to other rules and laws of the seat?

Partially overlapping this question and avoiding the theoretical discussion on this point is the fact that completely ignoring an insolvency order made in the seat country against one of the parties would most likely lead to setting aside of an award due to violation of public policy, § 1059(2)(2)(b) ZPO, based on Article 34(2)(b)(ii)) Arb.ML.[226] Arguing by way of *ordre public* could be seen as an implicit argument against the binding power of an insolvency in the seat on arbitration per se. The *ordre public* argument would be unnecessary if the tribunal were bound directly. Neither a sole reference to *ordre public* nor the blind application of the insolvency rules truly provides a conclusion on the relationship between the seat jurisdiction, c.q. in-seat insolvencies, and arbitration.

Aside from this, it should be noted that the *ordre public* arguments used here are also intrinsically bound to other questions, the answer to which this approach relies on, i.e., the existence or non-existence of a duty to deliver enforceable and non-annullable awards,[227] and the discussion regarding the contents of *ordre public*, in particular in the context of insolvency law.

2.1.1 The Relationship Between the Seat Jurisdiction and the Arbitration

The answer to the question of to what extent and how a tribunal is bound to take into account insolvency in the seat country relies on the perceived relationship between the arbitration and the seat. Select relevant theories are discussed here before providing a position and analysis (§ 2.1.2).

224. *See, e.g.*, *Award in CAM Case No. 2412*, A contribution by the ITA Board of Reporters, Kluwer Law International, where the CAM directly jumps to applying Italian insolvency rules.
225. *Martiny*, Anerkennung ausländischer Entscheidungen nach autonomem Recht, p. 264.
226. *Flöther*, Auswirkungen des inländischen Insolvenzverfahrens auf Schiedsverfahren und Schiedsabrede, p. 36; *Riedel*, Insolvenz in nationalen und internationalen Schiedsverfahren, p. 129.
227. *See, e.g.*, *Pérez Lozada*, Spain Arbitration Review 2016, 71–94.

How one typifies this relationship depends mainly on which of the arbitration theories, as introduced in Chapter 1 § 4, one favours. Crudely summarised, in a purely jurisdictional theory, all the procedural rules of the *lex loci arbitri* can be directly applied, as arbitration forms part of the local legal order and arbitrators perform a judiciary task. Applying the delocalised theory would not allow for the direct application of the law of the seat beyond what was agreed to by the parties and puts final control solely at the place of enforcement.[228]

Delocalisation theory, mainly advocated in French circles, essentially negates any relationship between the arbitration, c.q. the arbitration agreement, and the law of the seat jurisdiction. Ironically it is the UK Supreme Court that succinctly summarises the French approach in this context: 'arbitration agreements derive their existence, validity and effect from supra-national law, without it being necessary to refer to any national law'.[229] *Blackaby* et al. provide two arguments that are also requirements for this approach: first, that arbitration is sufficiently organised by the parties' agreement and international arbitration rules and second, that the only control should come from the place of enforcement.[230]

Although the word is usually avoided, German arbitration theory tends towards the jurisdictional approach.[231] German commentators, such as *Wagner* and *Flöther*, argue in favour of an automatic taking into account of the insolvency, much like the unspoken automatic recognition of domestic insolvencies by national courts.[232] *Schultze-Moderow* views 'German' arbitration as embedded in the German legal order.[233] Some authors, such as *Schütze*, even refer to a *lex fori* in arbitration.[234] As a consequence of this, the tribunal should automatically take into account domestic insolvency. Whereas in earlier commentaries, the nationality of arbitration was linked to the applicable procedural law,[235] *Wagner* states that with the incorporation of § 1025(1) ZPO and with it Article 1(2) Arb.ML, the idea that the chosen seat determines the nationality of arbitration has become law.[236] These articles do indeed provide for a quasi-nationality of arbitration, as they declare the German *lex arbitri* applicable to 'German' arbitration, i.e., arbitration seated in Germany.

---

228. *S.M. Kröll*, Chapter 18: Arbitration and Insolvency Proceedings – Selected Problems, 357, p. 362; *Blackaby et al.*, Redfern and Hunter on International Arbitration, p. 182.
229. *Supreme Court of United Kingdom*, 3.11.2010 – [2010] UKSC 46, No. 5; as cited by *Blackaby et al.*, Redfern and Hunter on International Arbitration, p. 180.
230. *Blackaby et al.*, Redfern and Hunter on International Arbitration, p. 181.
231. *Schlosser*, Das Recht des internationalen privaten Schiedsgerichtsbarkeit, p. 42.
232. *Flöther*, Auswirkungen des inländischen Insolvenzverfahrens auf Schiedsverfahren und Schiedsabrede, p. 36; *P.K. Wagner*, Abstimmungsfragen zwischen Internationalem Insolvenzrecht und Internationaler Schiedsgerichtsbarkeit, pp. 87–88.
233. *Schultze-Moderow*, Schiedsverfahren und Insolvenz, pp. 108–112.
234. MüKoZPO/*Münch* § 1051 ZPO, No. 1; *Schütze*, Armut im internationalen Schiedsverfahren, 867–876.
235. *K. Peter Berger*, RIW 39 (1993), pp. 8–9.
236. *P.K. Wagner*, Abstimmungsfragen zwischen Internationalem Insolvenzrecht und Internationaler Schiedsgerichtsbarkeit, p. 87.

In light of this, some German commentators view the choice of seat as formal incorporation of the arbitration into that legal order.[237] It regulates which court needs to be seized when assistance is required for evidence taking, the formation of the tribunal, security measures and much more. In this context, the choice of seat goes beyond the choice of a *lex arbitri* and involves the further rules of the *lex fori.*[238] Internationally and in practice, the necessity of the connection between the arbitration and the seat is still the prevailing view, *see also* Article 1(a) and (e) NYC.[239]

Schultze-Moderow has distilled the arguments for the embedding of arbitration into the seat's legal order into three main points.[240] First, by making legal determinations of substantive law, the tribunal is part of or takes over part of, the state's judicial monopoly and should, therefore, be bound to the same legal framework.[241] Second, all contractual freedom, including that to go to and organise an arbitration, flows from a state's legal order and therefore, they only exist within this legal order's framework.[242] The third argument is a Germany-specific argument. Several articles in the ZPO, i.e., §§ 1025, 1051 ZPO, address arbitral tribunals specifically. This arguably provides the tribunal with a *lex fori,* which provides it with a framework in which to operate.[243]

The first argument, which qualifies the tribunal as an enactor of the state's judicial monopoly, is no more and no less than the pure jurisdictional view of arbitration. Even in recent German commentary, *Münch* described awards as a '*delegierten staatshoheitlichen Urteilsakt*' or a 'judicial act based on delegated state sovereignty'.[244] For this first and second argument, Schultze-Moderow rightly finds that the root argument is state sovereignty – a state has the power to regulate what goes on within its borders.[245] The second argument, *Mann's* argument, is aptly reduced to the thought that 'Every right or power a private person enjoys is inexorably conferred by or derived from a system of municipal law [...].'[246]

The first argument focuses on the position of the tribunal, whereas the second argument focuses on the position of the parties and their agreements. *Mann* points out that any statement made by parties only has a contractual effect if and when a legal system gives effect to such a statement. Even a choice of law agreement only has a legal effect because a legal order recognises this choice and gives effect to it.[247] In other words, an arbitration agreement is only an arbitration agreement because a legal system recognises it as such. Outside of such a context, there is no frame of reference and it essentially loses all meaning unless one argues in favour of some elusive

237. *P.K. Wagner*, p. 87 citing; *Schwab/Walter*, Schiedsgerichtsbarkeit, Ch. 15 No. 39; Zöller/*R. Geimer* § 1025 ZPO, No. 2 and several others.
238. *Blackaby et al.*, Redfern and Hunter on International Arbitration, p. 183.
239. *Blackaby et al.*, Redfern and Hunter on International Arbitration, p. 182.
240. *Schultze-Moderow*, Schiedsverfahren und Insolvenz, pp. 107–112.
241. MüKoZPO/*Münch* § 1055 ZPO, Nos 2, 7; *Schmitz*, Schiedsverfahren und Insolvenz, p. 168.
242. *Mann*, Lex Facit Arbitrum, 157, 160 et seq; *Schlosser*, Das Recht des internationalen privaten Schiedsgerichtsbarkeit, p. 354; *Solomon*, Die Verbindlichkeit von Schiedssprüchen in der internationalen privaten Schiedsgerichtsbarkeit, p. 327.
243. *Schütze*, Armut im internationalen Schiedsverfahren, 867, p. 871.
244. MüKoZPO/*Münch* § 1055 ZPO, No. 7.
245. *Schultze-Moderow*, Schiedsverfahren und Insolvenz, pp. 109–110.
246. *Mann*, Lex Facit Arbitrum, 157, p. 160.
247. *Mann*, Lex Facit Arbitrum, 157, p. 161.

international or natural law framework.[248] That the relevant legal order should be that of the seat country seems clear to *Mann* and seems to flow primarily from the argument *Wagner* also made, i.e., that the court and, therefore, the legal order of the seat country generally 'controls' the arbitration.[249]

However, it is notable that the reasons for such embedding into a national legal order, as presented by *Schulze-Moderow*, do not necessarily combine and can also lead to a different sort of 'embedding into a national legal order'. If one takes the stand represented in the first argument, the tribunal represents state judicial sovereignty putting them in the same position as judges. This would make arbitration a procedure dominated by public law. The second reason provided merely embeds the arbitration agreement as a private contract and the arbitration as a private legal act being effectuated within the national legal order.

Schultze-Moderow's third argument is mostly a specific example of the argument *Wagner* made concerning the nationality of an arbitration. The arguments based on articles such as § 1025(1) ZPO addressing the tribunal mainly show that such articles represent a sovereignty claim to organise arbitration within the country.[250]

2.1.2 Position and Analysis

The above arguments must be considered and analysed as the outcome of this discussion provides the answer to whether and, if so, how an arbitral tribunal is bound to take into account an insolvency in the seat of arbitration. The fundamental view of an arbitrator as an enactor of state-derived justice or simply an enactor of a contractual duty is crucial to the dogmatic approach one takes to insolvency in arbitration. To come to a final position on the need to take into account in-seat insolvencies, a position will be taken on delocalisation (i) and the nature of arbitration (ii) below.

i Localised or Delocalised Arbitration

The above-discussed delocalisation of arbitration is only possible within the context of national law, with few exceptions such as International Centre of the Settlement of Investment Disputes (ICSID) arbitration.[251] Connecting arbitration to the law of its seat prevents the arbitration from 'floating in the transnational firmament, unconnected with any municipal system of law'.[252] The wording used by the UK Supreme Court shows as much, as only by applying French law, or within the French legal order, arbitration is delocalised, which is thus not true delocalisation at all. Congruently,

248. *Rubellin-Devichi*, L'Arbitrage: Nature juridique, droit interne et droit international privé, p. 365.
249. *Mann*, Lex Facit Arbitrum, 157, p. 161; *Schultze-Moderow*, Schiedsverfahren und Insolvenz, p. 111.
250. *Handorn*, Das Sonderkollisionsrecht der deutschen internationalen Schiedsgerichtsbarkeit, p. 25; *Schultze-Moderow*, Schiedsverfahren und Insolvenz, p. 111.
251. *Bělohlávek*, ASA Bull. 31 (2013), 262, p. 269; *Blackaby et al.*, Redfern and Hunter on International Arbitration, p. 182.
252. *England and Wales Court of Appeal*, Q.B. 1984, 291, p. 301.

aside from institutions such as ICSID, arbitrations cannot be viewed as separate from the legal order of the seat as this is where the arbitration agreement is enforced or at least performed, even if only fictively. Positions stating that arbitration needs no national law system whatsoever are like stating that there is no need for contract law, as parties create their own legal system by sheer force of will – akin to a natural law approach. As a basic concept of contract law, parties are free to agree on any terms they will. However, it is a legal system that provides legal operability, and for the parties to make, for example, a legally valid contract within this system, they will have to adhere to the requirements that the relevant legal order posits for validity.[253]

The Tribunal in ICC Case 5730 also considers that an arbitration agreement needs to be embedded in a legal order to be given any effect and that merely stating that the arbitration agreement is valid independent of any state jurisdiction does not suffice. The tribunal, in this case, seems to mainly link this to the law applicable to the arbitration agreement.[254] It is correct that the law applicable to the arbitration agreement will finally determine the validity of the arbitration agreement. However, it should be clear that a different law than that of the seat can only be applied to the validity of the agreement insofar as the law of the seat allows for it.[255] In ICC Case 5730, this is found to be possible under Article 1495 French Civil Procedural Code (NCPC).[256] Delocalisation is, therefore, only valid and possible to the degree allowed for by national legal systems in which arbitration operates.[257] This is also evidenced by the fact that annulment forums will apply their own *lex fori* to see if the parties could and have chosen a law applicable to the arbitration agreement. In conclusion, the basic legal constructs underpinning private commercial arbitration are always provided by the law of the seat. As such, arbitration must be viewed as intrinsically bound to the seat jurisdiction.

ii *Arbitration as the Performance of a Contract or Part of the Judicial Order*

Having considered that arbitration is bound to the seat jurisdiction, the next question concerns the nature of this relationship. Within the position that favours binding arbitration into the legal order of the seat, two different approaches need to be considered as they differ as to important consequences. One approach favours the view that the arbitral tribunal delivers state justice, while the other views the arbitration agreement as a contract performed within the boundaries the seat's legal order provides for it. The position that a tribunal performs part of the state sovereignty and forms part of the state's legal order, c.q. judicial order leads to the conclusion that all relevant rules of the *lex fori* apply, e.g., all procedural rules when not excluded by

253. *Blackaby et al.*, Redfern and Hunter on International Arbitration, p. 156.
254. *Award in ICC Case No. 5730*, Collection of ICC Awards II, 1994, 410, pp. 413-415.
255. *Award in ICC Case No. 5832*, Collection of ICC Awards II, 1994, 533, p. 534 note by G. Aquilar Alvarez; *Award in ICC Case No. 4504*, Collection of ICC Awards II, 1994, 279, p. 280; *Blackaby et al.*, Redfern and Hunter on International Arbitration, p. 182.
256. *Award in ICC Case No. 5730*, Collection of ICC Awards II, 1994, 410, pp. 414-415.
257. Except those directly based on treaty and international law, such as the previously mentioned ICSID arbitration.

superseding arbitration law. In the context of insolvency, this would logically include rules and procedures a national judge would be obliged to follow.[258] Whereas, when an arbitration proceeding is merely viewed as the consequence of the performance of a special type of contract, i.e., the arbitration agreement, given effect by the law of the jurisdiction in which it is performed, i.e., the arbitration law or *lex loci arbitri*, then only such rules as those that affect this contract and those performing the contract are relevant.[259]

The arbitrator in ICC Case 2321 seated in Sweden deals with this fundamental discussion decisively in a preliminary award on two procedural points. He finds that as an arbitrator, he is not an organ or a representative of the state but that his powers are based on the contract: 'As arbitrator I am myself no representative or organ of any State. My authority as arbitrator rests upon an agreement between the parties to the dispute and by my activities I do not, as State judges or other State representatives do, engage the responsibility of the State [...].'[260]

The arbitrator cited here arrives at the correct conclusion. The arguments that favour the approach equating an arbitrator to a judge, c.q. a dispenser of state justice, negate the mentioned contractual basis that is also visible in German arbitration law.[261] A primary example thereof can be found in the limitation on the arbitrability of non-economic interests, as provided in § 1030(1) ZPO, stating that these issues are only arbitrable if the parties could decide these matters amongst themselves, i.e., something that the parties could settle by contract. § 1055 ZPO, which is used to argue that the tribunal administers state justice because the award is equalled to a court decision, actually also provides that it only equals a court decision insofar as the parties are concerned. This follows the contractual law rule that parties cannot make a contract to the detriment of a third party. Aside from this, parties are arguably allowed to change or fully set aside the award by contractual agreement,[262] something rather unthinkable when it comes to a court decision. Furthermore, as *Solomon* states, the contractual nature of arbitration does not change that the arbitral tribunal makes an adjudication *in place* of the state court. However, this does not equate the tribunal to a court.[263]

If not a member of the judiciary or enactor of state authority, the question can be asked, are the parties, the arbitration, and with them the arbitrator, not subject to state sovereignty as any private person that wishes to give effect to a contract within a particular legal order and would thus be obliged to adhere to the relevant rules of the relevant legal order as such. This must be answered in the affirmative. In this line, the conclusion that arbitration and the arbitral tribunal do not as such perform part of the state sovereignty, i.e., take up the mantle of the judiciary, does not hinder the

258. *Solomon*, Die Verbindlichkeit von Schiedssprüchen in der internationalen privaten Schiedsgerichtsbarkeit, p. 304.
259. Cf. *Mankowski*, ZIP 2010, 2478, p. 2480.
260. *Preliminary Award in ICC Case No. 2321*, Collection of ICC Awards I, 1990, 8, p. 10.
261. MüKoZPO/*Münch* Vorbemerkung zu § 1025 ZPO, Nos 1–4; Musielak/Voit/*Voit* § 1025 ZPO, No. 11.
262. MüKoZPO/*Münch* § 1055 ZPO, No. 31; of another opinion is Voit, who correctly finds that will have unacceptable effects on third parties Musielak/Voit/*Voit* § 1055 ZPO, No. 6.
263. *Solomon*, Die Verbindlichkeit von Schiedssprüchen in der internationalen privaten Schiedsgerichtsbarkeit, pp. 319–320.

conclusion here that arbitration, as the performance of a special form of contract, is given effect within a chosen legal order. This integration of arbitration into a legal order as a private law-based agreement by choosing to effectuate the agreement within that legal order means that the parties to the arbitration and thus the tribunal cannot ignore the existence of insolvency in this legal order as it cannot ignore previous court decisions having legal effect, c.q. creating, altering or terminating legal relationships (German: *Gestaltungswirkung*). This would violate *ordre public*.[264] Consequently, *Wagner* is to be followed in his conclusion that German insolvency should be automatically 'recognised' and taken into account within the arbitration.[265] However, the only sanction for not doing so remains the setting aside of the award for violation of *ordre public*, as this is the only sanction provided by the legal framework. This does not affect the basic legitimacy of the arbitration based on the arbitration agreement.[266]

More in general, building on *Solomon* and *Mann*, the arbitration, the arbitration agreement and the award, as with any private act, depend on a legal order to be given effect.[267] What effect an arbitral award is given depends on the legal order. However, within that legal order, the reason that an award is binding still finally flows from the parties' agreement.[268] Therefore, if the parties involved aim at creating specific effects in a specific legal order, they cannot violate the basic principles of their elected legal order.[269] Arbitration can thus not ignore an in-seat insolvency and is bound by the decision ordering the opening of such procedures.

2.2 Standing and Representation: The Administrator

The role of an insolvency administrator is a fundamental part of an insolvency. In this subsection, his role in an ongoing arbitration involving the insolvent is discussed. His role, his binding (or lack thereof) to an arbitration agreement and his standing in arbitration fundamentally affect an arbitration and arbitration agreement upon opening of an insolvency.

Discussing the continued validity of the arbitration agreement in insolvency is a necessary part of deciding upon the arbitral tribunal's jurisdiction, and in this context, it is a preliminary question in arbitration.[270] This jurisdiction is limited *ratione materiae*

264. *Flöther*, Auswirkungen des inländischen Insolvenzverfahrens auf Schiedsverfahren und Schiedsabrede, p. 36; *P.K. Wagner*, Abstimmungsfragen zwischen Internationalem Insolvenzrecht und Internationaler Schiedsgerichtsbarkeit, p. 95.
265. *P.K. Wagner*, Abstimmungsfragen zwischen Internationalem Insolvenzrecht und Internationaler Schiedsgerichtsbarkeit, pp. 88–89; *Vorburger*, International Arbitration and Cross-Border Insolvency, p. 50.
266. Cf. *Flöther*, Auswirkungen des inländischen Insolvenzverfahrens auf Schiedsverfahren und Schiedsabrede, p. 36.
267. *Award in ICC Case No. 5730*, Collection of ICC Awards II, 1994, 410, pp. 413–414.
268. *Solomon*, Die Verbindlichkeit von Schiedssprüchen in der internationalen privaten Schiedsgerichtsbarkeit, 322–323, 332; Cf. *Born*, International Commercial Arbitration, p. 229.
269. Cf. *Mann*, Lex Facit Arbitrum, 157, p. 161; *Solomon*, Die Verbindlichkeit von Schiedssprüchen in der internationalen privaten Schiedsgerichtsbarkeit, 327 et seq; *Schultze-Moderow*, Schiedsverfahren und Insolvenz, p. 105.
270. *Partial Award in ICC Case No. 13764*, ICC International Court of Arbitration Bulletin 20, 2009, 108, Nos 139.

by the arbitrability of issues. The jurisdiction *ratione personae* in arbitration is generally limited to the parties to the agreement. However, the insolvency administrator has to take over the legal situation of the insolvent estate as it is found, including arbitration agreements.[271] This is generally viewed as the consequence of transference of dispositive power over the insolvent estate upon insolvency as codified in § 80 InsO.[272] This is relevant as the insolvent, or the regular representatives thereof, e.g., the board of directors, loses the capacity to represent the now insolvent estate.[273] In Germany, the right to administer the estate of the insolvent is transferred to the insolvency administrator based on the rule of § 80(1) InsO:

> Upon the opening of the insolvency proceedings the debtor's right to manage and transfer the insolvency estate shall be vested in the insolvency administrator.

For ongoing procedures express rules are made in §§ 85, 86 InsO. The insolvency administrator has a choice as to which proceedings that were ongoing when the insolvency was opened he will resume.[274]

It should be noted that, in several of the procedures not discussed in this book, this is not necessarily the case. When it comes to certain pre-bankruptcy frameworks and proceedings or restructuring procedures, those persons and bodies usually able to represent the company remain able to do so or can do so with supervision. Reorganisation plans can also create jurisdictional issues. For example, in the partial award in ICC Case 13764, the tribunal considered the assignment of claims and contracts and its effect on the standing of the relevant parties as a preliminary question of jurisdiction.[275]

As stated, the administrator is, in general, bound to the legal position of the insolvent. If a proceeding is continued, the administrator is, therefore, generally also bound to the previous procedural actions of the insolvent[276] unless such action can be disputed based on insolvency law, i.e., the insolvency disputation of §§ 129 et seq. InsO, known in other jurisdictions as the *actio pauliana*, is further explored in paragraph Chapter 2 § 4.2.4.[277] Aside from the more specific discussion on the binding of the arbitration agreement upon the insolvency administrator, which will be discussed further on,[278] two central arbitration-specific issues remain regarding the role of the administrator. The first question is how the above rules regarding the replacement of the party with the administrator function regarding arbitration proceedings (§ 2.2.1).

271. Uhlenbruck/*Mock* § 80 InsO, No. 71.
272. Uhlenbruck/*Mock* § 80 InsO, No. 71.
273. *Lazić*, Insolvency Proceedings and Commercial Arbitration, p. 109.
274. *KG Berlin*, SchiedsVZ 2013, 112–119 where an insolvency administrator is deemed to be able to enforce an award in the name of the insolvent; *Schiedsgericht des Deutschen Kaffeeverbands an der Handelskammer Hamburg*, Y.B. Com. Arb. 1994, 48, No. 4; *Sachs/Lörcher*, Part II: Commentary on the German Arbitration Law (10th Book of the German Code of Civil Procedure), Chapter V: Conduct of the Arbitral Proceeding, p. 295.
275. *Partial Award in ICC Case No. 13764*, ICC International Court of Arbitration Bulletin 20, 2009, 108, §§ 139–140.
276. *BGH*, NJW-RR 2007, 397, No. 9.
277. BeckOK InsO/*Cymutta* § 85 InsO, Nos 37–37a; HK-InsO/*Kayser* § 85 InsO, No. 57; Uhlenbruck/*Mock* § 85 InsO, p. 162.
278. For the specific discussion on if he is bound to the arbitration agreement, refer to § 3.3.

The second question regards the power of the administrator to enter into an arbitration agreement (§ 2.2.2), which was already implied above.

2.2.1 *Standing in the Arbitration Proceedings*

The rules concerning dispositive power and standing are relatively straightforward. Their application to arbitration is, however, not always straightforward. According to most insolvency laws, the debtor loses its *locus standi*, whereas the insolvency administrator gains *locus standi*.[279] However, the administrator is often not free to decide upon the (dis)continuation of arbitral proceedings or proceedings in general. For example, it might be the case that the administrator requires the consent of a bankruptcy court or a creditor's commission, e.g., under English Law, *see* section 314 Insolvency Act 1986.[280] As will be discussed further on, the usual ways a German administrator might dissolve or not perform a contract do not affect or apply to the arbitration agreement.[281]

The shifting of the right to administer the estate to the administrator from the now insolvent logically would also affect the ability of the regular representatives thereof to represent the insolvent party in the arbitration. The debtor's right to conduct proceedings concerning the estate, either by it or against it, is often transferred to the insolvency administrator, *see* §§ 80, 85–86 InsO. The insolvent, however, does not lose its passive or active legal capacity. The insolvent only loses the right to dispose of the assets in the insolvent estate. This negative consequence of the shift of dispositive power as stated in § 80 InsO is further reinforced by § 81 InsO, which states the general rule in § 81(1) InsO: that dispositive acts of the insolvent regarding assets of the insolvent estate after the opening of the insolvency are invalid. In a personal bankruptcy case, this leaves the insolvent room to litigate and dispose of the so-called insolvency-free assets, assets that are not encompassed in the insolvent estate.[282] Furthermore, if the insolvency administrator decides not to pursue an active claim, the insolvent is again free to pursue it, *see* § 85(2) InsO. On the passive side – as the insolvent does not lose passive legal capacity – the insolvent can still be a party to an arbitration. However, any arbitral award in such a case will not bind the estate but merely the insolvent.[283]

Considerations regarding the shift in standing can also be found in arbitral practice. For example, in a partial award in 2005, an ICC Tribunal decided that the insolvent could not continue the arbitration concerning a claim in the insolvency and

279. *Final Award in ICC Case No. 16369*, Y.B. Com. Arb. XXXIX, 2014, 169, No. 56; *Lazić*, Insolvency Proceedings and Commercial Arbitration, p. 112; *Lord*, Int'l Trade&Bus. L. Rev. 15 (2012), 316, pp. 331–333.
280. *Lazić*, Insolvency Proceedings and Commercial Arbitration, p. 112; *Yang*, Insolvency Proceedings and Their Effect on International Commercial Arbitration, p. 30.
281. *See* Chapter 2 § 3.5.
282. MüKoInsO/*Vuia* § 80 InsO, No. 11.
283. Cf. MüKoInsO/*Vuia* § 80 InsO, No. 11.

that only the insolvency administrator could continue the proceedings.[284] Similarly, the Tribunal in ICC Case 7337 deemed the estate, represented by the receiver, the right and proper party for post-insolvency claims.[285] In other cases, like ICC Case 3267, the replacement of the original party by its administrator, in this case, a trustee, seems to have been accepted implicitly and without further consideration.[286]

In conclusion, the insolvent will have to be replaced in the proceedings by the insolvency administrator as the representative of the estate.[287] In 2009, the German Federal Supreme Court made a ruling that concerned the interpretation of an arbitral award rendered after the opening of an insolvency. This topic is explored in Chapter 2 § 5.2. In this ruling, the German Federal Supreme Court found that failing to name the administrator officially as a party but factually treating him as such, c.q. the representative of the insolvent, will not lead to the setting aside of the award.[288] Such an approach is to be preferred, especially since no real damage was suffered if the administrator is factually representing the insolvent party. Similarly, the Tribunal in ICC Case 11714 tried to handle inconsistencies related to the insolvent's representation by the administrator in an effective and pro-arbitration fashion.[289] The Tribunal, as reported by *Vidal*, let the claimant continue the proceedings at the behest of the administrator after it had become unclear if the administrator, which had represented the claimant previously, had lost its powers.[290]

Conversely, this means that an administrator cannot successfully argue that a claim pending in arbitration should be dismissed just because the administrator was not mentioned as a party in the request for arbitration. In a similar discussion about a Japanese defendant, an ICC tribunal even concluded that addressing 'Company A' was a way to address the competent representative of the company, which included the insolvency administrator.[291] In ICC Case 11123, the Tribunal also did not take too formalistic an approach to the inclusion of the administrator. In this case, the administrator had been incorrectly appointed, and this was only rectified later. In the meantime, the administrator had been involved in the arbitration, but the tribunal

284. *Partial Award in ICC Case No. 12907*, ICC International Court of Arbitration Bulletin 20, 2009, 98, 25, 58, 65–67.
285. *Interim Award in ICC Case No. 7337*, Collection of ICC Awards IV, 2003, 308–320, p. 312; as further examples ICC Case 14753 and ICC Case 4629 can be mentioned. In the first, the Tribunal mostly tacitly accepted that the Trustee could represent the insolvent company and raise its rights in arbitration and in the latter case it merely mentioned that if the second Claimant were insolvent the administrator would have claimed the rights in the procedure, *see Final Award in ICC Case No. 14753*, Collection of ICC Awards VI, 2013, 973, 974, 982 note by F. Mantilla Serrano; *Final Award in ICC Case No. 4629*, Collection of ICC Awards III, 1997, 152, p. 156.
286. *Final Award in ICC Case No. 3267*, Y.B. Com. Arb. XII, 1986, 87, p. 88.
287. Jeager, InsO/*Windel* § 85 InsO, No. 68; *BGH*, NJW 2009, 1747–1750, No. 14; Cf. Musielak/Voit/*Stadler* § 240 ZPO, No. 1.
288. *BGH*, NJW 2009, 1747–1750, p. 14.
289. *Final Award in ICC Case No. 11714*, ICC International Court of Arbitration Bulletin 20, 2009, p. 85.
290. *Vidal*, ICC International Court of Arbitration Bulletin 20 (2009), 51, p. 59.
291. *Mantilla-Serrano*, Arbitration International 11 (1995), 51, p. 66; *Sutcliffe/Rogers*, Arbitration 76 (2010), 277, p. 287.

decided that this did not affect the arbitration.[292] In Case 10515, concerning the performance of contracts between a Swiss company and a Libyan respondent, the respondent argued that the claimant lacked standing as it had failed to add 'in liquidation' to its corporate name. Here the tribunal seated in France similarly did not let a formal flaw in representation, i.e., the omission of 'in liquidation' from the claimant's name, stand in the way of rendering an award. It considered that a company in liquidation is identical to the former company and that, furthermore, under the applicable Swiss company law, the omission was not sanctioned.[293]

In conclusion, although the insolvent under German law does not wholly lose its capacity nor legal standing per se, not replacing the insolvent, c.q. their representatives, with the administrator in ongoing proceedings concerning the estate would seriously endanger the proceedings and the results,[294] i.e., the binding power of the award upon the estate. Essentially one would have a procedure where one party is not represented correctly. This could lead to unenforceable awards. However, following the German Federal Supreme Court, one should be practical here and allow awards of proceedings in which the administrator has factually been (representing) a party to stand and be used to prove claims and register them to the insolvency table.[295]

2.2.2 *The Administrator's Power to Enter into Arbitration Agreements*

As a follow-up to the question of the insolvency administrator's standing in an ongoing arbitration, the question arises if an insolvency administrator can enter into arbitration agreements on behalf of the insolvent estate. Some arbitration or insolvency codes have specific rules regarding the question of the insolvency administrator entering into an arbitration agreement or, for that matter, starting an arbitration. At the same time, in other jurisdictions, this is viewed as part of the administrator's general duty and capacity vis-à-vis the estate and the creditors.[296]

In Germany, the insolvency administrator's power to enter into arbitration agreements primarily flows from the general dispositive power of the administrator over the estate, based on the general transfer of the right to administrate and dispose of the estate as incorporated in § 80 InsO.[297] Conversely, this transfer of powers excludes the regular representatives of the insolvent from further binding the estate after an insolvency, both in general and specifically to arbitration agreements.[298]

---

292. *Partial Award in ICC Case No. 11123*, ICC International Court of Arbitration Bulletin 20, 2009, pp. 79–80; *Vidal*, ICC International Court of Arbitration Bulletin 20 (2009), 51, p. 59.
293. *Final Award in ICC Case No. 10515*, ICC International Court of Arbitration Bulletin 20, 2009, 74, p. 75.
294. *Vorburger*, International Arbitration and Cross-Border Insolvency, p. 158.
295. *See* § 2.3.3; *BGH*, NJW 2009, 1747–1750, 7, 14.
296. *Lazić*, Insolvency Proceedings and Commercial Arbitration, p. 113; e.g., discussing the specific rules in France is *Fouchard*, Rev. Arb. 1998, 471, pp. 492–494.
297. *Riedel*, Insolvenz in nationalen und internationalen Schiedsverfahren, p. 8.
298. *S.M. Kröll*, Part IV: Selected Areas and Issues of Arbitration in Germany, Insolvency and Arbitration – Effects of Party Insolvency on Arbitral Proceedings in Germany, 981, p. 991; Cf. MüKoInsO/*Vuia* § 80 InsO, No. 11.

Regarding arbitrations concerning a significant value, the authority to enter into arbitration agreements is even made explicit. § 160(2)(3) InsO gives the administrator the power to enter into an arbitration agreement with the permission of the creditors' commission.[299] Notably, the lack of such permission, like other cases of justified reliance on the capacity of a representative, does not affect the effectiveness of such an agreement in relationships with third parties, *see* § 164 InsO.[300]

It is also significant to note again that the administrator will have the power to enter into arbitration agreements regarding issues that should be considered beyond the scope of any pre-insolvency arbitration agreement, such as the administrator's right to choose regarding mutually non-performed contracts. These issues were not at the free disposition of the relevant party pre-insolvency, but they are at the disposition of the administrator once insolvency is opened.[301] However, those decisions that can solely be made by the insolvency court are outside of the administrator's power to be subjected to an arbitration agreement.[302]

Insolvency administrators are generally bound to existing arbitration agreements and the state of ongoing arbitration agreements in which they will replace the insolvent if the arbitration concerns assets or claims of the estate. With the above-described restriction, an insolvency administrator can also enter into arbitration agreements for the insolvent estate. The general shift of dispositive power away from the insolvent towards the insolvency administrator significantly impacts standing and representation in ongoing arbitration and the power to bind the insolvent estate to any future arbitration agreements.

2.3 The Effect on the Proceedings

Beyond the question of recognition and the effect of insolvency on standing and representation, the question must be answered as to the effect of the insolvency on the proceedings themselves. The previous subsection has already discussed that the representation of the party changes, but what other effects does the opening of insolvency proceedings have on pending proceedings, specifically pending arbitration proceedings? The main issue here is a potential mandatory suspension of proceedings, which is the principal discussion in this subsection (§ 2.3.1). A potential suspension automatically leads to the question of resumption of those proceedings (§ 2.3.2).

The resumption of suspended arbitration proceedings during insolvency raises several ancillary issues, which will be discussed below, such as the need to register claims and the object of the resumed proceedings (§ 2.3.3), the special case of liabilities of the estate (§ 2.3.4), the scope of any resumed proceedings (§ 2.3.5), and finally, the arbitration specific issue of the choice of arbitrator in a resumed proceeding (§ 2.3.6).

---

299. MüKoInsO/*Görg/Janssen* § 160 InsO, No. 37; MüKoInsO/*Görg/Janssen* § 164 InsO, Nos 1-7.
300. *Riedel*, Insolvenz in nationalen und internationalen Schiedsverfahren, p. 9.
301. As discussed in Chapter 2 § 1.5.
302. *See* Chapter 2 § 3.6; Cf. *Schmitz*, Schiedsverfahren und Insolvenz, p. 53.

2.3.1 *Stay of Proceedings*

Most insolvency codes have clauses that suspend all ongoing legal proceedings concerning the estate in case insolvency proceedings are opened.[303] Based on the same consideration, such rules often also prevent further proceedings outside of the ongoing insolvency proceedings from being opened.[304] That consideration is the aim to centre all proceedings of the insolvent debtor in one forum. These rules are often found in the insolvency code and sometimes in the procedural law. They are often formulated generally, e.g., to apply to 'proceedings'. Many jurisdictions have concluded that they extend to arbitration proceedings.[305]

A stay or suspension of proceedings is often temporary: to replace the insolvent party's representative with the insolvency administrator or, as in Germany, until, and if, the administrator or another creditor disputes the claim, *see* § 180(2) InsO. This is further examined in the following subsection § 2.3.2, in particular under (iii). Similar systems can be found in many jurisdictions, *see, e.g.*, the Netherlands.[306]

In Germany, ongoing procedures are stayed in case insolvency is opened in accordance with § 240 ZPO:

> In the event of insolvency proceedings being opened against a party, the proceedings shall be interrupted to the extent they concern the insolvent estate until they can be resumed in accordance with the rules applying to the insolvency proceedings, or until the insolvency proceedings are terminated. The same shall apply if the authority to manage the debtor's assets and the power to dispose over them devolves upon a preliminary insolvency administrator.

However, this section is widely deemed not to apply to arbitration proceedings.[307] The same rule for foreign insolvencies is found in § 352 InsO:

> By opening foreign insolvency proceedings, an action shall be interrupted which is pending at the time of opening and concerns the insolvency estate. The interruption shall continue until the action is joindered by a person who in accordance with the law of the state of the opening of proceedings is entitled to continue the action, or until the insolvency proceedings have been terminated.

---

303. *Bělohlávek*, The Impact of Insolvency of a Party on Pending Arbitration Proceedings in Czech Republic, England and Switzerland and Other Countries, 145, p. 151; *Fouchard*, Rev. Arb. 1998, 471, pp. 475–476; *Mantilla-Serrano*, Arbitration International 11 (1995), 51, p. 57; *Yang*, Insolvency Proceedings and Their Effect on International Commercial Arbitration, p. 30.
304. *Vorburger*, International Arbitration and Cross-Border Insolvency, p. 179 for a discussion on the chosen jurisdictions *see* Chapter 3.
305. *Ferrari/S. Kröll*, Conflict of laws in international arbitration, p. 362; *Yang*, Insolvency Proceedings and Their Effect on International Commercial Arbitration, p. 32.
306. *Van Mierlo/van de Hel-Koedoot*, Ondernemingsrecht 2010, 39–43; *van Genugten*, Tijdschrift voor Curatoren 2015, 192, 3.1; *Rechtbank Noord-Nederland*, 27.3.2013 – ECLI: NL: RBNNE: 2013: BZ6109; *Rechtbank Den Haag*, JOR, 158.
307. *S.M. Kröll*, Part IV: Selected Areas and Issues of Arbitration in Germany, Insolvency and Arbitration – Effects of Party Insolvency on Arbitral Proceedings in Germany, 981, p. 984; *Longrée/Gantenbrink*, SchiedsVZ 2014, p. 21; *Nacimiento/Bähr*, NJOZ 2009, 4752, p. 4755; *Poudret/Besson*, Comparative Law of International Arbitration, p. 505; *Sachs*, Collected Courses of the International Academy for Arbitration Law, year 2011 1 (2013), 1–48, p. 26.

This section is also generally considered not to affect arbitration.[308] However, case law and commentary suggest that for reasons of procedural fairness and to prevent setting aside, tribunals should consider a stay of some sort.[309] § 240 InsO (i), its applicability to arbitration (ii), its potential analogous application (iv) and the need for a factual stay (iii) are further discussed in this subsection.

i *The Functioning of § 240 ZPO*

In case insolvency is opened or a so-called strong provisional administrator is appointed, § 240 InsO requires a stay of proceedings. This rule is strongly linked to the fact that the insolvent loses his power to dispose of the claims in question.[310] The stay of proceedings is mandatory and provides the parties and primarily the insolvency administrator the opportunity to consider how to proceed. After all, at the opening of the proceedings, the insolvency administrator is unlikely to be knowledgeable about any specific proceedings. Therefore, providing a stay of proceedings also touches upon the administrator's right to be heard, as enshrined in Article 103 of the GG.[311]

Interpreting § 240 ZPO provides us with two main requirements for its application. First, an insolvency proceeding needs to have been opened concerning the estate of one of the parties to the relevant proceedings. As mentioned, the appointment of a strong provisional administrator would also suffice. § 240 ZPO only considers domestic insolvency. However, foreign insolvencies would have the same effect based on § 352 InsO. Second, the case must directly or indirectly concern assets of the insolvent estate.[312]

If the administrator does not confirm the claims underlying the proceeding, the proceeding can continue. There are some exceptions to this rule. Proceedings concerning certain specific claims can immediately be continued by both the administrator and the debtor, *see* § 86 InsO. Such claims are separation, separate satisfaction and other claims incumbent on the estate's assets. However, 'normal' claims, which have now become insolvency claims, can only be continued after the claim has been registered and subsequently contested, *see* §§ 174, 180, 184, 189 InsO.[313]

ii *Applicability to Arbitration*

In some jurisdictions, the applicability of general stays of proceedings to arbitration is primarily one of interpretation. The question is if 'the proceedings', as used in the

308. *Nacimiento/Bähr*, NJOZ 2009, 4752, p. 4761.
309. *Kaufmann-Kohler/Lévy*, Insolvency and International Arbitration, 257, pp. 22-24; *Longrée/Gantenbrink*, SchiedsVZ 2014, p. 21; *Sachs*, Collected Courses of the International Academy for Arbitration Law, year 2011 1 (2013), 1-48, p. 26; *OLG Dresden*, SchiedsVZ 2005, 159-163.
310. Musielak/Voit/*Stadler* § 240 ZPO, No. 1.
311. *Schmitz*, Schiedsverfahren und Insolvenz, p. 58.
312. MüKoZPO/*Stackmann* § 240 ZPO, pp. 9-27; Musielak/Voit/*Stadler* § 240 ZPO, Nos 2-5.
313. *Schmitz*, Schiedsverfahren und Insolvenz, p. 65; Musielak/Voit/*Stadler* § 240 ZPO, p. 11.

relevant articles, also refer to arbitration. However, German scholars go about answering this question on a more fundamental level. The majority opinion is that the relevant articles can only directly apply to court proceedings.[314] The main argument is that arbitration, as proceedings based on party autonomy, is only bound to such rules as are found in the arbitration law, which is considered a choice by the parties due to their choice of the seat of arbitration. Thus, unless the parties have chosen to apply § 240 ZPO or the ZPO in general, the mandatory stay of proceedings therein cannot be applicable to them, regardless of the scope of the term 'proceedings' in § 240 ZPO.[315]

The same reasoning can be applied to § 352 InsO, mandating stays in the context of foreign insolvency proceedings.[316] Although, in the context of § 352 InsO, more voices argue that the term 'legal disputes' includes arbitration.[317] However, this seems to contradict the legislator's intent where it merely wanted to transfer the working of § 240 InsO to then § 392 InsO aF (now § 352 InsO).[318] Furthermore, such arguments based on interpretation ignore that even though one might interpret clauses outside of the arbitration code to include arbitration, there is no direct sanction for the parties or tribunal if they do not apply them. This would only differ if these clauses are deemed *ordre public* or mandatory law and, therefore, cannot be ignored without endangering the award's validity. However, this is not the case here, as until now, courts have not considered such articles to themselves constitute rules of *ordre public.*[319]

In other countries, such as France, courts have reached a different conclusion based on very similar articles. Therefore, it is far from unthinkable that another conclusion could be drawn. Case law on the French systems plainly states that the rule that prevents individual actions is in itself public policy, national and international, or part of mandatory law and such must be enforced in arbitration or otherwise upon the award by the court.[320]

iii *A Factual Stay of Proceedings*

Whereas neither § 240 ZPO nor § 352 InsO have been considered by themselves as mandatory rules or *ordre public*, the majority opinion is that the principle enshrined

314. *RGZ* 62, 24–25; *BGH*, KTS 1966, 246–249, p. 247; *OLG Hamburg*, IPrax 1985, 218–219; *BGH*, NJW 2009, 1747–1750; *Longrée/Gantenbrink*, SchiedsVZ 2014, p. 21; *Schmitz*, Schiedsverfahren und Insolvenz, pp. 66–70; *Sachs*, Collected Courses of the International Academy for Arbitration Law, year 2011 1 (2013), 1–48, p. 26; Musielak/Voit/*Stadler* § 240 ZPO, p. 6; *Strauch*, Schutz von Schiedsvereinbarung und vereinbarter Vertraulichkeit bei Insolvenzeröffnung, pp. 31–32; *G. Wagner*, KTS 2010, 39, p. 62; *OLG Dresden*, SchiedsVZ 2005, 159–163.
315. Vorwerk/Wolf/*Jaspersen* § 240 ZPO, No. 2.12; *Lazić*, Insolvency Proceedings and Commercial Arbitration, p. 292; MüKoInsO/*Schumacher* Vorbemerkungen vor §§ 85 bis 87, No. 53; *Nacimiento/Bähr*, NJOZ 2009, 4752, p. 4755.
316. *Nacimiento/Bähr*, NJOZ 2009, 4752, p. 4757; MüKoBGB/*Kindler* § 352 InsO, No. 6.
317. K. Schmidt InsO/*Brinkmann* § 352 InsO, No. 5; *Schultze-Moderow*, Schiedsverfahren und Insolvenz, p. 50; BeckOK InsO/*Weissinger* § 352 InsO, No. 10.
318. Entwurf einer Insolvenzordnung of 15.4.92, BT-Drs. 12/2443, p. 244; *Kraus*, Das Schicksal internationaler Schiedsverfahren in der Insolvenz des Schiedsbeklagten, p. 161.
319. *BGH*, NJW 2009, 1747–1750, No. 22.
320. *Cour de Cassation*, Arrêt of 2.6.2004 – Arrêt no. 873 (02-13.940) unnumbered, see the second and third paragraphs of the only ground mentioned; *Award in ICC Case No. 9163*, Collection of ICC Awards V, 2009, 703, pp. 704–705; *Berset/Lévy*, ASA Bull. 16 (1998), 664, p. 674.

within them cannot be ignored. This concerns the core legal principle of the right to be heard.[321]

The administrator, as discussed above, must join the proceedings and the arbitral tribunal must grant him the necessary time to realistically prepare for further proceedings in light of his right to be heard and the equality of parties, *see* § 1042 ZPO.[322] This means in practice that the tribunal has to at least temporarily suspend the proceedings insofar as they concern claims that can be considered part of the insolvency and grant a reasonable suspension of deadlines.[323] Technically the estimation of what is necessary to secure the administrator's right to be heard, i.e., primarily the length of the suspension, is within the tribunal's discretion. Nevertheless, when contrasted with the reality that not taking the appropriate measures, c.q. not providing an adequate suspension will be sanctioned with the setting aside of the subsequent award based on § 1059(2)(1)(b) ZPO,[324] this discretion becomes rather limited in practice.[325]

Notably, in normal circumstances, enough time should be given for the claim to be registered and go through the claim verification process, as based on the *paritas creditorum, see* § 87 InsO, which is part of German *ordre public* and gives every creditor and the administrator the right to challenge a claim.[326] Consequentially, the essence of § 240 ZPO is applied, as the arbitration should, in most instances, only be continued in case of a challenge.[327] A similar decision was made under French Law by a Paris-seated tribunal in ICC Case 13845 between two French companies. The administrator of the respondent had discontinued a contract with the claimant. The claimant submitted the claim for verification but also initiated arbitration for the same claim two months later.

321. *Nacimiento/Bähr*, NJOZ 2009, 4752, p. 4755; *Riedel*, Insolvenz in nationalen und internationalen Schiedsverfahren, pp. 112–113; *Schmitz*, Schiedsverfahren und Insolvenz, p. 70; *Schultze-Moderow*, Schiedsverfahren und Insolvenz, p. 50.
322. *Flöther*, DZWIR 2001, 89–95, p. 90; *S.M. Kröll*, Part IV: Selected Areas and Issues of Arbitration in Germany, Insolvency and Arbitration – Effects of Party Insolvency on Arbitral Proceedings in Germany, 981–1012; Berset and Lévy reach the same conclusion based on considerations of Swiss law, *see Badel*, ASA Bull. 25 (2007), 36–47; *Berset/Lévy*, ASA Bull. 16 (1998), 664, pp. 674–675.
323. *Flöther*, DZWIR 2001, 89–95, p. 92; *BGH*, NJW 2009, 1747–1750; *S.M. Kröll*, Part IV: Selected Areas and Issues of Arbitration in Germany, Insolvency and Arbitration – Effects of Party Insolvency on Arbitral Proceedings in Germany, 981, p. 1001.
324. *Nacimiento/Bähr*, NJOZ 2009, 4752, p. 4755; *S.M. Kröll*, Part IV: Selected Areas and Issues of Arbitration in Germany, Insolvency and Arbitration – Effects of Party Insolvency on Arbitral Proceedings in Germany, 981, p. 1001.
325. *S.M. Kröll*, Part IV: Selected Areas and Issues of Arbitration in Germany, Insolvency and Arbitration – Effects of Party Insolvency on Arbitral Proceedings in Germany, 981, p. 1001; *Strauch*, Schutz von Schiedsvereinbarung und vereinbarter Vertraulichkeit bei Insolvenzeröffnung, p. 33.
326. *BGH*, NZI 2002, 37–38, No. 9; NJW-RR 2007, 1693–1697, No. 12; NJW 2009, 1747–1750, 22–28; MüKoInsO/*Schumacher* Vorbemerkungen vor §§ 85 bis 87, No. 53; *Strauch*, Schutz von Schiedsvereinbarung und vereinbarter Vertraulichkeit bei Insolvenzeröffnung, 33, 65; *Schmitz*, Schiedsverfahren und Insolvenz, pp. 85–86; this rule is generally seen as a rule of ordre public, *see, e.g.*, France *Final Award in ICC Case No. 7205*, Collection of ICC Awards III, 1997, 622–628, 624–625, 628.
327. *Jestaedt*, Schiedsverfahren und Konkurs, p. 113; *S.M. Kröll*, Part IV: Selected Areas and Issues of Arbitration in Germany, Insolvency and Arbitration – Effects of Party Insolvency on Arbitral Proceedings in Germany, 981, pp. 1000–1001; *Riedel*, Insolvenz in nationalen und internationalen Schiedsverfahren, 47, 113; Cf. *Longrée/Gantenbrink*, SchiedsVZ 2014, pp. 21–23.

The tribunal denied jurisdiction with reference to the prohibition of individual claims in insolvency, as the verification was currently pending in the insolvency proceedings.[328]

A different conclusion could be reached insofar as the proceedings have factually ended, i.e., the hearings have been held, and submissions have been closed. In such circumstances, the only thing remaining is for the tribunal to render an award. Under similar circumstances, the tribunal in ICC Case 12805 ruled that it could continue and render the award.[329] The view of this tribunal is to be preferred as the test presented by the right to be heard in such articles as § 1059(2)(1)(b) ZPO is a factual one. Accordingly, it must be tested if the rights to be heard and equal treatment are violated in practice. In this vein, the fact that the submissions are closed and that the parties would not have any further opportunity in the case to express their views is a consideration when assessing if the continuation would violate the administrator's right to be heard. However, such considerations rely on the fact that no straightforward suspension rule as § 240 ZPO applies in arbitration, as such *de lege* suspensions are often not premised on such a factual test.[330]

iv *Analogous Application*

Some authors argue that instead of a factual suspension, as a necessary product of mandatory rules and the fundamental principle of the right to be heard, § 240 ZPO and implicitly § 352 InsO should be applied analogously to arbitration.[331]

They argue mainly that some of the reasoning of the German Supreme Court 1905 decision on the applicability of suspension rules to arbitration is not, or is no longer, fitting.[332] The Supreme Court argued that arbitration, unlike court proceedings, did not have the statutory terms and deadlines that § 240 ZPO is meant to interrupt.[333] Commentators point out that arbitration also works with deadlines, and it is contended that an analogous application of § 240 ZPO is necessary to secure the interruptions of these deadlines. In addition, they argue that arbitration has since become a full-fledged judicial process, as opposed to merely a private dispute resolution mechanism.[334]

Lenzen questions why one would not apply § 240 ZPO when one of the main conclusions is that the arbitral tribunal must essentially deliver the same effects as

328. *Final Award in ICC Case No. 13845*, ICC International Court of Arbitration Bulletin 20, 2009, 110, p. 113.
329. *Final Award in ICC Case No. 12805*, ICC International Court of Arbitration Bulletin 20, 2009, 97.
330. In ICC Case 12805, the consideration was had that insofar the Dutch rules on suspension of proceedings in case of insolvency apply to arbitration, an exception to interruption is found in Art. 30 Fw (Dutch Insolvency Code), stating that no interruption occurs when everything has been submitted to the judge to render a decision. *See Final Award in ICC Case No. 12805*, ICC International Court of Arbitration Bulletin 20, 2009, 97.
331. *Lenzen*, NZBau 2003, 428, p. 430; *G. Wagner*, KTS 2010, 39, 56 et seq; MüKoInsO/*Thole* § 352 insO, No. 16; *Riedel*, Insolvenz in nationalen und internationalen Schiedsverfahren, pp. 113–114.
332. *Lenzen*, NZBau 2003, 428, p. 430.
333. *RGZ* 62, 24–25, p. 25.
334. MüKoInsO/*Thole* § 352 insO, No. 16.

§ 240 ZPO through other means.[335] As far as this is to be understood as a call for direct application, the mere fact that a similar effect is reached through other means is not a dogmatic argument for the applicability of the rule and relies on circular logic: the effect of the rule is there so we should apply the rule. An arbitrator is not directly bound to apply any rule of the ZPO as a civil judge would be beyond the *lex arbitri*.[336]

Aufdermauer and *Schmitz* provide the most succinct argument as to why § 240 ZPO or, for that matter, § 352 InsO cannot be applied by analogy.[337] Application by analogy is subjected to several stringent criteria in German theory, mainly that the law has to contain an unintended legislative caveat.[338] Stating that there is no equivalent article to § 240 ZPO regarding arbitration is in itself insufficient. It needs to be shown that the arbitration code's lack of such a rule is unintended. Those arguing in favour postulate the argument that the underlying principle of § 240 ZPO, the right to be heard, also applies in arbitration.[339] However, this does not constitute a caveat in the law as the right to be heard is enshrined in the arbitration code, *see* §§ 1042(1) and 1059 ZPO. The fact that the arbitration code or agreement does not specify any further procedural rules cannot be considered a caveat or at least not a caveat to be closed by analogous application of § 240 ZPO, as under such circumstances, the tribunal decides by discretion, as stated in § 1042(4) ZPO.[340]

On the other hand, one could point out that the specific rule in § 240 ZPO was thought necessary even though there is already a general rule prescribing the right to be heard in German courts, namely § 103 GG. This then leaves room for an argument stating that as § 240 ZPO was deemed necessary even though § 103 GG applies, the legislature apparently did see a caveat or at least the need and room to create a specific rule to stay proceeding in case of insolvency. However, even if one were to see this as a caveat in the arbitration code, arguing in favour of an analogous application would still require this caveat to be unintended. While it would be hard to argue that the legislature, in the drafting of the arbitration code, actively considered adding an insolvency-specific rule, it should be considered that the rules in the arbitration code actively constitute the extent to which the legislator wishes to regulate the arbitration proceeding bindingly.[341] The legislator has positively stated in the arbitration code that beyond the principles of equal treatment and the right to be heard, the parties and subsidiarily the tribunal are free to organise the proceedings, following the maxim of party autonomy in arbitration.[342] Similarly, *Schmitz* argues that applying § 240 ZPO directly or indirectly contravenes arbitration's core concept of party autonomy. In

335. *Lenzen*, NZBau 2003, 428, p. 430; MüKoInsO/*Thole* § 352 insO, No. 16.
336. *See* ii above.
337. *Aufdermauer*, Schiedsgerichtsbarkeit und Insolvenz in Deutschland, pp. 279–281; *Schmitz*, Schiedsverfahren und Insolvenz, pp. 72–73; *Strauch*, Schutz von Schiedsvereinbarung und vereinbarter Vertraulichkeit bei Insolvenzeröffnung, pp. 33–34.
338. *BGHZ* 149, 165–178, p. 174.
339. *Lenzen*, NZBau 2003, 428, p. 430.
340. *Schmitz*, Schiedsverfahren und Insolvenz, p. 72.
341. Entwurf eines Gesetzes zur Neuregelung des Schiedsverfahrensrechts of 12.7.1996, BT-Drs. 13/5274, p. 26.
342. Entwurf eines Gesetzes zur Neuregelung des Schiedsverfahrensrechts of 12.7.1996, BT-Drs. 13/5274, pp. 26, 46–47.

particular, it collides with the freedom to shape the proceedings as found in §§ 1025 et seq. ZPO.[343] In conclusion, there is no caveat to be filled in as the legislator actively leaves every non-legislated procedural aspect to the parties beyond the principles it posits. Even if one does consider the absence of an insolvency-specific rule on the suspension of proceedings in the arbitration code a caveat, this cannot be considered an unintended caveat.

The line of argument presented above can be generalised to an argument against the direct or indirect application of non-arbitration-specific procedural rules in general to the extent the parties have not chosen these. However, this argumentation cannot prevent that the same result, i.e., suspension is still achieved by a practical application of the right to be heard and the *ordre public* principle of *paritas creditorum* by way of arbitration-specific rules. The fact that in most circumstances, the same effect as § 240 ZPO is reached and that, in parallel, its application directly would hardly provide a more stringent restriction of the autonomy of the parties cannot be sufficient for analogous application, as it does not negate the fact that the legislator did not leave an unintended caveat.[344] The conclusion remains that the arbitration code leaves no room for an analogous application of § 240 ZPO or § 352 InsO.

As such, §§ 240 and 352 InsO are neither directly nor indirectly applicable to arbitration. This does not change the fact that the tribunal is bound to suspend the arbitration proceedings – concerning the assets belonging to the insolvency estate – by way of *ordre public* and the right to be heard as examined in the previous subsection in a way similar to the operation of these sections of the InsO.

2.3.2 *Resumption of Proceedings*

As a logical consequence of the answer that arbitration should be suspended upon the opening of insolvency proceedings provided in the last subsection, follows the question of when an arbitration should then be resumed.[345] In insolvency, the challenging of claims that are the subject of ongoing court proceedings at the time of the opening of the insolvency proceeding leads to the resumption of those court proceedings, *see* §§ 179(1), 180(2), 184(1) InsO. This raises the question of whether this applies to arbitration as well. § 180 InsO, containing the primary rules concerning the jurisdiction for the determination of challenged claims, is discussed below. First, the application of § 180(2) InsO to arbitration (i), then the functioning of § 180(1) and (2) InsO (ii) and finally, § 180(1) and (2) InsO and arbitration (iii).

i Application of § 180(2) InsO to Arbitration

§ 180(2) InsO contains the general rule that a contested claim which was subject to ongoing proceedings at the moment of the opening of the insolvency is determined by the continuation of the suspended proceedings:

343. *Schmitz*, Schiedsverfahren und Insolvenz, pp. 72–73.
344. *Lenzen*, NZBau 2003, 428, p. 430; Cf. *Schmitz*, Schiedsverfahren und Insolvenz, p. 81.
345. For this discussion in the French context, *see Fouchard*, Rev. Arb. 1998, 471, pp. 487–488.

(1) An action for the determination of a claim shall be brought under the provisions governing ordinary civil proceedings. The local court where the insolvency proceedings are or were pending shall have exclusive jurisdiction for such action. If the subject-matter of the action does not fall under the jurisdiction of the local courts, the regional court in whose district the insolvency court is located shall have exclusive jurisdiction.

(2) *If an action concerning such claim was pending on the date when the insolvency proceedings were opened, determination of the claim shall be initiated by the joinder of such action.*[346] [Emphasis added]

Strong arguments favour the application of § 180(2) InsO and the similar rule concerning the disputation of claims by other creditors in § 184(1) InsO to arbitration. Insofar as the administrator and the challenging creditor are both bound to the arbitration agreement, as discussed further on,[347] they cannot ignore the ongoing arbitration proceedings. Furthermore, the fact that § 240 ZPO does not apply to arbitration makes no difference to the application of § 180(2) InsO, as the proceeding is suspended nonetheless and should generally only continue upon challenge, as otherwise, the dispute is moot.[348] First, § 180(2) InsO merely requires that a '*Rechtsstreit*' or 'legal procedure' was ongoing at the time of insolvency opening. The wording '*Rechtsstreit*' or legal dispute[349] is wider than just court procedures or '*Gerichtsverfahren*'. The correct assumption is that this also applies to arbitration as the debtor can only pursue his claims in insolvency via the route provided by the insolvency code. This leads to the conclusion that at least from the perspective of the insolvency proceedings, § 180(2) InsO or § 184(1) InsO also organise the resumption of arbitration proceedings.[350] As discussed in the previous section, the tribunal is bound to halt proceedings by way of § 1059(2)(2)(b) ZPO and § 87 InsO, i.e., the *ordre public* nature of the prohibition on individual enforcement and *paritas creditorum*. This also supports the conclusion that *ordre public* considerations provide further grounds for tribunals to generally respect the verification proceeding. Therefore, regard should be had for the regulation of the continuation of pending legal disputes in the insolvency code or *ordre public* will be violated and the award set aside.[351]

346. MüKoInsO/*Schumacher* § 180 InsO, No. 22; the author considers the wording '*joinder of such action*' a mistranslation of the German '*Aufnahme des Rechtsstreits*'. A more fitting translation is 'reopening of the proceedings'. Joinder has an established legal meaning, which is not equal to the German word '*Aufnahme*'. The word '*Aufnahme*' does not refer to the entry of a new party to the proceedings. In the German system the insolvency administrator replaces the insolvent.

347. *See* §§ 3.3 and 3.6.5.

348. *BGH*, NJW 2009, 1747–1750, No. 28; Jeager, InsO/*Gerhardt* § 180 InsO, Nos 61–62.

349. Translated as 'action' by *Reusch*, Insolvency Statute, http://www.gesetze-im-internet.de/englisch_inso/print_englisch_inso.html.

350. *Flecke-Gianmarco/C. Keller*, NZI 2012, 529, p. 532; Jeager, InsO/*Gerhardt* § 180 InsO, No. 62; *Longrée/Gantenbrink*, SchiedsVZ 2014, 21, p. 22; MüKoInsO/*Schumacher* § 180 InsO, No. 31; BeckOK InsO/*Zenker* § 180 InsO, p. 19.

351. *Aufdermauer*, Schiedsgerichtsbarkeit und Insolvenz in Deutschland, p. 53; *Jestaedt*, Schiedsverfahren und Konkurs, p. 113; MüKoInsO/*Schumacher* § 180 InsO, No. 31; Uhlenbruck/*Sinz* § 180 InsO, No. 37.

ii The Functioning of § 180(1) and (2) InsO: Continuation or New Proceedings

§ 180 InsO grammatically seems to provide a binary way forward: the continuation of suspended proceedings based on § 180(2) InsO or new verification proceeding based on § 180(1) InsO.[352] Aside from the application of § 180(2) InsO to ongoing arbitration, the question arises of whether § 180(1) InsO also includes claims that are challenged and subject to arbitration agreements. Insofar as no arbitration proceeding is pending, the question of whether proceedings under § 180(1) InsO should be referred to arbitration is answered positively, as is discussed in the next subsection.[353] As will be discussed in that discussion, the scope of the relevant arbitration agreement plays a key role.[354] However, before that discussion can be properly had, the relationship between § 180(1) InsO and § 180(2) InsO must be discussed as it provides a preliminary issue.

Regarding the continuation of pending proceedings, the Federal Supreme Court interprets the resumption of ongoing proceedings as meant in § 180(2) as mandatory when the claim is challenged,[355] regardless of the nature of the challenge. However, a large part of the academic opinions and related case law has come to a different conclusion regarding specific challenges and the scope of the continued proceedings. It is correctly posited that the discussion regarding the bare existence of the claim leads to a continuation of suspended proceedings, including arbitration, under § 180(2) InsO. There is, however, a debate on the question of to which extent disputes about registration, insolvency disputation and insolvency rank, or in other words, insolvency-specific questions that do not touch upon the existence of the claim itself, lead to a continuation of suspended proceedings. It is argued that such objections must be dealt with in the separate verification proceedings of § 180(1) InsO, as they do not fall under § 180(2) InsO.[356]

The wording of § 180(2) InsO is often used to argue this view. § 180(2) InsO, although using the wide-term 'legal dispute', specifies this as 'legal disputes concerning the claim'. Until recently, the majority opinion found that this at least excludes disputes that purely regard the rank of claim in insolvency as it is not the claim itself that is disputed in this case.[357] However, some go even further and argue that disputes that concern only insolvency-specific questions, such as registration and insolvency disputation, must lead to new disputes as meant in § 180(1) InsO.[358]

The Federal Supreme Court seems to have gone against the opinion presented above and disregards this separation of proceedings. During an appeal procedure, several of the defendants went into insolvency. The plaintiff entered claims into the

352. Uhlenbruck/*Sinz* § 180 InsO, No. 20.
353. Uhlenbruck/*Sinz* § 180 InsO, No. 16.
354. *See* §§ 3.3 and 3.6; Nerlich/Römermann/*Becker* § 180 InsO, No. 12; similarly in France, *see* *Cour de Cassation*, Arrêt of 2.6.2004 – Arrêt no. 874 (02-18.700).
355. *BGH*, NZI 2017, 300, No. 8.
356. *Häsemeyer*, Insolvenzrecht, 22.31; Uhlenbruck/*Sinz* § 180 InsO, No. 27 in the 2015 (14th) edition but differently in the 2019 (15th) edition.
357. *Häsemeyer*, Insolvenzrecht, 22.31; MüKoInsO/*Schumacher* § 180 InsO, No. 19.
358. *Häsemeyer*, Insolvenzrecht, 22.31; BeckOK InsO/*Zenker* § 180 InsO, No. 17.

insolvency of one defendant to which another defendant objects. The objecting defendant ended up making solely insolvency-related objections. The Federal Supreme Court seized the opportunity to discuss most of the relevant positions one can take on this subject. It decided that a creditor can resume a proceeding as meant in § 180(2) InsO if the objections are solely based on insolvency-specific issues. In this context, the court specifically mentions questions regarding the rank of the claim.[359] This approach is vastly preferable from both a legal and procedural economic point of view. However, it needs to be stated that the court explicitly does not decide that the opening of § 180(1) InsO proceedings is excluded when only insolvency-specific arguments are made, merely that all issues can be presented in the case continued as per § 180(2) InsO.[360]

The arguments that support the conclusion by the court are convincing. The relevant parties should be able to get a legally enforceable decision on the question of verification regardless of the sort of objection that is made. It cannot be that the resumed proceedings devolve into a dispute about the correct resumption of the proceedings and end up necessitating a separate proceeding just for the insolvency-specific questions.[361] The risk of such a problem is exacerbated by the fact that the ground for the disputation of a claim need not be specified, and new objections can be raised during the proceedings.[362] Consequently, an insolvency-specific objection can be raised after a proceeding has been continued in line with § 180(2) InsO, leading to discussions on whether new proceedings must be opened regarding the insolvency specific-objection under § 180(1) InsO.[363]

The Court concludes correctly that § 180(2) InsO aims to protect judicial efficiency and effective legal protection. It would go against the spirit of this regulation to force the creditor to go through two inefficient legal proceedings due to the nature of objections he might not even be aware of before starting the relevant proceedings.[364] A consistent application of the logic of the Court would lead to the conclusion that continuation of § 180(2) InsO proceedings is the preferred option, and choosing to pursue new proceedings under § 180(1) InsO should, if at all, only be allowed when an objector has finally bound himself to insolvency-specific objections. If the objector would not bindingly limit himself to such objections, he could raise a new non-insolvency-specific objection during the proceedings. This would force the halting of the § 180(1) InsO proceedings and the resumption of halted proceedings under § 180(2) InsO. This follows from the consideration of the Court that § 180(2) InsO provides a binding direction to continue suspended proceedings when objections as to the claim

359. *BGH*, NZI 2017, 300, Nos 11, 12, 14, 16.
360. *BGH*, NZI 2017, 300, No. 16.
361. *BGH*, NZI 2017, 300, 17, 18.
362. Cf. MüKoInsO/*Riedel* § 176 InsO, No. 27.
363. *BGH*, NZI 2017, 300, No. 20.
364. *BGH*, NZI 2017, 300, No. 21; In paragraph 3.4 it is discussed that the Canadian Supreme Court – in a very different context – even found that a multitude of court and arbitration proceedings can render the arbitration agreement inoperative for practical reasons including the risk of conflicting findings on related issues; *Supreme Court of Canada*, Judgment of 10.11.2022 – 2022 SCC 41, No. 175.

itself are made in which then all objections must be presented, to the exclusion of the separate verification proceeding of § 180(1) InsO.[365]

Aside from this, the rights of the creditor should be viewed holistically, i.e., registration, rank, and liability of the estate are all part of the 'right of the creditor' in the proceedings. The rank of a claim can mean the difference between getting full satisfaction and getting no satisfaction at all. As such, there is no partial legal force concerning the height of the claim when one only disputes the rank of the claim, as these are merely parts of the same right.[366] If there is a suspended proceeding as meant in § 180(2) InsO, all objections should be brought in that forum regardless of the specific nature. Accordingly, if an objection to a claim only concerns the rank of the claim, this should be seen as an objection against the creditor's right as a whole and lead to the continuation of the suspended proceedings per § 180(2) InsO.[367]

iii *§ 180(1) and (2) InsO and Arbitration*

In the context of § 180(1) InsO and arbitration, i.e., a claim is challenged and there is an arbitration agreement but no ongoing arbitration, it is argued that a challenge can and should be discussed in arbitration as the tribunal takes the place of the ordinary court meant in § 180(1) InsO as the insolvency administrator is bound to pre-existing arbitration agreements.[368] There is no convincing reason why this logic cannot be directly transposed to § 180(2) InsO. This leads to the conclusion that the same must count for the continuation of ongoing proceedings. As this is the case, the Federal Supreme Court's judgment, as mentioned above, can also be applied to suspended arbitrations. In which case, all that can be placed within the scope of the arbitration agreement can be discussed in the continued arbitration under § 180(2) InsO.

It is good to note that a pre-insolvency arbitration agreement cannot cover insolvency-specific claims, and as such, challenges based on such insolvency-specific claims cannot be dealt with by reopening a pre-insolvency arbitration.[369] The question that the Court has left open, the possible opening of new procedures based on § 180(1) InsO when insolvency-specific questions are raised, thus becomes extra problematic in arbitration. Depending on the effective scope of the arbitration agreement, the creditor might face a jurisdictional objection from the insolvency administrator if he tries to go to regular court as per § 180(1) InsO for the entire verification proceedings.[370] The administrator might argue that the verification itself should take place in the suspended arbitration. However, in the reverse situation, if an administrator attempts to bring insolvency-specific claims in arbitration, the creditor can object to a tribunal deciding

---

365. *BGH*, NZI 2017, 300, No. 8.
366. *Eckhardt*, Die Feststellung und Befriedigung des Insolvenzgläubigerrechts, 743, 34, 65.
367. *Eckhardt*, Die Feststellung und Befriedigung des Insolvenzgläubigerrechts, 743, No. 65; MüKoInsO/*Schumacher* § 180 InsO, No. 18.
368. Uhlenbruck/*Sinz* § 180 InsO, No. 16; *BGH*, NJW 2009, 1747–1750, No. 11 For the discussion on the binding power of the arbitration agreement *see* Chapter 2 § 3.3.
369. *BGH*, NZI 2013, 934–936, No. 9.
370. *See* the discussion in Chapter 2 § 3.6.

insolvency-specific issues on the ground that the arbitration agreement does not cover such issues.

The scope of the arbitration agreement forms the primary hurdle towards unifying all objections into one proceeding, as is the goal of § 180 InsO.[371] If one concludes, as above, that at least some of the insolvency-specific questions are covered by the arbitration agreement whereas other issues cannot be covered, this will lead to a strange and inefficient separation in proceedings. For example, based on § 180(1) InsO, this might lead to a situation where one must open a new arbitration for the disputations based on contractual arguments and another court proceeding, based on the same article, in front of a separate court for any insolvency-specific issues not covered by the arbitration agreement. If the scope of the arbitration agreement is correctly enforced in § 180 InsO's application, the situation might become even more complex if one considers that the administrator can make his own arbitration agreement for arbitrable insolvency-related issues that are also claims of the estate but do not fall under a pre-insolvency arbitration agreement, such as insolvency disputation in §§ 129 et seq. InsO that. In such circumstances, the administrator might be forced to open new arbitration proceedings merely for those issues if they cannot be added to the ongoing proceedings by later accord, even if arbitration was pending. Consequently, this could lead to a situation involving two arbitrations to determine the admission of one claim to insolvency.

In conclusion, insofar as the insolvency has suspended proceedings regarding a particular claim, these proceedings should be continued in arbitration or otherwise if the claim is disputed.[372] Insolvency-specific issues cannot be brought up based on pre-insolvency agreements. Consequently, the unification of the verification proceeding cannot be achieved. Whereas this contravenes the purpose of § 180 InsO, § 180(2) InsO cannot overrule that in arbitration the authority of the parties is limited to the scope of the arbitration agreement, which could not have included these issues.[373] As such, it is highly advisable for the insolvency administrator and the creditor to agree to bring all claims in either arbitration proceedings or a court proceeding.

In parallel to the conclusion that the arbitration proceedings can be continued as verification proceedings comes the conclusion that the arbitration should generally not be continued before the claim is disputed. The tribunal in ICC Case 13845 pointed this out in a discussion on similar French provisions.[374]

Although theoretically left unanswered by the court, the question of the possibility of new proceedings based on § 180(1) InsO should generally be answered negatively in the context of halted arbitration proceedings. This conclusion is supported by a teleological interpretation of § 180 InsO, judicial efficiency approach and a holistic approach to the creditor's right. To wholly determine the existence of a claim, a tribunal can and should decide as preliminary questions on the registration and rank

371. *See* the discussion in Chapter 2 § 3.6.
372. BeckOK InsO/*Zenker* § 180 InsO, No. 17.1.
373. *See* Chapter 2 §§ 1.4, 3.6.
374. *See* Chapter 2 § 2.3.1 iii; *Final Award in ICC Case No. 13845*, ICC International Court of Arbitration Bulletin 20, 2009, p. 110; *Jestaedt*, Schiedsverfahren und Konkurs, p. 113.

of the claim.[375] The situation is different in the narrow situation left open by the Supreme Court; the situation where objections are limited to those insolvency-specific objections, as these questions, as independent issues, are not covered by a pre-insolvency arbitration agreement, as discussed in Chapter 2 § 3.6.[376] *Zenker* finds with the author that the state court should be seized in those circumstances. In a quote that neatly summarises the issue:[377]

> Translation by author: When deciding on the existence of the claim, the arbitral tribunal can (and, if necessary, must) also decide on insolvency-specific questions of registrability and ranking as preliminary questions for determining mass liability (references). If, on the other hand, the existence of the claim is undisputed and the objection relates solely to the ranking under insolvency law, this is probably not covered by the arbitration agreement and should be clarified by the state courts appointed under § 180.

In the discussion above, the insolvency administrator is at least relatively actively engaged with the arbitration. However, there is also the situation, which is more common than one would want, wherein the insolvency administrator fails to respond or respond within a reasonable time to the important questions of insolvency in arbitration.[378] The question arises of how the continuation of arbitration should be considered under those circumstances. In ICC Case 10687 seated in France, where both parties went insolvent, the Tribunal had to extend multiple deadlines by way of five procedural 'reminders' to, after nine months, finally elicit a response from the respondent's administrator.[379] In such a situation, the French Supreme Court has decided that the administrator was estopped from relying on a violation of *ordre public* constituted by the continuation of the proceedings and the rendering of a subsequent award in insolvency, c.q. the violation of the principle of adversarial proceedings, which here partially overlaps with the right to be heard.[380] Although there seems to be no corresponding case law in Germany, the logic of the court, c.q. a version thereof, does fit within the German system and should be applied. As stated previously, the suspension of proceedings in Germany is based on the factual application of the right to be heard of the administrator based on § 1059(2)(1)(b) ZPO. Similar to the argument made regarding the non-necessity of the suspension in case arbitration is virtually closed,[381] the continuation of proceedings after having provided the administrator with all reasonable possibilities to participate in and decide concerning the arbitration and the underlying claim does not violate the right to be heard. Even if one was to consider

375. Citation aus Comment einfügen.
376. BeckOK InsO/*Zenker* § 180 InsO, No. 17.1.
377. BeckOK InsO/*Zenker* § 180 InsO, No. 4.3.
378. *Vidal*, ICC International Court of Arbitration Bulletin 20 (2009), 51, pp. 57–58.
379. *Final Award in ICC Case No. 10687*, ICC International Court of Arbitration Bulletin 20, 2009, 77–79; *Vidal*, ICC International Court of Arbitration Bulletin 20 (2009), 51, p. 58.
380. *Cour de Cassation*, Arrêt of 6.5.2009 – Arrêt no. 509 (08-10.281) unnumbered, but under the second paragraph of the first ground and similarly the third paragraph of the fifth ground.
381. *See* Chapter 2 § 2.3.1 iii.

it as such the insolvency administrator should be estopped from arguing this violation as stated by the French Supreme Court.[382]

2.3.3 *Claim Registration and Object of the Proceedings*

Proceedings that are continued or initiated under § 180 InsO must have as the object of those proceedings the verifications of the claim in the insolvency.[383] This subsection examines the nature of this rule and its relation to and implications for arbitration.

The suspension of proceedings and change in the object of proceedings both have a basis in the same legal principle, i.e., the principle of equality of creditors. This principle, as discussed above, is considered public policy in Germany.[384] The embodiment of this principle can be found in § 87 InsO and § 174 InsO, which state that all creditors in the sense of § 38 InsO must pursue their claims under the umbrella of the insolvency proceeding and must, in that context, register their claims with the insolvency administrator. The German Federal Supreme Court has stated in this respect that, based upon these rules of *ordre public,* it will set aside an award or, *in casu* parts thereof, that concern non-registered claims.[385]

If registered claims subject to arbitration are challenged, the arbitration can be continued. *See* the discussion in Chapter 2 § 2.3.2. However, as no individual enforcement is allowed in for insolvency claims, *see* the previously mentioned § 87 InsO, the prayer for relief in such cases must be changed from a prayer for the performance of the claim to a prayer for declaratory relief, namely a declaration that the claim exists.[386] Whereas these rules again would not directly apply to the arbitration, they will need to be followed in essence to avoid violating the equality of creditors principle. In arbitration, § 1046(2) ZPO explicitly allows for the amendment of claims. Naturally, an arbitral tribunal can also, by its own volition, render an award solely granting declaratory relief, even if there was a claim for monetary relief. Several ICC Awards can be found that apply similar rules applicable under other laws. Tribunals in France applying similar French provisions in cases concerning the insolvency of a party in the arbitration, for example, in ICC Cases 11876, 9163 and 7563, clearly state that they could only determine the claim and not order payment. They found that the Respondent was merely 'liable for the amount of [...]', i.e., they only determined the existence and height of the claim.[387] A tribunal seated in Düsseldorf, considering a

382. *See* § 2.3.1 iii; *Cour de Cassation,* Arrêt of 6.5.2009 – Arrêt no. 509 (08-10.281) unnumbered, but under the second paragraph of the first ground and similarly the third paragraph of the fifth ground; arguably also *Final Award in ICC Case No. 10687,* ICC International Court of Arbitration Bulletin 20, 2009, 77, pp. 78–79; *Vidal,* ICC International Court of Arbitration Bulletin 20 (2009), 51, Nos 18–19.
383. MüKoInsO/*Schumacher* § 180 InsO, No. 23.
384. *BGH,* NJW 2009, 1747–1750; MüKoInsO/*Schumacher* Vorbemerkungen vor §§ 85 bis 87, No. 53; *S.M. Kröll,* Part IV: Selected Areas and Issues of Arbitration in Germany, Insolvency and Arbitration – Effects of Party Insolvency on Arbitral Proceedings in Germany, 981, p. 999.
385. *BGH,* NJW 2009, 1747–1750, 21, 23.
386. *Longrée/Gantenbrink,* SchiedsVZ 2014, 21, p. 22.
387. *Partial Award in ICC Case No. 11876,* ICC International Court of Arbitration Bulletin 20, 2009, 85, 4.5, 5.3; *Award in ICC Case No. 9163,* Collection of ICC Awards V, 2009, 703, p. 707; *Final*

claim in insolvency, found similarly that under an application of Swedish law, it could also only determine the height of the claim for the purpose of a dividends calculation and explicitly could not order payment out of the estate.[388]

Furthermore, claiming monetary relief necessarily requires, as a first step, finding that a claim exists and, second, a determination of the height of the claim.[389] Thus, a tribunal can and should in insolvency merely find that the claim exists and determine its height and refrain from actually ordering any monetary relief. If a claim is not amended and the tribunal does order monetary relief, enforcing such an award literally and in full would go against public policy, *see* § 1059(2)(2)(b) ZPO.[390]

Whereas this remains true in theory, the German Federal Supreme Court has taken a softer approach in practice. The Court has found that awards awarding monetary relief concerning duly registered claims should be interpreted and enforced as merely stating the existence of the claim for the purpose of verification and registration in the insolvency table, in this sense curing the violation of public policy.[391] Another ICC Tribunal in France in Case 10687 found, based on similar French provisions that were applicable, that due to the suspension of individual enforcement proceedings, the claims had to be seen as 'modified', from claims of payment to merely a dispute over the height and existence of the claim.[392]

From another perspective, such an approach can also be seen as partial enforcement instead of an interpretation. As discussed, finding the existence of the claim is a necessary part and interim step of assessing damages, c.q. granting a claim of monetary relief.[393] Thus, instead of an interpretation of the operative part, which comes close to changing the award, one can see the enforcement of an award granting monetary relief as an award granting declaratory relief, as partial enforcement.[394] This perspective fits better with the fact that, when it comes to non-registered claims in awards and the decision on costs in case a part of the award is set aside, the German Federal Supreme Court chooses to partially enforce an award only for the part that concern claims that

---

Award in ICC Case No. 7563, Collection of ICC Awards III, 1997, 550, 553, 555; referring to the rule established in *Cour de Cassation*, Rev. Arb. 1989, 473; *Final Award in ICC Case No. 7205*, Collection of ICC Awards III, 1997, 622–628, pp. 624–625; *Gaillard/Savage*, Fouchard, Gaillard, Goldman on International Commercial Arbitration, No. 587587.

388. *Interim Award in ICC Case No. 7337*, Collection of ICC Awards IV, 2003, 308–320, No. 10.
389. *P.K. Wagner*, GWR 2010, 129, p. 130.
390. *Ehricke*, ZIP 2006, 1847–1854, p. 1850; *Longrée/Gantenbrink*, SchiedsVZ 2014, 21, p. 22; *S.M. Kröll*, Part IV: Selected Areas and Issues of Arbitration in Germany, Insolvency and Arbitration - Effects of Party Insolvency on Arbitral Proceedings in Germany, 981, p. 1000; *Schmitz*, Schiedsverfahren und Insolvenz, p. 86; similarly in France *Cour de Cassation*, Arrêt of 6.5.2009 - Arrêt no. 509 (08-10.281) *see* the fourth paragraph of the second ground.
391. *BGH*, NJW 2009, 1747–1750, 7–9, 16–17; *P.K. Wagner*, GWR 2009, pp. 44–45.
392. *Final Award in ICC Case No. 10687*, ICC International Court of Arbitration Bulletin 20, 2009, 77, II.2; Cf. *Fouchard*, Rev. Arb. 1998, 471, pp. 490–492.
393. *P.K. Wagner*, GWR 2010, 129, p. 130.
394. *BGH*, NJW 2009, 1747–1750, Nos 29–30; Vorwerk/Wolf/*Wilske/Markert* § 1059 ZPO, No. 76; Fouchard argues in favour of such an approach in France, *see Fouchard*, Rev. Arb. 1998, 471, pp. 490–491; Voit considers that a court, in the context of an annulment proceeding, is not allowed to change the award but is allowed to partially annul the award Musielak/Voit/*Voit* § 1059 ZPO, Nos 14–15, 32, 40.

a properly registered in the insolvency.[395] Consequently, the enforcement of an award minus all ordered monetary relief is closer to partial enforcement than to an interpretation. The court essentially enforces the decisions in the award on points on which the tribunal could decide in insolvency and, conversely, sets aside the decisions on issues it could not decide upon, such as the granting of monetary relief.[396]

2.3.4 The Special Case of Liabilities of the Estate

The discussion on the need for a stay of proceedings and resumption of those proceedings differs when a claim in dispute concerns a liability of the estate (*'Masseschuld'*). Creditors of the estate in the sense of §§ 53–55 InsO do not enjoy a 'rank' in the insolvency as their debts are not part of the insolvency debts but are debts incumbent upon the estate itself. Estate debts most prominently include obligations to administer the estate, *see* § 54 InsO.[397]

It is important to note that such debts can, in general, only be made when insolvency is already opened. However, this does not mean that such debts only flow from agreements and obligations, e.g., arbitration agreements, entered into by the insolvency administrator. The administrator can also continue specific contracts entered into by the insolvent, making accruing contractual debts from that point onwards debts of the estate. In those circumstances, a pre-insolvency arbitration agreement can cover such debts of the estate.

As a general rule, the estate's Liabilities must be paid when they become due.[398] Their enforcement at least is not bound to the special insolvency rules stemming from the prohibition on individual enforcement in § 87 InsO.[399] A creditor can try to enforce its claims in court. Similarly, insofar as a creditor can rely on a valid arbitration agreement, arbitration for estate liabilities can be started in insolvency.

In an international context, similar conclusions are reached. For example, in ICC Cases 11123 and 9163, the tribunals seated in Switzerland came to comparable conclusions regarding French law. They found that insofar as the claims consisted of debts created after the opening of the insolvency as meant in Article L. 631-32 French Commercial Code, i.e., debts of the estate, the tribunal was able to render an award ordering payment. Whereas it could not order payment of insolvency debts as meant in Article L. 621-40 French Commercial Code, i.e., claims encompassed in the insolvency.[400]

If an arbitration contains both sorts of claims the logical solution would be that the tribunal could not order payment for the pre-insolvency debts. Instead, if the proceeding is not suspended or is resumed after suspension, it could only confirm or

395. *BGH*, NJW 2009, 1747–1750, Nos 30–31, 35.
396. *BGH*, NJW 2009, 1747–1750, No. 31.
397. BeckOK InsO/*Erdmann* § 53 InsO, No. 3; MüKoInsO/*Hefermehl* § 53 InsO, No. 46.
398. *BGH*, NZI 2004, 435, p. 437; BeckOK InsO/*Erdmann* § 53 InsO, No. 4; similarly in France, *see Fouchard*, Rev. Arb. 1998, 471, p. 491.
399. MüKoInsO/*Hefermehl* § 53 InsO, No. 46.
400. *Partial Award in ICC Case No. 11123*, ICC International Court of Arbitration Bulletin 20, 2009, 79, pp. 82–83; *Award in ICC Case No. 9163*, Collection of ICC Awards V, 2009, 703, p. 707.

deny the insolvency claim's existence and height. However, it could order the payment of debts incumbent on the estate in the same award. This included, for example, the costs of the proceedings that occur when proceedings must be continued due to non-recognition of the claim by the administrator.[401] Theoretically, only the costs that occur after the opening of insolvency should be considered debts of the estate.[402] However, in Germany, the Federal Supreme Court and the Federal Labour Court have concluded that if such a proceeding is continued, the full costs of the proceedings, at least in that instance, become debts of the estate as meant in § 55(1) InsO. This includes both costs that accrued before and after the opening of the insolvency proceedings.[403] This conclusion is primarily based on the concept of the unity of the cost decision as meant in §§ 91 et seq. ZPO, i.e., no differentiation between costs can be made in the cost decision.[404]

§ 240 ZPO will apply for court proceedings concerning the suspension of a proceeding covering such mixed debts, as the proceedings do concern insolvency debts, even if only in part. For arbitration, the considerations do not change as § 240 ZPO does not apply directly, and the relevant criterion is still the right to be heard and the right to equal treatment. Under those principles, the insolvency administrator should be granted a reasonable amount of time to take a position, and inversely enough time must be granted to creditors to register the claim. Insofar as a mandatory suspension is applicable, as it might well be in other jurisdictions, dependent on the relevant law that prescribed the suspension, the claimant could be able to remove the proceedings from the scope of this suspension by changing the scope of the proceedings to be reduced to only the liabilities of the estate.

The nature of the claims in dispute, thus, affects the applicability of mandatory stay provisions, and there is no reason not to apply this to arbitration as well. In case mandatory stay provisions do not apply to arbitration, such as in Germany, this does not change this conclusion. In the case of debts incumbent on the estate, the reasons for a factual stay provided in Chapter 2 § 2.3.1 do not require a prolonged stay. The right to be heard should in such cases generally only justify a limited factual stay, such as also given when a change of party occurs. Furthermore, a tribunal does not need to change the object of the proceedings for such debts, as the prohibition of individual enforcement does not play a role in the context of such claims. Payment can be ordered even during insolvency.

2.3.5 *The Scope of the Proceedings: Preliminary Questions*

As discussed in the previous two topics, insolvency affects the object and, consequently, the arbitration proceedings' scope. This effect on the scope is further

401. *Award in ICC Case No. 9163*, Collection of ICC Awards V, 2009, 703, p. 707; *Procedural Order in Procedural Order No. 14*, ASA Bull. 23, 2005, 108–115, 4.9.
402. MüKoInsO/*Schumacher* § 85 InsO, No. 20; Uhlenbruck/*Mock* § 85 InsO, No. 166 with reference to a lot of first and second instance case law.
403. MüKoInsO/*Schumacher* § 180 InsO, No. 32.
404. *BAG*, NZI 2015, 462, Nos 9–11 and paragraphs 1–2 of the note by P. Meyer; *BGH*, NJW-RR 2007, 397, No. 14; differently MüKoInsO/*Schumacher* § 85 InsO, No. 20.

discussed here. From the perspective of the arbitration, insolvency-related issues also provide difficult (preliminary) questions for the tribunal, e.g., questions of jurisdictions and standing. The nature and, to some extent, the scope of the questions that the arbitral tribunal must answer to reach a substantive conclusion on the question before it changes. Most of these questions should be considered preliminary questions over which the arbitral tribunal has jurisdiction, even insofar as they have not in themselves been subjected to arbitration by the parties. In arbitration, it is understood that the tribunal has the jurisdiction to answer any preliminary question necessary to decide upon the claim submitted to it. Any other conclusion would be opposed to the parties' will as expressed in the arbitration agreement, c.q. the will to conclusively resolve the particular issue for which these preliminary questions are necessary.[405]

In ICC Case 13764, the tribunal had to answer questions regarding the assignment of specific contracts and claims due to a reorganisation scheme in a partial award. The Claimant argued that this was beyond the tribunal's jurisdiction as it constituted wholly new questions. However, the Tribunal correctly considered these questions preliminary questions as to jurisdiction, as the questions regarding the validity of the assignment were preliminary to the question of whether the parties were bound to the arbitration agreement.[406] In ICC Case 11519, the tribunal also effortlessly incorporated the insolvency issues into the determination of the claims in arbitration as they were necessary to answer the questions put before the tribunal.[407] Both these cases were seated in New York. However, the same logic applies in Germany, especially considering the approach to insolvency jurisdiction and arbitrability, *see* Chapter 2 § 1.5.[408]

ICC Case 12441 illustrates the significant extent to which a dispute can mutate due to insolvency.[409] In this case, the original claim concerned unsettled debts stemming from a licensing contract between a UK Claimant and a Dutch/American Respondent. The Respondent went into insolvency in both the Netherlands and the United States. The Dutch insolvency produced a composition with the creditors. The claimant's claim was initially accepted into the insolvency proceedings, but the Respondent then refused to transfer the shares into a new company which, as provided by the composition agreement, were to be transferred in satisfaction of the accepted claims. The arbitrators tried to steer clear of ruling on Dutch insolvency law. However, the arbitration mutated into a proceeding akin to an appeal of the Dutch composition and the underlying issues, such as the US Rejection Order regarding the relevant contract. As such, the arbitration incorporated insolvency-specific questions to a large extent.[410]

405. *R. Geimer/E. Geimer/Geimer*, Internationales Zivilprozessrecht, No. 38653865.
406. *Partial Award in ICC Case No. 13764*, ICC International Court of Arbitration Bulletin 20, 2009, 108–110.
407. *Final Award in ICC Case No. 11519*, ICC International Court of Arbitration Bulletin 20, 2009, 83–84.
408. *See* Chapter 2 §§ 1.3–1.4.
409. *Final Award in ICC Case No. 12441*, ICC International Court of Arbitration Bulletin 20, 2009, 90–95.
410. *Vidal*, ICC International Court of Arbitration Bulletin 20 (2009), 51, p. 57.

In very practical ways, Tribunals can also make substantially important considerations about the effect of insolvency on claims in arbitration beyond questions of jurisdiction. Although the case was rejected for other reasons, the Tribunal in ICC Case 13085, for example, considered that the attachment in dispute was without meaning under the insolvency law, and a successful claim could only result in a claim against the estate. In doing so, it essentially deliberated on a claim of insolvency preference.[411]

In light of the above, it is clear that the nature, scope and purpose of arbitration can be significantly impacted by insolvency. Beyond suspension and representation, insolvency leads to questions of jurisdiction, arbitrability and the object and nature of the proceedings and claims. However, the preferable conclusion is that insolvency-specific issues are in the scope of the arbitration if they must be considered preliminary issues to the dispute submitted to the tribunal. Any other conclusion would essentially defunct the arbitration and the will of the parties for effective and final dispute resolution.

2.3.6 The Choice of Arbitrator

In an ongoing arbitration, the insolvent has often already selected an arbitrator when insolvency is opened. It can be asked if this choice binds the insolvency administrator. Selecting one's own arbitrator is considered one of the main advantages of arbitration. It is also considered one of the primary rights of parties in arbitration. This has, for example, led to extensive discussions on multi-party arbitration and the way tribunals are composed in such cases, especially if parties join after the constitution of the tribunal, i.e., joinder or consolidation.[412]

The administrator, replacing the original party in the arbitration, is hard to categorise. It is not truly a new party, but it is also not, at least in Germany, an actual legal successor of the original party, *see* § 80(1) InsO and the discussion Chapter 2 § 2.2. Therefore, questioning whether the administrator is bound to the choice of arbitrator of the insolvent debtor is a valid question. However, the procedural relationship between the debtor and the arbitrator, c.q. the arbitration proceedings fall under the general principle that the administrator must enter into the legal relationships of the debtor as he finds them. It follows from this principle that he is also bound to the selection of the arbitrator made by the debtor.[413]

The Highest Regional Court in Berlin finds that this is only different in the unique circumstances in that the arbitrators had a special relationship with the original parties.[414] In this case, the arbitrator was considered equally close to both original parties, instead of equally 'far-removed', as his appointment was made by parties in a close corporate relationship – a bank on the one side and shareholding directors on the

411. *Final Award on Jurisdiction in ICC Case No. 13085*, Y.B. Com. Arb. XXXIV, 2009, 212, No. 3535.
412. *Born*, International Commercial Arbitration, p. 2568.
413. *KG Berlin*, SchiedsVZ 2005, 100–102; *P.K. Wagner*, GWR 2010, 129, p. 130; *S.M. Kröll*, Part IV: Selected Areas and Issues of Arbitration in Germany, Insolvency and Arbitration – Effects of Party Insolvency on Arbitral Proceedings in Germany, 981, pp. 1002–1003.
414. *KG Berlin*, SchiedsVZ 2005, 100, p. 102.

other side. Under such circumstances, the administrator does not have to accept this situation on the ground that the tribunal would now be skewed against the administrator as only the relationship with the other party would remain, in breach of the equal treatment of parties as embodied in § 1034(2) ZPO. However, this is not an insolvency-specific right and merely relates to the fact that the arbitral tribunal or one arbitrator is now closely related to only one of the parties due to a change of circumstances. Furthermore, it can be asked if the objection can still be brought outside of the two-week time limit for objections concerning a skewed appointment of the tribunal as given in § 1034(2) ZPO in case new facts come to light.[415] It could be argued that the substitution of the insolvent by the administrator is a new fact in this sense. However, *Voit* finds that it is generally not possible to bring further objections outside of the two-week period after the composition of the tribunal has been notified to the parties, as such a time limit would lose any meaning if this were possible.[416] However, outside the formal discussion of § 1034(2) ZPO, a tribunal should be hesitant to dismiss such arguments by the administrator too quickly if he has reasonable grounds to assume a skewed tribunal, as a court can refuse to enforce an award on those grounds, *see* § ZPO 1059(2)(2)(b).[417] In line with the above, the insolvency administrator will generally be bound to the choice of arbitrator, barring exceptional circumstances.

2.4 The Effect of the Dissolution of the Insolvent

The result or consequence of classical corporate insolvency is often the dissolution of the corporation.[418] It is not hard to imagine that the dissolution of a party in arbitration has a profound effect on the arbitration proceedings. This effect is discussed and examined in this subsection.

However, dissolution is not a necessary characteristic of the broader definition of insolvency proceedings.[419] Contemporary legislation and literature have focused more on reorganisation proceedings and turn-around proceedings wherein a corporation is not necessarily dissolved. These are now a common feature of insolvency or insolvency-related law. *See*, *e.g.*, Article 1(1) EIR and Annex A thereof. In ICC Case 19114, one finds an example of such a reorganisation proceeding within the context of arbitration: The French party is taken out of insolvency by a continuation plan, and the arbitration proceedings continue with the main discussion being on the question of whether the insolvency and reorganisation could allow for the termination of the underlying agreement. The Tribunal concluded that the German Party could, neither under the contract nor under French law, *see* L-622.13 French Commercial Code,

415. *KG Berlin*, SchiedsVZ 2005, 100, p. 102.
416. Musielak/Voit/*Voit* § 1034 ZPO, No. 7.
417. Musielak/Voit/*Voit* § 1034 ZPO, No. 7.
418. For example, *Fletcher*, The Law of Insolvency, Nos 19.
419. *Trunk*, Internationales Insolvenzrecht, p. 3; The definition of what is and what isn't an insolvency proceedings differs per jurisdiction and is as such hard to pin down, *see* Paulus/*Paulus* Art. 2 EuInsVO, No. 8.

terminate the agreement with the French party due to the bare fact of reorganisation.[420] From an economic perspective, such reorganisations are to be applauded. However, if reorganisation is not an option or fails, the company will generally be dissolved. The problem this creates for ongoing arbitration proceedings persists and is the subject of this discussion in this subsection.

In many jurisdictions, the dissolution of a company is often associated with insolvency. In general, insolvency proceedings end when the assets have been distributed and the insolvency court renders a decision lifting the insolvency. In Germany, the opening of insolvency proceedings leads to the 'dissolution' of the company and the closing of the insolvency, if there are no further assets,[421] leads to the striking of the company from the company register, *see* § 262(3) AktG, § 60(4). GmbHG and § 394(1) FamFG. For the purpose of this discussion, there is little difference between the way in which the insolvency was handled or came to an end, whether the estate has been divided amongst the creditors by either a 'creditors' accord', *see* § 258 InsO, or the normal insolvency division, § 200 InsO, or when the administrator finds that there are insufficient funds to administer the insolvency, *see* § 207 InsO. Insufficient funds at the point of the request to open insolvency proceedings can also lead to the rejection thereof, *see* § 26 InsO, and the immediate dissolution, *see* § 262(1)(4) AktG and § 60(1)(5) GmbhG. This is only different when an insolvent leaves insolvency because he is no longer insolvent, c.q. the reason for opening the insolvency has disappeared, *see* § 212 InsO, or when the creditors' accord includes the continuation of the company.[422] In the last case, the company will no longer be dissolved nor struck from the company register.

As used in the previous paragraph, the direct translation of dissolution, '*Auflösung*', describes what happens to a company at the opening of insolvency proceedings. *See* § 262(3) AktG and § 60(4) GmbHG. However, the German '*Auflösung*' is not the proper and full dissolution of the company in the meaning of 'seizing to exist', but merely a change of objective of the company towards dissolving the company. It does not immediately mean the '*Untergang der juristischen Person*' but merely starts a process of dissolution during which the company retains legal personality.[423] The actual 'seizing to exist' only happens when the insolvency procedure has come to an end and the company has been stricken from the company register in a second step, *see* § 262(3) AktG, § 60(4) GmbHG and § 394(1) FamFG.[424] This two-stepped process, also called '*Doppeltatbestand*', requires both the process of dissolution of the company, as described in the respective company laws, or in place thereof insolvency proceedings, and the act of striking the company from the record before the company truly ceases to

---

420. *Final Award in ICC Case No. 19114*, Y.B. Com. Arb. XLIII, 2018, 235, 75, 107–111; for another example, *see IUSCT*, Y.B. Com. Arb. 1988, 367, No. 8.
421. In general, it should be considered unlikely that a company remains viable after classical insolvency proceedings, not including here the option of selling the operations of the company as a going concern, e.g., *Final Award in SCC Case No. V079/2005*, Rev. Arb., 2011, 543, No. 667.
422. *BGH*, ZIP 2015, 1533, Nos 11–12.
423. Hölters/*Hirschmann* § 262 AktG, Nos 4–5.
424. BeckOK InsO/*Madaus* § 1 InsO, No. 19.

exist.[425] These two steps are differentiated between '*Beendigung*' and '*Vollbeendigung*' or '*Auflösung*' and '*Erlöschen*'.[426]

After the insolvency has ended and the company has truly been '*erlöscht*' by being stricken from the record, it lacks a legal personality, which presents some glaring potential issues for an ongoing arbitration. Insofar as arbitration was not yet pending when the company was dissolved, the company is no longer a valid party to be brought to arbitration as it does not legally exist anymore. Theoretically, insofar as an arbitration proceeding was pending or even has been opened during insolvency concerning an insolvency claim, this claim should have been dealt with in the insolvency proceedings. As discussed in Chapter 2 § 2.3.3 and § 3.6.4, the claim should be registered with the insolvency administrator and then dealt with in the verification procedure. This leads to either the administrator accepting the claim and the related arbitration losing its purpose or the administrator rejecting the claim and the arbitration being continued or started to verify the claim in the insolvency proceedings.[427] Presupposing that the estate has sufficient assets, it should be impossible for the insolvency proceedings to be closed before arbitration has finished, as the arbitration has become part of the verification and disputation proceedings. Consequently, the company losing its legal personality due to the insolvency proceedings being finished should not be an issue. In those circumstances, issues should only occur if the claim has not been properly introduced to the insolvency.

However, a company seizing to exist after a full-fledged insolvency proceeding is merely one option. There are several other ways a company can cease to exist in the middle of arbitration or before or during the enforcement of an award without the claim having been dealt with in a collective insolvency proceeding. In the German insolvency context, a prime example would be the termination of the insolvency proceedings due to a lack of assets leading to striking from the records, *see* § 207 InsO or § 24 InsO and § 394(1) FamFG.

In principle, the suspension of § 240 ZPO and the factual suspension of arbitration proceedings is lifted when termination of the insolvency proceedings is based on a lack of assets as meant in § 207 InsO.[428] Therefore, theoretically, the proceedings can be continued. However, according to § 394(1) FamFG, the company is to be stricken from the record ex officio after insolvency proceedings if there is no indication of further assets. There is an exception in case new assets are found in the future. In case of the closure of the proceedings due to insufficient assets, it is unlikely that a company has or will have assets in the sense of § 394(1) FamFG. Thus, it must be stricken from the record. Consequently, the company is properly and fully dissolved, and proceedings against this company must cease as it does not exist and has

425. BeckOK InsO/*Ruland* § 207 InsO, No. 26.
426. Hölters/*Hirschmann* § 262 AktG, No. 4; MünchKomm-AktG/*Koch* § 262 AktG, No. 14; BeckOK FamFG/*Otto* § 394 FamFG, No. 4.
427. *See* Chapter 2 §§ 2.3.1, 0 and 2.3.3; apparently this did not happen in the Iranian insolvency proceedings in IUSCT case 834, where after the lifting of the insolvency proceedings, the company was neither immediately dissolved nor was the claim finally dealt with in insolvency, *see IUSCT*, Y.B. Com. Arb. 1988, 367, No. 8.
428. MüKoInsO/*Hefermehl* § 207 InsO, No. 81.

no legal capacity.[429] Furthermore, the officers and representatives of the former company cannot represent the non-existent company. *See* § 50(1) ZPO and § 394(1) FamFG. For these reasons, the case law of the German Federal Supreme Court points towards the rejection of such cases on the basis of inadmissibility.[430] Barring specific situations such as the existence of other debtors, this leads to the outcome that the claim in the proceedings at least factually ceases to exist as the claim debtor has ceased to exist.[431]

Insofar as the dissolving company is actively pursuing a claim, this suffices to argue that there are at least potential assets in the company and, therefore, to stave off full dissolution according to the German Federal Supreme Court.[432] In cases where this ongoing proceeding, c.q. the claim at issue therein has not been dealt with in insolvency, as could theoretically happen in termination of such proceedings based on insufficient funds, § 207 InsO, the existence of such proceedings could be used to stave off the final dissolution of the company. However, such an outcome seems unlikely as in case the ongoing dispute would likely result in any significant assets, the insolvency proceedings would not have been closed for insufficient funds, and the claim would be handled in the insolvency proceedings by the administrator.

The remaining question is whether this logic can be transferred directly to arbitration. In a case before the Higher Regional Court of Düsseldorf, the court decided that an arbitration agreement had become incapable of being performed due to the fact that the company had no assets, all assets had been paid out, and the company was to be finally dissolved.[433] However, as the German Federal Supreme Court stated in the *Plumber* case and as *Leibner* notes in his commentary on the Düsseldorf case, the reasoning applied by the Düsseldorf court should not be followed stringently. In the *Plumber* case, the Court stated that the other party should have the option, as in court cases, to finance the proceedings and, in this way, counter the impossibility to perform.[434] *Leibner* states that actual impossibility to perform should not be coupled with a financial inability but with the final dissolution of the company, insofar as one takes this as the formal end of the capacity of a company to be a party in legal proceedings.[435] This is the correct approach, as at the moment the party is formally finally dissolved by the striking of the company in the company register it loses its legal personality and, with it, its capacity to be a party. The continuation of the operation of an arbitration agreement where one of the parties has ceased to exist should be deemed impossible. Consequently, an arbitral tribunal should deny jurisdiction over a company insofar as its final dissolution, as in § 394(1) FamFG, has occurred either in or before arbitration.

429. Scholz/*K. Schmidt/Bitter* § 60 GmbhG, 57, 62.
430. *BGH*, ZfBR 2015, 672, No. 19; NZG 2012, 916, No. 27; DStR 2010, 2643, Nos 21–22; NJW-RR 1996, 805, p. 806; NJW 1982, p. 238; NJW 1979, 1592, Nos 1–3.
431. *BGH*, NJW 1979, 1592, No. 2.
432. *BGH*, NZG 2012, 916, No. 27.
433. *OLG Düsseldorf*, ZIP 2004, 1956, p. 1962.
434. *BGH*, NJW 2000, 3720–3722, p. 3721; *Leibner*, EWiR 2004, 623, p. 624.
435. *Leibner*, EWiR 2004, 623, p. 624.

The High Court of England and Wales in *Silver Dry Company Ltd. v. Homer Hulbert Maritime Company Ltd* manages to phrase this conclusion masterfully: 'It takes two to arbitrate, just as it does to tango. There cannot be a valid arbitration when one of the two parties has ceased to exist: [...].'[436]

Barring special rules on litigation against dissolved entities,[437] an award against a non-existent company would generally be incapable of being enforced and should be considered null and void.[438] In this line, an LCIA tribunal declared one of its interim awards a nullity as it concerned a party that had ceased to exist.[439]

Arbitral practice has, however, not always drawn the same conclusion. In ICC Case 2139, the Tribunal found, based on the considerations the company was dissolved after the opening of the procedure and that the company had submitted its plea and that the administrator had signed terms of reference even after the date of alleged removal from the company register, that the arbitration could be continued.[440] However, in this case, it can be inferred that the arbitral tribunal was suspicious of the dissolution of the state-owned company in a developing country, which it calls the 'alleged' dissolution and striking from the company register. In the observations of this case, *Derains* states that it is generally accepted that the dissolution of a company does not, in principle, affect an arbitration agreement. It could, for example, be enforced against other parties. However, beyond these considerations, he is critical of what he interprets as an argument for a material rule that the final dissolution of the company does not affect the proceedings.[441] *Derains*, in his note, does state that the Tribunal could have denied effect to the judicial decision dissolving the company by relying on recognition rules of the seat.[442] This argument could also be used in regard to the decision opening insolvency, but not without endangering enforcement due to violation of *ordre public*. However, for a decision ordering final dissolution, its factual effect also features in the questions of legal capacity and personality and plays into arbitration by way of specific rules referring to legal personality regardless. This is key mainly in the decision on jurisdiction and later in the enforcement and annulment phase as an award has been made against a party that has no legal capacity according to the law of the state in which it has been incorporated or seated and can thus deny enforcement or find for annulment.[443] Tribunals would be hard-pressed to rely on (non-) recognition of dissolution decision as an argument to ignore dissolution, as rules surrounding legal personality are mostly understood to point to the 'personal law' of a

436. *Commercial Court*, Judgment of 18.1.2017 – [2017] EWHC 44 (Comm), No. 1; with reference to the same conclusion in *England and Wales Court of Appeal*, Judgment of 13.6.1991 – [1992] 1 QB 610.
437. *Supreme Court of British Columbia*, 7.3.2014 – 2014 BCSC 370, Nos 61–65.
438. *J.D.M. Lew/Mistelis/Kröll*, Comparative International Commercial Arbitration, 7.56.
439. As reported by the Court in *Commercial Court*, ArbLR 2006, 521, No. 35.
440. *Award in ICC Case No. 2139*, Collection of ICC Awards I, 1990, 24–25, 237–241, 24, 237.
441. *Award in ICC Case No. 2139*, Collection of ICC Awards I, 1990, 24–25, 237–241, pp. 238–239.
442. *Award in ICC Case No. 2139*, Collection of ICC Awards I, 1990, 24–25, 237–241, pp. 239–240.
443. *Jahn/Brian*, § 27 Geschäftsverkehr mit ausländischen Kunden, No. 17; Differently Born, who argues for a validation application of the relevant laws, *see Born*, International Commercial Arbitration, pp. 722–723; *Jahn/Brian*, § 27 Geschäftsverkehr mit ausländischen Kunden, No. 17.

company and not the effects of the law of the company as recognised in the seat country.[444] However, in regard to the arbitration agreement, some want to apply a validation principle to the legal capacity of the party.[445] The tribunal could technically continue arbitration, especially if no jurisdictional arguments can be brought anymore due to the phase of the procedure. However, the continuation of the proceedings based on the fact that the relevant decision is not recognised will most likely lead to unenforceable awards. Whether that be due to a violation of the rights to be heard and equal opportunity, as the company has not been recognised as dissolved but lacks proper representation as a fully dissolved company cannot be represented, or due to lack of jurisdiction based on the invalidity of the arbitration agreement vis-à-vis the dissolved party.[446] For this reason, it makes little sense to continue an arbitration solely against a dissolved company.

If one concludes, as is concluded here, that continuing an arbitration against a dissolved company is not possible or not to be preferred, the question can be asked if one could turn to another party. In another ICC Case, 1803, the Tribunal implicitly accepted that the dissolved party could no longer be a party and tried to apply succession rules to bring other parties into the arbitration as respondents.[447] Similarly, but from the opposing perspective, the previously mentioned LCIA tribunal, after stating that its award for the dissolved company was null, immediately turned to discuss the substitution of the claimant.[448]

In *Silver Dry Bulk Company Ltd. v. Homer Hulbert Maritime Company Ltd.*, the Court essentially formulated the question that the aforementioned LCIA tribunal was also trying to answer: 'There may be an issue whether, even though the claimant no longer continues in existence, its claims in arbitration can survive, for example by means of a principle of universal succession […] or some broadly equivalent principle […].'[449] The German courts have seen similar discussions as well, e.g., on enforcement against legal successors or shareholder-directors.[450] In ICC Case 2626, a Tribunal in Germany, in a case involving a corporate transformation, also found that legal succession had taken place and found the successor bound to the arbitration agreement.[451] There is no dogmatic argument based on insolvency or arbitration as to why

444. *See* Chapter 3 §§ 4.3–4.4; *Svea Hovrätt*, ITA Monthly Report 2008, s.l; *Moss*, Legal Capacity, Arbitration and Private International Law, 619, p. 628; Cf. Wolff/*Wilske/Fox* Art. V NYC, Nos 105–107.
445. Differently Born, who argues for a validation application of the relevant laws, *see Born*, International Commercial Arbitration, pp. 722–723.
446. *Moss*, Legal Capacity, Arbitration and Private International Law, 619, pp. 620–624; *Commercial Court*, Judgment of 18.1.2017 – [2017] EWHC 44 (Comm), No. 4.
447. *Award (Procedural Order) in ICC Case No. 1803*, Collection of ICC Awards I, 1990, 40, pp. 43–47; The Tribunal did not succeed as the Court in Geneva as confirmed by the Federal Tribunal denied it competence regarding the successor company and the state of Bangladesh, *see BGE*, Y.B. Com. Arb. 1980, 217, 217, 219–220.
448. *Commercial Court*, ArbLR 2006, 521, No. 35; *see also* CLC 2000, 470.
449. *Commercial Court*, Judgment of 18.1.2017 – [2017] EWHC 44 (Comm), No. 1.
450. *BGH*, NJW-RR 2007, 1366–1367; BeckRS 1969, 31173417; *OLG München*, BeckRS 2015, 9570.
451. *Award in ICC Case No. 2626*, Collection of ICC Awards I, 1990, pp. 316–318 note by Y. Derains; as another example of succession in arbitration ICC Case 3281 can be mentioned where a party is absorbed, *see Award in ICC Case No. 3281*, Collection of ICC Awards II, 1990, 453–456 note by Y. Derains.

the arbitration could indeed not be continued against a legal successor or if the dissolved party is substituted in another sense by a party bound to the arbitration agreement.

In consequence, an arbitration against or for a company that has been dissolved in arbitration should be stopped, and the arbitral tribunal should deny jurisdiction. Any awards against a company that has ceased to exist should be considered null and cannot be enforced regardless. Arbitration can continue if the party is substituted, or there are still parties left on both sides without substitution, c.q. another party can be considered bound to the arbitration agreement.

2.5 Conclusion and Position

In this section, a core topic of this book was examined: the effect of insolvency proceedings on arbitration. While the opening of insolvency proceedings should not invalidate ongoing proceedings, an arbitration can and should not ignore the insolvency of one of the parties. The arbitrator, not being an administrator of state justice, is not bound to apply the law as a judge would have to. Therefore, he does not need to follow procedural rules set out for state proceedings or apply procedural laws outside of those explicitly meant to apply to arbitration.

Prima facie, that conclusion can create significant tension in the context of insolvency, as it would lead to disputes using different sorts of dispute resolution mechanisms to resolve similar insolvency claims being treated differently. Such a result would violate not only principles of insolvency, such as the equality of creditors and the related principle of no-individual-enforcement, but it would also violate core principles of arbitration. Letting arbitration continue with indifference to insolvency would seriously endanger the right to be heard and the equality of arms in arbitration.

This does, however, not mean that to prevent this, one must violate the nature and position of arbitration and directly apply non-arbitration procedural rules to arbitration. Arbitration has several safety mechanisms to prevent the unwanted outcomes described above. First, arbitrability prevents arbitrations from directly arbitrating insolvency issues it has no business deciding upon, as discussed in § 1.4, and second, the public policy exception prevents the arbitration from trampling core concepts of national law.[452] *Wolff* points out that public policy can be misused to fend off undesired awards due to its opaqueness and fluidity. In regard to insolvency, however, it can be safely said that, at least in German practice, it is generally clear which principles are put in jeopardy and what steps would put them in jeopardy, e.g., the principle of equality of creditors is violated by given a single creditor an enforceable award, whereas other creditors cannot pursue individual enforcement. It can be concluded that the sword of Damocles that *Wolff* sees in the public policy exception has already fallen when it comes to insolvency in arbitration.[453] At any rate, his observation alerts us to a practical issue, not so much a dogmatic one.

452. Wolff/*Wolff* Article V(2)(b) NYC, Nos 569-579.
453. Wolff/*Wolff* Article V(2)(b) NYC, Nos 491-492.

This does not mean that there are no discussions left. On the contrary, there are fundamental discussions ongoing. This is, however, part of the natural development of law. In keeping with the previously used imagery, there is and should be a healthy debate on where Damocles' sword has made its cut. In more explicit terms, it should be debated when and how the relevant principles are genuinely put in jeopardy and what consequences this has for arbitration. This will also remain a largely case-by-case discussion.

For now, it is clear, however, that an administrator cannot freely ignore an arbitration, just as arbitration cannot freely ignore insolvency. The arbitrators must accept the administrator into the proceedings and provide the administrator with the possibility to decide on the proceedings and the underlying claim. The administrator, for his part, cannot simply dismiss the arbitration proceedings and must decide within a reasonable timeframe. If the claim is challenged, this challenge should result in the continuation of the arbitration proceedings. Finally, as will be discussed in the following section, the administrator, besides their inapplicability on other grounds, cannot use insolvency-related powers to undermine an ongoing arbitration by 'attacking' its contractual fundaments, i.e., the arbitration agreement but also the arbitrator contracts. This would undermine the core concepts of how ongoing proceedings are dealt with in insolvency.

In this way, arbitration and insolvency can co-exist and do co-exist, within the German legal order.

3 THE EFFECT OF INSOLVENCY PROCEEDINGS ON THE ARBITRATION AGREEMENT

In this section, the effect of the insolvency proceedings on an arbitration agreement is examined and discussed. After having established that a 'German' tribunal must take into account insolvency in Germany, the next step for the tribunal is to reflect upon the effects of this insolvency. The above discussion on the effects of insolvency on the arbitration proceedings is intrinsically entwined with the discussion on the effect of insolvency on the arbitration agreement, necessitating several references to the discussion in this section.

As the jurisdiction of the tribunal flows primarily from the parties' arbitration agreement, the basis for any arbitration, any effect of insolvency on the arbitration agreement might have repercussions on the tribunal's jurisdiction. This would drastically affect the arbitration and perhaps even lead to its termination. To examine this effect, one must first answer if an arbitration agreement 'survives' insolvency, c.q. if the opening of insolvency proceedings does not invalidate it. If the agreement is not per se invalidated, the follow-up question is if an arbitrator, in general, is bound to such agreements. If this is generally the case, it becomes relevant to deal with questions regarding special insolvency powers with which one could actively challenge or invalidate agreements. If the arbitration agreement remains valid, a discussion of its scope in regard to insolvency issues remains.

In line with this summation, the examination in this section starts with the necessary fundamental discussion on the nature of the arbitration agreement (§ 3.1), followed by an important topic in the context of insolvency in arbitration: the validity of the arbitration agreement (§ 3.2), the binding power of the arbitration agreement (§ 3.3), potential incapability to perform due to impecuniosity (§ 3.4), further possibilities to dissolve, defunct or otherwise challenge the arbitration agreement (§ 3.5), and finally the effective scope of the arbitration agreement (§ 3.6).

An example of those potential ways to defunct an arbitration agreement is the so-called right-to-choose (German: *Wahlrecht*) of the insolvency administrator set out in § 103 InsO. A topic regularly looked at in this context in German works. This is discussed in § 3.5.1.

3.1 The Nature of the Arbitration Agreement

Before more practical questions regarding the arbitration agreement can be answered, a clear concept of the nature of the arbitration agreement is necessary. In the German system, the law provides a few hints as to the nature of the arbitration agreement. § 1029(1) ZPO provides for the essential characteristics of an arbitration agreement as described above, a party agreement to submit certain disputes to an arbitral tribunal.[454] However, it does not unambiguously provide us with the legal nature of the arbitration agreement.

The legal nature of the arbitration agreement is disputed, and courts and academics have come to different conclusions. The discussions focus on the arbitration agreement's substantive, procedural, or dual nature.[455] To summarise the two sides, the substantive nature flows from the fact that the arbitration agreement is a private contract between parties and the procedural nature focuses on the fact that a procedure is created that takes away disputes from the jurisdiction of the courts.[456]

This discussion follows a similar line to the one above on the relationship between arbitration and the seat jurisdiction.[457] Similarly, it is argued that the arbitration agreement is nothing more than a contractual method to determine a dispute, which could have been settled by contract in any case, making it not much more than a determination mechanism.[458] The fact that under German law, *see* § 1055 ZPO, the arbitral award is given the same effect as a court decision between parties[459] does not change this. Even if this was not the case, the parties have agreed that the

454. *See* Chapter 1 § 3.2.
455. Musielak/Voit/*Voit* § 1029 ZPO, No. 3; *Schmitz*, Schiedsverfahren und Insolvenz, pp. 41–42; *J.D.M. Lew*, The Law Applicable to the Form and Substance of the Arbitration Clause, 114, p. 118.
456. *J.D.M. Lew*, The Law Applicable to the Form and Substance of the Arbitration Clause, 114, p. 118.
457. *See* Chapter 2 § 2.1.
458. Musielak/Voit/*Voit* § 1025 ZPO, No. 1; Musielak/Voit/*Voit* § 1029 ZPO, p. 3.
459. Some authors find that Art. 1055 ZPO states that awards are by nature legal rulings. However, Art. 1055 ZPO merely states that the award is provided the same effect and this only between the parties who contracted into the underlying arbitration agreement *Schmitz*, Schiedsverfahren und Insolvenz.

award has a binding effect between them as part of the arbitration agreement.[460] The older case law of the German Supreme Court categorises the arbitration agreement as a substantive law agreement with a procedural subject:[461]

> Allerdings beruht dort die Unterwerfung der Parteien unter die [schieds]richterliche Entsch. nicht, wie im Zivilprozeß, auf dem Gesetz, sondern auf einem zwischen ihnen abgeschlossenen gegenseitigen Vertrag. Aber auch durch eine Vereinbarung nach Maßgabe von § 1205 Abs. 1 ZPO [aF]- *einen materiellrechtlichen Vertrag über prozeßrechtliche Beziehungen* (RGZ 144, 96 [98]; 156, 101 [104]) – werden für die Beteiligten Pflichten begründet, die übrigens, soweit nicht besondere verfahrensrechtliche Bestimmungen eingreifen, nach den Grundsätzen des bürgerlichen Rechts zu beurteilen sind (Emphasis added).
>
> Translation by author: However, here the parties' submission to the judicial decision is not based on the law, as in civil proceedings, but on a mutual contract concluded between them. However, an agreement under § 1205 (1) of the Code of Civil Procedure [old edition] – *a substantive contract on procedural relations* (RGZ 144, 96 [98]; 156, 101 [104]) – also creates obligations for the parties, which, by the way, are to be judged according to the principles of civil law, unless special procedural provisions intervene.

The German Supreme Court more recently found that the arbitration agreement is a subtype of a procedural agreement:[462]

> Die Schiedsvereinbarung unterliegt nach altem wie nach neuem Recht als Unterfall des Prozessvertrages (BGHZ 99, 143, 147) materiellen Gültigkeitsgrenzen [...].
>
> Translation by author: The arbitration agreement is subject to substantive limits of validity under both the old and the new law as a subcategory of the procedural agreement (BGHZ 99, 143, 147) [...].

Where the German Federal Supreme Court did not explicitly mention this, the core of the argument in favour is that the nature of an agreement is determined by its primary effect and not by the modus of the agreement.[463]

Aside from this, in international literature, the procedural nature of the arbitration agreement is mainly discussed as opposed to the substantive nature of the underlying contract or relationship. Whereas the underlying contract qualifies the rights and duties of the parties involved, the procedural arbitration agreement provides a mechanism to determine these duties in case of a dispute finally. It, however, does not in itself qualify or determine these rights.[464]

This notwithstanding, it is widely agreed that an arbitration agreement, procedural as it may be, carries several substantive duties, such as a duty to cooperate with

460. Cf. Musielak/Voit/*Voit* § 1029 ZPO, p. 3.
461. *BGH*, NJW 1957, 589–591, p. 590; Cf. Musielak/Voit/*Voit* § 1029 ZPO, No. 3.
462. *BGH*, DNotZ 2009, 938, No. 17; with reference to NJW 1987, 651–653; Cf. MüKoZPO/*Münch* § 1029 ZPO, No. 13.
463. A common approach in civil law countries, *see Born*, International Commercial Arbitration, p. 1977; MüKoZPO/*Münch* § 1029 ZPO, No. 13.
464. *Leboulanger*, The Arbitration Agreement: Still Autonomous?, 3, pp. 13–14; *Born*, International Commercial Arbitration, 215, 359–360.

the arbitral process or a duty not to obstruct the proceedings.[465] Whether authors favour the procedural or substantive nature of the arbitration agreement, most do not deny that the agreement also has aspects pertaining to the other nature. Whereas *Voit* seems to favour the substantive, private nature, he does not deny the procedural aspects, albeit solely from the perspective of the relevant legal order.[466] *Münch*, in line with the more recent German Supreme Court cases, states that the arbitration agreement is a procedural contract but also does not deny substantive effects and the applicability of substantive-contract standards on the 'making and breaking' of the contract.[467]

In general, considering the arbitration agreement as a procedural agreement is a more convincing approach. The procedural purpose is the primary purpose of the agreement.[468] In general, a contract's nature should indeed, as *Münch* argues, be determined by its primary purpose. Otherwise, any mixed contract could not be categorised, which would present many issues in regard to applicable rules and regulations.

However, whatever nomenclature one prefers, an arbitration agreement has both procedural and substantial obligations under German law.[469] To qualify these substantive obligations as purely procedural duties and to thus legitimise a qualification of the arbitration agreement as a procedural agreement solely is a wilful misqualification and unnecessary. It also ignores other substantive contractual characteristics of the arbitration agreement, e.g., formation questions.[470] When following the rule that *Münch* discusses, stating that the contract's primary purpose qualifies its legal nature, a qualification as a pure material or procedural contact would not be necessary.[471] After all, one is only looking at the primary purpose of the contract, not the sole purpose of the contract. Applying this rule leads to the qualification of the arbitration agreement as a procedural agreement without disqualifying its substantive aspects.[472]

3.2 The Validity of the Arbitration Agreement

In this subsection, the effect of insolvency on the validity of the arbitration agreement is discussed. Potential invalidation of the arbitration agreement profoundly affects arbitration and could necessitate termination of the arbitration proceedings due to lack of jurisdiction.

465. *Wong, Venus, Valentina/Siwy*, Recalcitrant Parties and the Tribunal's Power to Order Cost Advance Payments, 201, p. 204; *Hanefeld/Trittman*, Part II: Commentary on the German Arbitration Law (10th Book of the German Code of Civil Procedure), Chapter II: Arbitration Agreement, § 1029 – Definition, pp. 81–82.
466. Musielak/Voit/*Voit* § 1029 ZPO, No. 3.
467. MüKoZPO/*Münch* § 1029 ZPO, Nos 12–15.
468. Cf. *BGH*, NJW 1987, 651, 3(c).
469. *Wong, Venus, Valentina/Siwy*, Recalcitrant Parties and the Tribunal's Power to Order Cost Advance Payments, 201, p. 207.
470. *Schmitz*, Schiedsverfahren und Insolvenz, p. 42; MüKoZPO/*Münch* § 1029 ZPO, Nos 13–15; Musielak/Voit/*Voit* § 1029 ZPO, p. 3.
471. *BGH*, NJW 1987, 651, 3(c); MüKoZPO/*Münch* § 1029 ZPO, No. 13.
472. MüKoZPO/*Münch* § 1029 ZPO, Nos 12–14.

In some jurisdictions, insolvency does indeed affect or invalidate an arbitration agreement, i.e., when a party goes insolvent, all arbitration agreements become void. This was the case under previous Polish law, as seen in the *Vivendi* cases,[473] and under older law in Spain and, some argue, in Lithuania.[474] This *ipso iure* invalidity must not be mistaken for an insolvency-specific possibility to avoid contracts. Like in Germany under § 103 InsO, as discussed in Chapter 2 § 3.5.1, the insolvency administrator can opt out of non-performed contracts in many countries.[475] These 'choice'-clauses could potentially be applied to arbitration agreements. For example, in Italy, based on § 72 Italian Bankruptcy Act, the insolvency administrator can avoid contracts that have not been fully performed, including an arbitration agreement. Under § 83bis Italian Bankruptcy Act, this terminates any proceedings based on these contracts.[476] However, the *ipso iure* invalidity of arbitration agreements purely due to the opening of insolvency proceedings is rare and, in fact, looks like a thing of the past. In most countries, the arbitration agreement remains valid upon the opening of insolvency proceedings.[477]

Germany does not have a rule in its insolvency code invalidating arbitration agreements. To the contrary, the German Federal Supreme Court has concluded in a case concerning separation rights based on a sale and cession contract subject to an arbitration agreement that the insolvency does not affect the validity of the arbitration agreement and that the questions could thus be arbitrated.[478] In the author's view, this is the only correct approach as no valid dogmatic reason exists to invalidate arbitration agreements upon insolvency.

3.3 Binding Power of the Arbitration Agreement

As the arbitration agreement is not invalidated *ipso iure* upon opening the insolvency proceedings in Germany, the more relevant question is whether arbitration agreements bind an insolvency administrator. Although legally different, the invalidity of the

473. Cf. *Fletcher*, Insolvency Intelligence 22 (2009), 60, p. 61.
474. *Cole et al.*, Legal Instruments and Practice of Arbitration in the EU, 96, 131–132; *Sachs*, Collected Courses of the International Academy for Arbitration Law, year 2011 1 (2013), 1–48, p. 19; *BGE*, ASA Bull. 2010, 104–110.
475. On § 103 InsO *see* § 3.5, especially § 3.5.1.
476. *Sachs*, Collected Courses of the International Academy for Arbitration Law, year 2011 1 (2013), 1–48, p. 20; *Tsvengrosh, Marta* Arbitration and Insolvency: Conflict of Laws Issues, p. 14; In an ICC Case the dissenting arbitrator found that under Italian law the administrator had no capacity to act in arbitration due to exclusive jurisdiction of the bankruptcy court, *see Interim Award in ICC Case No. 10507*, ICC International Court of Arbitration Bulletin 20, 2009, 71, § 10.
477. *Dorda*, Annals FLB – Belgrade Law Review Year LVII (2009), 83, p. 85; *Sachs*, Collected Courses of the International Academy for Arbitration Law, year 2011 1 (2013), 1–48, p. 17; e.g., for France *see Krause/Filhol*, International Arbitration and French Insolvency Proceedings: French Supreme Court Reiterates Importance of Public Policy, http://kluwerarbitrationblog.com/2009/10/28/international-arbitration-and-french-insolvency-proceedings-french-supreme-court-reiterates-importance-of-public-policy/; for Brazil *see W. Stuber/A.M.G. Stuber*, JIBLR 23 (2008), p. 116.
478. *Lord*, Int'l Trade&Bus. L. Rev. 15 (2012), 316, p. 338; *Sachs*, Collected Courses of the International Academy for Arbitration Law, year 2011 1 (2013), 1–48, p. 18; *BGH*, SchiedsVZ 2008, 148–150, No. 17; ZinsO 2004, 88, No. 1.

agreement and it not being binding upon the administrator would have similar effects. If the administrator is not bound to the arbitration agreement, it no longer serves any purpose in insolvency, as in that case, the agreement could neither be enforced against the insolvent - insofar as the agreement concerns claims assets and claims belonging to the insolvent estate - nor its administrator.

Following the principle that arbitration agreements bind only the parties, one could conclude that the pre-insolvency arbitration agreement does not bind the insolvency administrator. This conclusion would be supported by the view that the administrator is neither a party representative nor its legal successor under German law.[479] The leading theory under German law is that the insolvency administrator executes an office created explicitly by the insolvency code and that his powers flow from the insolvency code itself.[480] However, it is long-standing case law in Germany that the insolvency administrator must generally take over the legal situation of the insolvent as it is at the moment the insolvency order is made, including arbitration agreements.[481]

Other opinions insisting that the administrator is a representative or agent of the debtor or the estate would only facilitate the above conclusion that the administrator is generally bound, as representatives and agents within their function are generally bound to the agreements of the parties they represent.[482]

The binding of the administrator to such agreements should be viewed as an international standard, e.g., corresponding provisions are found anywhere from French doctrine to Chinese Law to US Law, *see, e.g.*, § 25(7) P.R.C. Bankruptcy Law and U.S.C.A section 541.[483] Although it needs to be noted that there is a difference between civil and common law countries (excluding the US). Whereas in civil law countries, like Germany, the administrator merely administrates the estate, whether it be in the capacity of a special office ('*Amtstheorie*')[484] or a representative or an agent. Whereas in England, the trustee retains the title to the assets, creating a more direct binding effect, as the trustee, in this case, could be viewed as a legal successor.[485] Interestingly, in the example case of England, there is a *lex specialis,* stating that upon adoption of a contract the trustee is bound by an arbitration agreement applicable to that contract.

Arbitral tribunals have also found that the insolvency administrator is bound to the arbitration agreement under the laws of various jurisdictions. This can be seen in

479. MüKoInsO/*Vuia* § 80 InsO, 27–28, 83; BeckOK InsO/*Riewe* § 80 InsO, No. 20.
480. MüKoInsO/*Vuia* § 80 InsO, No. 27.
481. *BGH*, NJW 2009, 1747–1750; NJW 1957, 791, No. 8; *Ferrari/S. Kröll*, Conflict of laws in international arbitration, p. 369; MüKoZPO/*Münch* § 1029 ZPO, No. 54; *Riedel*, Insolvenz in nationalen und internationalen Schiedsverfahren, p. 10; *Strauch*, Schutz von Schiedsvereinbarung und vereinbarter Vertraulichkeit bei Insolvenzeröffnung; Musielak/Voit/*Voit* § 1029 ZPO, No. 8.
482. MüKoInsO/*Vuia* § 80 InsO, 28, 73, 76; Cf. Musielak/Voit/*Voit* § 1029 ZPO, No. 8.
483. *Fouchard*, Rev. Arb. 1998, 471, p. 486; *Yang*, Insolvency Proceedings and Their Effect on International Commercial Arbitration, pp. 2–309.
484. MüKoInsO/*Vuia* § 80 InsO, No. 73.
485. *Lazić*, Insolvency Proceedings and Commercial Arbitration, p. 110.

the case law of ICC tribunals.[486] For example, an ICC Tribunal seated in Düsseldorf, in an arbitration between a Swedish and a Japanese party, found that succession takes place under Swedish law in case of insolvency and that, consequently, the estate and the estate administrator were bound to the arbitration agreement.[487] Similarly, in ICC Case 11123, the administrator, applying French law, went so far as to state it could not decide upon the claimed subject to an arbitration agreement as this was part of the jurisdiction of the arbitrators.[488] Insofar as this award is to be understood in a way that the administrator has lost all his authority over the claim, this is manifestly incorrect. He is still free within the convenes of insolvency law to accept the claim into insolvency and consequently negate the need for arbitration. However, as the French Supreme Court decided, the arbitration agreement should be respected upon challenging the claim.[489] Above, it was similarly discussed that under § 180(1) and (2) InsO, the challenging of a claim subject to an arbitration agreement in insolvency should lead to (continuation of the) arbitration in Germany.[490] That conclusion implies that the relevant arbitration agreement binds the insolvency administrator.

The fact that, in general, the administrator is bound by pre-insolvency arbitration agreements does not diminish the fact that some insolvency issues cannot be considered part of the effective scope of the pre-insolvency arbitration agreement. This mainly refers to issues which, under German theory, are either non-arbitrable or not of the free disposal of the debtor pre-insolvency and are directly based on powers vested in the administrator by virtue of the insolvency.[491]

3.4 Incapability to Perform the Arbitration Agreement

In the previous two subsections, it was established that the arbitration agreement remains valid and the insolvency administrator is generally considered bound to it. Having examined and answered those questions, potential insolvency-related issues that could otherwise frustrate – factually or legally – the performance of the arbitration agreement become relevant. A primary issue in that respect is the potential incapability to perform the agreement due to impecuniosity. Recently the Canadian Supreme Court also found arbitration agreements inoperable in insolvency due to reasons of practical complexity, efficiency and effectiveness. These issues are examined in this subsection.

486. *Final Award in ICC Case No. 12993*, ICC International Court of Arbitration Bulletin 20, 2009, 105, No. 9797 presumptively under Korean law; *Interim Award in ICC Case No. 7337*, Collection of ICC Awards IV, 2003, 308–320, pp. 312–313 considering the question under Swedish law.
487. *Interim Award in ICC Case No. 7337*, Collection of ICC Awards IV, 2003, 308–320, p. 313.
488. *Partial Award in ICC Case No. 11123*, ICC International Court of Arbitration Bulletin 20, 2009, 79–83; *Vidal*, ICC International Court of Arbitration Bulletin 20 (2009), 51, p. 63.
489. *Cour de Cassation*, Arrêt of 2.6.2004 – Arrêt no. 874 (02-18.700) unnumbered, *see* 3th and 4th paragraph of the second ground; *see also Final Award in ICC Case No. 7205*, Collection of ICC Awards III, 1997, 622–628, pp. 624, 627; *Final Award in ICC Case No. 6057*, ICC International Court of Arbitration Bulletin III, 1994, p. 487; *Final Award in ICC Case No. 4415*, Collection of ICC Awards I, 1990, 530, p. 532; *Fouchard*, Rev. Arb. 1998, 471, p. 488.
490. *See* Chapter 2 § 2.3.2.
491. *See* the discussion under Chapter 2 § 3.6.

Practically, insolvency might render the arbitration agreement incapable of being performed due to impecuniosity. This conclusion was reached by the German Federal Supreme Court in the *Plumber* case:

> Im Streitfall ist die Schiedsvereinbarung undurchführbar gewesen, weil der Kl. die Kosten des Schiedsverfahrens nicht hat aufbringen können und auch nicht anderweitig für Kostendeckung gesorgt gewesen ist.[492]
>
> Translation by author: In the case in dispute, the arbitration agreement was incapable of being performed because the plaintiff was unable to raise the costs of the arbitration proceedings and there was no other means of covering the costs.

The court decided not to enforce the arbitration agreement based on § 1032(1) ZPO, i.e., the incapability to perform.[493] However, insolvency merely means that the debtor can no longer pay all its debts, not that it has absolutely no funds. § 17(1) InsO speaks of '*Zahlungsunfähigkeit*', which is defined in § 17(2) InsO as 'the incapability of the debtors to pay those debts which are due. The incapability to make payments is generally to be assumed if the debtor has ceased to make payments'. Neither of those descriptions requires the debtor to be actually impecunious. It merely refers to situations where the debtor has fewer assets than the total debts due.[494] Thus, as insolvency does not necessarily mean impecuniosity, such decisions need to be made on a case-by-case basis.

Worth noting that the same case-by-case consideration has to be made for a request for security for costs. If the estate is shown to have sufficient funds, no such order should be made.[495] In both cases, the naked fact of insolvency per se is therefore not a sufficient argument. The argument has to be focused on actual impecuniosity and the consequential inability to pay for arbitration or, respectively, the inability to pay a potential cost award.

Decisions on the impecuniosity argument have to involve considerations on access to justice as it involves asking an impecunious party to stick to an arbitration agreement that it cannot afford to enact. It is imperative that a party, impecunious or not, should not be denied an effective legal remedy. However, most writers do not follow the logic of the *Plumber* case, and courts in many other jurisdictions, e.g., England, the US and France, have concluded that an impecunious party cannot rely on its own inability to perform the arbitration agreement.[496]

The question also arises if the impecuniosity defence can be used when the other party declares itself willing to take over the insolvent party's costs. Under previous law and case law on the incapability to perform the arbitration agreement, this possibility

492. *BGH*, NJW 2000, 3720–3722, p. 3721; *Strauch*, Schutz von Schiedsvereinbarung und vereinbarter Vertraulichkeit bei Insolvenzeröffnung, 65, 68–78; *G. Wagner*, SchiedsVZ 2003, pp. 206–207; *P. Wagner*, Disp. Resol. Int'l 5 (2011), 189, pp. 196–197.
493. *BGH*, NJW 2000, 3720–3722, p. 3721; *OLG Düsseldorf*, ZIP 2004, 1956, p. 1962.
494. MüKoInsO/*Eilenberger* § 17 InsO, 18a.
495. *Procedural Order in Procedural Order No. 14*, ASA Bull. 23, 2005, 108–115.
496. *Lord*, Int'l Trade&Bus. L. Rev. 15 (2012), 316, pp. 325–326; *England and Wales Court of Appeal*, Lloyd's Rep. 1981, 302, p. 305.

was provided to the non-impecunious party to still enable arbitration.[497] However, under the law before the renewal of arbitration law in Germany on 1 January 1998, the incapability to perform the arbitration agreement due to impecuniosity led to a right to terminate the arbitration agreement under § 1027a ZPO a.F, a non-automatic effect.[498] Whereas, according to the Federal Supreme Court in the *Plumber* case under § 1032(1) ZPO, the effect of impecuniosity makes the arbitration agreement *ipso iure* incapable of being performed, and no act of termination is required.[499] Accordingly, it can be argued that the non-impecunious party, under § 1032(1) ZPO, does not have the opportunity to declare itself willing to pay all the costs since the non-enforceability of the arbitration agreement is direct and by law.[500]

However, in the same *Plumber* case, the German Supreme Court decided it wanted to keep this possibility. An arbitral tribunal has 'competence-competence'. In other words, it has the authority to determine its own jurisdiction.[501] The question of incapability of being performed is part of the question of jurisdiction. When answering this question, the incapability of being performed due to non-coverage of the costs cannot be found if the other party declares itself willing to pay all costs.[502]

The German Federal Supreme Court was widely criticised for parts of its findings in the *Plumber* case, i.e., finding incapability to perform under the circumstance of impecuniosity.[503] However, if no party is willing to cover the costs of the impecunious party and no other solution is found, the court essentially just stated a practical reality. Arbitration remains a private dispute resolution method. Consequently, everyone involved in it is paid by the parties. If their wages, honorarium, and costs cannot be guaranteed, they would rightfully and legally be unwilling to perform their duties, and thus, the arbitral process is not capable of being performed in a very practical sense. Impecuniosity can, therefore, be a reason to find that the arbitration agreement cannot be performed, but the non-impecunious party should be offered a chance to cover the relevant costs.

Aside from impecuniosity, practical considerations can also be used to argue the inoperability of the arbitration agreements. In the recent *Peace River Hydro Partners v. Petrowest* case, the Canadian Supreme Court found that certain arbitration agreements had become inoperative for reasons of procedural efficiency and effectiveness or 'practicality'.[504] In determining the question if court proceedings should be stayed in favour of arbitration, the majority considered that the circumstances of the case justified finding the arbitration agreements inoperative. The receiver would have had to participate in at least four different arbitrations including at least seven counterparties. Certain claims would fall within the arbitration agreement others would not and

497. *Riedel,* Insolvenz in nationalen und internationalen Schiedsverfahren, 86 et seq., 97.
498. *BGH,* NJW 1988, 1215, No. I(2)(b).
499. *BGH,* NJW 2000, 3720–3722, No. II(1).
500. *Riedel,* Insolvenz in nationalen und internationalen Schiedsverfahren, p. 97.
501. *Born,* International Commercial Arbitration, p. 1047.
502. Similarly *Riedel,* Insolvenz in nationalen und internationalen Schiedsverfahren, p. 97; *BGH,* NJW 2000, 3720–3722, 17, 19 et seq.
503. *BGH,* NJW 2000, 3720–3722; *Strauch,* Schutz von Schiedsvereinbarung und vereinbarter Vertraulichkeit bei Insolvenzeröffnung, pp. 77–78; *G. Wagner,* SchiedsVZ 2003, 206, p. 208.
504. *Supreme Court of Canada,* Judgment of 10.11.2022 – 2022 SCC 41, No. 9.

thus would have to be determined in court. This would lead to parallel court proceedings and risk conflicting outcomes. The court determined that this would comprise the orderly conduct of the insolvency and potentially the integrity of the procedure. That again, would be contrary to the statutory goal of the insolvency administrator, to maximise recovery for creditor.[505]

While the logic of the Canadian Supreme Court is appealing at surface level, as it is likely that indeed the effectuation of the arbitration agreement would have been a severe strain on the insolvency procedure, the term inoperative should be regarded as an objective standard: factually no longer able of being performed. In this case, it seems that effectuating the arbitration agreements would not be impossible but merely complex and difficult. It cannot be denied that the factual effectuation of the arbitration agreement could be to the detriment of the estate, particularly in this case. However, there are other insolvency tools to decide which contracts can be dissolved or challenged on that ground – *see* the following paragraph – that is not a valid ground to find that an arbitration agreement is inoperative. The logic used in the Canadian case could lead to parties having to worry if their counterparty had not signed 'too many' arbitration agreements so that their application in insolvency would be so complex and burdensome that the courts would deem all the arbitration agreements inoperative. The court itself is quick to point out that the outcome is very context-specific.[506] That, however, does not negate that this ruling puts the rule that insolvency administrators are generally bound to pre-insolvency arbitration agreements on a slippery slope.

3.5 Possibilities to Dissolve, Defunct or Challenge an Existing Arbitration Agreement

Aside from the incapability to perform the arbitration agreement, German law provides the insolvency administrator several options to challenge or dissolve contracts and transactions made before the insolvency, which might be applied to and thus adversely affect the arbitration agreement and therewith the arbitration.[507] These are examined in this subsection: § 103 InsO (§ 3.5.1), § 115 InsO (§ 3.5.2), §§ 129–133 InsO (§ 3.5.3), and § 314 *Bürgerliches Gesetzbuch* (BGB) (§ 3.5.4).

It should be noted beforehand that the application to the material contract to which the arbitration agreement applies does not directly include the application to that arbitration agreement due to the concept of separability introduced in Chapter 1 § 3.2.[508]

3.5.1 § 103 InsO: The Right to Choose

§ 103 InsO incorporates the insolvency administrators the right to choose:

505. *Supreme Court of Canada*, Judgment of 10.11.2022 – 2022 SCC 41, No. 173.
506. *Supreme Court of Canada*, Judgment of 10.11.2022 – 2022 SCC 41, No. 10.
507. *See also* for a discussion on role of the articles below in this context *Schmitz*, Schiedsverfahren und Insolvenz, pp. 44–53.
508. *Strauch*, Schutz von Schiedsvereinbarung und vereinbarter Vertraulichkeit bei Insolvenzeröffnung, pp. 66–67.

(1) If a mutual contract was not or not completely performed by the debtor and its other party at the date when the insolvency proceedings were opened, the insolvency administrator may perform such contract replacing the debtor and claim the other party's consideration.
(2) If the administrator refuses to perform such contract, the other party shall be entitled to its claims for non-performance only as an insolvency creditor. If the other party requires the administrator to opt for performance or non-performance, the administrator shall state his intention to claim performance without negligent delay. If the administrator does not give his statement, he may no longer insist on performance.

Under § 103 InsO, the German Insolvency Administrator can reject the performance of mutual contracts. Although the claims are not dissolved under the current theory, they can merely not be enforced, c.q. enforced outside of insolvency.[509] Looking at this broad article, the question has to be raised if this applies to arbitration agreements as it does under the previously mentioned and similar Italian provisions. Two factors that play a significant role here are: Which contracts are covered by § 103 InsO, and how does German law view the nature of an arbitration agreement? Or in other words: Does the arbitration agreement fall under § 103 InsO?

§ 103 InsO applies to mutual contracts, i.e., the obligations that depend on each other, also called a synallagmatic contract.[510] However, in standing case law, the German Federal Supreme Court states that the arbitration agreement is not such a contract:[511]

> Der Konkursverwalter muß grundsätzlich die Rechtslage übernehmen, die bei Eröffnung des Verfahrens besteht. *Die Schiedsabrede ist weder ein gegenseitiger Vertrag* i.S. des § 17 KO noch ein Auftrag i.S. des § 23 KO (vgl. RG VII 463/05 Urt. v. 17. 4. 1906 = Nachschlagewerk des RG Nr. 26 zu § 274 ZPO; RGZ 137, 109) (Emphasis added)
>
> Translation by author: In principle, the insolvency administrator must adopt the legal situation existing at the opening of the proceedings. *The arbitration agreement is neither a mutual contract* within the meaning of § 17 KO nor a mandate within the meaning of § 23 KO (cf. RG VII 463/05 Urt. v. 17. 4. 1906 = RG reference no. 26 to § 274 ZPO; RGZ 137, 109).

This conclusion is further supported by the typification of the arbitration agreement as primarily a procedural agreement, as there is simply no interdependent performance. Accordingly, § 103 InsO cannot be applied to the arbitration agreement itself.[512]

Whereas § 103 InsO cannot be directly applied to the arbitration agreement, it can theoretically be applied to the underlying contract to which the arbitration agreement applies. The questions of whether that issue falls within the scope of a pre-insolvency

509. Uhlenbruck/*Wegener* § 103 InsO, Nos 8–9.
510. MüKoInsO/*Huber* § 103 InsO, No. 55.
511. *BGH*, NJW 1957, 791, No. 2; MüKoInsO/*Huber* § 103 InsO, No. 94.
512. *BGH*, NJW 1957, 791, No. 2; ZinsO 2004, 88, No. 1; *S.M. Kröll*, Part IV: Selected Areas and Issues of Arbitration in Germany, Insolvency and Arbitration – Effects of Party Insolvency on Arbitral Proceedings in Germany, 981, p. 993; *Schmitz*, Schiedsverfahren und Insolvenz, p. 45.

arbitration agreement and the consequences of its application are further explored in Chapter 2 § 3.6.2.

3.5.2 *§ 115 InsO: Expiration of Mandates*

Besides § 103 InsO, § 115 InsO might be applicable to the arbitration agreement. § 115(1) InsO states that mandates provided by the Insolvent before insolvency expire with the opening of the insolvency:

> (1) Any mandate ordered by the debtor referring to the property forming part of the insolvency estate shall expire upon the opening of the insolvency proceedings.

The relevance of § 115(1) InsO to the arbitration agreement, thus, depends on the question of whether an arbitration agreement can be classified as a mandate provided by the insolvent.

In the same case as cited above, where the German Federal Supreme Court states that the arbitration agreement is not a mutual contract as meant under § 103 InsO, it also states that it is not a mandate:

> Translation by author: In principle, the insolvency administrator must adopt the legal situation existing at the opening of the proceedings. *The arbitration agreement is neither a mutual contract within the meaning of § 17 KO nor a mandate* within the meaning of § 23 KO (cf. RG VII 463/05 Urt. v. 17. 4. 1906 = RG reference no. 26 to § 274 ZPO; RGZ 137, 109).[513]

Therefore, the arbitration agreement does not qualify for expiration under § 115 InsO. This conclusion is correct, as, between the parties, the arbitration agreement is primarily a procedural agreement, as discussed above in Chapter 2 § 3.1, and consequently not a mandate.

3.5.3 *§§ 129–133 InsO: Contesting Pre-insolvency Transactions*

§§ 129–133 InsO provide a further potential option to challenge and affect the arbitration agreement. §§ 129–133 InsO allow for the challenging of certain transactions that negatively impacted the estate made by the insolvent before the opening of insolvency proceedings.[514] § 129(1) InsO states generally:

> (1) Transactions made prior to the opening of insolvency proceedings and disadvantaging the insolvency creditors may be contested by the insolvency administrator under sections 130 to 146

513. *BGH*, NJW 1957, 791, No. 2; ZinsO 2004, 88, No. 1; *S.M. Kröll*, Part IV: Selected Areas and Issues of Arbitration in Germany, Insolvency and Arbitration – Effects of Party Insolvency on Arbitral Proceedings in Germany, 981, p. 992; *Schmitz*, Schiedsverfahren und Insolvenz, p. 48.
514. BeckOK InsO/*Raupach* § 129 InsO, under 'Grundsatz'.

In Germany, this is commonly known as '*Insolvenzanfechtung*'. In some jurisdictions, this concept is more commonly known under the name '*actio pauliana*' after its Roman roots.[515]

§§ 130 and 131 InsO, on congruent and incongruent coverage, cannot apply to the arbitration agreement per se as it does not constitute payment or security as necessary for their application.[516] However, the rules of §§ 132 and 133 InsO concerning actions directly disadvantaging the creditor and wilfully disadvantaging the creditor can be considered.[517]

The core question in §§ 132 and 133 InsO, or at least a fundamental part of these rules, is the requirement introduced in § 129 InsO that the creditors have been unduly disadvantaged, c.q. the insolvency estate has been adversely impacted.[518] The adverse impact of the insolvency estate is meant in the literal sense: a negative effect on the estate's value.[519] The arbitration agreement, as organised in § 1029(1) ZPO, represents a party agreement to derogate from their right to go to court and to organise a method of alternative dispute resolution. The right to have access to a state court cannot be qualified as a property right nor valued economically in itself. Consequently, one cannot speak of a negative effect on the financial value of insolvency estate due to a contract derogating from this right in favour of arbitration.[520]

Aside from this, one can take a wider view and look at the potential adverse effect on the insolvency estate beyond purely financial interests. Hence one should ask if it can be stated that the derogation from court dispute resolution in favour of arbitration can be viewed as a net negative value to the estate. In general, this question has to be answered in the negative.[521] The German legislator perceives arbitration to be a true alternative to state courts and hence of 'equal value':[522]

> Der Abschluß der Schiedsvereinbarung als solcher kann unter der Prämisse einer Gleichbehandlung der Parteien sowohl bei der Zusammensetzung des Schiedsgerichts als auch bei der Durchführung des schiedsrichterlichen Verfahrens keine Benachteiligung einer Partei darstellen. Die in § 1025 Abs. 2 erste Alternative ZPO vorgesehene Rechtsfolge der Nichtigkeit des Schiedsvertrages für den Fall, daß eine Partei ihre wirtschaftliche und soziale Überlegenheit dazu ausgenutzt hat, die andere Partei zum Abschluß der Schiedsvereinbarung zu nötigen, erscheint angesichts der Tatsache, daß die Schiedsgerichtsbarkeit einen der staatlichen Gerichtsbarkeit grundsätzlich gleichwertigen Rechtsschutz bietet. [...]
>
> Sieht man die Schiedsgerichtsbarkeit als eine der staatlichen Gerichtsbarkeit im Prinzip gleichwertige Rechtsschutzmöglichkeit an, liegt es nahe, sie nur

515. *U. Keller*, Insolvenzrecht, No. 14311431.
516. Cf. BeckOK InsO/*Raupach* § 130 InsO, No. 7.
517. *Strauch*, Schutz von Schiedsvereinbarung und vereinbarter Vertraulichkeit bei Insolvenzeröffnung, pp. 81–109.
518. MüKoInsO/*Kayser/Freudenberg* § 129 InsO, No. 76.
519. MüKoInsO/*Kayser/Freudenberg* § 129 InsO, No. 76.
520. *Schmitz*, Schiedsverfahren und Insolvenz, p. 49.
521. *Strauch*, Schutz von Schiedsvereinbarung und vereinbarter Vertraulichkeit bei Insolvenzeröffnung, p. 87.
522. Entwurf eines Gesetzes zur Neuregelung des Schiedsverfahrensrechts of 12.7.1996, BT-Drs. 13/5274, p. 34; *BGH*, NJW 2004, 2898, p. 2899; *S.M. Kröll*, Part IV: Selected Areas and Issues of Arbitration in Germany, Insolvency and Arbitration – Effects of Party Insolvency on Arbitral Proceedings in Germany, 981, p. 993.

insoweit auszuschließen, als der Staat sich im Interesse besonders schutzwürdiger Rechtsguter ein Entscheidungsmonopol vorbehalten hat.

Translation by author: The conclusion of the arbitration agreement as such cannot, under the premise of equal treatment of the parties both in the composition of the arbitral tribunal and in the conduct of the arbitral proceedings, constitute a disadvantage of one party. The legal consequence of the nullity of the arbitration agreement provided for in § 1025 (2) first alternative of the Code of Civil Procedure, if one party has exploited its economic and social superiority to coerce the other party into concluding the arbitration agreement, appears to be unacceptable in view of the fact that arbitration offers legal protection equivalent in principle to state jurisdiction. [...]

If arbitration is seen as a legal protection option equivalent in principle to state jurisdiction, it is obvious to exclude it only to the extent that the state has reserved a decision-making monopoly in the interest of legal interests that are particularly worthy of protection.

Consequently, an arbitration clause will generally not fall under the scheme of §§ 129–133 InsO.[523] However, under certain circumstances, one could argue that an arbitration agreement negatively impacts the insolvency estate, c.q. disadvantage the creditors. These would take the form of arbitration agreements that, in their *accidentialia negotii*, i.e., its secondary terms, including choice of law, place of arbitration, choice of arbitrator and costs scheme, purposefully, significantly and abnormally heighten the practical or financial difficulty of pursuing claims.[524] The operation of § 132 InsO would furthermore require that the insolvent was already in a position of illiquidity at the moment of the contract conclusion and that the other party was aware thereof and of the possibility that the arbitration agreement would disadvantage creditors, *see* § 132(1) InsO.[525] If these conditions are fulfilled and the arbitration agreement falls within the three-month scope of § 132(1)[526] InsO, a challenge based on § 132(2) InsO can be successful.[527]

If the arbitration agreement has been agreed upon more than three months before the insolvency request and was not made between the insolvency request and the

523. MüKoInsO/*Kayser/Freudenberg* § 129 InsO, No. 124.
524. *Strauch*, Schutz von Schiedsvereinbarung und vereinbarter Vertraulichkeit bei Insolvenzeröffnung, pp. 88–109.
525. *Dahl/Thomas*, NZI 2012, p. 534; *S.M. Kröll*, Part IV: Selected Areas and Issues of Arbitration in Germany, Insolvency and Arbitration – Effects of Party Insolvency on Arbitral Proceedings in Germany, 981, p. 993; *Strauch*, Schutz von Schiedsvereinbarung und vereinbarter Vertraulichkeit bei Insolvenzeröffnung.
526. § 132(1) in its official translation reads as follows: *(1) Legal transactions on the part of the debtor constituting a direct disadvantage to insolvency creditors may be contested if they were made*

   1. *during the last three months prior to the request to open insolvency proceedings, if the debtor was illiquid on the date of such transaction, and if the other party was aware of such insolvency on this date, or*
   2. *subsequent to the request to open insolvency proceedings, and if at the time when the legal transaction was made the other party was aware of such insolvency or of the request to open insolvency proceedings.*

527. *Strauch*, Schutz von Schiedsvereinbarung und vereinbarter Vertraulichkeit bei Insolvenzeröffnung, p. 109.

actual opening of the insolvency, it falls outside the scope of § 132(1) InsO. In that case, § 133 InsO could still provide an option. § 133(1) InsO can be applied to transactions taking place up to ten years before the request to open insolvency proceedings. However, under this section, beyond the aforementioned negative impact, the insolvent is required to have had a certain degree of intent to disadvantage his creditors according to:

> (1) A transaction made by the debtor during the last ten years prior to the request to open insolvency proceedings, or subsequent to such request, *with the intention to disadvantage his creditors* may be contested if the other party was aware of the debtor's intention on the date of such transaction. Such awareness shall be presumed if the other party knew of the debtor's imminent insolvency, and that the transaction constituted a disadvantage for the creditors. [Emphasis added]

This intent can be provided by willingly and knowingly accepting that creditors might be disadvantaged.[528] In contrast, this intent is not found insofar as the insolvent reasonably expected and wanted these adverse effects not to materialise.[529] The other party must have also positively known this intent. No fixed objective standard of 'should have known' applies here.[530] However, this knowledge is assumed if the party is already in a position of illiquidity, which is not a requirement for § 133 IsnO. In such circumstances, an arbitration agreement can be affected by § 132(1) and (2) InsO.[531] Any arbitration agreement that would fulfil these criteria would be abusive, and the invalidation thereof by application of § 133 InsO should not be lamented but encouraged. In conclusion, generally, a market practice arbitration agreement will not be challengeable under §§ 129–133 InsO, but there are exceptional circumstances under which a challenge could be considered.

3.5.4 *§ 314 BGB: Terminating Continuing Contracts for Compelling Reasons*

The final insolvency-induced potential challenge to the arbitration agreement discussed here is § 314(1) BGB. § 314(1) BGB is not an insolvency-specific rule and can be found in the more general Civil Code (BGB). Accordingly, it is not *ipso iure* dependent on the state of insolvency. However, it is worth asking if insolvency as a factual state can be a 'compelling' reason as meant in § 314(1) BGB:

> (1) Each party may terminate a contract for the performance of a continuing obligation *for a compelling reason* without a notice period. There is a compelling reason if the terminating party, taking into account all the circumstances of the specific case and weighing the interests of both parties, cannot reasonably be expected to continue the contractual relationship until the agreed end or until the expiry of a notice period. [Emphasis added]

528. *BGH*, NZI 2014, 863, p. 864; NZI 2014, 762, p. 764; NJW 2009, 1601–1603; BeckOK InsO/*Raupach* § 133 InsO, No. 16; *Strauch*, Schutz von Schiedsvereinbarung und vereinbarter Vertraulichkeit bei Insolvenzeröffnung, p. 104.
529. *Uhlenbruck/Borries/Hirte* § 133 InsO, No. 39.
530. *BGH*, NZI 2011, 684, p. 686.
531. *Strauch*, Schutz von Schiedsvereinbarung und vereinbarter Vertraulichkeit bei Insolvenzeröffnung, p. 109.

As mentioned above, the German Federal Supreme Court has already, under § 1032(1) ZPO, found that an arbitration agreement can be performed in case of insolvency and, under specific circumstances, in case of impecuniosity.[532] Again, the difference must be made between impecuniosity and insolvency. The administrator will have to argue that he factually lacks the funds to pursue arbitration, c.q. cannot pay the advance on cost.[533] This would impede access to justice and arguably provide a compelling reason to dissolve the contract under § 314(1) BGB.[534]

The German Federal Supreme Court has previously found that non-payment of the advance on costs is a valid reason to dissolve the contract.[535] However, parallel to the argument of incapability of being performed due to impecuniosity, the impecuniosity ceases to be a valid reason or argument when another party declares itself willing to pay the costs.[536] In regard to § 314 BGB, it has to be noted as well that the German Federal Supreme Court, in the previously discussed *Plumber* case, has shown a preference for placing this discussion in the context of § 1032(1) ZPO, the incapability of being performed, over an argument under § 314(1) BGB, the termination of the contract for a compelling reason.[537]

The placing of impecuniosity in the context of the incapability to perform instead of termination due to a compelling reason under § 314(1) BGB changes the relevant process and operational logic even where it might not practically alter the outcome. *Wagner* rightly points out that under the previous logic, i.e., the application of § 314(1) BGB, impecuniosity gave the parties the right to challenge the validity of the arbitration agreement.[538] It is, in the view of the author, not inherently logical that outside of insolvency-specific rules and certain exceptions, a party's current financial situation can alter the validity of a validly concluded contract, especially when there is no objective relation between that financial situation and the contract in question which would justify this. This would conflict with the basic tenet of *pacta sunt servanda.*

However, the logic of § 1032(1) ZPO is different. It does not speak to the validity of the agreement per se. It merely states that, in some way, the process described therein is not capable of being performed.[539] In the case of impecuniosity, the payments, c.q. the advance on costs, part of the process described in the arbitration agreement, is not practically possible. Thus, the arbitration agreement cannot be performed. However, the agreement itself remains valid, as evidenced by the fact that

532. *BGH*, NJW 2000, 3720–3722.
533. *BGH*, NJW-RR 1994, 1214–1215; *Flöther*, Auswirkungen des inländischen Insolvenzverfahrens auf Schiedsverfahren und Schiedsabrede, p. 78; *Riedel*, Insolvenz in nationalen und internationalen Schiedsverfahren, p. 93; *Schmitz*, Schiedsverfahren und Insolvenz, p. 50; *Strauch*, Schutz von Schiedsvereinbarung und vereinbarter Vertraulichkeit bei Insolvenzeröffnung, pp. 68–69.
534. *Sachs*, Collected Courses of the International Academy for Arbitration Law, year 2011 1 (2013), 1–48, p. 22.
535. *BGHZ* 41, 104–113, p. 108; NJW 1968, 1622–1625; *Strauch*, Schutz von Schiedsvereinbarung und vereinbarter Vertraulichkeit bei Insolvenzeröffnung, p. 69.
536. *BGH*, NJW-RR 1994, 1214, p. 2115; *Strauch*, Schutz von Schiedsvereinbarung und vereinbarter Vertraulichkeit bei Insolvenzeröffnung, p. 69.
537. *BGH*, NJW 2000, 3720–3722.
538. *G. Wagner*, SchiedsVZ 2003, 206, p. 208.
539. *G. Wagner*, SchiedsVZ 2003, 206, p. 208.

if the problem posed by the impecuniosity is solved, for example, by the other party covering the costs, it can no longer be deemed incapable of being performed and in that sense can be enforced again.[540] In conclusion, the application of § 1032(1) ZPO is rightly preferred over that of § 314(1) BGB. It represents impecuniosity more accurately as not affecting validity but as a, perhaps temporary, incapability to perform a contract due to practical financial reasons. The application of § 314(1) BGB to the arbitration agreement based on impecuniosity should consequently be considered excluded.

3.6 The Effective Scope of the Arbitration Agreement in Insolvency

As seen above in Chapter 2 § 1.5, the German concept of arbitrability provides for an extensive range of objectively arbitrable insolvency issues. Therefore, the question of whether these issues lay within the material jurisdiction of the tribunal and which can also factually be arbitrated depends primarily upon the interpretation of the scope of the arbitration agreement. This topic is discussed in this subsection with particular attention to rights of separation and separate satisfaction (§ 3.6.1), § 103 InsO (§ 3.6.2), §§ 129–133 InsO (§ 3.6.3), insolvency verification (§ 3.6.4), and the objecting creditor in verification proceedings (§ 3.6.5).

In this examination, a differentiation needs to be made between arbitration agreements entered into after the insolvency proceedings have been opened and those made before the opening, i.e., generally those entered into by the debtor and those entered into by the administrator. Arbitration agreements often contain inclusive language such as 'all disputes related to this contractual relationship', which could grammatically be interpreted to contain insolvency issues. Beyond the question of dispositive power, i.e., could the insolvent have subjected such issues to arbitration, as discussed in Chapter 2 § 2.2.1, the effective scope of the arbitration agreement becomes a matter of interpreting the will of the parties. It is undoubtedly easier to argue that parties had insolvency issues in mind when entering into an arbitration agreement after insolvency or perhaps shortly before insolvency than it is to argue that the parties had the intent to include insolvency-related claims in the scope of the arbitration agreement if the agreement was entered into when insolvency was not on the horizon.

However, the relevant discussion centres primarily on the dispositive power of the insolvent and the administrator. Part of this discussion is provided and analysed in the section on arbitrability of insolvency-issues Chapter 2 § 1.5 and § 2.2.1, and the arguments will not be repeated in their entirety here.

Courts and commentators have come to several important conclusions based on the principle of dispositive power and the closely related argument that the pre-insolvent parties cannot make an arbitration contract regarding claims that did not yet exist.[541] Insolvency-specific claims come into being at the moment of insolvency and are often at the sole disposal of the administrator. First, the insolvency debtor cannot dispose of rights rooted solely in insolvency law, the state of insolvency, or the

540. *BGH*, NJW 2000, 3720–3722, II.1.a.
541. Hk-ZPO/*Saenger* § 1030 ZPO, No. 5; Musielak/Voit/*Voit* § 1030 ZPO, Nos 2, 6; Vorwerk/Wolf/*Wolf/Eslami* § 1030 ZPO, No. 3.

administrator's role.[542] Second and conjunctive, the insolvency administrator can enter into arbitration agreements concerning all the insolvency-specific rights that he is granted under insolvency law.[543] A *contrario*, insolvency-specific actions that are not at the administrator's disposal cannot be within the scope of an arbitration agreement, aside from the fact that they are usually considered non-arbitrable on other grounds, e.g., the opening and closing of the proceedings.[544]

After insolvency is opened, an administrator could theoretically enter into an arbitration agreement with a very narrow scope that concerns only insolvency-specific rights.[545] However, the conclusions become a lot less clear when it comes to pre-insolvency arbitration agreements. Beyond objective arbitrarily, it is not only harder to factually argue that the parties had the specific application of actions under the insolvency code in mind when agreeing to the arbitration agreement it is also more likely that the administrator is opposed to the arbitration, as he did not agree to it himself.

Based on the above conclusions and those reached in Chapter 2 § 1.5 on the arbitrability of insolvency-related claims in Germany, when looking at the effective scope of a pre-insolvency arbitration agreement, the relevant test is if the relevant claims are based on powers rooted solely in insolvency and or solely at the disposition role of the administrator.[546] A positive answer would preclude them from the effective scope of a pre-insolvency arbitration agreement regardless of how broad the wording and intended scope of the arbitration agreement is. This is because such issues were not at the dispositive power of the insolvent pre-insolvency. The German Federal Supreme Court in 2013 considered similarly:

> Translation by author: Arbitration agreements from the time before the opening of insolvency proceedings do not cover such rights of the administrator that do not arise directly from the contract concluded by the debtor but are based on the Insolvency Code. This includes in particular the avoidance in insolvency [references]. The claim of insolvency contestation (§ INSO § 143 INSO § 143 paragraph I InsO) does not follow from the contract concluded subject to avoidance, but from an independent right of the insolvency administrator separate from the debtor's dispositive power [references]. The debtor is not involved in the material dispute of the insolvency avoidance claims; he cannot dispose of them [references].[547]

Therefore, the debate below focuses on whether a pre-insolvency arbitration agreement could, regardless of its wording, encompass the discussed insolvency-related issues based on the dispositive power of the insolvent pre-insolvency.

542. *BGH*, NJW 1956, 1920, p. 1921; ZinsO 2004, 88, No. 1; SchiedsVZ 2008, 148–150; GPUR 2012, 95, No. 14; NZI 2013, 934–936, No. 9; Musielak/Voit/*Voit* § 1029 ZPO, No. 8.
543. *Schmitz*, Schiedsverfahren und Insolvenz, p. 51; Zöller/*R. Geimer* § 1029 ZPO, No. 65.
544. *Schmitz*, Schiedsverfahren und Insolvenz, p. 53.
545. This presupposes that an insolvency administrator has the authority to enter into arbitration agreements, which, as stated in the previous chapter, he has in Germany as a consequence of transferal of the right to administrate and dispose of the estate as found in § 80 InsO. *See* § 2.2.2 and *S.M. Kröll*, Part IV: Selected Areas and Issues of Arbitration in Germany, Insolvency and Arbitration – Effects of Party Insolvency on Arbitral Proceedings in Germany, 981, No. 991.
546. *S.M. Kröll*, Part IV: Selected Areas and Issues of Arbitration in Germany, Insolvency and Arbitration – Effects of Party Insolvency on Arbitral Proceedings in Germany, 981, p. 994.
547. *BGH*, NZI 2013, 934–936, No. 9.

3.6.1 *Rights of Separation and Separate Satisfaction*

Rights of separation and separate satisfaction play a significant role in insolvency. This subsection examines if these rights can fall within the scope of a pre-insolvency arbitration agreement. Rights of separation, in §§ 47–48 InsO, or to separate satisfaction §§ 49–51 InsO, for example, in case of right of a pledge § 50 InsO with reference §§ 1204 et seq. BGB, only come into existence with the opening of insolvency and the creation of the insolvent mass. They grant a specific right of separation from that mass or separate satisfaction out of the estate:

> *Section 47 Right to Separation:*
>
> Anyone entitled to claim the separation of an object from the insolvency estate under a right in rem or in personam *shall not form part of the insolvency creditors. Entitlement to separation of such object shall be governed by the legal provisions applying outside the insolvency proceedings*
>
> [...]
>
> *Section 50 Separate Satisfaction of Pledgees*
>
> (1) *Creditors holding a contractual pledge, a pledge acquired by attachment or a legal lien in an object forming part of the insolvency estate shall be entitled to separate satisfaction* in respect of the main claim, interest and costs from the pledged object under sections 166 to 173 [...] [Emphasis added]

However, as indicated by the text, these qualifications stem from rights existing pre-insolvency or separate from insolvency. The rights in rem or personam referenced in § 47 InsO are specifically referred to the rules applying to them outside of insolvency, and the rights of §§ 49–51 InsO all concern security rights that can be established outside of insolvency: mortgages (§ 49 InsO), pledges (§ 50 InsO) other security and retention rights (§ 51 InsO). These rights are not rooted in insolvency. The establishment of such rights is at the disposal of the insolvent pre-insolvency. Thus, such rights are deemed to fall within the scope of pre-insolvency arbitration agreements. The administrator will, therefore, be bound to arbitrate these claims.[548]

3.6.2 *§ 103 InsO: The Right to Choose*

The right to choose can fundamentally affect the rights subject to an arbitration. It is, therefore, relevant to examine if this right can be adjudicated under a pre-insolvency arbitration agreement.

If the question of § 103 InsO, the right to choose, is raised, a different conclusion must be reached as to the rights of separation and separate satisfaction even if it is raised in defence against claims otherwise arbitrable.[549] § 103 InsO, discussed above in

548. *BGH*, NJW 2004, 2898, p. 2899; *RGZ* 137, 109, p. 111; *KG Berlin*, SchiedsVZ 2012, 218, p. 219; *S.M. Kröll*, Part IV: Selected Areas and Issues of Arbitration in Germany, Insolvency and Arbitration – Effects of Party Insolvency on Arbitral Proceedings in Germany, 981, p. 995.
549. *KG Berlin*, SchiedsVZ 2012, 218, p. 219; *BGH*, GPUR 2012, 95–99; *S.M. Kröll*, Part IV: Selected Areas and Issues of Arbitration in Germany, Insolvency and Arbitration – Effects of Party Insolvency on Arbitral Proceedings in Germany, 981, p. 995.

Chapter 2 § 3.5.1, is a primary example of an insolvency-specific right vested solely in the administrator.

The right to choose is not at the disposition of the insolvent pre-insolvency. It is, thus, not surprising that the right to choose whether to perform certain contracts under § 103 InsO, discussed in Chapter 2 § 3.5.1, is often mentioned as not covered by a pre-insolvency arbitration clause.[550]

Although the right to choose affects claims and contracts outside of insolvency, the action itself is purely based on insolvency and solely vested in the administrator. In comparison, § 49 InsO provides a creditor with the right to enforce a pre-existing right in insolvency and does not in itself create the underlying right, while § 103 InsO gives the administrator the power to choose to perform certain contracts that did not exist pre-insolvency. The right to choose was never at the disposal of the insolvent. This bars its inclusion in an arbitration agreement by the insolvency debtor.[551]

Aside from the application of § 103 InsO to the underlying contract, thus, falls outside of the scope of pre-insolvency arbitration agreements.[552] However, within the determination of its jurisdiction, a tribunal could deliberate the question of whether, in the case at hand, a right to choose under § 103 InsO exists as a preliminary question because only if the right exists does the tribunal lack jurisdiction, *see also* the discussion in Chapter 2 § 2.3.5.[553]

Application of the right to choose the contract subject to arbitration creates a potentially problematic situation: The arbitration agreement is still valid, but the application of § 103 InsO per se cannot be arbitrated. The consequences of this finding are further examined here.

In the author's opinion, the tribunal's jurisdiction is not negated in case § 103(2) InsO is applied to the underlying contractual relationship. The arbitration agreement remains unaffected. However, arbitration is significantly affected by the application of § 103 InsO to the underlying contractual relationship of the arbitration.[554] First, any decision the tribunal could make would not affect the application of § 103 InsO. However, this is not the same as the insolvency administrator not being bound by the arbitration agreement, as *Schmitz* formulates it.[555] On the contrary, the arbitration agreement endures and is binding upon the administrator. It merely does not encompass the question of the application of § 103 InsO in its scope, as also follows from the cases *Schmitz* cites.[556]

Second, the application of § 103 InsO results in a verifiable claim for non-performance of the relevant contract, as stated in § 103(2) InsO, which needs to be

550. *BGH*, GPUR 2012, 95–99; *S.M. Kröll*, Part IV: Selected Areas and Issues of Arbitration in Germany, Insolvency and Arbitration – Effects of Party Insolvency on Arbitral Proceedings in Germany, 981, p. 996; In the newer editions it is acknowledged that there view is not shared by the German Federal Supreme Court, Cf. Musielak/Voit/*Voit* § 1029 ZPO, p. 2.
551. *Strauch*, Schutz von Schiedsvereinbarung und vereinbarter Vertraulichkeit bei Insolvenzeröffnung, p. 11.
552. *Wellensiek*, § 13 Der Bauvertrag in der Insolvenz, No. 152.
553. *Hombeck/Schneider*, NZI 2020, 449, p. 452; *BGH*, NZI 2018, 106, No. 22.
554. *BGH*, GPUR 2012, 95, No. 19; *Schmitz*, Schiedsverfahren und Insolvenz, p. 47.
555. *Schmitz*, Schiedsverfahren und Insolvenz, p. 47.
556. *BGH*, GPUR 2012, 95, §§ 3(a), 3(c).

registered to the insolvency table. It is debatable if this claim is arbitrable under a pre-insolvency arbitration agreement. There are opposing views on the nature of the non-performance claim mentioned in § 103(2) InsO: Whether it is a reference to the claim for non-performance of a contract as provided for in the civil code, i.e., §§ 280 et seq. BGB, or if it flows from this specific insolvency code rule, i.e., §§ 38, 45, 103(2) InsO.[557] The German Federal Supreme Court seems to leave the question of the legal nature open arguably because of a perceived lack of practical relevance.[558] However, as discussed here and in Chapter 2 § 1.5, the legal nature of the claim is pivotal for whether a tribunal can have jurisdiction over the issue under a pre-insolvency arbitration agreement. If the non-performance claim referenced in § 103 InsO is an insolvency-specific right, the insolvent could not have the dispositive power to subject it to arbitration. *Wegener*, however, posits that the majority view is that this right concerns a damages claim based on non-performance due to either subsequent impossibly to perform, §§ 280(1)(3), 283 BGB, damages due to default of the debtor, §§ 280(1)(3) 281 BGB or as damages to breach due to delay of performance.[559] The legislator for, then § 117 a.F. InsO and now § 103 InsO, refers to § 103(2) InsO 'clarifying the legal consequences of a refusal to perform'.[560] Whereas perhaps this is not the strongest indication that the non-performance claim flows from the civil code rules, it is, in this author's opinion, certainly not the wording one would choose to create a new right under the insolvency law. In light of the above, a lack of conclusive indications that the legislator wanted to create an insolvency-specific claim and the fact that there is simply no need for that insolvency-specific damages claim for non-performance, it can be concluded that the majority opinion is to be followed and this non-performance claim should be viewed as derived from the civil code rules. As such, it is a non-insolvency-specific claim and can fall under an arbitration clause that encompasses disputes concerning the contract and related claims. As such, verification of this non-performance claim can be achieved by arbitration. *See* the discussion on § 180 InsO in Chapter 2, §§ 2.3.2–2.3.3.

In conclusion, for a dispute regarding the application of § 103 InsO, a state court needs to be seized. However, if the administrator accepts the underlying contract, he also accepts the arbitration agreement.[561] If the performance of the contract is refused based on § 103(2) InsO, the non-performance claim that flows from that is not insolvency-specific and can be arbitrated under a pre-insolvency arbitration agreement.

It is important to note that the choice of non-performance does not dissolve a contract or finally and bindingly free the insolvent of its performance, as is sometimes the case in other jurisdictions with similar rules and the latter being the case according

557. MüKoInsO/*Huber* § 103 InsO, No. 184.
558. *BGH*, NJW 1977, 1345–1346; NJW 1987, 1702–1703; NJW 1986, 1176–1178; Uhlenbruck/*Wegener* § 103 InsO, No. 166; MüKoInsO/*Huber* § 103 InsO, No. 184.
559. Uhlenbruck/*Wegener* § 103 InsO, No. 166.
560. Entwurf einer Insolvenzordnung of 15.4.92, BT-Drs. 12/2443, paragraph 145.
561. *Dahl/Thomas*, NZI 2012, 534, p. 536; *Riedel*, Insolvenz in nationalen und internationalen Schiedsverfahren, p. 77.

to old doctrine in Germany.[562] If a party is no longer a party to the underlying contract, the reason for which falls outside of the jurisdiction of the tribunal arbitration cannot be meaningful. Not dissimilar is the decision in a Partial Award in Case 12452. An ICC tribunal decided that no award could be made against the insolvent as he was no longer a party to the underlying contract.[563] In that case, the arbitration clause was part of the shareholder agreement to which the tribunal considered the estate no longer bound as the shares had been sold based on a share purchase agreement referring to the state court.

3.6.3 §§ 129–133 InsO: Insolvency Contestation

The insolvency administrator has the right to challenge certain pre-insolvency contracts. Its application to a contract subject to arbitration has potentially fundamental consequences for that arbitration. In Chapter 2 § 3.5.3, the application of this right to the arbitration agreement was examined. Here the primary question to be examined is if the question of its application could fall within the scope of a pre-insolvency arbitration and thus could be answered in an arbitration based on such an arbitration agreement.

The application of the insolvency contestation per se is not in the scope of the pre-insolvency arbitration agreement. The right to choose was never at the disposal of the insolvent. This bars its inclusion in an arbitration agreement made by the insolvency debtor.[564] The German Federal Supreme Court acknowledged this over sixty-five years ago, calling the lack of dispositive power of the insolvent in regard to the insolvency contestation the decisive point why the pre-insolvency arbitration agreement did not apply to insolvency contestation.[565] It should be noted that this case was adjudicated under the old ZPO, in which dispositive power was the central term in the determination of arbitrability. However, as discussed in Chapter 2 § 1.5, the key factor in the determination of the arbitrability of insolvency disputes in Germany is if they flow solely from insolvency and, thus, could not be subjected to arbitration by the insolvent. This is clearly the case for §§ 129–133 InsO, as the insolvent did not have the right to challenge transactions based on these rights pre-insolvency. Thus, it is not surprising that besides the right to choose whether to perform certain contracts under § 103 InsO, the insolvency contestation of §§ 129–133 InsO, discussed in Chapter 2 § 3.5.1 and Chapter 2 § 3.5.3 respectively, is often mentioned as not covered by a

562. MüKoInsO/*Huber* § 103 InsO, No. 8.
563. *Partial Award in ICC Case No. 12452*, ICC International Court of Arbitration Bulletin 20, 2004, 95, p. 96 some discussion can be had in regard to the decision of the tribunal to declare itself incompetent ratione personae, this arguably negates the separability between the arbitration agreement and the underlying contract. However, the factual outcome would be same if the tribunal would have declared itself incompetent ratione materiae due to the insolvency effects on the contract.
564. Differently Uhlenbruck/*Hirte* § 143 InsO, No. 66 (13th ed.); In the newer editions it is acknowledged that the German Federal Supreme Court does not share this view, *see* Uhlenbruck/*Borries/Hirte* § 143 InsO, p. 143; *Strauch*, Schutz von Schiedsvereinbarung und vereinbarter Vertraulichkeit bei Insolvenzeröffnung, pp. 9–12.
565. *BGH*, NJW 1956, 1920, p. 1921; ZinsO 2004, 88, Juris-No. 3; SchiedsVZ 2008, 148–150, No. 17.

pre-insolvency arbitration clause.[566] Consequently, these questions fall beyond the jurisdiction of an arbitral tribunal based on a pre-insolvency arbitration agreement.

3.6.4 *Insolvency Verification: §§ 174 Et Seq. InsO*

Central to insolvency proceedings is the verification of claims. Here it is examined if this central part of the insolvency proceedings could be considered within the scope of a pre-insolvency arbitration agreement.

Several insolvency-related issues are based on pre-insolvency contracts or rights. One of the most relevant ones is the verification and disputation of claims, found in §§ 174 et seq. InsO. Such claims are purely about the assessment of rights existent before insolvency.[567] Thus, the German Federal Supreme Court finds that such claims fall within the scope of a pre-insolvency arbitration agreement:[568]

> Translation by author: 8. b) The insolvency administrator is bound by the arbitration agreements of the insolvency debtor if he asserts contractual rights [references] The arbitration agreement is neither a mutual contract (§ INSO § 103 InsO) nor a mandate (§ INSO § 114 InsO). Therefore, the administrator can neither refuse performance nor does the arbitration agreement expire by the opening of the insolvency proceedings [references]. The arbitration agreement also applies in verification proceedings [references].

A minority view wants to exclude verification disputes from the scope of an arbitration agreement. They characterise the dispute under § 179 InsO as a dispute not on the existence of a claim but on the creditor's right to receive a share of the estate.[569] It is furthermore argued that even if the question were to concern the existence of the claim, the arbitration agreement would not be binding as the intended procedural efficiency would be lacking, i.e., some of the verification procedures would be held in state court, others in the arbitration.[570]

This minority view is to be rejected. Verification disputes in arbitration are just that, disputes to verify the existence of a pre-existing claim. The legal instrument of verification does not offer any insolvency-specific instruments to invalidate a claim, unlike § 103 InsO for example. Instead, the arguments here are solely based on non-insolvency-specific arguments concerning the claim's existence, c.q. the legal nature of the arguments is the same as before insolvency, and they could have been raised by the insolvent to contest the claim before insolvency. Any further consequences that the insolvency code attaches to the verification are irrelevant to the nature of the claims disputed in the verification procedure. Accordingly, the verification

566. *BGH*, GPUR 2012, 95–99; *S.M. Kröll*, Part IV: Selected Areas and Issues of Arbitration in Germany, Insolvency and Arbitration – Effects of Party Insolvency on Arbitral Proceedings in Germany, 981, p. 996; In the newer editions it is acknowledged that there view is not shared by the German Federal Supreme Court, Cf. Musielak/Voit/*Voit* § 1029 ZPO, p. 2.
567. *S.M. Kröll*, Part IV: Selected Areas and Issues of Arbitration in Germany, Insolvency and Arbitration – Effects of Party Insolvency on Arbitral Proceedings in Germany, 981, pp. 995–996.
568. *BGH*, NJW 2004, 2898, p. 2899; NZI 2013, 934–936, No. 8.
569. HambKomm/*Herchen* § 179 InsO, No. 17.
570. HambKomm/*Herchen* § 180 InsO, No. 12.

procedure is not in itself a claim for the right to receive a certain part of the estate that is merely a consequence of the claim's existence. The verification procedure has merely reaffirmed or rejected the existence of a claim.

The second argument concerning a lack of procedural efficiency must be dismissed out of hand. As discussed earlier, the legislator has established that arbitration should be viewed as a full and equal dispute resolution mechanism, equivalent to state court proceedings.[571] Thus, it cannot generally be stated that verification of claims insolvency by arbitration is detrimental to procedural efficiency.

Insolvency verification of claims subject to arbitration is, thus, encompassed by the relevant arbitration agreement. This is in line with the discussions in Chapter 2 §§ 2.3.2 and 3.3, where it was respectively concluded that verification of a disputed claim subject to arbitration should be done by (continuing the) arbitration and that the arbitrator is generally bound to the arbitration agreement.

3.6.5 Insolvency Verification and Objecting Creditors

Another creditor in the same insolvency can also dispute a registered claim. *See* §§ 177(1), 178(1) 179(1) InsO. This poses a problem in the context of the discussion in this subsection as the objecting creditor is (generally) not directly a party to the arbitration agreement between the insolvent and the claiming creditor.[572]

As the administrator, in general, is bound to pre-insolvency arbitration agreements, and the challenge proceeding can fall within the scope of such proceedings, there is no issue there. However, other creditors can also challenge claims submitted by other creditors. As generally accepted, an arbitration – barring certain exceptions – does not bind third parties.[573] Another creditor will often, if not in most circumstances, be a third party to the arbitration agreement between a creditor and the insolvent.

The situation where the disputation of a claim against the estate either has to be arbitrated or not depending on the challenger is an unwanted one from the perspective of legal certainty and efficiency. The challenging creditor is most likely not a party to the arbitration agreement between the party with the claim and the insolvent. He is also not directly bound via § 80 InsO. However, the right view here is that the creditor is enforcing a right that belongs to the debtor, c.q. the insolvent estate. Beyond the arbitration agreement, the objecting party is also not likely a party to the contract or claim it is disputing. Accordingly, the objector is essentially disputing the claim's existence in the relationship between the claim creditor and the insolvent. Personally, the objecting creditor would have had no right to dispute the claim between the debtor and creditor outside of insolvency. In enforcing the rights of the debtor, c.q. the estate,

571. *See* § 3.5.3; Entwurf eines Gesetzes zur Neuregelung des Schiedsverfahrensrechts of 12.7.1996, BT-Drs. 13/5274, p. 34.
572. *S.M. Kröll*, Part IV: Selected Areas and Issues of Arbitration in Germany, Insolvency and Arbitration – Effects of Party Insolvency on Arbitral Proceedings in Germany, 981, p. 996.
573. Musielak/Voit/*Voit* § 1029 ZPO, Nos 8–9.

the objector is also bound to the same relationships that exist between the estate and the creditor, including any arbitration agreements.[574]

Arguments based on the prohibition of contracts to the detriment of third parties should be dismissed.[575] Many rights of other creditors are indirectly detrimental to the other creditors by binding the insolvency debtor, e.g., securities, right of separation. Such rights, c.q. the contracts they are based on, are not considered contracts to the detriment of third parties, precisely because it is the estate that is bound, and the other creditors are only indirectly affected. An arbitration agreement that binds the debtor, in general, is not binding upon third parties such as the other creditors. However, it should be considered binding upon a creditor exercising the right to dispute another creditor's claim, a right that he did not have outside of insolvency and is purely based on the rights and legal position of the debtor and the estate.[576]

In conclusion, the objecting creditor is acting in a role not unlike the administrator, arguing that the estate is not liable for the relevant claim. Within the verification discussion, both take over the legal situation of the insolvent and have at their disposal the same arguments the insolvent would have to dispute the existence of a claim. The insolvency code itself also does not differentiate between the procedural position of administrator as an objector and a creditor as an objector, confer §§ 176, 179 InsO, preciously because they both claim the same thing: The claim between the creditor and the insolvent does not exist or is invalid.[577] As such, the verification of a claim subject to arbitration in the case of an objecting other creditor is also encompassed by the relevant arbitration agreement.

3.7 Conclusion on the Arbitration Agreement in Insolvency

This section examined the effect of insolvency proceedings on the arbitration agreement. While there are many debates regarding the arbitration agreement, especially surrounding its nature, it is relatively uncontested that it 'survives' insolvency. While it is only right that an arbitration agreement as a procedural agreement survives the insolvency, impecuniosity for very practical reasons can and should be a different case. The new approach of the German Federal Supreme Court that, in the author's opinion, focuses on the operability of the arbitration agreement and not its validity as a procedural agreement is correct. If the procedure, being one of private dispute settlement, cannot in all reasonability be financed, binding an impecunious party to it would significantly infringe on its right to access justice. Previous approaches that

574. MüKoInsO/*Schumacher* § 180 InsO, 11, 31; *S.M. Kröll*, Part IV: Selected Areas and Issues of Arbitration in Germany, Insolvency and Arbitration – Effects of Party Insolvency on Arbitral Proceedings in Germany, 981, pp. 995–996; Uhlenbruck/*Sinz* § 180 InsO, No. 16 Schumacher states that only the existence of the claim is covered by the scope of the arbitration, Sinz finds that also the registration and rank are covered; *Schultze-Moderow*, Schiedsverfahren und Insolvenz, p. 41.
575. *Longrée/Gantenbrink*, SchiedsVZ 2014, 21, p. 23; Uhlenbruck/*Sinz* § 180 InsO, p. 16.
576. *Riedel*, Insolvenz in nationalen und internationalen Schiedsverfahren, p. 40; Cf. on the binding power of awards on other crediters *Ristelhuber*, ZinsO 2004, 427, p. 430.
577. *Schultze-Moderow*, Schiedsverfahren und Insolvenz, p. 42.

focus on the contract's validity, providing parties with de jure means to dissolve the agreement in case of insolvency, are to be rejected.

None of the articles that one might consider to dissolve or adversely affect an arbitration agreement due to insolvency discussed above apply to an arbitration agreement being a procedural agreement. Although the Federal Supreme Court did not clearly deny the application of § 314 BGB, the application of § 1032(1) ZPO should be viewed as taking precedent. As the operational ratio of the two articles differs, where one affects the validity of the contract by providing a means to dissolve the contract, the other merely states that the otherwise valid arbitration agreement cannot be enforced as it cannot be performed. In conclusion, impecuniosity instead creates a situation parallel to impossibility or frustration, which blocks the enforcement of a contract but does not allow for the dissolving of the contract or otherwise affects the validity thereof.

However, the arbitrator could apply insolvency-specific rules to the underlying contract, i.e., § 103 InsO. Since this rule is insolvency specific, its application could not be challenged in front of an arbitral tribunal based on a pre-insolvency arbitration agreement.

4 THE EFFECT OF THE INSOLVENCY PROCEEDINGS ON THE ARBITRATOR'S CONTRACT

The topic of this section is the effect of insolvency proceedings on the arbitrator's contract. Besides the procedural relationship between the parties and the arbitrators, there is also a contractual relationship. This relationship is embodied in the so-called arbitrators' contracts or agreements. In ad hoc arbitration, such contracts are between the parties and the arbitrators. In the case of institutional arbitration, such a contract can also be between the arbitral institution and arbitrators. In that last case, the parties have a contract with the institution, which acts not unlike an arbitrator's agreement except that many specifics can now be found in the institutional rules.[578] Much like the separability of arbitration agreements from their underlying contracts or non-contractual legal relationships, these contracts are independent and separate contracts.[579] Such contracts contain everything relevant to the relationship between the parties and the arbitrator and, when relevant, an institution. In general, they provide for the duty of the arbitrators to participate in the arbitration and arbitrate the relevant dispute to the best of their abilities, within the framework as provided for in the arbitration agreement and the relevant legal principles, and to deliver a final award.[580]

The above discussed what effect the opening of insolvency proceedings could have on the arbitration agreement. It is equally interesting to investigate the effect of

578. *S.M. Kröll*, Part IV: Selected Areas and Issues of Arbitration in Germany, Insolvency and Arbitration – Effects of Party Insolvency on Arbitral Proceedings in Germany, 981, p. 1002.
579. *BGH*, NJW 1953, 303; *OLG München*, IBRS 2007; *Breetzke*, NJW 1968, 1113, p. 1115; *Born*, International Commercial Arbitration, pp. 1975–1977; *Riedel*, Insolvenz in nationalen und internationalen Schiedsverfahren, p. 116; Musielak/Voit/*Voit* § 1035 ZPO, No. 20.
580. *RGZ* 74, 321–325; *Schmitz*, Schiedsverfahren und Insolvenz, pp. 94–95; MüKoBGB/*Heermann* § 675 BGB, No. 101.

insolvency on the arbitrator's contract in an ongoing arbitration. As if the arbitrator's contract is compromised, the arbitration could come to a full stop as this has the potential to frustrate the proceedings completely. It is not hard to imagine the potential problems presented by arbitrators no longer being bound to arbitrate the case and having no contractual claim for payment upon the insolvent.

The majority view is that the administrator is also bound to the arbitrator's contract for essentially the same reasons as for which he is bound to the choice of arbitrator, discussed in Chapter 2 § 2.3.6, he takes over the estate 'as is' from the insolvent in line with § 80 InsO, *see* Chapter 2 § 2.2.[581] However, depending on the nature of an arbitrator's agreement, the insolvency-specific rules to dissolve, defunct or challenge contractual relationships or pre-insolvency transactions based on §§ 103, 115, 116, 129 et seq. InsO or 314 BGB might be applied to it. As such, the nature of the arbitrator's contract is discussed in this section (§ 4.1), after which the potential application of these rules is discussed (§4.2).

4.1 The Nature of the Arbitrator's Contract

The nature of the arbitrator's agreement is of significant importance to its fate in insolvency and thus warrants further scrutiny. However, the nature of arbitrators' agreements is highly debated, and several significantly differing views are espoused.[582]

As a first step, it must be determined if the arbitrator's contract constitutes a procedural or material contract. In the discussion on the nature of the arbitration agreement, the viewpoint was taken that a contract's primary function determines its nature, *see* Chapter 2 § 3.1. The arbitrator's agreement mainly deals with the material obligations of the parties: e.g., payment, availability and the duty to arbitrate. As such, it can be established that an arbitrator's contract is a material contract and not a procedural one. *Schwab*'s thesis that the arbitrator's contract constitutes the procedural role of the arbitrator and thus constitutes a procedural agreement, or at least an agreement with a dual nature, is to be rejected.[583] The procedural role of the arbitrator is an aspect of the arbitration agreement, which is, as discussed above, a procedural agreement.[584]

In general, it is widely agreed that the arbitrator's contract constitutes a contract of a material nature.[585] The follow-up question is then: What sort of material contract? Several different material contracts can be considered: service contracts, agency contracts, employment contracts or a contract sui generis.[586]

581. *G. Wagner*, KTS 2010, 39, p. 64; *S.M. Kröll*, Part IV: Selected Areas and Issues of Arbitration in Germany, Insolvency and Arbitration – Effects of Party Insolvency on Arbitral Proceedings in Germany, 981, p. 1002.
582. *Schmitz*, Schiedsverfahren und Insolvenz, pp. 96–97.
583. *Schwab/Walter*, Schiedsgerichtsbarkeit, Ch. 11 No. 9.
584. *See* § 3.1; *Schwab/Walter*, Schiedsgerichtsbarkeit, Ch. 11 No. 9.
585. MüKoZPO/*Münch* Vorbemerkungen zu § 1034 ZPO, No. 5; Musielak/Voit/*Voit* § 1035 ZPO, No. 20.
586. *Schöldström*, The Arbitrator's Mandate, 83 et seq; *Born*, International Commercial Arbitration, p. 1977; *Schmitz*, Schiedsverfahren und Insolvenz, pp. 96–97.

Two forms can be rejected relatively quickly, the employment contract and the agency contract. The examination here starts with the employment contract, which has not been seriously considered in German theory. The position of an arbitrator is, in many aspects, utterly different from that of an employee. To name a few main differences, an arbitrator is not personally dependent on the party, an arbitrator does not need to take instruction, and performs a goal-orientated task, i.e., delivering an award, as opposed to the general and broad nature of employment contracts.[587]

The second material contract to be considered, the agency contract, has several features that do not fit an arbitrator's contract function, especially in the German context. In Germany, agency contracts are organised in §§ 675 et seq. BGB. In this context, an agency agreement constitutes an economic activity that goes beyond that of service in the sense that it requires the representation and safeguarding by the agent of the economic interests of the principal.[588] However, this is in direct opposition to the role of an arbitrator, as he does not represent the party who selected him or even directly represent the interests of both parties. He is obliged to act as a neutral arbiter of the relevant dispute.[589] This neutrality cannot coexist with the representation of interests and necessitates independence. In fact, independence and neutrality are core values of arbitration, the lack of which can lead to the dismissal of arbitrators, *see* § 1036(2) ZPO. A direct right of instruction, as existent in an agency relationship, *see* § 665 BGB, is lacking in arbitration as this would directly violate this neutrality and independence. Arbitrators, aside from in the form of reasoning their award and decisions, do not have a duty to give an account of their actions to a principal, certainly not as meant in § 666 BGB.[590]

A contract for services prima facie seems to be a reasonable categorisation since, in a practical sense, the arbitrators indeed provide the parties with a service.[591] Some authors do indeed see an arbitrator's contract as a service agreement or argue that the differentiation between the arbitrator's agreement as a service agreement or a sui generis contract is irrelevant.[592] This view is to be rejected. The concept of service provider simply does not fit an arbitrator. First, unlike an arbitrator, a service provider is rarely largely immune from liability and suit. Second, regardless of the contractual basis for arbitration, arbitration as adjudication cannot be viewed as a regular service, as besides a service to the parties, it is also a substitute for public court adjudication,[593] even though this adjudication generally does not bind third parties.[594]

587. *RGZ* 59, 247-252, p. 249; *Supreme Court of the United Kingdom*, 27.7.2011 - [2011] UKSC 40, 75 et seq; ErfK/*Preis* § 611a BGB, 32-40, 96.
588. MüKoBGB/*Heermann* § 675 BGB, p. 8.
589. MüKoBGB/*Heermann* § 675 BGB, p. 102; Musielak/Voit/*Voit* § 1035 ZPO, No. 20.
590. *Born*, International Commercial Arbitration, p. 1978; MüKoBGB/*Heermann* § 675 BGB, p. 102.
591. *H. Prütting*, SchiedsVZ 2011, 233, p. 235.
592. *Lachmann*, Handbuch für die Schiedsgerichtspraxis, No. 41754175; *Schmitz*, Schiedsverfahren und Insolvenz, p. 97; Musielak/Voit/*Voit* § 1035 ZPO, No. 20.
593. However, this does not rise to arbitration being part of the state adjudication system, as it remains a private instrument. Arbitration as dispute resolution mechanism is a full equivalent of state court proceedings, *see* Chapter 2 § 3.5.3.
594. *Born*, International Commercial Arbitration, p. 1978; Regarding arbitration as a full equivalent to court proceedings *see* Entwurf eines Gesetzes zur Neuregelung des Schiedsverfahrensrechts of 12.7.1996, BT-Drs. 13/5274, p. 34; *BGH*, NJW 2004, 2898, p. 2899; *S.M. Kröll*, Part IV:

Aside from these dogmatically fundamental differences, *Voit* and *Schmitz* state that there is no practical difference between considering the arbitrator's contract as a service contract or as a contract sui generis.[595] However, with the categorisation of a contract as one for services, the application of several sections of the German Civil Code is implied, i.e., §§ 611 et seq. BGB. More importantly, this classification might trigger the application of certain insolvency-specific rights for the administrator, specifically § 113 InsO, which regulates the termination of service contracts. Furthermore, *Münch* correctly states that many of the rules the German Civil Code prescribes for service contracts cannot be applicable to arbitrator's contract, i.e., §§ 615–625, 629, 630, 672, 674 BGB. Some of these rules are not applicable because there are specific and overlapping rules for arbitrators, i.e., §§ 1038–1039 ZPO as opposed to §§ 672–674 BGB concerning the replacement of respectively the arbitrator or the service provider. Others cannot apply simply because they would disturb the nature of an arbitrator's contract. Most glaringly of these are perhaps the rules on termination of service agreements in §§ 620–625 BGB. Aside from one-sided termination, any application that would lead to one-sided optimisation of the 'service' would violate the principle of neutrality.[596]

The German Supreme Court in 1904 was already on the right track, as pointed out by Lord Mance of the UK Supreme Court: It does not seem permissible to treat the arbitrator as equivalent to a representative or an employee or an entrepreneur. His office has an entirely special character, which distinguishes him from other persons handling the affairs of third parties. He has to decide a legal dispute in the same way as and instead of a judge, identifying the law by matching the relevant facts to the relevant legal provisions. The performance expected from him is the award, which constitutes the goal and outcome of his activity. It is true that the extent of his powers depends on the arbitration agreement, which can to a greater or lesser extent prescribe the way to that goal for him. But, apart from this restriction, his position is entirely free, freer than that of an ordinary judge.' [Translation by *Lord Mance* within his ruling][597]

The opinion that an arbitrator's contract is a contract sui generis is the correct one, or at least the preferable one. In many ways, it does resemble a service contract. However, several key differences point toward the arbitrator's contract being a contract in its own category, i.e., a contract sui generis.[598]

Selected Areas and Issues of Arbitration in Germany, Insolvency and Arbitration – Effects of Party Insolvency on Arbitral Proceedings in Germany, 981, p. 993.

595. *Schmitz*, Schiedsverfahren und Insolvenz, p. 97; Musielak/Voit/*Voit* § 1035 ZPO, No. 20.
596. MüKoZPO/*Münch* Vorbemerkungen zu § 1034 ZPO, No. 6.
597. *RGZ* 59, 247–252, p. 9; *Supreme Court of the United Kingdom*, 27.7.2011 – [2011] UKSC 40, No. 76.
598. *RGZ* 59, 247–252, p. 248; *RGZ* 74, 321–325, p. 323; *RGZ* 94, 210–213, p. 213; *BGH*, NJW 1953, 303; *Schwab/Walter*, Schiedsgerichtsbarkeit, Ch. 11 No. 8; *H. Prütting*, SchiedsVZ 2011, 233, pp. 234–235; *Born*, International Commercial Arbitration, pp. 1978–1980; MüKoBGB /*Heermann* § 675 BGB, No. 102; MüKoZPO/*Münch* Vorbemerkungen zu § 1034 ZPO, No. 6.

4.2 Possibilities to Dissolve, Defunct or Challenge an Existing Arbitrator's Agreement

After establishing the nature of the arbitrator's agreement, the specific rules that could potentially adversely affect the arbitrator's agreement and, consequently, arbitration in insolvency can be discussed. Many of the same articles discussed regarding the possibility of affecting the arbitration agreement can be thought of in the context of the arbitrator's contract as well, i.e., §§ 103, 113, 115–117 and 129 et seq. InsO. In this subsection § 103 InsO (§ 4.2.1), § 113 InsO (§ 4.2.2), §§ 115–117 InsO (§ 4.2.3), §§ 129–133 InsO (§ 4.2.4), and §§ 314, 626 et seq. BGB (§ 4.2.5) are discussed.

4.2.1 § 103 InsO: The Administrator's Right to Choose

Applying the administrator's right to choose, which was discussed in the context of the arbitration agreement and its scope §§ 3.5.1 and 3.6.2, could significantly disrupt an ongoing arbitration. However, it is mostly agreed that § 103 InsO does not apply – cannot be applied – to the arbitrator's contract, just as it does not apply to an arbitration agreement.[599] However, the relevant reasoning is different. Whereas one of the main arguments for the non-application of § 103 InsO to arbitration agreements is that such a contract does not form a synallagmatic or mutual dependent contract, this is not true for an arbitrator's agreement. In arbitrators' contracts, there is a clear relationship between the performance of the parties and that of the arbitrator.[600]

The non-applicability of § 103 InsO to arbitration contracts, thus, must be based on other arguments. Some argue that an application of § 103 InsO cannot be accepted as it would allow the administrator to unilaterally defunct a tri-party agreement, c.q. dismiss the arbitrators.[601]

Others conclude based on an argument that the right to choose in § 103 InsO can only be applied to rights for which the 'chooser', i.e., the administrator, could sue. In other words, it can only be applied to rights he could potentially enforce.[602] Outside of the regulations of §§ 1031 and 1032 ZPO, it is understood that a party cannot sue an arbitrator for the performance of the contract, i.e., for the rendering of a final award.[603]

A third approach focuses on the nature of the arbitrator's contract. *Berger* argues that the arbitrator's contract is irrevocably bound to the faith of the arbitration proceedings. Accordingly, § 103 InsO does not apply as the rules of § 85 InsO have to

599. *G. Wagner*, KTS 2010, 39, p. 64; *C. Berger*, Schiedsrichtervertrag und Insolvenz der Schiedspartei, 903–913; *S.M. Kröll*, Part IV: Selected Areas and Issues of Arbitration in Germany, Insolvency and Arbitration – Effects of Party Insolvency on Arbitral Proceedings in Germany, 981, p. 1002; Musielak/Voit/*Voit* § 1035 ZPO, No. 20.
600. *Jestaedt*, Schiedsverfahren und Konkurs, p. 149; *Hoffman*, Der Internationale Schiedsrichtervertrag – eine kollisionsrechtliche Skizze, 143, p. 144.
601. Musielak/Voit/*Voit* § 1035 ZPO, p. 20; Cf. MüKoZPO/*Münch* Vorbemerkungen zu § 1034 ZPO, No. 13.
602. Cf. MüKoInsO/*Huber* § 103 InsO, 93, 104–105.
603. *Jestaedt*, Schiedsverfahren und Konkurs, pp. 149–150; MüKoInsO/*Huber* § 103 InsO, Nos 104–105.

apply. § 85 InsO provides the administrator with a choice, proceed with the proceedings or recognise the relevant claim. This specific rule regarding ongoing proceedings supersedes § 103 InsO as its application would hollow out § 85 InsO.[604]

Whereas neither the related suspension of proceedings in § 240 ZPO nor § 85 InsO itself directly apply to arbitration, the same principles apply in arbitration, as argued above.[605] It is argued that this choice, whether to proceed or not, also decides the faith of the arbitrator's agreement. The administrator's choice to continue the arbitration would also bind the estate to the arbitrator's contracts made to perform the arbitration agreement, making the related costs and debts incumbent on the estate in the sense of § 55(1)(1) or (2) InsO. A *contrario* not pursuing the arbitration would also affect the arbitrator's contract, i.e., it would not bind the administrator going forward, c.q. the estate.[606]

Schmitz provides a similar argument by rightly pointing out that the arbitrator's contract is, although a separate contract, indispensable to, and undeniably linked with, the arbitration agreement. Therefore, the finding that the administrator is bound to the arbitration agreement must also lead to the conclusion that he is bound to the arbitrator's agreement.[607] Any other finding can, under circumstances, provide the insolvency administrator with the option to significantly undermine the arbitration proceedings by dissolving the arbitrator's contract and consequently materially hollow out the established rule that the insolvency administrator is bound to the arbitration agreement.[608]

This third argument is the most compelling and should be viewed as decisive. Although *Schmitz* has qualified the arbitrator's contract as a service contract and uses the above argumentation to exclude the application of § 113 InsO,[609] the above argumentation showcases the unique nature of the arbitrator's contract. It clearly shows that it is not merely a common services agreement, or for that matter, an agency agreement. The argument is correct precisely because it considers the arbitrator's contract as an integral part of the ongoing dispute resolution. In conclusion, the administrator should be bound to the arbitrator's contract as long as he is bound by the arbitration agreement.

4.2.2 § 113 InsO: Dissolution of Service and Employment Contracts

The application of § 113 InsO with which the insolvency administrator can dissolve employment and service contracts as meant in §§ 611 et seq. BGB to the arbitrator's

604. *C. Berger*, Schiedsrichtervertrag und Insolvenz der Schiedspartei, 903, p. 909.
605. *See* § 2.3.1; *Schmitz*, Schiedsverfahren und Insolvenz, pp. 106–107.
606. *C. Berger*, Schiedsrichtervertrag und Insolvenz der Schiedspartei, 903, pp. 909–910; *S.M. Kröll*, Part IV: Selected Areas and Issues of Arbitration in Germany, Insolvency and Arbitration – Effects of Party Insolvency on Arbitral Proceedings in Germany, 981, p. 1002; *Schmitz*, Schiedsverfahren und Insolvenz, pp. 105–106.
607. *Schlosser*, SchiedsVZ 2004, 21, p. 23; *Schmitz*, Schiedsverfahren und Insolvenz, p. 98; Cf. *Jestaedt*, Schiedsverfahren und Konkurs, pp. 68-69.
608. *See* Chapter 2 § 3.3.
609. *Schmitz*, Schiedsverfahren und Insolvenz, pp. 96–99.

contract could significantly and adversely affect ongoing arbitration. However, the application of § 113 InsO is already excluded by its categorisation as a sui generis contract, c.q. it not being an employment contract within the scope of § 113 InsO.

Would one, however, qualify the arbitrator's contract as *Schmitz* did, i.e., as a service contract, the argument provided by *Schmitz* discussed in the previous subsection also excludes the application of § 113 InsO to the arbitrator's contract by the administrator. That argument is that the administrator cannot apply § 113 InsO to the arbitrator's agreement as this would undermine the arbitration agreement to which he is bound.[610]

Both sides could theoretically apply the right to annul the contract in case of insolvency in § 113 InsO. However, § 113 InsO could not be applied by the arbitrator. Such an application would directly violate their duty to facilitate arbitration.[611] Whereas naturally, one cannot expect the arbitrator to work for free, this cannot be an argument here as the costs of the arbitration would become a debt incumbent on the estate if the administrator pursues arbitration, and if the arbitration is not pursued the arbitrator has no reason to annul the contract as arbitration will not be continued.[612] § 113 InsO can, therefore, neither be applied by the administrator nor the arbitrator to the arbitrator's agreement.

4.2.3 §§ 115, 116, 117 InsO: Dissolution of Mandates, Agencies and Proxies

§§ 115–117 InsO represent further insolvency-specific rules that trigger upon insolvency that could be used to affect the arbitrator's agreement adversely. §§ 115, 116 and 117 InsO organise the dissolution of respective mandates, agency agreements and proxies. They would, like § 113 InsO, already be excluded from applying to arbitrators' contracts if one follows the qualification of the arbitrator's agreement as a sui generis contract. On top of this, the argumentations by *Berger* and *Schmitz* provided in the previous two paragraphs concerning the link between the arbitrators' contract and the proceedings and the arbitration agreement would also exclude their application, *see* §§ 4.2.1, 4.2.2.

However, there is a third major argument to exclude the application of §§ 115–117, which could theoretically be used to dissolve the irrevocable proxy given to the other party to make a binding choice of arbitrator.[613] This argument is based on a teleological approach, as it argues that the arbitrator's contract simply does not fall within the scope of the goal that these articles mean to achieve. §§ 115–117 InsO are all meant to achieve a situation wherein the administrator is the only one that has the right

610. *Schmitz*, Schiedsverfahren und Insolvenz, p. 98.
611. *C. Berger*, Schiedsrichtervertrag und Insolvenz der Schiedspartei, 903, pp. 908–909; *S.M. Kröll*, Part IV: Selected Areas and Issues of Arbitration in Germany, Insolvency and Arbitration – Effects of Party Insolvency on Arbitral Proceedings in Germany, 981, p. 1003.
612. *BAG*, NZI 2015, 462, No. 9 and paragraphs 1 and 2 of the note by P. Meyer; *BGH*, NJW-RR 2007, 397, No. 14; *Procedural Order in Procedural Order No. 14*, ASA Bull. 23, 2005, 108–115, 4.9; differently MüKoInsO/*Schumacher* § 85 InsO, No. 20; Cf. *Schmitz*, Schiedsverfahren und Insolvenz, p. 105.
613. *C. Berger*, Schiedsrichtervertrag und Insolvenz der Schiedspartei, 903, pp. 907–909.

to dispose of the estate.[614] However, the arbitrator's contract does not interfere with the administrator's sole right of 'administration'. The duty of an arbitrator to finally resolve a dispute by an award falls outside of the administrator's powers, i.e., the administrator could not himself bindingly settle the dispute by the award. Therefore, the contract cannot be seen to interfere with the administrator's powers.[615]

In conclusion, the application of these articles is excluded as the arbitrator's contract does not fall within their substantive or teleological scope. Furthermore, such an application would interfere with the arbitration, c.q. the arbitration agreement, which follows superseding rules regarding ongoing disputes in insolvency, as concluded regarding § 103 InsO in Chapter 2 § 4.2.1.

4.2.4 §§ 129–133 InsO: Insolvency Contestation

This leaves §§ 129–133 InsO as the last insolvency-specific right to be discussed here, the disputation of pre-insolvency transactions. As is the case with the previous sections of the insolvency code discussed in this subsection, a successful contestation of the arbitrator's agreement under §§ 129 et seq. InsO could significantly and adversely affect the arbitration by creating a right of rescission in regard to the arbitrator's agreement.

As discussed previously, under the potential application of §§ 129–133 InsO to arbitration agreements, its application requires an economic disadvantage to the debtor.[616] Whereas this does not apply to arbitration agreements, there is a prima facie reason to believe that this could apply to the arbitrator's contract concerning the arbitrator's fees.[617]

However, the potential application of §§ 129–133 InsO to arbitrators' fees seems restricted at best. Regarding the payment of future fees, § 132(1) InsO could potentially apply.[618] First, there are the limits posed by the disputation rules themselves. The prima facie potentially applicable article of § 132(1) InsO provides a three-month limit and requires an awareness of the illiquidity.[619] Meaning that the contract can only be disputed in case it was entered into within three months of the insolvency petition and that the arbitrator must have had knowledge of the debtor's lack of funds. Finally, a challenge of this kind would only affect the part of the contract that is unbalanced,[620] i.e., that part of the price that does not reasonably match the service. In the case of an

614. Braun/*Kroth* § 115 InsO, No. 1; Braun/*Kroth* § 116 InsO, No. 1; Braun/*Kroth* § 117 InsO, No. 1.
615. *C. Berger*, Schiedsrichtervertrag und Insolvenz der Schiedspartei, 903, pp. 907–908; *S.M. Kröll*, Part IV: Selected Areas and Issues of Arbitration in Germany, Insolvency and Arbitration – Effects of Party Insolvency on Arbitral Proceedings in Germany, 981, pp. 1002–1003.
616. *See* § 3.5, in particular § 3.5.3.
617. *C. Berger*, Schiedsrichtervertrag und Insolvenz der Schiedspartei, 903, p. 910.
618. In contrast to §§ 130–131 InsO, Cf. MüKoInsO/*Kayser/Freudenberg* § 132 InsO, No. 5 For a broader discussion and introduction of these rules refer to the discussion Chapter 2 § 3.5.3.
619. MüKoInsO/*Kayser/Freudenberg* § 132 InsO, No. 18.
620. *BGH*, NJW 1980, 1962, pp. 1963–1964; *C. Berger*, Schiedsrichtervertrag und Insolvenz der Schiedspartei, 903, p. 911; MüKoInsO/*Kayser/Freudenberg* § 129 InsO, No. 164; *S.M. Kröll*, Part IV: Selected Areas and Issues of Arbitration in Germany, Insolvency and Arbitration – Effects of Party Insolvency on Arbitral Proceedings in Germany, 981, p. 1003.

arbitrator's contract, this means only that part of the fee, which is not reasonable according to market standards, e.g., the fees-tables used by institutions, can be challenged.[621] In conclusion, one can say that not only is a successful challenge under § 132(1) InsO unlikely under normal circumstances, but it would also not free the administrator from the arbitrator's contract proper and, thus, will typically not interfere with the operation of the arbitration directly.

The already paid costs, primarily the advance on costs or potential security for costs, could be challenged under § 130 InsO. As the arbitrators have a contractual ground for such costs, § 131 InsO cannot be considered.[622] § 130(1) InsO provides a right to challenge transactions that provide securities or satisfaction of claims in case there was awareness of the illiquidity and the payment happened after or within the three months preceding the insolvency. However, the application of this article to payments flowing from the arbitrator's contract will, in the vast majority of circumstances, be excluded by § 142 InsO.[623] § 142 InsO excludes certain 'cash transactions' from insolvency disputation, namely owed performances made by the debtor in direct exchange for 'equal' performance. However, the German Federal Supreme Court has interpreted the term 'direct exchange', which could prima facie cause some trouble with the application of § 142 InsO to pre-payments quite widely. '*Unmittelbar*' [German: direct] should be interpreted as requiring a close temporal connection between the two performances. The acceptable amount of time between performances depends on the relevant market standards.[624] In a ruling from 2006 concerning the prepayment of attorney's fees by a client who later became insolvent, the German Federal Supreme Court reinforces that the exception of § 142 InsO can also encompass relationships of continuing obligations and provision of services over an extended period.[625] The payment of an advance on costs within the relationship between the parties, the arbitrators and often an arbitral institution is a usual step in arbitration. It is also usual that a prepayment is made at the beginning of arbitration.[626] The time between this performance and that of the arbitrators, although variable from case to case, therefore, should be considered as market-conform. In conclusion, under most circumstances, an advance on costs would fall under the exception of § 142 InsO.[627]

621. *C. Berger,* Schiedsrichtervertrag und Insolvenz der Schiedspartei, 903, p. 911; *S.M. Kröll,* Part IV: Selected Areas and Issues of Arbitration in Germany, Insolvency and Arbitration – Effects of Party Insolvency on Arbitral Proceedings in Germany, 981, p. 1003.
622. MüKoZPO/*Münch* Vorbemerkungen zu § 1034 ZPO, No. 48.
623. Only in case direct intent to disadvantage creditors on part of the debtor can be proven would this not be the case, *see* §§ 133(1), 142 InsO.
624. *BGHZ* 167, 190–203, No. 31; MüKoInsO/*Kirchhof/Piekenbrock* § 142 InsO, No. 27; K. Schmidt InsO/*Ganter/Weinland* § 142 InsO, No. 27; Braun/*Riggert* § 142 InsO, No. 18.
625. *BGHZ* 167, 190–203, No. 32; *C. Berger,* Schiedsrichtervertrag und Insolvenz der Schiedspartei, 903, p. 912.
626. *See, e.g.*, §§ 16, 37(2) and Appendix III of the Arbitration and Mediation Rules of 3.1.2017; or Art. 55(3) of the Arbitration Rules of 1.1.2015; or for a German example, §§ 34(3), 35 of the Arbitration Rules 2018 of 3.1.2018 administrative fee as mentioned in § 5 DIS-Rules, should be treated similarly in this context.
627. *C. Berger,* Schiedsrichtervertrag und Insolvenz der Schiedspartei, 903, p. 912; *S.M. Kröll,* Part IV: Selected Areas and Issues of Arbitration in Germany, Insolvency and Arbitration – Effects of Party Insolvency on Arbitral Proceedings in Germany, 981, p. 1003.

Arbitration Rules also often consider the advance of costs as security for future fees and expenses. This is, for example, literally stated in § 35(1) of the German DIS-Rules 2018. Other rules use the wording *'deposit'*, *see, e.g.*, Article 55 NAI-Rules 2015, which normally also indicates a security measure. This is relevant because if one views the advance on costs as a security for the later full payment of costs, § 142 InsO should be applied regardless of the prior discussion. Reasonable (cash) securities for undisputable obligations are not disputable by means of § 142 InsO.[628]

Viewing the advance on costs as a security is the correct view, as this is clearly what the parties intended when they agreed to implement rules that incorporate an obligation into their agreement stating that: 'The parties shall provide a security for the fees and expenses of the arbitrators by paying an amount [...]', *see* § 35(1) DIS-Rules 2018.[629] Aside from the intent and the wording of specific rules, in practice, the advance on costs also functions as a security for the claim of arbitrators, who might otherwise have to try to enforce their claims on unwilling parties after rendering an award.[630] In conclusion, when it comes to advances on costs, § 142 InsO generally applies.

Except in certain circumstances concerning unbalanced and unfair arbitrator's agreements, an arbitrator's agreement cannot be contested under §§ 129 et seq. InsO.

4.2.5 §§ 314, 626 et seq. BGB: Termination for Compelling Reason

Regular rules for the annulment of a contract as stipulated in the BGB may also be used to affect the arbitrator's agreement adversely. However, the multi-party nature of the agreement would already take this decision away from the sole authority of the administrator, for the application of, e.g., §§ 626 et seq. BGB, the termination of service relationships, one would need a second termination declaration, as in § 627(1) BGB, from the other party to the arbitration.[631]

The qualification of the arbitrator's contract as a contract sui generis already excludes §§ 626 et seq. as these apply to service and employment contracts.[632] Furthermore, §§ 314 and 626 et seq. BGB call for a compelling reason to terminate. However, it is widely and correctly understood that insolvency itself does not constitute a compelling reason under such BGB articles, neither in general nor in the context

628. Jeager, InsO/*Henckel* § 132 InsO, No. 19; *C. Berger*, Schiedsrichtervertrag und Insolvenz der Schiedspartei, 903, p. 912; Cf. MüKoInsO/*Kirchhof/Piekenbrock* § 142 InsO, Nos 21, 31.
629. Under the leading theory, the obligation to pay advances on costs is incorporated into the arbitration agreement by reference [to relevant arbitration rules] *Darwazeh/Greenberg*, Journal of International Arbitration 31 (2014), 557, p. 560.
630. *Schlosser*, SchiedsVZ 2004, 21, p. 24; *Born*, International Commercial Arbitration, pp. 2247–2248; *Buchwitz/Schütt*, SchiedsVZ 2015, 1, p. 2.
631. *Flöther*, Auswirkungen des inländischen Insolvenzverfahrens auf Schiedsverfahren und Schiedsabrede, p. 127; *Schmitz*, Schiedsverfahren und Insolvenz, p. 99; *Lachmann*, Handbuch für die Schiedsgerichtspraxis, No. 43684368; *Schütze*, Schiedsgericht und Schiedsverfahren, No. 132132.
632. MüKoBGB/*Henssler* § 626 BGB, No. 6.

of an arbitrator's contract.[633] Since the considerations for the conclusion are similar to those made for the arbitration agreement, *see* Chapter 2 § 3.5.4, there is no need to discuss these articles further.

4.3 Conclusion: Effect of the Insolvency on the Arbitrator's Contract

This section examined the effect of insolvency proceedings on the arbitrator's agreement. The guiding perspective regarding the effect of the insolvency on the arbitrator's contract should be that the administrator should generally not be able to hollow out the arbitration agreement, insofar as he is bound to it, by avoiding or otherwise defuncting the arbitrator's contract. Following from the above, insolvency provides neither an insolvency-specific nor regular right to avoidance, annulment or dissolution applicable to the arbitrator's contract.[634]

Notwithstanding this, it is not impossible under German law to terminate the arbitrator's contract. This termination, however, would require all parties to agree based on standard contract law rules.

5 EFFECT OF THE INSOLVENCY PROCEEDINGS ON POST-AWARD PROCEEDINGS AND AWARDS

This final section of Chapter 2 examines the effect of insolvency on post-award proceedings and awards from a broad selection of perspectives. The previous sections showed that insolvency profoundly affects arbitration proceedings and arbitration agreements. However, even after an award has been rendered, insolvency can fundamentally affect arbitration, i.e., post-award proceedings and the award.

In the previous sections, it was already discussed that arbitration proceedings could not push forward with a prayer for monetary relief in case an insolvency proceeding is opened. In Chapter 2 § 2.3.3, it was discussed that any monetary relief would be unenforceable and should be changed to a claim for declaratory relief. The German Federal Supreme Court has in the past taken a liberal approach by interpreting an award granting monetary relief in a way that merely granted declaratory relief and was meant to prove and verify the claim within the insolvency proceedings.[635] Beyond an ongoing arbitration in which prayers for relief can be changed,[636] it is worth considering how this affects an already granted award.

However, the above primarily considers claims and subsequent awards against the insolvency debtor and not an award in favour of the insolvent. Indeed, the latter appears less problematic as §§ 85 et seq. InsO, on the prohibition of independent

633. *BGH*, NJW 2005, 1360, p. 1361; *Schmitz*, Schiedsverfahren und Insolvenz, p. 99; MüKoBGB/*Gaier* § 314 BGB, No. 10; Baumbach/Lauterbach/Albers/Hartmann/*Hartmann* Anh § 1035 ZPO, No. 14; Vorwerk/Wolf/*Wolf/Eslami* § 1035 ZPO, No. 43.
634. *Schmitz*, Schiedsverfahren und Insolvenz, p. 110.
635. *BGH*, NJW 2009, 1747–1750, 7–9, 16–17.
636. Especially when speaking about changing a monetary claim to a claim for declaratory relief, which in effect merely constitutes lowering the requested damages to zero, but still maintaining the same basic claim that the other party violated an obligation.

enforcement against an insolvent party, are generally irrelevant in a direct sense in the context of an award in favour of the insolvency debtor. This, however, does not mean that adjustments are not necessary when the award creditor goes insolvent.

This section will discuss the effect of insolvency on arbitration in the post-award stage, mainly differentiating on the basis of the legal status of the award in insolvency by discussing it in the context of the different phases of arbitration. The first topic discussed is the often left-out topic of an arbitration that did not finish during insolvency and delivers an award after insolvency (§ 5.1). Second, awards rendered during insolvency will be discussed (§ 5.2). Third, pre-insolvency awards will be discussed (§ 5.3), after which more specific situations will be discussed: awards in enforcement (§ 5.4) and annulment procedures (§ 5.5), insolvency-specific grounds for annulment and non-enforcement (§ 5.6), correction, interpretation and additional awards proceedings (§ 5.7), the specific considerations concerning an award that has already been enforced (§ 5.8), an award in execution (§ 5.9), and an executed award (§ 5.10). Finally, the situation in which the award creditor goes insolvent will be discussed separately (§ 5.11) to explore the issue from the other side.

5.1 Awards Rendered Post-insolvency

The first discussion of this section concerns awards that are rendered post-insolvency. The problems such awards pose in the context of the rules and practicalities of insolvency are discussed here.

In many discussions on insolvency in arbitration the topic of awards rendered after the closing of the insolvency, c.q. arbitration that did not finish during the insolvency, is often ignored in discussions. Instead, the main focus is often on ongoing proceedings and awards rendered during insolvency.[637] Why this is done is relatively straightforward and understandable; the situation of awards being rendered after insolvency proceedings have been closed is relatively unlikely and irrelevant in practice. In corporate insolvency, the corporation will often be dissolved in insolvency and fully dissolved after insolvency, whether it be in two steps as in Germany, *see, e.g.*, § 60(1)(4) GmbHG or § 262(1)(3) AktG and § 394(1) FamFG and the discussion in Chapter 2 § 2.4, or a single step. As such, it cannot continue to be a party in proceedings, and even if proceedings would somehow proceed, the dissolved company could not be enforced against.[638] A post-insolvency award would also suggest that the proceedings were ongoing during insolvency, as one can generally not start proceedings against a non-existing corporation. Proceedings that were opened or ongoing in insolvency but only produce an award after the insolvency is closed did not take into account the insolvency as was concluded above that it should, i.e., stay the proceedings, substitute the debtor with the administrator and change the purpose of the

637. *See, e.g., Vorburger,* International Arbitration and Cross-Border Insolvency, pp. 201 et seq; or *Schmitz,* Schiedsverfahren und Insolvenz, pp. 91–94.
638. *See* Chapter 2 § 2.4.

proceedings towards registration and confirmation of the claim. These rules are rules generally considered *ordre public* or designed to implement other rules of *ordre public* such as the equality of creditors.[639] This alone can form a bar to enforcement of the award. *See* § 1059(2)(2)(b) ZPO.

As a side note, the reopening of liquidation proceedings due to previously unknown assets as described in § 273(4) AktG for the Aktiengesellschaft (AG) - as a rule similarly applied to the GmbH[640] - could perhaps provide an opportunity for a post-insolvency award creditor. Newly discovered assets will be dispersed amongst the recognised creditors, not per se on a pro-rata basis,[641] and after that, the shareholders, per § 273 AktG. The temporary revival of the company does not change that the award,[642] c.q. the arbitration, violated several rules of *ordre public*, making any enforcement of the award unlikely.

Regarding assets 'free of insolvency', or claims that do not involve the insolvent estate, which plays a significant role in personal insolvency, *see* § 35 InsO, the above could be different. In the sense that proceedings could be held over the insolvency-free assets and subsequently enforced. Furthermore, if active proceedings were paused and the administrator has decided not to pursue the ongoing proceeding, *see* §§ 55, 85(2) InsO, the debtor and the creditor can pursue these active proceedings. In that case, the underlying claim will be considered as against the debtor/insolvent personally, c.q. the assets free of insolvency.[643] A natural person in insolvency will also not dissolve after an insolvency, barring some unfortunate events. Enforcement is, thus, not impossible. However, due to the residual debt discharge common in most modern personal insolvency proceedings, *see* §§ 286 et seq. InsO, awards concerning the estate rendered after the insolvency has been closed, will fare no better than if the debtor was a corporation, i.e., the award and underlying claim will become unenforceable, §§ 286, 301(1) InsO.

Thus, barring exceptions, awards rendered post-insolvency can generally not be enforced due to violations of the right to be heard and *ordre public* rules related to insolvency. Aside from this, enforcement against a post-insolvency company is practically unlikely as the company, in most circumstances, would cease to exist after the insolvency as it will be dissolved.

---

639. *See* the discussions in §§ 2.2.1, 2.3.1 and 2.3.3.

640. MükoGmbhG/*H.-F. Müller* § 74 GmbhG, Nos 41–42. *See, e.g., BGH*, NJW 1970, 1044, pp. 1445–1446 Beyond this example, this discussion is beyond the scope of this book. I also note that technically, the assets do not have to have been unknown previously.

641. Henssler/Strohn GesR/*Drescher* § 273 AktG, No. 20.

642. It is disputed how to classify the continuation of the company in the case of reopening of the liquidation as meant in § 273 AktG. This dispute is beyond the scope of this book; Henssler/Strohn GesR/*Drescher* § 273 AktG, No. 18.

643. Jeager, InsO/*Henckel* § 55 InsO, No. 25; MüKoInsO/*Hefermehl* § 55 InsO, No. 47; MüKoInsO/*Schumacher* § 86 InsO, No. 26; *Schmitz*, Schiedsverfahren und Insolvenz, pp. 105–106; *see* Schmidt for § 240 ZPO, requirement of 'related to the insolvent mass' in relation to corporate insolvencies *K. Schmidt*, Prozessunterbrechung und Prozessaufnahme in der Gesellschtsinsolvenz - Ungelöste Probleme im Umgang mit § 240 ZPO, §§ 85 ff. InsO, 503, p. 509.

5.2 Awards Rendered During the Insolvency Proceedings

Awards can also be rendered during insolvency. These come with their own insolvency-specific considerations, which are further examined here.

An award rendered during the insolvency can have been rendered in several situations, only two of which can be considered in line with the governing public policy principles of equality of creditors and the right to be heard. These are: (i) an award against the administrator where he participated wholly in the proceedings; and (ii) an award against the insolvency debtor regarding assets not encompassed in the insolvency, the insolvency-free assets. Any award against the estate or administrator, which did not include the administrator as a party or did not provide an adequate amount of time to him, will be rejected on public policy grounds.[644] However, the same exception as above must be made, i.e., awards against the insolvency-free assets.[645]

In the below, a separation is made between awards that consider insolvency claims (§ 5.2.1) and awards that consider exceptions rights and debts incumbent on the estate (§ 5.2.2), as these warrant different considerations.

5.2.1 Insolvency Claims

Rendering a 'useful' award in insolvency against the administrator, c.q. the estate, presupposes several steps taken during the proceedings, as discussed in Chapter 2 § 2.3. First, it presupposes that the underlying claim has been duly registered with the administrator, *see* § 174 InsO.[646] Second, it presupposes that the arbitration proceedings provided the administrator with a reasonable amount of time. Generally, this means suspension until the creditors' meeting has been held, *see* § 176 InsO.[647] When the claim is an insolvency claim, the arbitration will generally only continue after it has been challenged. This could theoretically be different if, for certain reasons, e.g., insurance or foreign enforcement, the creditor has other motives to pursue an award. Third, when the arbitration continues, this can only be with the goal of verifying the claim, *see* § 180 InsO, not with the goal of enforcing against the estate. Consequently, declaratory relief must be requested instead of monetary relief. However, the Federal Supreme Court has shown a willingness to interpret awards regarding the registered claim, which erroneously lists the debtor instead of the administrator or those that order monetary relief, in an insolvency-law conform way.[648]

Again, it has to be noted that § 180(1) InsO, which creates jurisdiction for the disputation of claims, does not exclude arbitration, according to the majority opinion. Thus, the dispute regarding claims covered by an arbitration agreement must be arbitrated.[649]

644. *See* the discussions in §§ 2.2.1 and 2.3.1.
645. *See* Chapter 2 § 5.1.
646. *See* Chapter 2 § 2.3.3.
647. *See* Chapter 2 § 2.3.1 iii.
648. *See* Chapter 2 § 2.3.3; *BGH*, NJW 2009, 1747–1750, 9, 14.
649. *See* Chapter 2 § 2.3, specifically §§ 2.3.1-2.3.3; MüKoInsO/*Schumacher* § 180 InsO, Nos 9–11; *Riedel*, Insolvenz in nationalen und internationalen Schiedsverfahren, pp. 28–29.

In this context, awards rendered during insolvency will be based on an arbitration agreement or at least arbitration proceedings conducted with the administrator's participation. There is little doubt that the administrator, c.q. the estate is bound to awards rendered in proceedings based on agreements he himself agreed to *qualitate qua* (within his role as administrator). However, in both circumstances, the argument for the binding effect of the award upon the administrator is the same: Those who are bound to the arbitration agreement are bound to the subsequent award, barring setting aside.[650] Under § 1055 ZPO, an award has the same effect on the parties as a judicial decision.[651] As discussed in Chapter 2 § 3.3, following from § 80 InsO, the administrator is generally bound to the arbitration clause agreed to be the debtor pre-insolvency. However, this connection works both ways in the sense that the estate will be bound to proceedings conducted by the administrator.[652]

5.2.2 Claims Regarding Exception Rights and Debts Incumbent on the Estate

The process described above does not come into play for claims that or not insolvency claims found in §§ 47–51, 53–55, 86 InsO, e.g., rights of separation. Awards that embody such claims can be enforced during insolvency. The administrator could challenge this right and enforcement in the appropriate proceedings. § 89 InsO does not prevent such enforcement.[653] Even though the process of separation is insolvency specific, the rights on which it is based exist outside of insolvency and are untouched by it, *see* § 47 InsO and Chapter 2 §§ 1.5, 3.6.1. It is for this reason that, although, in general, the right of separation is discussed in the insolvency code, there is no particular procedure for 'separation rights' as a whole. Specific procedures for a certain right can instead be found in its own organisation, for example, in the Civil Procedural Code.[654] For awards, this would mean a proceeding in accordance with § 1060 ZPO and subsequent execution proceedings. Even though § 240 ZPO applies, these proceedings can then be continued in insolvency by the creditor based on § 86(1) InsO.[655] Consequently, the claimant or award creditor can pursue enforcement proceedings and execution proceedings. It is, however, still highly advisable to provide the administrator time to take a position on the claim to prevent unnecessary costs.

Awards rendered during insolvency can, thus, be effective and remain effective if they take into account the insolvency-specific rules concerning the claims that they mean to arbitrate. These rules have been thoroughly discussed in the previous sections of this Chapter 2, primarily § 2.3.

---

650. *See* §§ 2.3.1 0, 2.3.3 and 3.3.
651. MüKoZPO/*Münch* § 1055 ZPO, Nos 23–24.
652. Jeager, InsO/*Windel* § 80 InsO, p. 147; MüKoInsO/*Vuia* § 80 InsO, p. 95.
653. MüKoInsO/*Ganter* § 47 InsO, Nos 492–493; *Schultze-Moderow*, Schiedsverfahren und Insolvenz, p. 56.
654. Uhlenbruck/*Brinkmann* § 47 InsO, Nos 2–3.
655. *BGH*, NZI 2013, 886, No. 10; BeckRS 2016, 15487, No. 4; Vorwerk/Wolf/*Jaspersen* § 240 ZPO, Nos 29–30; Cf. Musielak/Voit/*Stadler* § 240 ZPO, No. 11.

5.3 Non-enforced Pre-insolvency Awards

After discussing awards rendered post-insolvency and during insolvency, one can take one more step back in time and consider awards rendered pre-insolvency. The insolvency-specific considerations for such awards are discussed here.

An arbitration proceeding ends with the award and opens the way for enforcement proceedings. However, does this change when insolvency occurs before enforcement proceedings have started? Claims need to be registered with the insolvency administrator, following from the system in §§ 37, 38, 85, 87, 174 et seq. InsO. Consequently, one can conclude that an award embodying a claim against the insolvent should be registered with the administrator following §§ 174 et seq. InsO. This, on its own, is not controversial as the claim embodied in the award cannot be individually enforced in insolvency, *see* § 87 InsO.[656]

The examination below is made in two stages: first, the status of pre-insolvency awards in the insolvency is considered (§ 5.3.1), and second, it is discussed what role an award plays in case the claim it represents is disputed in the insolvency (§ 5.3.2).

5.3.1 The Status of the Award

A pre-insolvency final court decision often provides an advantageous position in insolvency for the verification of the claim confirmed or granted in the decision, *see* § 179(2) InsO. In this paragraph, it is discussed if this is also true for a pre-insolvency award.

An arbitral award is equalled to a judicial decision by German law, *see* § 1055 ZPO. There is some discussion regarding the status of the award, especially regarding the moment the award gains legal effect and what this might mean. This is especially relevant when it comes to how a challenge to the claim is handled. § 179(2) InsO provides that registered claims, based on executable titles or final legal decisions, enjoy a special status. This status ensures that the objector must pursue the insolvency disputation if he wishes to dispute the claim.[657]

The core of the discussion on the status and effects of awards in Germany is the perceived tension between § 1055 ZPO and § 1060 ZPO. § 1060 ZPO organises the enforcement of awards and requires a declaration of enforceability for compulsory enforcement, § 1060(1) ZPO, by the appellate court, § 1062(1)(4) ZPO. Regular judicial decisions do not need an enforcement proceeding to gain the status of executable title; they merely need to have gained legal effect. Some scholars, therefore, bind the two together and argue that since an award needs to be enforced via § 1060 ZPO, the status that it is granted under § 1055 ZPO does not provide the award with full legal effect. They further support this argument by describing that, in several ways, § 1055 ZPO does not provide the award with actual identical treatment as compared to a judicial

656. *S.M. Kröll*, Part IV: Selected Areas and Issues of Arbitration in Germany, Insolvency and Arbitration – Effects of Party Insolvency on Arbitral Proceedings in Germany, 981, p. 1010.
657. *Schmitz*, Schiedsverfahren und Insolvenz, p. 88; Musielak/Voit/*Voit* § 1055 ZPO, No. 11; Musielak/Voit/*Voit* § 1060 ZPO, No. 2.

decision.[658] It is argued that the parties could still deny the award effect by mutual agreement, something unthinkable in regard to judicial decision. Furthermore, scholars point out that, unlike a judicial decision, the award is not in itself enough to effectuate registrations in the civil registers, e.g., the land registry.[659]

First, *Voit* is correct in stating that this argument - the binding together of the legal effect and executability - obfuscates and seems to ignore that legal effect and executability are two different things that do not necessarily have to come into being at the same time. Second, the argument that parties can still set aside the award by consent and that this proves that the awards have no legal effect is to be rejected. Whereas parties can set aside an award in setting aside proceedings, they cannot decide to do this extrajudicially. This would violate the legal status of the award as provided by § 1055 ZPO and potentially the interest of certain third parties, e.g., legal successors.[660] Arguably, without § 1055 ZPO, writers like *Schütze* are correct in stating that parties could privately agree to 'annul' their award.[661] At that point, one could discuss the finality of arbitral awards. However, § 1055 ZPO provides the award with a status outside of the autonomous control of parties.[662]

Be that as it may, *Jestaedt* is correct in pointing out that if executability was the only factor in § 179(2) InsO - at that point in time found in § 146(6) KO - the above discussion is irrelevant as executability and legal effect need not be directly coupled. Legal effect or not, an award needs an enforcement proceeding to become executable.[663] In conclusion, only an award that has already gone through enforcement proceedings will fall under the scope of 'executable title' as meant in § 179(2) InsO.[664]

In practice, the more relevant question is, however, if the award can be seen as falling under the scope of the second category of claims as mentioned in § 179(2) InsO, final judgments. The German term '*Endurteilen*' does not mean that the case must have gone to all instances or even that a ruling must have gone into effect. Neither does it mean that it must have become executable. If this was meant, this second category, final judgments, would be a superfluous addition to the first category, executable titles.[665] *Schumacher*'s opinion that awards only form titles under § 179(2) InsO after enforcement can, therefore, not be followed when he uses this argument to exclude awards from the scope of final decisions.[666] '*End-*' or final, merely means that the claim has been finally decided at the instance it was being litigated at. In this context, partial

658. MüKoZPO/*Münch* § 1055 ZPO, Nos 35-36.
659. *BayObLGZ*, 45-49; Baumbach/Lauterbach/Albers/Hartmann/*Hartmann* § 1055 ZPO, Nos 7-8.
660. Zöller/*R. Geimer* § 1055 ZPO, No. 2; Musielak/Voit/*Voit* § 1055 ZPO, Nos 6, 11; Musielak/Voit/*Voit* § 1060 ZPO, No. 2.
661. Wieczorek/Schütze/*Schütze* § 1055 ZPO, No. 14.
662. *Gaul*, Die Rechtskraft und Aufhebbarkeit des Schiedsspruchs im Verhältnis zu Verbindlickkeit des staatlichen Richterspruchs, 285, pp. 324-325.
663. *Jestaedt*, Schiedsverfahren und Konkurs, p. 109; *Schmitz*, Schiedsverfahren und Insolvenz, p. 88.
664. *Ristelhuber*, ZinsO 2004, 427, p. 429; MüKoInsO/*Schumacher* § 179 InsO, No. 23; Uhlenbruck/*Sinz* § 179 InsO, No. 20.
665. Uhlenbruck/*Sinz* § 179 InsO, No. 21; *Seehawer*, Das Verfahren zur Vollstreckbarerklärung von Schiedssprüchen, p. 82.
666. MüKoInsO/*Schumacher* § 179 InsO, No. 24.

judgments can finally determine a claim, they merely do not adjudicate the entire case before the court or tribunal, but preliminary judgments do not do so *ipso iure*.[667]

§ 1056 ZPO states that arbitration is ended by the final award. Aside from declaratory relief, a final award generally determines the (non)existence of a claim. This award has legal effect as discussed above and as meant in § 322 ZPO, i.e., at least between the parties.[668] Furthermore, when it comes to claim-verification proceedings, the arbitration agreement binds the other creditors insofar as they dispute a claim against the insolvent covered by that agreement.[669] Similarly, the award binds the administrator and the other creditors in the context of determining a claim against the estate.[670]

In conclusion, the award has the same effect as an '*Endurteil*' within the relevant context of § 179(2) InsO, leaving no other correct conclusion than to apply § 179(2) InsO to awards enforced or not.[671] Accordingly, the award creditor of an award duly registered will not need further proof of the claim embodied therein. Thus, if the claim is not disputed, the award creditor should receive payment when the estate is paid out, as his claim will count as registered and accepted.

5.3.2 *Disputing the Claim*

Even if it is accepted - as argued here - that the award falls under § 179(2) InsO, the claim provided therein can still be disputed. This is examined here.

If the claim adjudicated in the award is disputed, this leads to a verification proceeding against the award and the claim embodied therein. The administrator, c.q. the disputing creditor is restricted to arguments that the insolvency debtor could have made to counter the verification.[672] The verification proceeding is also bound to the procedural status of a disputed claim, i.e., a decision might be appealed in case the appeal deadlines have not yet passed.[673] In the context of an award, this means that the disputer, the administrator or another creditor is limited to the framework of a setting-aside procedure, *see* § 1059 ZPO.[674]

However, § 180(1) InsO and § 1062 ZPO superficially might seem to provide different jurisdictions when it comes to the verification of the claim embodied in the

667. BeckOK InsO/*Zenker* § 179 InsO, No. 12.
668. Wieczorek/Schütze/*Schütze* § 1055 ZPO, No. 13; Zöller/*R. Geimer* § 1055 ZPO, Nos 4–7.
669. *See* Chapter 2 § 3.6.5.
670. *See* Chapter 2 § 3.5, especially § 3.5.3; *Ristelhuber*, ZinsO 2004, 427, p. 430; *Seehawer*, Das Verfahren zur Vollstreckbarerklärung von Schiedssprüchen, p. 83.
671. *Jestaedt*, Schiedsverfahren und Konkurs, pp. 110–111; *Flöther*, Auswirkungen des inländischen Insolvenzverfahrens auf Schiedsverfahren und Schiedsabrede, pp. 116–117; *Ristelhuber*, ZinsO 2004, 427, p. 430; *Heidbrink/Groeben*, ZIP 2006, 265–272, p. 270; *Nacimiento/Bähr*, NJOZ 2009, 4752, p. 4757; *Schmitz*, Schiedsverfahren und Insolvenz, p. 89.
672. *Seehawer*, Das Verfahren zur Vollstreckbarerklärung von Schiedssprüchen, p. 83.
673. In regard to insolvency-specific objections, these cannot be precluded by such deadlines as they could not have been brought up and similarly could not have been adjudicated pre-insolvency.
674. *BGH*, NZI 2017, 774, Nos 22–23; *Jestaedt*, Schiedsverfahren und Konkurs, p. 144; Musielak/Voit/*Voit* § 1060 ZPO, No. 8.

award. However, this prima facie contradiction should pose no problem if the approach used concerning judicial decisions is correctly extended to arbitration.

Although one might, at first glance, think that a claim that has already led to a decision by a court has nothing to do with § 240 ZPO's suspension of ongoing proceedings, this would be a mistake. § 240 ZPO interrupts procedures that have not been concluded with legal effect (German: *Rechtskraft*).[675] Since a judicial decision only gains legal effect after the appeal term has expired, § 240 ZPO also interrupts the legal appeal terms.[676] In case the appeal term has not yet passed before the opening of the insolvency, § 180(2) InsO can be applied in the sense that the 'interrupted proceeding' can be continued by appealing the decision in the relevant instance.[677]

Applying this logic to arbitration, c.q. and award made before the insolvency, this would point towards starting an annulment procedure against the award at the relevant Higher Regional Court (OLG), as per §§ 1059 and 1063 ZPO. The fact that the set-aside procedure does not constitute a full review of the arbitration makes no difference. It is, in its own wording, the only legal remedy against arbitration awards, as stated in § 1059(1) ZPO:[678]

> Gegen einen Schiedsspruch kann nur der Antrag auf gerichtliche Aufhebung nach den Absätzen 2 und 3 gestellt werden.
>
> Translation by author: The *only remedy* against an arbitral award shall be an application for setting aside by the court in accordance with paragraphs 2 and 3. [Emphasis added]

Using the argument that the set-aside procedures do not constitute a true appeal of the award as the procedure does not review the facts and has limited grounds for 'appeal' must fail. Accepting such an argument would also exclude revision proceedings by the Federal Supreme Court, which also has a limited set of arguments and excludes factual review. It is, however, standing case law that § 180(2) InsO does apply to such revision procedures. The Court, in a case in 2012 where it specially considered the question of whether the insolvency rules on continuation apply to disputes that are currently in the revision phase, argues that it is the legislator's choice to give the § 180(2) ZPO resumption of proceedings precedence over new procedures under § 180(1) InsO as a choice of procedural economy. Interwoven with this is the fact that the debtor or objector is bound to the procedural position of the creditor and is thus similarly barred from relitigating the facts of the case.[679]

If the appeal period provided by § 1059(3) ZPO or the parties' agreement has passed, the award can no longer be challenged. In the above-cited case, the Court also stated that, as another consequence of the administrator taking over the procedural circumstances of the debtor, he and any objecting creditor are bound to the terms

675. Musielak/Voit/*Stadler* § 240 InsO.
676. Uhlenbruck/*Sinz* § 180 InsO, No. 40.
677. *BGH*, NJW 1953, 1144, p. 1145; MüKoInsO/*Schumacher* § 179 InsO, No. 33; MüKoInsO/*Schumacher* § 180 InsO, No. 16; Uhlenbruck/*Sinz* § 180 InsO, No. 40 *See* for a discussion on the applicability of § 180 InsO to arbitration Chapter 2 § 2.3.2.
678. MüKoZPO/*Münch* § 1059 ZPO, No. 1.
679. *BGH*, NJW-RR 2007, 397, No. 9; NJW 2012, 3725, Nos 8, 12, 17–18.

provided for in the law.[680] Although running terms are suspended, a term that has already passed before the insolvency was opened has a binding effect on the administrator and objectors, barring certain procedures.[681] In insolvency, this would mean that the administrator could not 'resume' the proceedings as there would be no proceeding to resume. In conclusion, he would be able to start proceedings under § 180(1) InsO, however, merely regarding the insolvency-specific issues that cannot have been bindingly decided in the pre-insolvency proceedings.[682]

As a final question in this regard, one could ask what the role of § 1060 ZPO or enforcement proceedings is in this context. In other words, could the administrator not achieve the annulment of the award via § 1060 ZPO if the deadline for proper set-aside proceedings has passed? There is, after all, no deadline for enforcement procedures. There are several considerations here. First, the set-aside grounds of § 1059(2)(1) ZPO cannot be argued anymore, leaving only the grounds that the court has to check ex officio, arbitrability and *ordre public*. Second, if the award represents a claim against the estate, the administrator would want the award to be set aside. Whereas the first consideration can merely be seen as an exclusion of arguments, just as the new factual litigation is already generally excluded in annulment proceedings, the second consideration proves more problematic.

§ 1060 ZPO procedures are opened by a request of either party for enforcement of the award. *See* the first sentence of § 1060(2) ZPO. Whereas the enforcement procedure can indeed still lead to annulment due to non-arbitrability or non-compliance with the *ordre public*,[683] a party could not start such procedures with a request for non-enforcement or the annulment of the award. The procedure in § 1060 ZPO is meant to enforce the award actively and can only be started with this goal; compare § 1064(1) ZPO.[684] Especially when compared to § 1059 ZPO, § 1060 ZPO should not be seen as a further possibility to challenge the award. The legislator consciously bound the set-aside proceedings to a three-month term in § 1059(3) ZPO. Any interpretation of § 1060 ZPO that provides the award debtor with a deadline-free option to challenge the award would make § 1059 ZPO redundant. As such, it is the author's opinion that after the three-month period mentioned in § 1059(3) ZPO, the award must be treated as a final decision as meant in § 179(2) InsO regardless of potential arguments that can be brought in enforcement proceedings as meant in § 1060 ZPO. As stated above in this paragraph, this means that a challenge should be made under § 180(1) InsO on only the insolvency-specific ground.

In conclusion, an award made before insolvency can be challenged by opening the annulment proceedings meant in § 1059 InsO if the insolvency was opened within the granted period to start annulment, i.e., three months or the term agreed. Suspended annulment proceedings can similarly be continued. One can conclude on § 1060 ZPO in the context of appeal proceedings that a § 1060 ZPO proceeding is simply not a

680. *BGH*, NJW-RR 2007, 397, No. 9; NJW 2012, 3725, No. 17.
681. *BGH*, NJW-RR 2007, 397, No. 9; NJW 2012, 3725, No. 17.
682. MüKoInsO/*Schumacher* § 179 InsO, No. 34; Uhlenbruck/*Sinz* § 179 InsO, No. 33.
683. Hk-ZPO/*Saenger* § 1064 ZPO, Nos 1–2; Musielak/Voit/*Voit* § 1060 ZPO, No. 15; Vorwerk/Wolf/*Wilske/Markert* § 1064 ZPO, No. 1.
684. Cf. *Schütze*, Schiedsgericht und Schiedsverfahren, 512 et seq.

means of appeal that is available to the award debtor and that after the three-month of § 1059 InsO, the award must be seen as a final decision as meant in § 179(2) InsO. This does not subtract from the conclusions reached in the next section, § 5.4, that enforcement proceedings should be seen as proceedings concerning the estate in the sense of § 240 ZPO and that, as such, they are suspended and can be resumed under § 180(2) InsO in case they were ongoing during the opening of insolvency.

5.4 Awards in Enforcement Proceedings

Aside from whether an award has been granted before, during or after insolvency, the award may also be subject to one of several post-award proceedings when the insolvency is opened. This subsection discusses the enforcement proceedings in this context while the other post-award proceedings are the subject of the following subsections. As this subsection concerns an ongoing proceeding, the first question to be discussed is the potential suspension of these proceedings (§ 5.4.1). The next question discussed is the resumption of those proceedings (§ 5.4.2).

5.4.1 Suspension of the Proceedings

As discussed above in Chapter 2 § 2.3.1, ongoing court proceedings concerning claims or assets belonging to the estate are suspended according to § 240 ZPO. In this paragraph, it is discussed if this rule can be applied to enforcement proceedings.

Enforcement proceedings in Germany are based on § 1060 ZPO and require the enforcing party, generally, the award creditor, to submit a corresponding request to the competent higher regional court. Thus, this enforcement proceeding, which is necessary to gain an executorial title in Germany, is a state court proceeding, unlike arbitration. Consequently, whereas § 240 ZPO did not apply to the arbitration proceeding, it does apply to enforcement proceedings against the estate.[685]

There has been some discussion in the literature as to the applicability of § 240 ZPO to enforcement proceedings. *Eberl* argues that § 240 ZPO cannot apply to § 1060 ZPO proceedings due to the nature of the enforcement proceedings, i.e., enforcement proceedings are closely related to the arbitration proceedings.[686] This argument must be rejected, as shown when this argument is inverted and expanded: the enforced proceedings are closely related to the arbitration proceedings for the very reason that the legislator wanted to give the state courts a final check on awards created by private proceedings. Whereas the German civil procedural code does not directly affect these private proceedings, it will directly affect any court proceedings, i.e., the enforcement proceedings.[687] Aside from this, as discussed,[688] the suspension described in § 240 ZPO

685. *BGH*, KTS 1966, 246–249.
686. *Eberl*, InVO 2002, 393, p. 394.
687. *Nacimiento/Bähr*, NJOZ 2009, 4752, p. 4755; *Seehawer*, Das Verfahren zur Vollstreckbarerklärung von Schiedssprüchen, p. 85; Cf. Baumbach/Lauterbach/Albers/Hartmann/*Hartmann* § 240 ZPO, p. 7.
688. *See* Chapter 2 § 2.3.1.

is more or less achieved by other means in regard to arbitration proceedings, narrowing *Eberl*'s argument purely to the theoretic dogma that § 240 ZPO would not apply to arbitration and enforcement proceedings per se.

A more disputed point is the necessity of an oral hearing for a procedure encompassed by § 240 ZPO, especially in the context of the enforcement proceedings of § 1060 ZPO. This debate is rooted in a 1966 decision by the German Federal Supreme Court in which it found that § 240 ZPO applied to enforcement proceedings as they did not differ from other civil procedures. Considering that in case grounds for setting-aside are invoked, this will lead to an oral hearing, after which the court will make a decision[689]

This led several authors to conclude that for an enforcement proceeding to be affected by § 240 ZPO, it must involve oral hearings, which only happens when set-aside grounds have been invoked.[690] However, this conclusion is erroneous. The Court merely stated that 'in any case' § 240 ZPO will apply insofar as oral hearings take place in the setting aside or enforcement proceeding.[691] This has to be differentiated from § 240 ZPO 'only' applying when there are oral hearings. § 240 ZPO applies to other proceedings with facultative oral hearings.[692] Accordingly, there is no valid reason to interpret the Court's wording restrictively when it comes to enforcement or set-aside proceedings.[693] Time must be provided to substitute the debtor with the administrator and provide him with a reasonable preparation and decision time in light of his right to be heard. That this is also the purpose of § 240 ZPO also provides a teleological argument to apply § 240 to set-aside and enforcement proceedings.[694]

In line with the above, the Court in 2017 reaffirmed the 1966 ruling, with no mention of the need for an oral hearing.[695] Instead, it merely pointed out that the suspension of § 240 ZPO is needed to facilitate the proper incorporation of the claim embodied in the award being enforced into the insolvency, *see* § 87 InsO. This proper incorporation means registering the claim and suspending proceedings until the claim is disputed.[696]

Enforcement proceedings regarding insolvency claims and rights of exemption in the sense of § 47 InsO are not treated differently when it comes to the application of the § 240 ZPO-suspension.[697] One could, however, argue that one of the requirements of § 240 ZPO, i.e., that the proceedings must affect the estate, is not present regarding proceedings enforcing rights meant in § 47 InsO. The exemption rights in § 47 InsO are essentially based on the argument that the relevant asset does not belong to the estate

689. *BGH*, KTS 1966, 246–249, p. 247 second paragraph under I.
690. *Schwab/Walter*, Schiedsgerichtsbarkeit, Ch. 16 No. 49; *Nacimiento/Bähr*, NJOZ 2009, 4752, p. 4755.
691. *BGH*, KTS 1966, 246–249, p. 247.
692. *Heidbrink/Groeben*, ZIP 2006, 265–272, p. 271; Vorwerk/Wolf/*Jaspersen* § 240 ZPO, No. 2 et seq; Musielak/Voit/*Stadler* § 239 ZPO, No. 1.
693. *Heidbrink/Groeben*, ZIP 2006, 265–272, p. 271; *Schmitz*, Schiedsverfahren und Insolvenz, pp. 90–91; *Seehawer*, Das Verfahren zur Vollstreckbarerklärung von Schiedssprüchen, p. 86.
694. *Ristelhuber*, ZInsO 2004, 427, p. 431; Uhlenbruck/*Mock* § 85 InsO, No. 1.
695. *BGH*, NZI 2017, 774, No. 12.
696. *BGH*, NZI 2017, 774, No. 14.
697. MüKoInsO/*Ganter* § 47 InsO, No. 474.

and does, from this perspective, not subtract from the estate or diminish the ability of other creditors to get satisfaction, as the relevant asset did not belong to the estate in the first place.[698]

However, the requirement of 'concerning the estate' as posited in § 240 ZPO is rightly interpreted widely: an indirect connection to the estate suffices.[699] Essentially, § 240 ZPO applies to procedures concerning economic rights that could be part of the estate.[700] Since the proceedings concerning rights mentioned in § 47 InsO finally decide if the relevant right is part of the estate or not, § 240 ZPO applies.[701] The other side of the medal is that the application of exemption rights presupposes that the administrator has at least preliminarily claimed the right in some way or another for the estate.[702] There is a practical interest here, which is that the suspension allows the administrator to decide on the right in question and, if necessary, substitute the debtor with the administrator. It makes little sense to directly continue these proceedings before the administrator has had the chance to decide whether or not to contest the claimed exemption. If the administrator decides to accept the exemption, the relevant asset is no longer part of the estate, and the enforcement proceedings can continue between the original parties.[703] Thus, in line with the above considerations, § 240 ZPO generally suspends the enforcement proceedings insofar as these concern the estate.

5.4.2 Resumption of the Proceedings

Having established that the enforcement proceedings must generally be suspended, it is logical to ask when and if they can be resumed. This is discussed here.

There is a difference between the resumption of proceedings concerning exemption rights and those concerning insolvency rights. Due to § 86 InsO, both the administrator and the creditor can resume proceedings regarding rights as meant in § 47 InsO.[704] Whereas regarding insolvency claims, the creditor is obliged to wait for the verification meeting, and the proceedings will only be taken up if the claim is disputed, *see* §§ 179 and 180(2) InsO. This also requires that the insolvency claims have been duly registered, §§ 174 et seq. InsO, whereas this is not necessary for rights of exemption.[705]

Thus, in this situation, much like in the discussion above regarding non-enforced awards, there will only be further proceedings regarding the relevant insolvency claim when they are registered and if they are disputed. If enforcement proceedings covering insolvency claims are ongoing, these should be halted until disputed under § 180(2)

698. *Riedel,* Insolvenz in nationalen und internationalen Schiedsverfahren, pp. 81–82.
699. *BGH,* NJW 2010, 2213–2216, No. 17; Stein/Jonas/*H. Roth* § 240 ZPO, p. 11.
700. Zöller/*Greger* § 240 ZPO, No. 8; Stein/Jonas/*H. Roth* § 240 ZPO, No. 11.
701. *BGH,* NJW 2008, 2580–2581, No. 14; NJW-RR 2015, 433–434, 14–15, 18; Jeager, InsO/*Henckel* § 47 InsO, No. 164; Jeager, InsO/*Windel* § 86 InsO, No. 2; Stein/Jonas/*H. Roth* § 240 ZPO, No. 12.
702. Jeager, InsO/*Henckel* § 47 InsO, No. 164; MüKoInsO/*Ganter* § 47 InsO, 35a, 474.
703. MüKoInsO/*Ganter* § 47 InsO, p. 474; Cf. Jeager, InsO/*Windel* § 86 InsO, No. 2.
704. Jeager, InsO/*Henckel* § 47 InsO, No. 164; *Börtinghaus,* NZM 2010, 326, p. 327; MüKoInsO/*Ganter* § 47 InsO, No. 473; Musielak/Voit/*Stadler* § 240 ZPO, No. 11.
705. MüKoInsO/*Schumacher* § 86 InsO, No. 10.

InsO.[706] Regarding enforcement proceedings of awards covering exemption rights solely, these should be halted and can then be continued by both parties.

In the 2017 case discussed in the previous paragraph regarding the applicability of § 240 ZPO, the Federal Supreme Court also considered the verification of contested claims in the context of enforcement proceedings. In this decision, it decided that the enforcement proceedings in front of the higher regional court, as meant in §§ 1060–1062 ZPO, were not the correct forum to pursue a claim for registration to the insolvency table.[707] The continuation of the enforcement proceedings as per § 180(2) InsO can only determine the validity and enforceability of the award, i.e., the claim.[708] Whereas regular insolvency verification proceedings, § 180(1) InsO, must be started for insolvency-specific questions and the final registration to the table. However, the administrator will be bound by § 179(2) ZPO, meaning he cannot dispute the height or existence of the claim in the verification procedure.

Furthermore, this decision seems to consider that the award creditor is to start both proceedings. This seems to negate that a non-enforced award already falls under § 179(2) ZPO as a final decision. § 179(2) InsO provides that when a final decision, or an executorial title, is presented, it is the objector that should start verification proceedings.[709] At any rate, from the position of the creditor, if this reasoning is followed, registration to the insolvency table cannot be achieved by the continuation of the enforcement proceedings, and thus, there is no interest in pursuing these further. His position under § 179(2) InsO will not change as a non-enforced award already falls under this article and can only weaken if the proceedings are continued and find that the award is non-enforceable. In their note to this decision, *Pohlmann* and *Clausen* conclude that it is unlikely that the Court wanted to deny the award final-decision status and that, accordingly, the reversal of the procedural burden would remain in place.[710] However, the court's logic would still lead to two separate forums: the higher regional court for the § 1060 ZPO procedure for arguments regarding the validity of the award and the relevant court for a § 180(1) InsO procedure regarding insolvency-related arguments and registration to the table.[711]

This discussion here is mostly the same as the one concerning the resumption of (arbitral) proceedings discussed above. The conclusion that two different fora would have jurisdiction over different sets of arguments in what is essentially one dispute can be rejected on the same grounds: judicial efficiency and economy, a teleological interpretation of § 180 InsO and a holistic approach to the creditor's right.[712] However, the core of the enforcement-specific argument rests in the alleged limitations of § 1060 ZPO proceedings. The regional court in a § 1060 ZPO proceeding is limited to declaring an award enforceable or non-enforceable based on the existence or absence of the

706. *BGH*, NZI 2017, 774, Nos 14–15; Vorwerk/Wolf/*Wilske/Markert* § 1060 ZPO, No. 19; Musielak/Voit/*Voit* § 1060 ZPO, No. 8.
707. *BGH*, NZI 2017, 774, 16 et seq.
708. *BGH*, NZI 2017, 774, No. 23.
709. *BGH*, NZI 2017, 774, No. 22.
710. 2017, p. 776 note by Pholmann and Clausen.
711. *BGH*, NZI 2017, 774, p. 776 note by Pholmann and Clausen.
712. *See* § 2.3.1 0.

ground laid down in § 1059(2) ZPO, *see* § 1060(2) ZPO and thus, cannot judge if a claim should be registered to an insolvency table.[713] This leaves only the way of § 180(1) InsO for such disputes.[714]

Zenker does not find this reasoning convincing. He does not see why the insolvency-specific questions cannot be taken up in the § 1060 ZPO proceedings and also points to the issue of judicial economy.[715] He specifically points to the case law of the Supreme Court discussed in this paragraph,[716] which argues in favour of unifying procedures and the taking up of insolvency-specific arguments in interrupted proceedings as meant in § 180(2) InsO and thus not giving room to separate and new proceedings under § 180(1) InsO.[717] § 180 InsO does not differentiate between insolvency-specific and non-specific objections to a claim. It merely states that the suspended proceedings should continue if an objection is made.

The view that the enforcement forum can decide on verification is preferable. It is true that for the decision regarding enforcement or non-enforcement, the relevant court in the § 1060 ZPO proceedings is limited to the grounds mentioned in § 1059(2) ZPO, as stated in § 1060(2) ZPO.[718] This does, however, not lead to the unfounded conclusion that the court could not take up any other matters besides the question of enforceability.[719] This is even more convincing when one views § 180(2) InsO as providing the court where the relevant proceedings are ongoing with an expanded material jurisdiction to specifically include insolvency-specific arguments and disputes. § 180(2) InsO, as it does not differentiate between categories and disputes or kinds of ongoing proceedings, states that the verification should be decided by resuming the suspended proceedings. § 180(2) only requires that the ongoing procedure concerns the relevant claim, which cannot be denied regarding enforcement proceedings of an award embodying the claim. This view is further reinforced as in another case in 2008 the Supreme Court did decide that a proceeding to enforce a foreign judgment – in this case a Canadian judgment from the Superior Court of the Province of Ontario – also falls under § 180(2) InsO, stating that disputation of the relevant claim would lead to these proceeding being continued to conclude the claim verification.[720]

Consequently, the conclusion is similar to that reached earlier in this work regarding the ongoing arbitration proceedings, *see* Chapter 2 § 2.3.2. However, one remaining significant difference is used to argue against the conclusion above. The

713. *BGH*, NZI 2017, 774, p. 19; Vorwerk/Wolf/*Wilske/Markert* § 1060 ZPO, No. 19; some interpretation of the award itself is however considered possible, especially concerning the substitution of the debtor and an possible order for payment *S.M. Kröll*, Part IV: Selected Areas and Issues of Arbitration in Germany, Insolvency and Arbitration – Effects of Party Insolvency on Arbitral Proceedings in Germany, 981, p. 1007 *see also* 2.3.3 and 5.3.
714. Cf. BeckOK InsO/*Zenker* § 180 InsO, No. 17.
715. BeckOK InsO/*Zenker* § 180 InsO, No. 19.1.
716. *BGH*, NZI 2017, 300, Nos 10 et seq.
717. BeckOK InsO/*Zenker* § 180 InsO, Nos 17.1, 19.1.
718. In this context the prohibition of so-called 'révision au fond', or no revision of the case proper, *see Hammer*, Überprüfung von Schiedsverfahren durch staatliche Gerichte in Deutschland, No. 709709.
719. Similarly, BeckOK InsO/*Zenker* § 180 InsO, No. 19.1.
720. *BGH*, NZI 2008, 681, No. 12.

procedural burden is reversed in case § 179(2) InsO is applied. This becomes problematic when one regards § 179(2) InsO as protecting the creditor from being forced to reargue what has already been determined by a court or, in the case of arbitration, by a tribunal. A pre-insolvency award cannot have bindingly discussed insolvency-specific objections to the claim. Thus, only the existence and the height of the claim have been determined in the context of insolvency. This has led to the conclusion that the reversal of the procedural burden only extends to the height and existence of the claim and not to these insolvency-specific issues.[721]

In the author's opinion, this argument can also not lead to a separation of procedures. The reasons for this are already mentioned in the decision by the Supreme Court of the German Empire in 1927 concerning a company that went bankrupt while defaulting on tax payments.[722] One of the discussions in that case was if a claim arguably subject to an executable title and a preferential right could lead to both the creditor and the administrator having to open proceedings under rules similar to what is now § 179(1) and (2) InsO. The court answered in the negative as this is not in line with the goals of the relevant legislation.[723] The logic here is similar to the argument made here in regard to § 180 InsO in Chapter 2 § 2.3.2. As also argued above regarding the bifurcation of proceedings when there are suspended (arbitration) proceedings, it is the goal of the insolvency code and that of its predecessor in effect in 1927 to streamline the verification proceedings in such a way that there is only one proceeding. The goal of the verification procedure is to accept or reject a liability of the estate. This liability is intrinsically bound to its rank, as this will determine the height of the actual payment.

Similarly, the verification or rejection based on insolvency disputation §§ 129 et seq. InsO is a crucial part of the whole that is the creditor's right in insolvency.[724] Therefore, the differentiation between kinds of objections must not lead to two different proceedings with two different procedural burdens.[725]

Furthermore, the insolvency code, particularly § 179(2) InsO, does not give any grounds for such a differentiation. This is further strengthened by the fact that § 179(2) InsO does not only serve to effectuate the claim provided by the title but also to ensure the procedural position of the creditor. He has already proven his claim in a court of law or in arbitration. Thus, the fact that the award does not state anything about, for example, the insolvency rank does not factor into the position provided by § 179(2) InsO.[726] Shifting the procedural burden back to the award creditor if insolvency-specific objections are raised would significantly hollow out the strong position the legislator provided the award creditor in § 179(2) InsO.

721. *BGH*, NJW 1954, 31, No. 17; *BSG*, NJW 1961, 1087, p. 1088 this decision is cited in support for this assertion but only states that the creditor also has the option to start proceedings when the insolvency administrator does not. *Häsemeyer*, Insolvenzrecht, 22.34; MüKoInsO/*Schumacher* § 179 InsO, No. 31.
722. *RGZ* 116, 368–377.
723. *RGZ* 116, 368, p. 374.
724. *Eckhardt*, Die Feststellung und Befriedigung des Insolvenzgläubigerrechts, 743, No. 43.
725. *RGZ* 116, 368, p. 374; *Eckhardt*, Die Feststellung und Befriedigung des Insolvenzgläubigerrechts, 743, No. 65; MüKoInsO/*Schumacher* § 179 InsO, No. 32.
726. MüKoInsO/*Schumacher* § 179 InsO, No. 32.

Consequently, the insolvency administrator or objector will have the procedural burden for all his objections when an award is present and certainly when an award has been enforced. When enforcement proceedings have been suspended due to insolvency, all these arguments must be made in the resumed enforcement proceedings. Enforcement proceedings can thus be resumed upon a challenge for which the burden lays with the challenger, be it the administrator or an objecting creditor.

5.5 Awards in Annulment Proceedings

A party can start annulment proceedings to annul an award in the jurisdiction an award was rendered. In this subsection, the effect of insolvency of the award-debtor upon such proceedings is examined.

Annulment proceedings are organised in § 1059 ZPO. The procedure is essentially a challenge to the validity of the award. Arguments in these proceedings are confined to a handful of fundamental legal grounds, *see* § 1059(2) ZPO: no valid arbitration agreement, violation of the arbitration agreement, violation of jurisdiction, violation of fundamental rights and violation of basic principles of law and public policy. Amongst them are the oft-mentioned right to be heard and the equality of creditors found in respectively § 1059(2)(1)(b) ZPO and § 1059(2)(2)(b) ZPO.

In a 1966 decision discussed in the previous section, the German Federal Supreme Court stated that both enforcement and annulment procedures are within the scope of § 240 ZPO. This was confirmed again by the 2017 decision also discussed in the previous section.[727] The Court also alludes to the point that the same arguments will be available to the parties in both proceedings, as stated in § 1060(2) ZPO.[728] However, more importantly, § 240 ZPO must apply from a teleological point of view, based on the same arguments as for the enforcement proceedings.[729]

In line with the application of § 240 ZPO, the same applies as discussed in the previous subsection on enforcement proceedings; the claim encompassed in the award must be pursued within the insolvency, and the proceedings will generally only proceed if the claim is disputed.[730] As such, this does not merit further discussion here.

However, one big difference is that insofar as set-aside proceedings have been opened regarding an award against the estate, such proceedings have likely been opened by the debtor. As it is generally the award debtor that will be interested in setting aside the award, in contrast, it is generally the award creditor that will initiate enforcement proceedings. In this context, the set-aside proceedings will be an 'active' proceeding from the perspective of the insolvent. In conclusion, the continuation of such proceedings is organised in § 85 InsO.[731] § 85 InsO provides that the administrator

727. *BGH*, KTS 1966, 246–249, p. 14; NZI 2017, 774, No. 12.
728. *BGH*, KTS 1966, 246–249, No. 14.
729. *BGH*, NZI 2017, 774, 12, 14–15; MüKoInsO/*Schumacher* Vorbemerkungen vor §§ 85 bis 87, No. 55.
730. *BGH*, NZI 2017, 774, pp. 14–15; *see* § 5.4.
731. *OLG München*, BeckRS 2008, 10260, Nos 18–19 the OLG in § 19, does apply oral hearings as a requirement for § 240 ZPO, in reference to the authors and discussion above. However, as stated this is to be rejected as a requirement as also reflected in the discussed BGH decision of 2017; *BGH*, NZI 2017, 774–776.

can continue the proceedings, § 85(1) InsO, or relinquish the proceedings to the insolvent and the debtor, § 85(2) InsO. § 85(1) InsO, referencing § 239(2)-(4) ZPO, also provides the debtor with the possibility to force the insolvency administrator to take a position on continuing the proceedings, i.e., the annulment proceedings in the context of this discussion proceedings, within a reasonable time.

5.6 The Grounds for Annulment and Non-enforcement in Insolvency

After discussing annulment and enforcement proceedings, this seems the appropriate place to discuss insolvency context-specific grounds for annulment and non-enforcement that could be raised in such proceedings. In the above-discussed set-aside and enforcement proceedings and within the framework of the insolvency verification proceedings of § 180(1) InsO, several insolvency-specific set-aside grounds can be raised. Most of these have been discussed in other contexts above. Thus, here they will merely be put within the context of § 1059(2) ZPO and actual setting-aside or non-enforcement proceedings.

Insolvency in arbitration could primarily lead to set-aside grounds in four categories: non-arbitrability, lack of jurisdiction, violation of the right to be heard, and public policy violation, as found in § 1059(2) ZPO. The arbitrability of insolvency issues was discussed above in Chapter 2 §§ 1.4–1.5. Thus it suffices to say here that in case the award violates the arbitrability rules discussed there, by attempting to adjudicate issues deemed non-arbitrable, this will be a ground on which to set aside the award and reject enforcement under respectively §§ 1059(2)(2)(a) and 1060(2) ZPO.[732]

While, in the German context, an administrator is in principle bound to the pre-insolvency arbitration agreement as discussed in Chapter 2 § 3.3. Jurisdiction *ratio materiae* plays a prominent role in the discussion above. *See* Chapter 2 §§ 1.5 and 3.6. The debtor pre-insolvency cannot effectively agree to arbitrate rights that are vested solely in the role of insolvency administrator within the framework of insolvency. Therefore, discussion awards on such issues can be challenged on the ground of § 1059(2)(1)(c) ZPO as being outside of the scope of the arbitration agreement simply because they could not be within the scope of the arbitration agreement.[733] It should be mentioned that the administrator, in certain circumstances, might be required to raise an objection during the proceedings or otherwise be precluded from doing so later. Regarding jurisdiction, this concerns the procedure of § 1040(3) ZPO.[734] It is also relevant that lack of jurisdiction could lead to a partial setting-aside instead of full annulment, i.e., a set-aside of that part of the decision for which there was no jurisdiction.[735] However, as discussed in Chapter 2 §§ 2.3.2, 3.6.4, arbitration can be used to verify claims in insolvency and, in that context, can in a limited way deal with these insolvency-specific questions, i.e., preliminary questions.

---

732. *See* § 1.4.
733. *See* § 3.6.
734. *BGH*, IBRRS 2003, 1118.
735. Musielak/Voit/*Voit* § 1059 ZPO, No. 15; Vorwerk/Wolf/*Wilske/Markert* § 1059 ZPO, No. 47.

The right to be heard, although it should also be considered part of procedural public policy in § 1059(2)(2)(b) ZPO,[736] is considered explicitly under § 1059(2)(1)(b) ZPO.[737] The right to be heard has played a crucial role in many of the discussions above. The right to be heard was the key to the conclusion that a suspension similar to that of § 240 ZPO should be observed in arbitration proceedings. Consequently, as an insolvency-specific ground for setting-aside, this ground will be highly relevant if a suspension is not or is improperly observed in the arbitration.[738]

In tandem with the right to be heard, public policy is likely the most significant source of insolvency-related set-aside grounds. Most prominently mentioned in the previous discussions is the equality of creditors, which is also expressed in the prohibition on individual enforcement in § 89 InsO. It is this principle that forces an award creditor or (counter-) claimant in the arbitration to pursue their claim within the framework of the insolvency or risk a challengeable award under § 1059(2)(2)(b) ZPO.[739] Consequently, to not violate this principle, a claim must be registered, and awards rendered in insolvency cannot order monetary relief. Furthermore, they must address the administrator. Otherwise, they must at least be interpreted to address the administrator and not to order monetary relief in enforcement proceedings.[740]

5.7 Correction, Interpretation and Additional Award Proceedings

While enforcement and annulment proceedings receive more attention in discussions, such as the ones in this book, there are several other post-award proceedings that could be ongoing when insolvency is opened: correction, interpretation and additional award proceedings. First, the suspension of such proceedings (§ 5.7.1) is examined, then the resumption of those proceedings (§ 5.7.2), and finally, the status of additional awards in insolvency (§ 5.7.3) is discussed.

5.7.1 Suspension of Ongoing Proceedings

Similar to the discussion regarding annulment and enforcement proceedings, the correction, interpretation and additional award proceedings can potentially fall under § 240 ZPO and thus might need to be suspended upon the opening of insolvency proceedings. This question is discussed further in this paragraph.

Correction, interpretation and additional awards proceedings are organised in § 1058 ZPO and reopen the arbitration proceedings, albeit merely for the purposes allowed by § 1058 ZPO. The stipulations in § 1058 ZPO do not change that the parties

736. *Schwarz/Ortner*, 'Chapter III: The Arbitration Procedure – Procedural Ordre Public and the Internationalization of Public Policy in Arbitration', 133, 138. 189 et seq.
737. MüKoZPO/*Münch* § 1059 ZPO, No. 27; Musielak/Voit/*Voit* § 1059 ZPO, Nos 13, 27.
738. *See* § 2.3.1 especially iii thereof.
739. *See* § 2.1 and *BGH*, NJW 2009, 1747–1750, No. 22; *Ehricke*, ZIP 2006, 1847–1854, p. 1850; *Schmitz*, Schiedsverfahren und Insolvenz, p. 126; MüKoZPO/*Münch* § 1059 ZPO, No. 56.
740. *See* § 2.3.3; *BGH*, NJW 2009, 1747–1750, 7 et seq.

can agree to different procedures, as they often do in the form of correction rules, which are a regular part of arbitration rules, e.g., § 40 DIS-Rules 2018.[741]

In the above discussion, it was argued that enforcement proceedings and set-aside proceedings are subject to the mandatory suspension of proceedings, mainly as the proceedings are entirely based on the ZPO and not separated from the norms therein as arbitration proceedings.[742] The proceedings under § 1058 InsO proceedings must be treated similarly to the original arbitration proceedings when it comes to the direct applicability of § 240 ZPO because the same considerations apply: the proceedings are held before the original arbitral tribunal, which follow the procedural rules established in the arbitration agreement and not that of the code of civil procedure, barring those rules specific to arbitration.[743] Consequently, there is no suspension based on § 240 ZPO, but there can still be one based on the same considerations that point toward the suspension of arbitration proceedings upon opening the insolvency, the right to be heard, and the equality of creditors, *see* Chapter 2 § 2.3.1.

As far as this author could find, there is currently no precedent regarding the possible suspension of § 1058 InsO proceedings. Theoretically, one can argue that suspension and thus the resumption should function similar to the suspension and resumption of regular arbitral proceedings. This, as the § 1058 InsO proceedings are arguably a resumption of those proceedings. This means that the suspension should last until the administrator and other creditors have decided to challenge the underlying claim or not.

For corrections as meant in § 1058(1)(1) in particular, one could also argue that in most correction proceedings, there is no need to provide the practical suspension argued for concerning the original arbitration proceedings, as they do not decide on the existence of the claim and as such do not affect the estate per se. However, barring the correction of obvious mistakes, which the tribunal can do without the parties based on § 1058(4) ZPO, e.g., typographical errors, there is still a right to be heard within the interpretation and additional award proceedings provided in § 1058(2)-(3) ZPO.[744] In particular, a proceeding for an additional or amending arbitration award as meant in § 1058(3) ZPO can lead to the granting or dismissing of a claim. Thus, insofar as they relate to insolvency claims, such proceedings conflict with the equality of creditors and the prohibition on individual enforcement. *See also* Chapter 2 § 2.3.1 iii. Ignoring these principles can lead to the setting aside or non-enforcement of the award.[745] Therefore, based on the discussed principles, the interpretation and additional award proceedings will have to be suspended.

Aside from this, the correct view is that § 1058 ZPO proceedings do alter the effect of an award and, thus, the treatment of the claim therein.[746] § 1058 ZPO proceedings

741. Cf. MüKoZPO/*Münch* § 1058 ZPO, No. 19.
742. *See* §§ 5.4 and 5.5; Cf. *Nacimiento/Bähr*, NJOZ 2009, 4752, p. 4755.
743. Baumbach/Lauterbach/Albers/Hartmann/*Hartmann* § 1058 ZPO, No. 3.
744. *OLG Frankfurt*, SchiedsVZ 2005, 311, p. 312; *Lachmann*, Handbuch für die Schiedsgerichtspraxis, 2031–2032, 2036; Musielak/Voit/*Voit* § 1058 ZPO, No. 6.
745. Musielak/Voit/*Voit* § 1058 ZPO, No. 6.
746. *Lachmann*, Handbuch für die Schiedsgerichtspraxis, No. 20312031; *Born*, International Commercial Arbitration, p. 3127.

cannot be seen as separated from the original arbitration. Accordingly, if the original arbitration considered claims, which are insolvency claims, the correction proceeding should be considered to do so by extension as well – reaffirming that a suspension is necessary to not violate public policy in the cases where there is a right to be heard.[747]

5.7.2 *Resumption of Proceedings and the Original Award*

Having discussed the suspension of proceedings in the previous paragraph, the natural follow-up question regards the resumption of proceedings. Since the administrator will have to accept the procedure in the state that it is in, he will only be able to influence the amendment and interpretation proceedings and not as such on the main dispute encompassed in the award.

However, § 1058 ZPO proceedings do not suspend the effect of § 1055 ZPO per se, meaning that they do not suspend the legal effect of the award. Not dissimilar, correction of state court decisions, as organised in § 319 ZPO, also does not suspend time limits to start appeal procedures and appeal is considered possible while correction proceedings are ongoing.[748] Correction in arbitration essentially functions similarly to how they function in court proceedings.[749] While leading to a new and separate award, amendment proceedings do not affect the potential legal force of the claims decided in the principal award,[750] which is not strange as the amendment proceedings are meant to decide issues that were erroneously not decided in the principal award. In conclusion, the administrator should be able to start set-aside procedures as meant in § 1059 ZPO in the context of § 180(2) InsO as discussed in Chapter 3 § 5.3, while correction but also interpretation and amendment proceedings are ongoing, arguing against the verification of the claims represented in the award as per § 179(2) InsO.[751] In the interest of judicial economy, the court in the set-aside procedure could, where the objections are the subject of the corrections proceedings, decide to defer to the pending § 1058 ZPO proceedings. In the end, as with § 319 ZPO corrections, if annulment proceedings are started, but the grounds for those proceedings fall away because they are corrected by a § 1058 ZPO proceedings decision or an additional award, the annulment proceedings will be dismissed, and the costs will be payable by the estate as the losing party.[752]

5.7.3 *The Status of Additional Awards in Insolvency*

Corrections and interpretations made in the proceedings described in § 1058 ZPO form part of the original award and do not create new awards.[753] However, in amendment

747. As discussed in § 2.3.1 iii.
748. *BGH*, NJW 1991, p. 1834; NJW-RR 2017, 55, No. 6; Vorwerk/Wolf/*Elzer* § 319 ZPO, No. 58; Musielak/Voit/*Musielak* § 319 ZPO, No. 18.
749. Musielak/Voit/*Voit* § 1058 ZPO, p. 2; Vorwerk/Wolf/*Wilske/Markert* § 1058 ZPO, p. 1; Cf. MüKoZPO/*Münch* § 1058 ZPO, Nos 1, 22.
750. Musielak/Voit/*Voit* § 1058 ZPO, No. 9.
751. *See* Chapter 2 § 5.3.
752. Cf. Musielak/Voit/*Musielak* § 319 ZPO, No. 18.
753. Entwurf eines Gesetzes zur Neuregelung des Schiedsverfahrensrechts of 12.7.1996, BT-Drs. 13/5274, p. 58; MüKoZPO/*Münch* § 1058 ZPO, p. 22; Musielak/Voit/*Voit* § 1058 ZPO, No. 7.

proceedings, an additional award is made in the sense of § 1058(3) ZPO.[754] The additional or amending award makes a final decision about a subject not decided in the original award. Therefore, the additional award forms a separate award from the original award.[755] The question arises of how this additional award is treated in insolvency.

The additional award procedure presents a more straightforward situation regarding its treatment in insolvency. The correct view is that both the original and the additional awards will form separate (partial-) awards that can be separately enforced or set aside in the sense of §§ 1059–1060 ZPO.[756] Thus, they can also be separated in their treatment of insolvency. The fact that the original award can now be identified as a partial award has no adverse effect on its enforceability. Partial awards make final determinations on issues, as opposed to preliminary awards, and are enforceable under § 1060 ZPO.[757]

Therefore, in the context of additional awards, the original award should be treated as any other pre-insolvency award.[758] The ongoing proceeding regarding the additional award should be considered ongoing arbitral proceedings, and be treated as such.[759]

5.8 Enforced Awards

After discussing the opening of insolvency during the post-award proceedings, one can also examine the considerations that arise when insolvency is opened after such post-award proceedings. This subsection shortly examines what special considerations an enforced award represents.

Enforced awards are largely treated the same as non-enforced awards. At the opening of insolvency proceedings, the claim embodied within the award must be registered. As discussed, the award falls under § 179(2) InsO. *See* Chapter 2 § 5.3.1. After the enforcement proceeding of § 1060 ZPO, the award will now fall under the first alternative of § 179(2) InsO, the 'executorial title'.[760] Procedurally, the considerations for an enforced award differ little from a non-enforced award as a 'final decision'.[761] When duly registered and not challenged, the claim will count as proven and accepted, entitling the award creditor to a payout. However, the administrator and other creditors

754. Confusingly, called an amendment in the English version of the ZPO. However, the source text found in Art. 33 of the UNCITRAL Model Law correctly speaks of additional award.
755. Entwurf eines Gesetzes zur Neuregelung des Schiedsverfahrensrechts of 12.7.1996, BT-Drs. 13/5274, p. 58; MüKoZPO/*Münch* § 1058 ZPO, No. 22; Musielak/Voit/*Voit* § 1058 ZPO, No. 7.
756. *OLG München*, Beschluss of 20.12.2006 - 34 Sch 27/06, II(2); *OLG Düsseldorf*, SchiedsVZ 2008, 156–160, II(1)(a); MüKoZPO/*Münch* § 1058 ZPO, p. 22.
757. *OLG Koblenz*, BeckRS 2010, 8387; *Schwab/Walter*, Schiedsgerichtsbarkeit, Ch. 21 No. 18; *Lachmann*, Handbuch für die Schiedsgerichtspraxis, No. 20402040; MüKoZPO/*Münch* § 1058 ZPO, No. 22.
758. *See* § 5.3.
759. *See* § 2 especially § 2.3 and therein § 2.3.1 on the stay of proceedings.
760. Musielak/Voit/*Voit* § 1060 ZPO, No. 8.
761. *See* Chapter 2 § 5.3.1.

can still challenge the claim. They will then bear the procedural burden, *see* Chapter 2 § 5.3.2.

The difference is the scope of the challenge. As the grounds to refuse enforcement are the same as that to set aside the award, a successful enforcement procedure under § 1060 ZPO precludes a request for annulment and, in the context of insolvency disputation, must, in the opinion of the author, preclude as adjudicated the grounds for setting-aside grounds as meant in § 1059 ZPO.[762] The arguments left to the administrator or disputing other creditors are only the insolvency-specific issues, which could not have been argued before in enforcement, annulment or arbitration and, thus, cannot be considered precluded, e.g., the ranking and registration itself.[763]

5.9 Awards and Execution Proceedings

After an award has been enforced, it can be executed. The execution proceedings provide a few unique considerations in case insolvency is opened when such proceedings are pending. These are discussed in this paragraph

In Germany, an award is considered to only grant an executorial title after it has been declared enforceable in the context of § 1060 ZPO proceedings.[764] It is important to note that, within execution proceedings, it is consequently not the award that is being executed but the decision made by the court in the § 1060 ZPO enforcement proceedings. It is the affirmative decision in the enforcement proceedings that forms a title in the sense of § 794(1)(4a) ZPO.[765]

Such proceedings are not covered by § 240 ZPO[766] but rather by § 89 InsO, which prohibits execution proceedings in insolvency. Awards generally award damages and costs, i.e., monetary claims. § 89(1) InsO blocks execution of monetary relief.[767] Thus, insofar as an execution proceeding is pending during insolvency, the request should be referred to the insolvency court, based on § 89(3) InsO, and then denied with reference to § 89(1) InsO. As such, the same situation is reached as discussed in the previous paragraph concerning enforced awards. As a side note, however unlikely in the context of awards, it is still relevant to mention that executions establishing securities made shortly before insolvency are also voided by § 88 InsO.[768]

5.10 Enforced and Performed or Executed Awards

A further step forward in time from the execution proceedings brings the discussion to awards that have both been enforced and executed or performed without the need for

762. Musielak/Voit/*Voit* § 1059 ZPO, No. 33; Musielak/Voit/*Voit* § 1060 ZPO, No. 8.
763. MüKoInsO/*Schumacher* § 179 InsO, No. 34; Uhlenbruck/*Sinz* § 179 InsO, Nos 33-34.
764. Musielak/Voit/*Voit* § 1060 ZPO, No. 2; Vorwerk/Wolf/*Wilske/Markert* § 1060 ZPO, No. 1.
765. Hk-ZPO/*Saenger* § 1060 ZPO, No. 1; Vorwerk/Wolf/*Wilske/Markert* § 1060 ZPO, No. 1.
766. MüKoZPO/*Stackmann* § 240 ZPO, No. 3.
767. MüKoInsO/*Breuer/Flöther* § 89 InsO, No. 27.
768. Musielak/Voit/*Stadler* § 240 ZPO, No. 6; MüKoInsO/*Breuer/Flöther* § 88 InsO, No. 14.

such proceedings. The considerations provided by the opening of insolvency at the post-execution stage are represented here.

The main discussion on post-award insolvency focuses on the situation wherein an award is rendered, but subsequent proceedings of enforcement or execution are still either not started or still in progress, e.g., questions about the binding power of the award upon the administrator. The situation wherein awards have already been enforced and duly executed leaves little to discuss. The insolvency under such circumstances does not present procedural questions, as all the arbitration-related procedures are closed, and the award no longer represents a claim to be registered in the insolvency proceedings.

An award is granted equal status to a court decision in § 1055 ZPO and a judge in the proceedings in §§ 1060 et seq. ZPO will ex officio have to find the award is in line with public policy, i.e., implicitly and a *contrario* by not finding that it violates public policy. The procedure of §§ 1060 et seq. ZPO also provides the award creditor with an executable title.[769] However, § 141 InsO clearly states that the right to dispute transactions in the sense of §§ 129 et seq. InsO is not extinguished by the mere fact that there is an executable title.[770] In fact, the challenges in §§ 131 et seq. InsO mainly focus on the means and timing of satisfaction.

Therefore, payment and securities achieved through the execution of a valid title are viable targets of insolvency disputation. In case such execution was achieved in the last three months before insolvency, the transaction can be considered under § 131 InsO 'Incongruent Coverage'.[771] What specific considerations could be made for an award's performance relies on case-specific facts. As a specific example, the award ordering performance that per the parties' agreement only becomes final and binding under the suspensive condition that no court appeal is launched in three months, as in one of the cases mentioned above,[772] could fall under § 131 InsO within the three-month period.[773]

Payments made and executions achieved based on an enforced award can be challenged via insolvency disputation without any arbitration-specific aspects. However, due to the nature of §§ 129 et seq. InsO challenges, a successful challenge of a pre-insolvency transaction does not necessarily prejudge the validity of the underlying claim. As such, if an award-creditor is forced to restitute the received payment to the debtor, *see* § 143 InsO, he should follow the same course as discussed regarding enforced awards. He should register the claim, which is 'revived' according to § 144 InsO, in the insolvency proceedings.[774] Consequently, the award, c.q. the decision to enforce the award will again have the status of § 179(2) InsO, an executable title, in the verification procedure.[775]

769. MüKoZPO/*Münch* § 1060 ZPO, No. 1; Musielak/Voit/*Voit* § 1060 ZPO, No. 2.
770. Uhlenbruck/*Hirte/Borries* § 141 InsO, No. 2.
771. *BGH*, NJW 1997, p. 3445; NJW 2006, 1870, No. 9; *Dahl/Schmitz*, NJW 2017, pp. 1505–1506.
772. *BGH*, SchiedsVZ 2007, 160–162; *see also* § 3.1.
773. BeckOK InsO/*Raupach* § 131 InsO, No. 20.
774. *OLG Brandenburg*, ZinsO 2004, 504, p. 506; Uhlenbruck/*Hirte/Borries* § 144 InsO, No. 2.
775. *See* §§ 5.4 and 5.5.

In conclusion, with regard to the above considerations, a performed award can still be challenged in the same way other pre-insolvency transactions can. However, after the performance of the award, the arbitration and award no longer represent procedural considerations for insolvency or vice versa.

5.11 Award in Favour of the Insolvency Debtor

The above almost exclusively considers awards against the insolvent, c.q. the estate. This is often the implicit premise for discussions on awards in insolvency. This implicit premise is easily explained by the fact that the situation wherein an award creditor goes insolvent is far less problematic than the insolvency of an award debtor. This is because of the simple fact that § 89 InsO does not apply to enforcement by and for the estate. The prohibition on execution in insolvency is purely one-sided. It exists solely to protect and preserve the estate and consequently the ability of the creditors collectively to get satisfaction and their equality *inter se*, *par conditio creditorum*, in doing so.[776] An award in favour of the insolvency debtor or the estate also generally does not constitute any insolvency claims, so not only § 89 InsO but also §§ 174 et seq. InsO on the filing of claims loses relevance in this context.

However, some insolvency-specific considerations do need to be made. Most significantly, the replacement of the debtor by the administrator in proceedings relating to the estate. In consequence of § 80 InsO, when an award is rendered before insolvency or insolvency, the administrator will need to be the party to any enforcement proceedings and generally any other post-award proceedings, e.g., correction, interpretation and additional award proceedings and execution proceedings.[777]

The most relevant of those subsequent proceedings are the annulment and enforcement proceedings.[778] As discussed more extensively, an award in the German context is generally given the same effect as a court decision by § 1055 ZPO. However, an executable title based on this award can only be acquired through enforcement proceedings, *see* §§ 1060 et seq. ZPO.[779] Whereas, as discussed, the arbitration proceedings themselves are not caught in the snare of § 240 ZPO directly, it is generally and correctly understood that enforcement proceedings are, *see* the paragraph above Chapter 2 § 5.4.1. For that matter, all post-award proceedings that are state court proceedings, except execution proceedings, should be considered within the scope of § 240 ZPO, be it either in favour or against the estate, c.q. enforcement or annulment proceedings.[780]

776. MüKoInsO/*Breuer/Flöther* § 89 InsO, No. 1.
777. *Heidbrink/Groeben*, ZIP 2006, 265–272, p. 270; *S.M. Kröll*, Part IV: Selected Areas and Issues of Arbitration in Germany, Insolvency and Arbitration – Effects of Party Insolvency on Arbitral Proceedings in Germany, 981, p. 1005; *Schmitz*, Schiedsverfahren und Insolvenz, pp. 87–88.
778. Not to be confused with execution proceedings.
779. MüKoZPO/*Münch* § 1060 ZPO, No. 1; Musielak/Voit/*Voit* § 1060 ZPO, Nos 1–4.
780. *S.M. Kröll*, Part IV: Selected Areas and Issues of Arbitration in Germany, Insolvency and Arbitration – Effects of Party Insolvency on Arbitral Proceedings in Germany, 981, p. 1006; Uhlenbruck/*Mock* § 85 InsO, No. 1; *Schmitz*, Schiedsverfahren und Insolvenz, p. 90.

The resumption of proceedings will mostly follow from § 85 InsO, which nominally organises the resumption of procedures 'for the debtor'. This is often translated as procedures in which the debtor is the plaintiff.[781] However, this is erroneous as it is the common understanding that the party's role is not decisive for the application of § 85 InsO. It is the object of the proceedings that is decisive.[782] If the claim in the proceedings would actively lead to an enrichment of the estate, § 85 InsO applies to the resumption of such proceedings.[783] Consequently, the insolvency of the award-debtor provides more substantive legal issues, e.g., claim verification via arbitration, but arbitration and post-award proceedings also do not remain unaffected by the insolvency of the award creditor or claimant.

5.12 Conclusion and Summary: Effects of the Insolvency on Post-arbitration Proceedings

In this section, the effect of insolvency on awards before, during and after the opening of insolvency is discussed, as well as the opening of insolvency during post-award proceedings and during execution.

One might be forgiven for assuming that there is little possibility left for the two fields of insolvency and arbitration to clash when the principal arbitration proceeding has closed with the rendering of the award. However, it has become clear that this is far from the case by extensively going through most if not all of the possible post-award proceedings and examining the influence of insolvency thereon.

All post-award proceedings are affected by the opening of insolvency in one way or another. Not only is an award creditor of an insolvent award debtor prohibited from starting many procedures but ongoing procedures will also generally be suspended, except for execution and correction proceedings. Moreover, the award creditor will be largely dependent on the decisions of others in the sense of insolvency verification. Only if one can argue that one's claim is not part of the insolvency proceedings, i.e., exemption rights, can one be partially freed from being dragged into the insolvency proceedings, c.q. the long road of registration and verification of insolvency claims.

Insolvency also exposes the award to several insolvency-specific grounds for setting aside. This is most certainly the case when such awards have been rendered during the insolvency proceedings. However, even if all the arbitration relation proceedings have been completed, i.e., all the proceedings found in Book 10 ZPO, the claim granted by the award is not 'safe'. This is because one of the principles of insolvency is the prohibition on individual execution. Going one step further, even after execution or performance, the insolvency can come back to haunt the award

781. *Reusch*, Insolvency Statute, http://www.gesetze-im-internet.de/englisch_inso/print_englisch_inso.html.
782. *BGH*, NJW 1995, 1750, 1750 [I.1]; NZBau 2005, 399, 399 [II.1]; BeckRS 2017, 136174, No. 16; MüKoInsO/*Schumacher* § 85 InsO, Nos 3–4.
783. *BGH*, NZI 2010, 811, No. 22; BeckRS 2017, 136174, 14, 16; MüKoInsO/*Schumacher* § 85 InsO, pp. 3–4.

creditor as the transactions made before insolvency can be challenged in the insolvency. In conclusion, insolvency has a very long and broad reach when it comes to interfering with the arbitration of claims, reaching from the time before the proceedings begin to after an award has been performed.

When an award is caught up in arbitration, it is forced into the straitjacket that is the insolvency proceeding. The relevant claim must be duly registered, and any ongoing proceedings must generally be suspended until the verification meeting, which could take years, as practice has shown. However, awards, especially enforced awards, are given special status within insolvency. Due to the application of § 179(2) InsO, the disputer, be it the administrator or another creditor, must pursue litigation to challenge the claim provided by the award. This could mean both the start of new proceedings or the resumption of suspended proceedings.

6 CONCLUSORY REMARKS TO CHAPTER 2

The above attempts to provide, in a holistic way, a broad and deep understanding of the specific issues associated with the occurrence of insolvency in arbitration proceedings. In conjunction with the first part, the above provides both the legislative background and a thorough discussion of the relevant legal questions.

If the interaction between insolvency and arbitration is imagined as a clash of two different worlds or two different sets of principles, this author would conclude from the above that insolvency is the clear victor. It is not the insolvency proceedings that must accommodate the arbitration proceedings. It is the arbitration proceeding that must thoroughly accommodate the insolvency. If it fails to do so, an award will be non-enforceable or set aside. Of course, there is always the argument that the arbitrators do not have the absolute duty to provide an enforceable award. However, in practice, especially in a national context, as was discussed above, arbitrators will almost always aim to do so.[784] In fact, the parties will expect them to do so, as otherwise, the arbitration will be rendered mostly pointless.[785]

Two factors give arbitration in insolvency in Germany more relevance than it would have had in a more restrictive system. First, the concept of arbitrability in Germany is quite broad and provides the parties and especially the insolvency administrator, with a wide array of insolvency-related issues that could be arbitrated. Second, Germany's minimal concept of *vis attractiva concursus* provides a relatively significant role for arbitration in insolvency. Challenge proceedings will be conducted through arbitration for claims covered by an arbitration agreement, even if another creditor makes the challenge. Challenges can also lead to arbitration proceedings being resumed where they were suspended, and the challenge of awards can lead to arbitration typical proceedings, i.e., set-aside proceedings, for the verification of insolvency claims.

784. *Vidal*, ICC International Court of Arbitration Bulletin 20 (2009), 51, p. 66.
785. Further discussion thereof in Chapter 2 § 3.3.1 i.

Many questions of insolvency in arbitration are relatively well explored within the German context. Notwithstanding that some of these questions have not been definitively answered and that some of the discussions and conclusions skirt the big underlying theoretical discussions. The discussion around the applicability of § 240 ZPO, the suspension, to arbitration, is a prime example. This, in the opinion of the author, overlays a fundamental discussion of the role of arbitration and the arbitrator within the national legal order but is often relegated to a mere interpretation question of the wording of § 240 ZPO ignoring that deeper and fundamental question.

That underlying discussion will also prove key in the upcoming discussions on international aspects of insolvency in arbitration. The view one has of the relationship the arbitration has to the relevant legal orders will largely define conclusions reached concerning applicable law and conflict of law rules.

CHAPTER 3

Insolvency in Arbitration: International Aspects

In this Chapter 3 of this book, insolvency in arbitration will be examined in the international context. Unlike in the discussion above, which was deliberately kept within the confines of a single jurisdiction, the chosen jurisdictions being the German jurisdictions with a few relevant references to other jurisdictions, many commercial arbitrations are international in one way or another. In fact, at the ICC, the most renowned commercial arbitration institution, only 20% of cases in 2018 featured parties of just one nationality.[786] However, at the DIS, or German Arbitration Institute, the situation in 2016 is still reversed, with 68% of arbitrations involving just German parties.[787]

Insolvency in arbitration is already complex within the boundaries of just one jurisdiction. The factor of internationality adds an entirely new dimension to this complexity. To provide some boundaries to the discussion, the theoretical discussion below will reference primarily German law and with that European law for international cases. However, the awards cited will not be limited to German seated arbitration. First, this approach is taken for the scientific reason that beyond the references to the German seated arbitration and thus primarily the German legal system, this research is meant to provide internationally relevant discussions and conclusions. The second reason is the practical reason that there are not enough published international arbitration awards or 'case law' from tribunals seated in Germany for a meaningful discussion. The awards cited, primarily ICC awards, will thus not be limited to arbitration seated in Germany. At any rate, many international awards, in particular awards from European jurisdictions, will also be relevant to the German legal system, e.g., because EU law applies.

786. *ICC – International Chamber of Commerce*, ICC Dispute Resolution Bulletin 2018, 51, p. 55.
787. *DIS*, DIS-Statistics 2016, http://www.disarb.org/upload/statistics/DIS%20Statistics%202016.pdf.

Using the same order as above, the sections below are ordered in such a way as to broadly represent the order in which a tribunal would systematically have to deal with them in case a party goes insolvent. Therefore, the discussion below starts with recognition (§ 1), which essentially asks whether the tribunal will take the (foreign) insolvency into account in the arbitration. The all-important question of applicable law follows this question. For every insolvency-related question, the tribunal tries to answer, it must first answer the question of which law it should apply to the question. This question is split up into several parts: first, a discussion of the insolvency-specific conflict-of-laws rules (§ 2); second, a discussion on the relationship between conflict-of-laws rules and arbitration and tribunals (§ 3); third, the question of applicable law before a tribunal (§ 4).

1 RECOGNITION OF INSOLVENCIES

The first subject of Chapter 3 is the recognition of insolvencies. This section examines the role of recognition of insolvencies in (international) arbitration. The international context adds the question of recognition to the discussion on the relationship between a tribunal and its seat jurisdiction, as put forward in Chapter 2. The instrument of recognition is the conventional method for a state court to act upon foreign insolvency, i.e., it will lend assistance to the foreign insolvency if the foreign insolvency, c.q. the relevant decision opening insolvency proceedings passes a recognition test. In the context of arbitration, this begs the question: Must a 'foreign' insolvency be recognised in the seat jurisdiction before the tribunal can take it into account, or can the tribunal recognise the insolvency itself or even bypass the entire question of recognition?

Recognition of insolvencies plays a significant role in the world of international insolvency. The theories prevailing in insolvency and its international dimension have been discussed in the first part of this book. It is primarily due to the fact that most countries, at least to a certain extent, adhere to a territorial dogma concerning insolvencies, that 'foreign' insolvencies need to first go through a process of recognition before they can be given effect in the domestic jurisdiction. However, even more universalistic countries, like Germany, have some safety-valve recognition regulations to deny effect to abusive, fraudulent or otherwise undesirable foreign insolvencies.

The fact that many countries attempt to give their own insolvencies universal effect while not extending such effect to foreign insolvencies does not change the necessity of recognition and, in actuality, is a logical prerequisite for effective recognition. There would be no to little need to recognise a foreign insolvency if the foreign insolvency did not aim to have substantive effects in the recognising jurisdiction.[788] Arguably, however, recognition in those circumstances could still serve to give effect to non-jurisdiction bound general effects of insolvency so that a court could recognise the effects on, for example, the legal personality of a company. Furthermore, recognition

788. An exemption to this logic would be a jurisdiction that provides in its own laws for specific effects for recognised foreign insolvencies and do not refer to the effects prescribed by the *lex fori concursus*.

could still be a requirement for the recognising jurisdiction to give the insolvency specific autonomous effects, independent of the effects its home jurisdiction ascribes to it.

To deal with recognition by a tribunal in general (§ 1.5) and particularly for Germany-seated tribunals (§ 1.6), a group of other topics needs to be examined first. This starts with, first, the relevant concepts of recognition (§ 1.1). Second, recognition under the UNCITRAL Model Law on Cross-Border Insolvency will be discussed (§ 1.2). After which, recognition under the EIR (§ 1.3) and German Insolvency Law (§ 1.4) will be examined.

1.1 Relevant Concepts of Recognition

Recognition can be used in different contexts and, in consequence, can refer to different things. In general, it can be said that recognition in the context of international law means the recognition of foreign legal acts and consequently providing those acts with legal effect in the recognising jurisdiction.[789] However, beyond this general description, the question remains, what sort of legal acts are to be recognised, and what sort of effect should these acts be given within the recognising jurisdiction?[790]

Within international civil procedural law, it refers to the recognition of a foreign judgment, order or ruling, collectively 'acts of foreign public authority', and the related extension of its effects to the territory of the recognising state.[791] This recognition, thus, can, by extending those effects, lead to the creation, change or even end of legal relationships within the recognising state.[792]

Within private international law, such recognition is not available, as private law acts are not made in the capacity of a judge or other official role. Recognition, in the context of international private law, concerns itself with the recognition of foreign acts of private law, e.g., the founding of a company, as opposed to the recognition of acts of public authority.[793] This substantive recognition is regulated by the private international law conflict-of-laws rules of the forum state.[794]

For this book, the most important concept of recognition is the concept of recognition that pertains to cross-border insolvency. There is no single concept of recognition within international insolvency law in the sense that procedures and

789. *Graf,* Die Anerkennung ausländischer Insolvenzentscheidungen, p. 258; *Martiny,* Anerkennung ausländischer Entscheidungen nach autonomem Recht, No. 264264.
790. Cf. *Graf,* Die Anerkennung ausländischer Insolvenzentscheidungen, p. 258; *P.K. Wagner,* Abstimmungsfragen zwischen Internationalem Insolvenzrecht und Internationaler Schiedsgerichtsbarkeit, p. 39.
791. *Martiny,* Anerkennung ausländischer Entscheidungen nach autonomem Recht, No. 6868; *P.K. Wagner,* Abstimmungsfragen zwischen Internationalem Insolvenzrecht und Internationaler Schiedsgerichtsbarkeit, p. 40.
792. *J.D.M. Lew/Mistelis/Kröll,* Comparative international commercial arbitration; *Vorburger,* International Arbitration and Cross-Border Insolvency, p. 17; *P.K. Wagner,* Abstimmungsfragen zwischen Internationalem Insolvenzrecht und Internationaler Schiedsgerichtsbarkeit, p. 40; *BGE,* Urt. of 11.3.2004 - BGE 130 III 336, p. 342.
793. *Trunk,* Internationales Insolvenzrecht, p. 263.
794. *Vorburger,* International Arbitration and Cross-Border Insolvency, p. 17.

effects vary between jurisdictions.[795] That being said, within cross-border insolvency laws, recognition is mentioned in reference to the recognition of the insolvency procedure or the judicial acts surrounding insolvency, in particular, the act, order or ruling opening insolvency proceedings. In conclusion, compared to the two concepts of recognition mentioned above, it is clearly a recognition of the procedural kind.[796]

Below three manners of recognising insolvency or the effect thereof will be examined: recognition of insolvency rulings and decisions (§ 1.1.1), recognition of the substantive effects of insolvency (§ 1.1.2), and recognition of insolvency as fact (§ 1.1.3).

1.1.1 Recognition of Insolvency Rulings and Decisions

The first manner in which insolvency can be recognised to be discussed here is the recognition of insolvency rulings and decisions. The recognition of an insolvency ruling is the formal way of recognising an insolvency and generally provides the most inclusive way of incorporating the effects of an insolvency into the recognising jurisdiction.

Although some insolvency codes, such as those based on the model law, *see* Articles 15, 17 Ins.ML, speak of the recognition of the insolvency 'proceedings' the object of recognition in the context of international insolvency is not the proceedings but the judicial decision opening the insolvency proceedings and, to an extent, relevant other decisions linked to this decision.[797] Thus, the recognition of an insolvency judgment or ruling and the insolvency proceedings are generally meant to refer to the same recognition, i.e., the recognition of the relevant orders.[798] The proceedings themselves cannot be seen as separate from the opening order and, as such, do not provide their own separate object of recognition.

Nevertheless, even if one wanted to recognise insolvency 'proceedings', insolvency proceedings are usually officially initiated by court order or ruling. Therefore, the recognition of judgments or rulings and that of the procedure amount to the same thing in a practical sense, as the recognition of the proceeding would automatically give effect to the opening order.[799] Thus recognition here, similar to recognition in the international civil procedure, remains the recognition of the judicial decision. This recognition is based upon the ruling to be recognised meeting certain formal criteria, including regularly one of comity. Courts in most regimes are not allowed to

795. *Graf,* Die Anerkennung ausländischer Insolvenzentscheidungen, p. 257.
796. *Trunk,* Internationales Insolvenzrecht, p. 263; *P.K. Wagner,* Abstimmungsfragen zwischen Internationalem Insolvenzrecht und Internationaler Schiedsgerichtsbarkeit, p. 41.
797. *P.K. Wagner,* Abstimmungsfragen zwischen Internationalem Insolvenzrecht und Internationaler Schiedsgerichtsbarkeit, p. 41.
798. *See, e.g.,* preamble 65 of the EIR and compare the title of Chapter II thereof, speaking of recognition of insolvency proceedings with the test of Art. 19 EIR, speaking of recognition of judgments opening insolvency proceedings; Regulation (EU) 2015/848 on insolvency proceedings of 20.5.2015, OJ L 141/19.
799. Cf. *Vorburger,* International Arbitration and Cross-Border Insolvency, p. 18.

substantively recheck the opening order, i.e., no *révision au fond*, although minimal checks of due process and public policy are often prescribed.

The concept of comity is a recurring theme and requirement in cross-border insolvency, c.q. cross-border insolvency recognition. The principle of comity describes the idea that states should do their best to give effect to foreign legislative, executive or judicial acts as a matter of necessity and goodwill towards each other. Furthermore, it is often used in the sense that recognition should and can only take place insofar as recognition is also extended to similar orders made in the recognising state by the jurisdiction in which the act to be recognised originated.[800]

Chapter III of the Model Law on Cross-Border Insolvency deals with recognition. Article 17 Ins.ML, discussed further in the next section, provides the requirements for recognition, notably absent there is comity. Considering the above, recognising an insolvency ruling is quite similar to the general recognition of civil procedural rulings. However, international insolvency often has its own specific conflict-of-laws systems, including recognition rules, which provide a more insolvency-specific system, e.g., the EIR and the Model Law for Cross-Border Insolvency.

Whereas the previous provides an understanding of the reasons and process of recognition, the question as to its effects remains unanswered. The answer to that question mainly depends on the conflict-of-laws rules of the recognising state or potentially those applied by the tribunal,[801] which will determine the applicable laws. The applicable law referred to by such rules can differ per issue or question. *See, e.g.*, Articles 7 et seq. EIR.

Recognition in the context of this book, i.e., international commercial arbitration, is not as straightforward as described above. In contrast, in the purely domestic situation, i.e., national courts in the jurisdiction in which the insolvency ruling has been made, the situation is relatively straightforward. In such cases, one cannot truly speak of any recognition of the insolvency as a national court must by virtue of being part of the same judicial order consider and give effect to the insolvency ex officio and de jure, *see, e.g.*, Article 20(3) GG. Furthermore, the question of the relevant law is non-existent, i.e., the national insolvency law applies. Courts in the context of international insolvency still have a relatively easy job. They are obliged to follow the rules of their jurisdiction, the *lex fori*. Therefore, the *lex fori* will be the starting point for them to rule on the potential recognition and the effect of foreign insolvency. As stated, many jurisdictions have specific conflict-of-laws rules for insolvencies. Such rules are often found in treaties. As such, the courts will have to either refer to such treaty rules, e.g., as are found in the EIR, or national law, e.g., national laws based on the Model Law for Cross-Border Insolvency. First, in this context, setting aside shortly the peculiarities of dualist and monist approaches to international treaties vis-à-vis domestic law, rules found in treaties are generally given precedence over rules in the national

800. *U.S. Supreme Court*, 3.6.1895 – 159 U.S. 113, pp. 163–164; *Gottwald*, Internationales Zivilprozessrecht, p. 621.
801. *Vorburger*, International Arbitration and Cross-Border Insolvency, p. 19.

law, *see* Article 27 of the Vienna Convention on the Law of Treaties.[802] Second, where such specific rules on recognition and applicable law exist, recognition based on regular civil procedural recognition is generally rejected.[803] This prevents parallel and perhaps different systems of recognition from applying. As a general principle of law, specific rules are given precedence over general rules, a principle often known by the Latin maxim, *lex specialis derogat legi generali.*[804] Thus, even where one could argue based on a grammatical interpretation that the civil procedural recognition rules include the recognition of insolvency rulings, this would be to no avail insofar as specific rules exist.

In the context of the recognition of insolvency orders or procedures, a specific problem can be identified when the question of such recognition surfaces in an ongoing court proceeding. Insofar as recognition is not an automatic de jure effect, jurisdictions mostly require a separate recognition proceeding before a specific court. Consequently, the court in an ongoing civil procedure and perhaps a tribunal in arbitration must defer this question to the competent court and likely suspend proceedings until this question is solved, as recognition of the insolvency can have far-reaching effects on the proceeding. To a certain level, the court could avail itself of either substantive or factual recognition as described below.[805]

1.1.2 Recognition of the Substantive Effects of Insolvency

Aside from the formal recognition of the insolvency orders, there is the recognition of the effects of the insolvency. In such a recognition, the object of recognition is not the procedure or the order of insolvency but merely its subsequent substantive effects as described in the foreign law applicable. For example, a court might recognise that the company's board or representative thereof can no longer represent the company or recognise the termination of legal relationships by the administrator. Such substantive effects, which go beyond insolvency-specific effects, in the sense that they can also occur outside of insolvency, are capable of recognition based on international private law rules. In comparison, the insolvency-specific effects can generally only be recognised based on insolvency-specific recognition.[806]

In Germany, an example of the substantive recognition of insolvency effects could be the application of the court of the established rule that refers issues of legal personality to the law state in which the company has its seat or law of the state of

802. For EU Law, this principle is found in the famous *Costa v. ENEL* case *CJEU*, Judgment of 15.7.1964 - Case 6-64.
803. *Vorburger*, International Arbitration and Cross-Border Insolvency, p. 22.
804. *See* for an explanation and discussion of this rule and other conflict rules *Vranes*, ZaöRV 2005, 391–405.
805. *Vorburger*, International Arbitration and Cross-Border Insolvency, p. 24.
806. *BGHZ* 95, 256–273, I(1)(b); *Staehelin*, Die Anerkennung ausländischer Konkurse und Nachlassverträge in der Schweiz, 15 et seq.; *Vorburger*, International Arbitration and Cross-Border Insolvency, p. 22.

incorporation or seat.[807] These rules could be used to recognise that a company has been dissolved due to insolvency in those jurisdictions without recognising the insolvency procedure per se.[808] Such recognition does generally not require a separate procedure and is achieved by merely applying, for example, the relevant rules of legal personality applicable in the recognising court when this question becomes relevant in the case before it.

1.1.3 Recognition of Insolvency as a Fact

Finally, certain effects of the insolvency could be recognised as facts in an ongoing procedure in the recognising jurisdiction. Due to the territorial approach that most jurisdictions retain in their approach to foreign insolvency proceedings or orders, insolvencies are generally not taken into account in courts when they are not somehow recognised in the jurisdiction of the seized court.[809] However, some authors advocate for 'recognition' without any actual recognition, i.e., factual recognition. This argument is primarily made in case non-recognition would lead to highly unwanted results, i.e., contradictions between the laws of the relevant countries, which cannot be justified.[810] The description 'recognition without any actual recognition' or 'recognition as fact' flows from the circumstance that no rules of recognition are applied, but specific effects are taken into account as simple facts. In this context, this type of recognition can thus only occur within the framework of answering preliminary questions, most prominently perhaps that of capacity and standing.[811]

Whereas the obvious efficiency and effectiveness argument in favour of factual recognition cannot be denied, factual recognition presents several issues and should only be considered in limited circumstances. The possibility of factual recognition depends entirely on the jurisdiction, i.e., how that jurisdiction balances the strict application of its rules with principles such as efficiency and effectiveness.[812] However, some general considerations can be made as to under which circumstances a court could contemplate factual recognition. The first consideration must be that the relevant insolvency or substantive effect is not capable of being recognised based on the rules of the *lex fori*. Insofar as it is capable of recognition by applying the rules of the *lex fori*, such recognition should always be preferred, and factual recognition should not be considered due to its nature as an *ultimum remedium*. Second, non-recognition must lead to fundamental legal issues and differences between the relevant jurisdictions. The issue of representation mentioned before is a good example: An insolvent who has lost all legal capacity or dispositive powers according to the *lex fori concursus*, but

807. *Jahn/Brian*, § 27 Geschäftsverkehr mit ausländischen Kunden, No. 17; *Schack*, Internationales Zivilverfahrensrecht, No. 600600.
808. Cf. MüKoBGB/*Lipp* Art. 7 EGBGB, 92 et seq.
809. Compare Chapter 1 §§ 2.4–2.5.
810. *Schwander*, ZIER 10 (2000), 382, p. 388.
811. *Schwander*, ZIER 10 (2000), 382, p. 288; *Vorburger*, International Arbitration and Cross-Border Insolvency, p. 22.
812. Factual recognition as described here comes from Swiss authors based on the decision of Swiss courts.

would somehow still be seen as the proper representative of the party, could be classified as an unbearable contradiction.

Insolvency or its effects can, thus, be recognised either by formal recognition of the insolvency order, recognition of specific effects of the insolvency by application of the relevant rules, or the recognition of insolvency or its effects as mere facts. Recognition of insolvency is commonly used to refer to the first of these three. Formal recognition also generally provides the broadest integration of insolvency effects into the recognising jurisdiction. Therefore, the relevant rules of recognition of insolvency are discussed in the following subsections.

1.2 Recognition under the UNCITRAL Model Law on Cross-Border Insolvency

The first rules of recognition to be examined here are found in the UNCITRAL Model Law on Cross-Border Insolvency. Every jurisdiction determines for itself under which circumstances it recognises an insolvency it classifies as foreign. Whereas it is neither possible nor necessary to discuss all possible systems here,[813] the UNCITRAL Model Law on Cross-Border Insolvency provides a good insight into the system of every adopting country and those which have other derivative legislation. It also provides a good view of what can be considered a growing international consensus.

The regulation of recognition of foreign insolvencies can be found in the third chapter of the model law, Articles 15–25 Ins.ML. The recognition proceedings start with a request by the insolvency administrator, as regulated by Article 15(1) Ins.ML. Therefore, it is important to note that recognition is not automatic, c.q. by autonomous operation of law, i.e., not *ipso jure*, but requires an application and subsequent recognition procedure.

A request, as described in Article 15 Ins.ML must include a certified copy of the decision opening the proceedings, including the appointment of the insolvency administrator. In the absence thereof, the existence of the proceedings and appointment of the administrator can be certified by the relevant court in a different way. Aside from the previous two options, the recognising court could rule that it is satisfied with some other form of proof, as provided by the three possibilities in Article 15(2) Ins.ML.

The basis for the recognition decision itself is found in Article 17 Ins.ML. The operation of this article does not provide any significant extra hurdles. Its first subclause, Article 17 Ins.ML provides the requirements for a recognition decision. It provides that the recognition shall be granted when the relevant insolvency is indeed actual insolvency within the definition of the law, the correct court has been addressed, the correct person, i.e., the insolvency administrator, has made the request, and the request satisfies the above-described proof requirements of Article 15(2) Ins.ML. As discussed previously,[814] the proceedings can be recognised as either main or non-main, secondary proceedings based on Article 17(2) Ins.ML.

---

813. For a discussion of international instruments, *see Wessels/Boon*, Cross-Border Insolvency Law.
814. *See* Chapter 1 § 1.2.3.

In light of the system described above, it can be stated that recognition is relatively easily obtained within model law jurisdictions. In addition, the model law contains an article prescribing a suspension of proceedings if a foreign proceeding is recognised, *see* Article 20 Ins.ML. However, it does not consider the questions of applicable law holistically for insolvency or any of the specific aspects of insolvency, in contrast to the EIR.[815]

1.3 The European Insolvency Regulation

The second system that provides rules for the recognition examined here is the EIR. Recognition of foreign insolvencies in Germany and other EU Member States, except Denmark, regarding insolvencies in other such EU Member States, is based on the EIR.[816] The current EIR is the second iteration of the EIR.[817] The 2015 regulation replaced the regulation from 2000 in 2017.[818] As described in the first chapter of this book,[819] the Regulation does not prescribe a uniform and coherent insolvency procedure but primarily facilitates recognition and coordination.[820] The EIR organises when, where, and which kind of procedure can be started. By doing so, it prevents a run to court to secure a procedure in the most favourable jurisdiction, i.e., forum shopping.[821]

Aside from mandating of and coordinating between primary and secondary proceedings, the EIR provides a conflict-of-laws ruleset to determine the applicable law for cross-border issues, which will be investigated properly in the next section.[822] However, the cornerstone of the EIR and the focus of this section is the automatic recognition of insolvencies EU-wide.[823] This concept is incorporated in Articles 19 et seq. EIR.[824]

Whereas Article 19(1) EIR does indeed *ipso jure* recognise Member State insolvencies, it mentions some basic procedural requirements, which deserve some discussion. Furthermore, an exception to this automatic recognition is made in Article 33 EIR. Recognition can be denied on an *ordre public* ground. Consequentially, a state can deny recognition when, under its laws, the relevant decision violates the minimum standard of material and procedural justice.[825]

The *ordre public* exception in international arbitration and the EIR should be viewed in their separate context. The fact that the EIR operates in a closed quasi-federal system based on the EU treaties and serves the recognition of judgments of courts that

815. *P.K. Wagner*, Abstimmungsfragen zwischen Internationalem Insolvenzrecht und Internationaler Schiedsgerichtsbarkeit, p. 148.
816. Cf. §§ 102, 102a EGInsO.
817. Regulation (EU) 2015/848 on insolvency proceedings of 20.5.2015, OJ L 141/19.
818. Council Regulation (EC) No 1346/2000 on insolvency proceedings of 29.5.2000, Official Journal of the European Communities L 160; *Wessels*, International Insolvency Law, p. 356.
819. *See* Chapter 1 § 1.2.1.
820. *Wessels*, International Insolvency Law, pp. 347–349; *see* § 1.2.1.
821. *Wessels*, International Insolvency Law, pp. 346–347.
822. *See* § 2.1; *Wessels*, International Insolvency Law, pp. 348–349.
823. Mankowski/Müller/J. Schmidt, EuInsVO 2015/*M. Müller* Art. 19 EuInsVO, No. 2.
824. *Nacimiento/Bähr*, NJOZ 2009, 4752, pp. 4758–4759.
825. Mankowski/Müller/J. Schmidt, EuInsVO 2015/*M. Müller* Art. 33 EuInsVO, No. 2.

must all meet certain common EU criteria serves to put a more restrictive light on the *ordre public* exemption. Moreover, literature rightly interprets the exemption restrictively, as the principle of trust is deeply embedded in the EIR.[826] *See, e.g.*, No. 65 of the preambles that states explicitly:

> [...] The recognition of judgments delivered by the courts of the Member States should be based on the principle of mutual trust. [...]

For an understanding of the requirements of recognition Article 19(1) EIR needs to be analysed. Article 19(1) EIR reads as follows:

> 1. *Any judgment opening insolvency proceedings handed down by a court of a Member State which has jurisdiction pursuant to Article 3* shall be recognised in all other Member States *from the moment that it becomes effective in the State of the opening of proceedings.* [Emphasis added]

The underlined parts constitute separate requirements, which will be discussed in the following paragraphs.

1.3.1 'Any judgment opening insolvency proceedings'

First, there needs to be a judgment opening the insolvency proceedings. Two things need to be noted here. First, a request for insolvency proceedings is not capable of recognition.[827] Second, the to-be-opened 'insolvency' proceedings need to be proceedings within the definition of the EIR; *see* Article 1(1) EIR and Annex A to the EIR. Proceedings that, for example, do not grant a stay of individual execution proceedings are excluded as no true insolvency proceedings as meant in the EIR.

In the *Eurofood* case by the Court of Justice of the European Union (CJEU), the Court discussed whether or not the concept of 'any judgment opening insolvency proceedings' includes the decision to appoint a preliminary insolvency administrator, such as the strong and weak preliminary insolvency administrator in the German system.[828] The Court decided that not only formal decisions opening insolvency proceedings but also decisions based on an application for insolvency that cause the divestment of the debtor and the appointment of a 'liquidator' (insolvency administrator) as in Annex C of the EIR could be recognised.[829] Whereas some writers remain adamant that even after *Eurofood*, only the official opening of insolvency proceedings can be recognised based on Article 19(1) EIR, this view is to be dismissed as the CJEU could not have been clearer in stating that not only those decisions fall under the definition of Article 19(1) EIR and that it applies a wider reach to this article:[830]

> 54 In those circumstances, *a 'decision to open insolvency proceedings' for the purposes of the Regulation must be regarded as including not only a decision which*

826. MüKoBGB/*Kindler* Art. 33 EuInsVO, No. 21.
827. Mankowski/Müller/J. Schmidt, EuInsVO 2015/*M. Müller* Art. 19 EuInsVO, No. 8.
828. *CJEU*, 2.5.2006 - C-341/04.
829. *CJEU*, 2.5.2006 - C-341/04, No. 54.
830. *CJEU*, 2.5.2006 - C-341/04, No. 54.

> *is formally described as an opening decision by the legislation of the Member State of the court that handed it down, but also a decision handed down following an application, based on the debtor's insolvency, seeking the opening of proceedings referred to in Annex A to the Regulation, where that decision involves divestment of the debtor and the appointment of a liquidator referred to in Annex C to the Regulation.* Such divestment involves the debtor losing the powers of management which he has over his assets. In such a case, the two characteristic consequences of insolvency proceedings, namely the appointment of a liquidator referred to in Annex C and the divestment of the debtor, have taken effect, and thus all the elements constituting the definition of such proceedings, given in Article 1(1) of the Regulation, are present.

From the CJEU's wording in *Eurofood*, it becomes clear that the decision to appoint a strong preliminary administrator under §§ 21(2)(1) and 22(2) InsO, where the executive power is fully transferred to the administrator, should be seen as falling under the definition. For the so-called 'weak administrator', *see* § 22(1) InsO, this remains debatable as the rights to administer and dispose of the estate are not fully transferred. However, following *Müller*, the correct conclusion here is that the appointment of a weak administrator would also be sufficient, as the Article 2(5) EIR and Annex B state that the 'supervision' of the debtor's business dealings suffices to fall under the regime of the EIR.[831]

Paulus is fervently critical of this point of view, mainly because the debtor has not been legally recognised as insolvent when a preliminary administrator is appointed. Second, he argues that the preliminary administrator already has certain powers based on the EIR and, therefore, does not need the 'extra options' provided by the official recognition per Article 19(1) EIR. More importantly, a recognition based on Article 19 EIR takes away the meaning and purpose of Article 32 EIR, which provides for the recognition of security measures. Accordingly, literature rightly criticises *Eurofood* as being systemically incoherent.[832] There would simply be no reason for securities and preliminary measures to be recognisable before the opening of proceedings if they themselves are viewed as the opening of the proceedings. However, this critique fails to recognise *Müller*'s argument regarding the widening of the criterion of the insolvency order to those orders that merely provide supervision of the debtor's business dealings. Second, recognising such orders does not negate the need to have a system for recognition of orders for other preliminary and security measures, e.g., an order to seize any or certain business activities, as these orders can still be made separate from any opening order a preliminary appointment. However, even if this critique was well-founded, the Court has not made any judgment overturning the rule of the *Eurofood* decision, and it remains standing case law to be followed by the national courts in the EU. Decisions appointing a preliminary administrator are thus still eligible for recognition as decisions opening insolvency proceedings under the autonomous EIR concept.[833]

831. Mankowski/Müller/J. Schmidt, EuInsVO 2015/*M. Müller* Art. 19 EuInsVO, No. 8.
832. Mankowski/Müller/J. Schmidt, EuInsVO 2015/*M. Müller* Art. 19 EuInsVO, No. 8; *Paulus*, NZG 16 (2006), 609, p. 613.
833. FK-InsO/*Wenner/Schuster* Art. 19 EuInsVO, No. 4.

1.3.2 *'handed down by a court of a Member State which has jurisdiction pursuant to Article 3'*

This partial sentence prescribes that the court handing down the judgment must have jurisdiction under Article 3 EIR. The jurisdictional concept in the EIR is separate from that of the Member States themselves. Article 3(1) EIR describes which court has jurisdiction to open main or secondary/territorial proceedings.

The courts in the country where the so-called COMI or Centre of Main Interests is located have the jurisdiction to open main proceedings.[834] This is an expression of the real seat theory, as opposed to the incorporation theory, i.e., the main proceedings will take place in the jurisdictions where the company's economic and administrative 'centre of gravity' is situated. The rebuttable assumption is that this is also the jurisdiction where the company is registered, *see* Article 3(1) EIR. This, in contrast to the COMI approach, is a clear reference to the incorporation theory. However, it is not a legal definition but merely an evidential assumption.[835] If there is a presence that does not amount to the COMI of a company but merely to an establishment, a territorial proceeding can be opened, which, in case a main proceeding is opened, is referred to as a secondary proceeding.[836]

The distinction between main and secondary proceedings has little to no consequences in terms of the actual effect and practical application within a given jurisdiction. However, within the EU and the EIR framework, it leads to several conclusions about the relation of the proceedings with foreign proceedings and a possible extension of effects to foreign assets insofar as no proceeding is opened in the relevant jurisdiction. Both main and secondary/territorial proceedings are automatically recognised under EU Law. Insofar as a main proceeding is recognised, the law of the opening state is applicable EU-wide, a sort of 'internal universalism'. All debtors and assets are to be included in this main proceeding.[837] The recognition of territorial proceedings has no cross-border effect as such, except that when a main proceeding is opened, this territorial proceeding, then to be called a secondary proceeding, will deny the main proceeding universal effect in the jurisdiction of the secondary proceedings.[838]

1.3.3 *'from the moment that it becomes effective in the State of the opening of proceedings'*

This last part of the subclause provides for a final requirement, the requirement that the decision mentioned before has become effective. This requirement is mostly of a procedural nature and ensures the integrity of the recognition system and the EIR system as a whole. Recognising orders that have not yet become effective can lead to unwanted results, especially in relation to procedures opened in other EU jurisdictions.

834. *Wessels,* International Insolvency Law, p. 365.
835. MüKoInsO/*Thole* Art. 3 EuInsVO, No. 36.
836. *Wessels,* International Insolvency Law, p. 365.
837. *Wessels,* International Insolvency Law, pp. 366-368.
838. *Wessels,* International Insolvency Law, p. 368.

Procedures opened elsewhere can be denied or given the status of secondary proceedings, even though the decision opening insolvency might still be overturned.

However, it is important to note here that, unlike the discussion on the definition of the to recognise act above stemming from *Eurofood*,[839] the term 'effective' does not have an autonomous meaning within the EIR. Accordingly, it solely matters if the decision to open proceedings has become effective within the jurisdiction where the decision has been made, c.q. effective based on the *lex fori concursus*.[840] This is relevant as jurisdictions can, for example, set different periods for appeals and orders usually are not considered effective before the appeal period has lapsed. In the context of this effectiveness requirement, a further important aspect of appeals is that decisions that are challenged or appealed often have their effectiveness suspended until a decision is reached on the challenge or appeal.

1.3.4 Interim Conclusion: Recognition Based on the EIR

Recognition based on the EIR, although automatic, has a few requirements. It is perhaps due to this automatic recognition that the EIR and its Annexes describe relatively extensively what is to be recognised and when. However, the requirements themselves are not hard to meet and could be summarised by stating that effective insolvency orders made in the EU will be recognised. Although, based on the discussion above, it is clear that the terms in this description do hide some discussion as to what an insolvency order is.

The consequences of recognition are the implementation of a system of secondary and main proceedings and the applicability of a conflict-of-laws system that determines which law is to be applied to which aspect of the insolvency and the potential assets in question.

1.4 Recognition Based on the German Insolvency Code

The recognition rules examined here are the recognition rules of the German Insolvency Code. For other foreign insolvencies, i.e., extra-EU insolvencies, Germany has an autonomous international insolvency ruleset found in §§ 343 to 353 InsO.[841] The German rules of recognition are not an adoption of the UNCITRAL Model Law on Cross-Border Insolvency, as described above. However, they take a similar, if not more, universalist approach, particularly when considering its automatic recognition.

The mechanism for recognition is found in § 343(1) InsO. Based on this article, foreign insolvencies are automatically recognised, not unlike in the EIR system. Although recognition is automatic, i.e., does not require a separate legal procedure, recognition still requires certain requirements to be met.

839. *CJEU*, 2.5.2006 – C-341/04.
840. MüKoBGB/*Kindler* Art. 19 EuInsVO, No. 8.
841. *S.M. Kröll*, Part IV: Selected Areas and Issues of Arbitration in Germany, Insolvency and Arbitration – Effects of Party Insolvency on Arbitral Proceedings in Germany, 981, pp. 984–986.

§ 343(1) InsO reads as follows, with the underlined elements presenting separate requirements or exceptions:

(1) *Die Eröffnung eines ausländischen Insolvenzverfahrens* wird anerkannt. Dies gilt nicht,
   1. wenn die *Gerichte des Staats der Verfahrenseröffnung nach deutschem Recht nicht zuständig sind;*
   2. *soweit die Anerkennung zu einem Ergebnis führt, das mit wesentlichen Grundsätzen des deutschen Rechts offensichtlich unvereinbar ist, insbesondere soweit sie mit den Grundrechten unvereinbar ist.* [Emphasis added]

   Or in English;

(1) *The opening* of *foreign insolvency proceedings* shall be recognised. This shall not apply,
   1. if *the courts of the state of the opening of proceedings do not have jurisdiction in accordance with German law;*
   2. *where recognition leads to a result which is manifestly incompatible with major principles of German law, in particular where it is incompatible with basic rights.*[842] [Emphasis added]

The elements of this rule are discussed separately in the following paragraphs.

1.4.1 'The Opening of a Foreign Insolvency Proceeding'

The requirements mentioned in § 343(1) InsO seem relatively easily met. However, some requirements are merely implicit in the text. In regard to this first element, the text promulgates that a decision to open insolvency proceeding is required. However, it is implicit in this element that the decision must have become effective[843] and must claim to have an international effect, c.q. claims to have an effect in Germany.[844] A second complication is the definition of the term 'insolvency proceeding' as used in § 343(1) InsO. § 343(1) InsO concerns an international context and does not merely refer to the insolvency procedure as described in the German Insolvency Code.

Consequently, the question needs to be asked what the relevant rules and definitions are to determine if the relevant proceeding is an insolvency proceeding within the meaning used here. Whereas the principle of automatic recognition in § 343(1) InsO functions mostly similar to that of Article 19 EIR, discussed above, the InsO does not provide us with a similar list or annex of foreign proceedings that qualify for recognition.

In the context of foreign insolvency having to be categorised in the German system, the first question is which of the two relevant laws provides the qualification of the term insolvency.[845] The legislator's discussion of an autonomous qualification

842. *Reusch,* Insolvency Statute, http://www.gesetze-im-internet.de/englisch_inso/print_englisch_inso.html.
843. Braun/*Ehret* § 343 InsO, No. 5; BeckOK InsO/*Weissinger* § 343 InsO, No. 8.
844. *BGHZ* 95, 256–273, 29,41; *Graf,* Die Anerkennung ausländischer Insolvenzentscheidungen, p. 286.
845. *Graf,* Die Anerkennung ausländischer Insolvenzentscheidungen, pp. 262–263; Cf. *R. Geimer/E. Geimer/Geimer,* Internationales Zivilprozessrecht, No. 329; Differently Kindler, who states that mere territorial proceedings can be recognised as well, without providing them with effects within the German jurisdiction MüKoBGB/*Kindler* § 343 InsO, No. 35.

under insolvency law in the legislative draft documentation leads to the conclusion that it does not want to rely on the qualification made by the foreign jurisdiction.[846] Furthermore, an independent qualification works as a filter that screens out foreign orders that merely operate under the guise of insolvency to achieve a specific effect in the (German) jurisdiction.[847]

Consequently, the term in § 343(1) InsO needs to be further qualified based on German law to provide specific requirements a foreign insolvency proceeding needs to meet to be qualified as an insolvency proceeding.[848] However, the German legislator here does not apply the term insolvency as defined by German substantive insolvency law and states that the main question should be if the relevant proceedings have largely the same purpose as German insolvency proceedings. Therefore, it is the function of the proceedings that provides the main criterion. The legislator describes this purpose and function as the collective satisfaction of creditors and refers to § 1 InsO. Consequently, similarity to this purpose is the primary requirement for proceedings to be recognised as insolvency proceedings under § 343(1) InsO.[849]

Further criteria and specifications have been developed based on case law and texts by the legislator.[850] Literature has reduced these criteria to a list of three requirements which provide an adequate summary of the contemporary approach. The first additional point is that the opening of the insolvency proceedings must be bound to specific criteria, e.g., insolvency or financial difficulty.[851] The second point is that the proceeding is a public law proceeding. However, not necessarily a judicial proceeding.[852] The third point, the primary requirement discussed above, is that the purpose of the proceedings is generally similar to that of German insolvency.[853]

The first requirement, which constitutes the necessity of specific opening criteria, does not flow from the wording of § 1 InsO but is still a necessary consequence of the reference by the legislator that the proceedings must generally have the same goal. The purpose of insolvency, including German insolvency,[854] is to organise the procedure to be followed when a party can no longer meet its obligations or, in some cases, is foreseeably near to such a situation.[855] In consequence, similar opening requirements must be present.

846. Entwurf einer Insolvenzordnung of 15.4.92, BT-Drs. 12/2443, p. 236; Entwurf eines Gesetzes zur Neuregelung des Internationalen Insolvenzrechts of 25.10.2002, BT-Drs. 15/16, p. 21.
847. *Graf,* Die Anerkennung ausländischer Insolvenzentscheidungen, p. 263; *Pielorz,* Auslandskonkurs und Disposition über das Inlandsvermögen, p. 66.
848. *R. Geimer/E. Geimer/Geimer,* Internationales Zivilprozessrecht, No. 33603360.
849. Entwurf einer Insolvenzordnung of 15.4.92, BT-Drs. 12/2443, p. 236; Braun/*Ehret* § 343 InsO, No. 4.
850. Braun/*Ehret* § 343 InsO, p. 4; MüKoInsO/*Thole* § 343 InsO, No. 14; MüKoBGB/*Kindler* § 343 InsO, Nos 6–9.
851. *Graf,* Die Anerkennung ausländischer Insolvenzentscheidungen, p. 270.
852. Entwurf eines Gesetzes zur Neuregelung des Internationalen Insolvenzrechts of 25.10.2002, BT-Drs. 15/16, p. 21.
853. MüKoBGB/*Kindler* § 343 InsO, No. 6; MüKoInsO/*Thole* § 343 InsO, No. 14; BeckOK InsO/*Weissinger* § 343 InsO, No. 7.
854. *R. Geimer/E. Geimer/Geimer,* Internationales Zivilprozessrecht.
855. *See* § 2.1; *R. Geimer/E. Geimer/Geimer,* Internationales Zivilprozessrecht, No. 33603360; *Graf,* Die Anerkennung ausländischer Insolvenzentscheidungen, pp. 270–271; *Wessels,* International Insolvency Law, p. 1.

The second requirement that the proceeding must be state administrated is provided directly by considerations of the legislator.[856] As stated, this does not require a court per se and could be presided over by a specially dedicated government body. Aside from the fact that the legislator mentions this as a requirement, this is also a common characteristic of insolvency that differentiates it from private debt enforcement. Finally, the proceeding needs to be collective, i.e., including all creditors and aimed at freeing the debtor of all debts.[857]

1.4.2 Unless the Court of Opening Is Not Competent under German Law

In case a foreign insolvency fulfils the two requirements discussed above and the primary requirement that the purpose of the proceeding is the collective satisfaction of creditors, the insolvency is to be recognised under § 343(1) InsO. This recognition can only be frustrated when one of the two exemptions applies. The first exemption is found in § 343(1)(1) InsO. It provides an exemption to recognition if the court giving the order is not competent under an analogous application of the German rules concerning competence. This test requires the fictional application of the German Insolvency Code to see if the courts in the relevant county would have had jurisdiction, the so-called mirror image principle.[858]

This test, importantly, does not stretch to test which specific court in the country is competent but is only a test of international competence; to test if the courts in the relevant country as a whole are competent under a fictive application of the German rules.[859] In conclusion, the actual test centres around whether the relevant party has its centre of main interests in the relevant country, *see* § 3(1)(2) InsO.[860]

1.4.3 Unless It Constitutes a Violation of Public Order or Constitutional Rights

The second exemption concerns the violation of public law or constitutional rights. Although the wording of this exemption seems broader and primarily focused on principles of German law, the exemption is fundamentally similar to the one mentioned in the EIR.[861] The German Federal Supreme Court has a restrictive view of the public order exemption for recognition of insolvencies. In the 2015 case, the German Federal

856. Entwurf eines Gesetzes zur Neuregelung des Internationalen Insolvenzrechts of 25.10.2002, BT-Drs. 15/16, p. 21.
857. BeckOK InsO/*Weissinger* § 343 InsO, Nos 7-8.
858. Braun/*Ehret* § 343 InsO; BeckOK InsO/*Weissinger* § 343 InsO, No. 10; *BGH*, NJW 1993, 1073, 1073, 1075.
859. Such as the fictive application of § 71(I) KO on a Swiss insolvency; *see*, *BGH*, NJW 1993, 2312, p. 2313; Cf. Braun/*Ehret* § 343 InsO, No. 9; *Graf*, Die Anerkennung ausländischer Insolvenzentscheidungen, p. 293; MüKoInsO/*Thole* § 343 InsO, Nos 26-27.
860. *Graf*, Die Anerkennung ausländischer Insolvenzentscheidungen, p. 293.
861. *Vorburger*, International Arbitration and Cross-Border Insolvency, p. 26; MüKoInsO/*Thole* § 343 InsO, No. 44; Cf. Entwurf einer Insolvenzordnung of 15.4.92, BT-Drs. 12/2443, p. 241.

Supreme Court put forward a high standard in the context of the exception in the EIR. To deny recognition, recognition must lead to:[862]

> Translation by author: Results which are manifestly incompatible with the public policy of the recognising state, in particular with the fundamental principles or the constitutionally guaranteed rights and freedoms of individuals.

Therefore, the public policy exception can only be applied if the:[863]

> Translation by author: result of the recognition or enforcement of the judgment given in another Member State would be contrary to an essential principle of law and would therefore be in unacceptable conflict with the legal order of the Member State of recognition or enforcement. This infringement must be a manifest breach of a rule of law considered to be essential in the legal order of the Member State of recognition or enforcement or of a right recognised as fundamental in that State.

The *ordre public* exemption is one of *ultima ratio* and requires a severe transgression against fundamental principles[864] and can only be applied in exceptional cases:[865]

> Translation by author: The public policy proviso of Art. 26 EuInsVO can therefore only be relevant in exceptional cases.

Even a violation of German *ordre public* does not necessarily lead to non-recognition as the court states that even in the event of fraud, if the creditors have remedies in the opening state, as in the case cited here, a German court will have to recognise the insolvency.[866]

The view that there needs to be a further local connection, e.g., a German party involved or German assets, for this exemption to be applicable is still partially represented.[867] However, this view should be rejected as the recognition itself presents the local connection, as the consequences of recognition have a legal effect in the German jurisdiction regardless of further practical connections.[868]

1.4.4 *Interim Conclusion: Recognition Based on the German Insolvency Code*

In this subsection, the recognition rules of the German Insolvency Code were examined. Recognition in the German autonomous insolvency law is relatively straightforward and open. Unlike many other jurisdictions, recognition in Germany is automatic. Optically the mechanism for recognition in the insolvency code resembles the recognition in the EIR. Upon further inspection, some differences emerge. These differences

862. *BGH*, NZI 2015, 93, No. 9.
863. *BGH*, NZI 2015, 93, No. 10.
864. *BGH*, NJW 1969, 369, p. 370.
865. *BGH*, NZI 2015, 93, No. 10.
866. *BGH*, NZI 2015, 93, Nos 27–29.
867. This view is represented in both case law and literature MüKoBGB/*Kindler* § 343 InsO, No. 17; Cf. *BGH*, NJW 1960, 189, p. 171; NJW 1973, 417, p. 419.
868. MüKoInsO/*Thole* § 343 InsO, No. 48.

stem primarily from the place, role and nature of recognition as organised in the insolvency code as opposed to its role in European legislation. The debate about the meaning and qualification of the term insolvency is a consequence of the international and autonomous context of this mechanism. Any difference in the understanding of *ordre public* between the two is also a consequence of this mechanism being rooted in German law instead of European regulation.

1.5 Recognition of Insolvency in Arbitration in General

In this subsection, recognition in arbitration will be discussed in general, while the following subsection will further specify this examination to Germany. The above discussion represents the recognition mechanisms as found in laws and regulations that courts are obliged to apply as part of their *lex fori*.[869] The courts and not arbitral tribunals are the addressees of these norms.[870] For this reason and the fact that tribunals are not bound to these rules of the *lex fori* as the rules to which the court is bound do not directly apply to the arbitral tribunal. Recognition by arbitral tribunals, if at all possible, presents its own problems and would necessarily have a different legal foundation than that of state courts due to arbitral tribunals being based on private law. Whereas the state courts are based upon public law,[871] the arbitration agreement is a contract that parties choose to effectuate within a chosen jurisdiction. The foundation for the binding of the tribunal to recognition or recognition rules can, therefore, be found in the basis for contracts and arbitration, i.e., the will of the parties. It is generally seen as the implicit will, c.q. interests, of the parties to have an award that will not be set aside and is enforceable to a certain extent.[872] Based on this, it is primarily the grounds for set-aside and enforcement, as the only provided sanctions, that could provide a ground for incorporation of recognition into the arbitral proceedings, i.e., violation of *ordre public* or mandatory law.[873]

It is argued that from the concept that arbitral tribunals have no true *lex fori*, the conclusion follows that one cannot identify an insolvency as foreign or domestic from the tribunal's perspective.[874] On the other hand, others argue in favour of viewing the seat jurisdiction as the 'home' jurisdiction of the arbitration. Previously, the relationship between the arbitration, the tribunal and the seat was discussed, *see* Chapter 2 § 2.1. As the seat jurisdiction is the legal order giving effect to the agreement to arbitrate, one could speak of home jurisdiction but not of *lex fori* as the tribunal is not a court. Thus, one can speak to a degree about home and foreign insolvencies but not within

869. *R. Geimer/E. Geimer/Geimer*, Internationales Zivilprozessrecht, No. 3364; *P.K. Wagner*, Abstimmungsfragen zwischen Internationalem Insolvenzrecht und Internationaler Schiedsgerichtsbarkeit, p. 45.
870. *Riedel*, Insolvenz in nationalen und internationalen Schiedsverfahren, p. 128.
871. *BGE, Fomento de Construcciones y Contratas S.A. v. Colon Container Terminal S.A.* of 14.5.2001 – BGE 127 III 279, 2(c)(aa).
872. For more on this *see* § 3.3.1 i.
873. *P.K. Wagner*, Abstimmungsfragen zwischen Internationalem Insolvenzrecht und Internationaler Schiedsgerichtsbarkeit, p. 105.
874. *Lévy*, Insolvency in Arbitration – Swiss Law, 87–106, p. 93.

the same legal meaning as used in a court. Beyond the semantics and theory of this discussion, the public policy and mandatory law of the seat jurisdiction in practice continue to play an important role, primarily for the court in annulment proceedings. Consequently, this distinction between 'domestic' and 'foreign' as seen from the perspective of the seat remains relevant.

Case law also makes a clear difference between insolvencies within the seat jurisdiction and those outside of said jurisdiction.[875] Insolvencies in the arbitral seat are often automatically taken into account or, in that sense, recognised, much like in court proceedings, often without any reasoning by the tribunal as to why they do so. The effect of insolvency is, in these cases, the main point of discussion.[876]

While it is legally questionable not to reason this recognition, failing to 'recognise' insolvency in the arbitral seat could severally endanger the award rendered, aside from the fact that ignoring the judicial decision in the seat opening insolvency would constitute a violation of *ordre public.*[877] Insolvency law or aspects thereof are often considered part of the state's public policy,[878] in particular, the principle of equality of creditors and the prohibition on individual enforcement linked to that equality.[879] Hence, ignoring the insolvency in the seat risks annulment under the adoption of Article 34(2)(b)(ii) Arb.ML or similar provisions in national laws, e.g., § 1059(2)(2)(b) ZPO.[880]

However, taking into account insolvencies from outside the seat of arbitration seems to be more problematic, especially insofar as the insolvency has not, or has not yet, been recognised in the seat jurisdiction.[881] This constellation produces fundamental questions. Primarily, the question arises if a tribunal has a need to recognise non-seat insolvencies and, second, if it has the ability to recognise such insolvencies independently. First, the less complicated issue of arbitration and recognised 'foreign' insolvencies will be further examined (§1.5.1) before turning to non-recognised 'foreign' insolvencies (§ 1.5.2).

1.5.1 Arbitration and Recognised 'Foreign' Insolvencies

The relation between arbitration and a recognised foreign insolvency provides fewer issues than if such recognition is lacking. This is further discussed in this paragraph.

875. *Final Award in ICC Case No. 7205*, Collection of ICC Awards III, 1997, 622–628; *Final Award in ICC Case No. 6057*, ICC International Court of Arbitration Bulletin III, 1994, 487–489; *Baizeau*, Arbitration and Insolvency: Issues of Applicable Law, pp. 97, 100, 103 referring to the unpublished award of; *Award in ICC Case No. 8133*, unpublished, 2000.
876. *Procedural Order in Procedural Order No. 14*, ASA Bull. 23, 2005, 108–115, p. 109; *Final Award in ICC Case No. 7205*, Collection of ICC Awards III, 1997, 622–628; *Mantilla-Serrano*, Arbitration International 11 (1995), 51, p. 56.
877. *Flöther*, Auswirkungen des inländischen Insolvenzverfahrens auf Schiedsverfahren und Schiedsabrede, p. 36.
878. *Baizeau*, Arbitration and Insolvency: Issues of Applicable Law, pp. 97, 100.
879. *Award in ICC Case No. 9163*, Collection of ICC Awards V, 2009, 703, p. 704.
880. France for example considers at least parts of its insolvency law as public policy *see Cour de Cassation*, 6.5.2009 – No. 08-10.281.
881. Cf. *Baizeau*, Arbitration and Insolvency: Issues of Applicable Law, pp. 97, 105–106.

Unlike under German law and the system of the EIR, the recognition of foreign insolvencies in most jurisdictions requires an application to the competent court.[882] Insofar as such recognition has been granted by court order or a similar act of public authority, the arguments for following such recognition are similar to that of domestic insolvencies. The act of recognition presents a domestic judicial decision extending the foreign legal effects into the domestic jurisdiction.[883] Ignoring this decision means risking a violation of *ordre public*.

Baizeau argues that an award ignoring the recognition of foreign insolvency can only lead to a violation of public policy or mandatory law if, upon recognition, the insolvency law of the seat or parts thereof become applicable to the insolvent party, i.e., new domestic effects originate in the decision to recognise. Otherwise, the award can only be challenged insofar as foreign international public policy provides a ground for annulment.[884] In most European jurisdictions, it is correct to say that it is not the recognition itself that provides the insolvency effects domestically, but the recognition merely provides that the foreign insolvency decision has effects in the jurisdiction.[885] This is different in, for example, jurisdictions that follow the UNCITRAL Model Law, *see* Article 20 Ins.ML and similarly in the US, *see* section 1520 United States Bankruptcy Code (USBC), where the recognition itself is provided with effects.[886]

Baizeau's view has to be followed at least partially. Generally, only the violation of the public policy or mandatory law of the seat state can be considered relevant in the context of setting-aside procedures. This leads to the conclusion that insofar as the act of recognition itself has no independent effects flowing from the law of the seat, which could constitute public policy, the tribunal could theoretically ignore the insolvency recognition.[887] Although, it could not actively deny the existence of the recognition as denying the recognition would be a direct contradiction of a judicial decision, which would most likely constitute a violation of *ordre public*.

There is, however, a caveat. Jurisdictions mostly tend to refer to the home jurisdiction of a foreign party for issues such as representation and legal personality. Consequently, ignoring the foreign insolvency effects on those issues would still

882. *Baizeau*, Arbitration and Insolvency: Issues of Applicable Law, pp. 97, 104.
883. *Gottwald*, Internationales Zivilprozessrecht, pp. 602–603; Cf. *Schönau*, Die Anerkennung von Urt.en aus Mehrrechtsstaaten nach § 328 Abs. 1 ZPO am Beispiel der USA und Kanadas, pp. 41–42.
884. *Baizeau*, Arbitration and Insolvency: Issues of Applicable Law, pp. 97–120.
885. *Graf*, Die Anerkennung ausländischer Insolvenzentscheidungen, 259 et seq; *P.K. Wagner*, Abstimmungsfragen zwischen Internationalem Insolvenzrecht und Internationaler Schiedsgerichtsbarkeit, p. 66.
886. *P.K. Wagner*, Abstimmungsfragen zwischen Internationalem Insolvenzrecht und Internationaler Schiedsgerichtsbarkeit, p. 67.
887. *See also Mantilla-Serrano*, Arbitration International 11 (1995), 51, p. 60; Wagner himself does not seem to make a difference between the effects of recognition and merely states that a tribunal could not safely ignore a recognition decision *P.K. Wagner*, Abstimmungsfragen zwischen Internationalem Insolvenzrecht und Internationaler Schiedsgerichtsbarkeit, p. 89.

constitute a ground for setting aside, when not on grounds of public policy, then on the ground of the violation of the right to be heard.[888]

A further caveat is that aside from the *ordre public* of the seat, the parties have an interest in not violating the *ordre public* of the state of likely enforcement, which is often the jurisdiction of the foreign insolvency, i.e., most likely the home state of one of the parties.[889]

1.5.2 Arbitration and Non-recognised 'Foreign' Insolvencies

In case there is no judicial act that recognises foreign insolvency, the question can be asked what need an arbitral tribunal has to recognise a foreign insolvency, c.q. take it into account. If it can be stated that this need exists (i), further questions arise. Primarily it should be asked then if the tribunal is capable of answering the question of recognition (ii), c.q. if it is arbitrable. Furthermore, the question arises as to which law it should apply to the question of the arbitrability of the recognition issue (iii). These questions are examined here.

i The Need for Recognition

Before asking how a tribunal might recognise a foreign insolvency, first, the need for that recognition must be examined. Recognition of foreign insolvencies in arbitration primarily plays a role as a preliminary question. It is a necessary preliminary question to the central question of the effects of insolvency on the case at hand. The tribunal is not bound to recognise foreign proceedings or even bound to apply the recognition mechanism directly since it lacks a proper *lex fori*. However, to answer questions about the potential application of mandatory stay provisions in the law of the seat, it needs to deal with the question of recognition as a preliminary question. More generally, recognition is often a preliminary question about the effect of a foreign insolvency in the seat jurisdiction, e.g., the effects on assets in a particular jurisdiction.[890] As such, in the deliberation of a claim that might or might not be encompassed in a foreign insolvency, recognition becomes an essential preliminary question.

Ignoring decisions opening foreign insolvency proceedings can lead to several grounds for annulment: violations of equal treatment, the right to be heard, and the *ordre public*.[891] Aside from the circumstances in which the cross-border insolvency

888. Cf. *Flöther*, Auswirkungen des inländischen Insolvenzverfahrens auf Schiedsverfahren und Schiedsabrede, 30 et seq; *P.K. Wagner*, Abstimmungsfragen zwischen Internationalem Insolvenzrecht und Internationaler Schiedsgerichtsbarkeit, p. 101.
889. More on the interest in enforceable awards in § 3.3.1 i. The home jurisdiction of party is generally a place of likely enforcement, cf. *Award in ICC Case No. 2879*, Collection of ICC Awards I, 1990, 346, pp. 350–351.
890. *P.K. Wagner*, Abstimmungsfragen zwischen Internationalem Insolvenzrecht und Internationaler Schiedsgerichtsbarkeit, p. 85.
891. *P.K. Wagner*, Abstimmungsfragen zwischen Internationalem Insolvenzrecht und Internationaler Schiedsgerichtsbarkeit, p. 101; Cf. *Flöther*, Auswirkungen des inländischen Insolvenzverfahrens auf Schiedsverfahren und Schiedsabrede, pp. 31–43.

regime is considered binding mandatory law or public policy, the main argument for applying a rule of recognition is the parties' interest in awards that can be enforced and cannot be annulled.[892]

Wagner and *Vorburger* both discuss the possible application of the doctrines of res judicata and *lis pendens* to constitute a necessity for recognition. Res judicata (Latin: an adjudicated matter) is the principle that a matter should not be adjudicated twice, whereas *lis pendens* (Latin: pending case) promulgates the principle that a case should not be heard insofar as it is already pending elsewhere. The questions as to their potential application in this context could be summarised as follows: Should the tribunal be held to recognise insolvency due to the fact that either a court has already decided upon it or the question is currently pending?[893] Whereas an arbitral tribunal would, insofar as it concerns a court in the seat jurisdiction, already be bound to respect the decisions or pending decisions, due to grounds of *ordre public*, the question remains to what extent it can be forced to recognise the foreign decision to open proceedings based on these doctrines.

It is debatable how res judicata and *lis pendens* apply in international arbitration.[894] For the tribunal to be bound to foreign decisions based on the principle of res judicata by way of the *ordre public* of the seat jurisdiction generally requires the decision to have been recognised or otherwise have effect in the seat jurisdiction.[895] The same goes for foreign awards.[896] Such requirements can be loosened, e.g., as stated in Swiss and American decisions, the tribunal can and should test itself if the decision is capable of recognition.[897] As such, the applicability of the principle of res judicata to the preliminary question of recognition would depend on prior recognition.[898] Consequently, the principle of res judicata could not form the basis of such recognition, as that would provide a circular reasoning. Even in those jurisdictions where the tribunal should independently verify if the award or decision could be recognised, res judicata can hardly be said to play an independent role.

Wagner and *Vorburger* dismiss the applicability of these principles because their goal does not cover providing a binding effect to a foreign decision opening insolvency in a way that would force their recognition in the arbitral proceedings. They argue

---

892. *See* § 3.3.1 i; *Vorburger*, International Arbitration and Cross-Border Insolvency, pp. 55–58; *P.K. Wagner*, Abstimmungsfragen zwischen Internationalem Insolvenzrecht und Internationaler Schiedsgerichtsbarkeit, p. 105.
893. *Vorburger*, International Arbitration and Cross-Border Insolvency, pp. 53–55; *P.K. Wagner*, Abstimmungsfragen zwischen Internationalem Insolvenzrecht und Internationaler Schiedsgerichtsbarkeit, pp. 93–98.
894. Born identifies a sui generis form of this principles, separate from those of national jurisdictions being developed in international arbitration; *Born*, International Commercial Arbitration, 3733 et seq.
895. *Award in ICC Case No. 5954*, Arbitration International (Article by Mantilla-Serrano) II, 1994, 58, p. 59; *Ly/Sheppard*, Arbitration International 25 (2009), 35, p. 51.
896. *Ly/Sheppard*, Arbitration International 25 (2009), 67, p. 73; *P.K. Wagner*, Abstimmungsfragen zwischen Internationalem Insolvenzrecht und Internationaler Schiedsgerichtsbarkeit, 98–97.
897. *BGE*, Urt. of 19.12.1997 – BGE 124 III 83, p. 86; *U.S. District Court for the Southern District of New York*, F. Supp. 1983, 367, p. 372; Cf. *P.K. Wagner*, Abstimmungsfragen zwischen Internationalem Insolvenzrecht und Internationaler Schiedsgerichtsbarkeit, 84, fn. 346.
898. *P.K. Wagner*, Abstimmungsfragen zwischen Internationalem Insolvenzrecht und Internationaler Schiedsgerichtsbarkeit, p. 97.

primarily that res judicata serves to prevent the relitigating of substantive claims and *lis pendens* serves to avoid contradicting decisions. However, a tribunal deciding upon recognition is not deciding upon substantive rights, nor does it contradict the foreign court in case of denial of recognition. In consequence, these principles cannot be used to force recognition.[899]

However, an argument against the applicability of these principles that is mostly similar to the one *Wagner* and *Vorburger* make can be stated simpler: The question the tribunal puts to itself when deciding upon recognition as a preliminary question is not the same as the question that the court that opened the insolvency proceedings asked itself. Whereas the opening court decided upon the substantive existence of the insolvency based on requirements of its own *lex fori*. The tribunal will be answering the question of recognition, which, as discussed above, is a question of procedural recognition, a question of the extension of the effect of the jurisdiction to a particular jurisdiction, based upon requirements for recognition and not for insolvency per se.

The non-applicability of *lis pendens* and res judicata arguments as described above does not change that a tribunal has a need to answer the question of recognition of whether this is a preliminary issue to key issues it needs to decide upon which are within its jurisdiction. A discussion on preliminary issues and the scope of the arbitration agreement can be found in Chapter 2 § 2.3.5.

Kraus argues that the step of recognition is unnecessary, even as a preliminary question, for a tribunal as, finally, considerations of annulment and enforcement will decide whether or not a tribunal will take into account specific insolvency rules.[900] It is indeed correct that a tribunal should, for example, consider a stay of proceedings if this is an *ordre public* rule in the insolvency jurisdiction, but the insolvency is not recognised in the seat jurisdiction. Nevertheless, it is incorrect to state that the recognition is consequently not to be considered. To answer, for example, if an asset in the seat jurisdiction can be disposed of, it must be established if it is part of the insolvency. To answer that question, the tribunal must look at the recognition rules of the seat jurisdiction as a preliminary question if it wants to give a legally sound answer. As if the insolvency is not recognised, it cannot be said to have an effect in the seat jurisdiction. Consequentially, even if recognition is not the only reason to consider foreign insolvency-specific rules in international arbitration, it remains a preliminary step in answering many legal questions that can be posed to a tribunal.

ii The Ability to Recognise Foreign Insolvencies: Arbitrability and Scope

Having established that a need for recognition by a tribunal exists, the question arises if the tribunal can answer the recognition, c.q. if this issue is arbitrable. The question regarding the tribunal's ability to recognise foreign insolvency proceedings is twofold.

899. *Lévy*, Insolvency in Arbitration – Swiss Law, 87–106, p. 101; *Vorburger*, International Arbitration and Cross-Border Insolvency, p. 55; *P.K. Wagner*, Abstimmungsfragen zwischen Internationalem Insolvenzrecht und Internationaler Schiedsgerichtsbarkeit, p. 97.
900. *Kraus*, Das Schicksal internationaler Schiedsverfahren in der Insolvenz des Schiedsbeklagten, pp. 205–206.

First, it is a question of objective arbitrability and second, a question of jurisdiction, c.q. can it be said that the arbitral tribunal has the authority under its arbitration agreement to answer questions of recognition?

The question as to the objective arbitrability of recognition is highly dependent on the seat jurisdiction and, insofar as they differ, the law applicable to the arbitration procedure.[901]

The arbitrability of insolvency issues has been discussed previously; *see* Chapter 2 §§ 1.4–1.5. However, not with specific regard for the issue of recognition.[902] It was considered before that issues for which the state has provided a specific and exclusive jurisdiction should be considered non-arbitrable.[903] Regarding insolvency issues, this was further specified with the concept of *vis attractiva concursus*, meaning that all such issues that were 'attracted' by the insolvency proceedings, i.e., issues that could only be decided upon by the insolvency court, are to be considered non-arbitrable.[904]

Based on these considerations, it can be concluded that, insofar as the relevant rules of recognition do not provide exclusive and absolute jurisdiction to a specific court, the question of recognition should be arbitrable.[905] Applying this consideration leads to the conclusion that the recognition of foreign insolvencies is arbitrable in countries such as Germany, France and England, where no exclusive jurisdiction is given to a specific court but not in, for example, the United States, *see* 11 U.S.C. § 1515 and countries applying the Ins.ML, *see* Article 4 Ins. ML.[906]

As discussed in the previous subsection, the German rules do not require a recognition decision from a specific court for an insolvency to be recognised. In such circumstances, the question of recognition could be considered generally arbitrable, in accordance with the considerations in Chapter 2 §§ 1.3, 1.5. However, another condition must be considered before reaching a conclusion on that point, the parties' ability to settle the issue amongst themselves.

First, parties would only rarely explicitly include the recognition of foreign insolvencies in the arbitration agreement, the terms of reference, or other documents that describe and limit the extent of the tribunal's substantive jurisdiction. The question arises if the tribunal would have the authority to decide upon recognition in such circumstances. Furthermore, as *Wagner* considers, recognition per se cannot be considered at the disposition of the parties even.[907] Recognition, in such a case of automatic recognition, is based on a legal rule and cannot legally be 'decided' by the parties *inter se*. As such, the parties cannot make recognition the object of proceedings as this must be considered non-arbitrable, *see* the discussion in Chapter 2 §§ 1.3–1.5, where the dispositive power of the parties plays a crucial role. However, it is generally

901. *Vorburger*, International Arbitration and Cross-Border Insolvency, p. 76.
902. *See* Chapter 2 § 1.4.
903. *See* Chapter 2 § 1.3; Musielak/Voit/*Voit* § 1030 ZPO, No. 2.
904. *See* Chapter 2 § 1.4.
905. *P.K. Wagner*, Abstimmungsfragen zwischen Internationalem Insolvenzrecht und Internationaler Schiedsgerichtsbarkeit, p. 89.
906. Cf. *Vorburger*, International Arbitration and Cross-Border Insolvency, p. 76.
907. *P.K. Wagner*, Abstimmungsfragen zwischen Internationalem Insolvenzrecht und Internationaler Schiedsgerichtsbarkeit, pp. 91–93.

and correctly considered that tribunals have the authority to answer the necessary preliminary questions to answer the questions they have been tasked with, *see* Chapter 2 § 2.3.5. Insofar as the recognition is a necessary preliminary question, it is both arbitrable and part of the implicit will and in the parties' interest to consider this within the tribunal's jurisdiction.[908]

In that same line, *Wagner* argues that answering the question of recognition as a preliminary question should be considered possible.[909] *Günter* seems to go a step further and argues that a tribunal can still consider insolvency even if a state court decision is necessary for formal recognition.[910] In his discussion, this concerns Switzerland. However, unlike what *Kraus* states,[911] *Günter*'s 'considering the insolvency' differs from using recognition as a preliminary question as *Wagner* proposes. *Günter* proposes that even if no formal recognition has taken place, one can still take insolvency into account to protect the enforceability of the award.[912] While *Günter* links this closely to enforceability in the seat jurisdiction, this is also particularly important in case non-consideration would result in the unenforceability of the award in the home jurisdiction of the insolvent. *Kraus,* who argues for taking into account foreign insolvency as a fact - without recognition - also mentions this as a significant consideration.[913] Consideration of the insolvency on other grounds such as enforceability neither negates the necessity of insolvency as a preliminary legal question nor does it affect the capability of the tribunal to answer this preliminary question.[914]

While recognition per se should not be deemed at the disposition of the parties, as *Wagner* also argues,[915] it can and must be answered as a preliminary question to answer any question that requires that could be affected by the recognition of the insolvency.

iii Applicable Law

After discussing the need for recognition and the capacity to recognise foreign insolvencies above, the question arises as to which law should be applied to the recognition.

As to which concepts of arbitrability are relevant and thus which law should be applied by the tribunal in the context of recognition, *Wagner* merely provides the options of the law of the procedure and the law of the seat, insofar as they differ. He

908. *R. Geimer/E. Geimer/Geimer,* Internationales Zivilprozessrecht, No. 3865.
909. *P.K. Wagner,* Abstimmungsfragen zwischen Internationalem Insolvenzrecht und Internationaler Schiedsgerichtsbarkeit, p. 89.
910. *Günter,* Internationale Schiedsgerichtsbarkeit und Insolvenz, pp. 117–118.
911. *Kraus,* Das Schicksal internationaler Schiedsverfahren in der Insolvenz des Schiedsbeklagten, p. 202.
912. *Günter,* Internationale Schiedsgerichtsbarkeit und Insolvenz, pp. 135–136.
913. *Kraus,* Das Schicksal internationaler Schiedsverfahren in der Insolvenz des Schiedsbeklagten, p. 206.
914. Differently *Kraus,* Das Schicksal internationaler Schiedsverfahren in der Insolvenz des Schiedsbeklagten, p. 206.
915. *P.K. Wagner,* Abstimmungsfragen zwischen Internationalem Insolvenzrecht und Internationaler Schiedsgerichtsbarkeit, pp. 91–93.

argues in favour of the law of the seat. *Vorburger* mentions the broader range of options that have been proposed in practice and literature, which add the law applicable to the arbitration agreement and the law applicable to the merits of the case to the discussion.[916]

Both *Wagner* and *Vorburger* prefer the application of the law of the seat, and there seems to be some agreement in the literature on this point.[917] The application of the law of the seat to the question of recognition is largely correct. For example, regarding the potential suspension of proceedings, the preliminary question should be if the insolvency is recognised according to the rules of the state where the suspension is to take place. For this reason, it is the recognition ruleset of the seat that must be looked to for preliminary questions for procedural issues. However, the critical point in that example remains that the primary question is about the effect of the insolvency on the arbitration proceedings and that such arbitration proceedings are localised in the seat. In conclusion, the question essentially asks after the effects of the foreign insolvency in the seat jurisdiction. The effects of the insolvency in the seat jurisdiction are intrinsically linked to the preliminary question of recognition in this jurisdiction, and that question can only be correctly answered by applying the recognition rules of that jurisdiction.

Authors arguing in favour of applying the recognition rules of the seat also mention several practical benefits that such an application has. Most importantly, in applying this law, the tribunal follows the *lex fori* of the court in which any potential set-aside procedure would have to be held and, in so doing, provides better insulation against annulment than the application of any other law.[918] Using the recognition rules of the seat jurisdiction would also provide a measure of predictability, which must be considered in the parties' interests,[919] as the parties choose the seat of arbitration, and the application of its law to these questions would be foreseeable.[920]

Whereas these arguments should be followed, the core argument presented above remains the most convincing: the law of the seat, c.q. the recognition system of the seat is the only logical option for the question as to the effect of the insolvency on arbitrations seated in the seat jurisdiction. Formulated more academically, extending the effects of a foreign insolvency to jurisdiction is a matter of sovereignty and must be referred to the rules promulgated therefor by the legitimate legislator. Extending on this logic, a different recognition system is more appropriate when discussing the effects of

916. *Vorburger,* International Arbitration and Cross-Border Insolvency, p. 77; Cf. *Mourre,* Arbitrage et droit de la faillite – Réflexions sur l'office du juge et de l'arbitre, 153, p. 166.
917. *Trunk,* Internationales Insolvenzrecht, p. 128; *Vorburger,* International Arbitration and Cross-Border Insolvency, p. 78; *P.K. Wagner,* Abstimmungsfragen zwischen Internationalem Insolvenzrecht und Internationaler Schiedsgerichtsbarkeit, p. 109; A similar conclusion but based on differing view of arbitration *Riedel,* Insolvenz in nationalen und internationalen Schiedsverfahren, pp. 129–130.
918. *Trunk,* Internationales Insolvenzrecht, p. 127; *Vorburger,* International Arbitration and Cross-Border Insolvency, p. 78; *P.K. Wagner,* Abstimmungsfragen zwischen Internationalem Insolvenzrecht und Internationaler Schiedsgerichtsbarkeit, p. 110.
919. *See* § 3.3.1 ii.
920. *Vorburger,* International Arbitration and Cross-Border Insolvency, p. 78; *P.K. Wagner,* Abstimmungsfragen zwischen Internationalem Insolvenzrecht und Internationaler Schiedsgerichtsbarkeit, p. 109.

insolvency on procedures and assets localised outside of the seat country. The main question in such circumstances is the effect of the insolvency on those procedures or assets, i.e., the effect of the insolvency in the jurisdiction where they are localised. Regardless of which material law governs these assets, the relevant preliminary question is if the insolvency has effect, i.e., is recognised, in the jurisdiction that governs these assets.[921]

Applying a 'foreign' recognition system to such assets and procedures can hardly pose a risk to the award in the context of setting-aside, as one is not asking questions regarding effects in the seat jurisdiction. Second, recognition following the rules of recognition of the seat jurisdiction generally has a territorial effect.[922] This means that the recognition of an insolvency in the seat jurisdiction has no direct intrinsic effect on assets and procedures outside of that jurisdiction.

However, applying the relevant foreign recognition rules will positively affect the enforceability of the award. When assets or procedures located in a different jurisdiction than the seat jurisdiction are the subject of arbitration, this jurisdiction is also a likely place of enforcement. Consequentially, applying the recognition system of this jurisdiction protects the enforceability of the award.[923] In conclusion, it is suggested here that the central question as to the applicable law to the preliminary question of recognition should be: Which jurisdiction exercises jurisdiction over the relevant asset or procedure? This rests on a similar sovereignty argument as described by Solomon regarding the application of applicable conflict-of-laws rules: recognition rules can only extend the effect of recognition to relevant sovereign territory, and thus the recognition rules of the relevant territory must be applied.[924] This is not to be confused with the law that materially governs such assets or procedures, which only apply because the jurisdiction wherein these are localised allows for the material applicability of foreign laws within its jurisdiction. Furthermore, for this purpose, arbitration procedures should be seen as tied to the jurisdiction of the seat.

As a result of globalisation and the information age, it is sometimes hard to pinpoint the location of assets and possibly even procedures. This can result in several jurisdictions operating different rules of localisation claiming jurisdiction over certain assets. Therefore, in the interest of the parties, the tribunal should first look at the seat and countries of likely enforcement to see if their rules regarding the locations of assets and procedures provide that the relevant procedure or asset is legally located in these jurisdictions or where else they consider it to be located. Otherwise, and in parallel, considering the effectiveness of the award, the tribunal should consider which court has the factual power to enforce against the relevant assets or authority to intervene in the procedure.

921. Not entirely dissimilar *Mourre*, Arbitrage et droit de la faillite – Réflexions sur l'office du juge et de l'arbitre, 153, p. 166.
922. MüKoInsO/*Thole* § 343 InsO, p. 67.
923. Wagner seem to leave room for such an argument *P.K. Wagner*, Abstimmungsfragen zwischen Internationalem Insolvenzrecht und Internationaler Schiedsgerichtsbarkeit, p. 110.
924. Cf. *Solomon*, Die Verbindlichkeit von Schiedssprüchen in der internationalen privaten Schiedsgerichtsbarkeit, p. 347.

iv *Analysis*

In the above subsection, recognition of insolvency in arbitration was discussed in a general context. The role of recognition in arbitration depends to an extent on the view of arbitration that one holds. For those who consider arbitration as a legal construct entirely disconnected from any national jurisdiction, the concept of recognition either does not exist, is irrelevant or must be built wholly autonomously, as all insolvencies and jurisdictions, in general, are equally foreign or domestic to the arbitration.

However, that is not the view represented here. Whereas a tribunal is not part of the judiciary or somehow exercises state authority, the arbitration agreement and awards have their effects provided to them by a legal order defined in national laws. Those national laws have universally sanctioned breaking their mandatory rules or the *ordre public* of their jurisdiction with the non-effectiveness of the contract's final product, i.e., the non-enforceability and annulment of the award, within the respective legal order. Insofar as recognition has already taken place in the jurisdiction, the tribunal can hardly directly defy such a recognition without violating *ordre public* and thereby jeopardising the effectiveness of the award.

The extent to which 'foreign' decisions opening insolvency play into arbitration will again depend largely on the effect on the effectiveness of the arbitration. To correctly investigate the legal questions it is faced with, the tribunal will have to answer the question of recognition as a preliminary question. Whether a tribunal can do so itself without violating the *ordre public* of the relevant jurisdiction or whether it has to wait for a court decision will depend on the law of the locale where the relevant effect is investigated.

It is important to note that even when not considering the recognition of the insolvency per se, the tribunal can consider the substantive recognition of many of the insolvency's effects without arbitrating the question of recognition. For example, by way of substantive recognition, it could find that the insolvency administrator is the correct representative of the party. This would not be a controversial conclusion as based on international private law rules, which the tribunal is free to apply, it is generally the law applicable to the party that regulates representation. *See, e.g.*, Article 7 EGBGB for natural persons and similar rules developed for legal persons in Germany that refer to the law of the seat of the company or the law of incorporation.[925]

1.6 Recognition of Insolvency by Tribunals in Germany

This subsection discusses the recognition of insolvency by tribunals in Germany. As many questions surrounding the issue of recognition of foreign insolvency proceedings depend on the seat of arbitration and the laws applicable to the arbitration, it remains interesting to see how recognition in arbitration would function in a specific jurisdiction. Therefore, in keeping with the orientation point of this research, recognition in an

925. *Schack*, Internationales Zivilverfahrensrecht, No. 598; there is a discussion in German doctrine between the seat theory and the incorporation theory. This discussion is, however, beyond the scope of this book.

arbitration seated in Germany is discussed below. Recognition of foreign insolvency in Germany is divided into two sets of rules: those of the InsO (§ 1.6.1) and those of the EIR (§ 1.6.2). These rules in the context of arbitration are discussed separately below.

1.6.1 Recognition in the Context of the InsO

This paragraph discusses the recognition of a foreign insolvency based on the InsO in an arbitration. Most of the relevant theoretical discussion has been represented above. Ignoring German insolvency in a Germany-seated arbitration would lead to a violation of *ordre public*.[926] *Kröll* states that § 343 InsO, recognition of foreign insolvencies, is also 'relevant' to arbitral tribunals.[927] This is incorrect insofar as this is meant as an argument for direct application. § 343 InsO does not apply directly to arbitration, c.q. arbitral tribunals, as it is not part of the German *lex arbitri*. However, *Kröll*'s avoidance of the word 'applicable' is likely on purpose. He refers to the rule as 'relevant', which should be understood as referring to the indirect effect of § 343 InsO in arbitration.

Although there is a debate in German literature, Article 20(3) GG, the article that binds courts to apply German law and abide by the German legal order, does not apply to arbitral tribunals.[928] This is due to the nature of arbitration, as discussed above, i.e., the tribunal does not perform acts derived from state authority or have a position somehow analogous to a court.[929] Therefore, § 343 InsO could not directly apply to arbitral tribunals.

A decision by the OLG Hamburg of 11 November 1983 concerning the enforcement of an ICC award in Germany, which is often cited to support statements that § 343 InsO is relevant for tribunals, is actually ambiguous on this point.[930] The claimant argued that she had not been represented adequately in the special administrative proceedings that were opened for which a 'state comptroller' had been assigned to the claimant. In this context, the role and recognition of these special administrative proceedings became relevant to the case's outcome. As stated, however, the ruling is not unambiguous on the point of recognition of an insolvency in arbitration. The court does not even use a phrasing close to 'recognition of insolvency'. The relevant German phrasing translates roughly to 'having regard for the insolvency'.[931] There is indeed a suggestion that the court applies the requirements of § 343 InsO, c.q. the equivalent thereof under the then applicable law and concludes that these are not met. The court, in this sense, states that the Italian administration proceeding does not have the goal of satisfying creditors but of securing jobs.[932]

926. *Flöther*, Auswirkungen des inländischen Insolvenzverfahrens auf Schiedsverfahren und Schiedsabrede, p. 36; *Trunk*, Internationales Insolvenzrecht, p. 127.
927. *S.M. Kröll*, Part IV: Selected Areas and Issues of Arbitration in Germany, Insolvency and Arbitration – Effects of Party Insolvency on Arbitral Proceedings in Germany, 981, p. 986.
928. *P.K. Wagner*, Disp. Resol. Int'l 3 (2009), 56, p. 62.
929. *See* § 4 and §§ 2.1 and 2.1.
930. *OLG Hamburg*, IPrax 1985, 218–219.
931. German: [...] *zu berücksichtigten seien* [...] (p. 6).
932. *OLG Hamburg*, IPrax 1985, 218–219 pp. 5–6 of the decision available online at newyorkconvention1958.org.

The court explicitly states that even if one follows the view that the Italian administration rules had to be considered by German courts, this would not mean that non-consideration by the tribunal would automatically violate German *ordre public.*[933] As such, this case would rather imply that § 343 InsO itself is not the relevant test for the tribunal and that instead, the test should be if ignoring the insolvency would lead to independent violations of German *ordre public.*[934] Consequently, recognition itself is not an obligatory test for the tribunal. However, it remains a necessary test for the investigation of the effects of insolvency within the German jurisdiction.[935] Accordingly, the test of § 343 InsO remains relevant as a preliminary question and for the application of German *ordre public.* Ignoring a foreign insolvency, which is unequivocally recognisable in Germany, can easily violate the German *ordre public*, e.g., the equality of creditors. However, since § 352 InsO, the suspension of proceedings is not found to apply to arbitration directly, the relevance of recognition as a preliminary question regarding suspension is diminished.[936]

As a final remark on this subject, it is good to mention an observation by *Trunk,* which has sometimes been restated in German literature in a way that would suggest that it was meant as a rule.[937] The observation states that a tribunal seated in Germany, applying German conflict-of-laws rules and German procedural law, will have to apply § 343 InsO, similar to the courts.[938] However, this is merely an example as, as will be discussed later, the tribunal is not directly forced to apply either German conflict-of-laws rules or procedural law.[939] For that reason, this conclusion is only correct insofar as the tribunal finds that it must apply German conflict-of-laws rules and German procedural law, which is certainly not given merely by the fact that the tribunal is seated in Germany.[940]

1.6.2 Recognition in the Context of the EIR

In arbitrations seated in Germany, or generally in the EU, confronted with insolvency elsewhere in the EU, it will not be the considerations of § 343 InsO that form the centre of recognition considerations but those of the EIR.

However, the arbitral tribunal is not directly bound to apply the EIR. The addressees of the EIR are national courts. The primary consideration for tribunals concerning recognition and the cross-border insolvency rules, in general, is that of enforceability and avoiding grounds for annulment. This leads to the conclusion that

933. *OLG Hamburg*, IPrax 1985, 218–219, p. 6.
934. *Nacimiento/Bähr*, NJOZ 2009, 4752, p. 4761; of a different opinion are previously cited authors such as Schmitz and Riedel, primarily due to different views on the role of arbitration within the seat jurisdiction *Schmitz*, Schiedsverfahren und Insolvenz, pp. 211–212.
935. MüKoInsO/*Reinhart* Vorbermerkungen vor §§ 335 ff. InsO, No. 27.
936. See § 2.3.1 in particular 'ii' thereof; *Nacimiento/Bähr*, NJOZ 2009, 4752, p. 4761.
937. *Vorburger*, International Arbitration and Cross-Border Insolvency, p. 50.
938. *Riedel*, Insolvenz in nationalen und internationalen Schiedsverfahren, p. 133; *Trunk*, Internationales Insolvenzrecht, p. 127.
939. *See* § 3.
940. *See* §§ 3 and 4; *P.K. Wagner*, Abstimmungsfragen zwischen Internationalem Insolvenzrecht und Internationaler Schiedsgerichtsbarkeit, 75–76, 85.

the question as to the relevance of the EIR is that of the extent to which its non-application could lead to the non-enforceability or annulment of the award.[941]

The CJEU has confirmed in standing case law since the *Nordsee* case, e.g., the 1999 *Eco Swiss* case, that an arbitral tribunal based on a private contract is not a court of a Member State.[942] In the *Nordsee* case, the Hanseatic Higher Regional Court Bremen had referred this question to the CJEU concerning an arbitrator appointed by the Bremen Chamber of Commerce. The CJEU links its reasoning clearly to the voluntary nature of arbitration, in the sense that, without a contract, no one is obligated to arbitrate:[943]

> 10. It is true, as the arbitrator noted in his question, that there are certain similarities between the activities of the arbitration tribunal in question and those of an ordinary court Or tribunal inasmuch as the arbitration is provided for within the framework of the law, the arbitrator must decide according to law and his award has, as between the parties, the force of res judicata, and may be enforceable if leave to issue execution is obtained. However, those characteristics are not sufficient to give the arbitrator the status of a 'court or tribunal of a member state' within the meaning of Article 177 of the Treaty.
> 11. *The first important point to note is that when the contract was entered into In 1973 the parties were free to leave their disputes to be resolved by the ordinary courts or to opt for arbitration by inserting a clause to that effect in the contract. From the facts of the case it appears that the parties were under no obligation, whether in law or in fact, to refer their disputes to arbitration.*
> 12. *The second point to be noted is that the German public authorities are not involved in the decision to opt for arbitration nor are they called upon to intervene automatically in the proceedings before the arbitrator. The Federal Republic of Germany, as a Member State of the Community responsible for the performance of obligations arising from Community law within its territory pursuant to Article 5 and Articles 169 to 171 of the Treaty, has not entrusted or left to private individuals the duty of ensuring that such obligations are complied with in the sphere in question in this case.*
> 13. It follows from these considerations that the link between the arbitration procedure in this instance and the organization of legal remedies through the courts in the Member State in question is not sufficiently close for the arbitrator to be considered as a 'court or tribunal of a member state' within the meaning of Article 177. [Emphasis added]

A similar conclusion was reached regarding investment-treaty-based tribunals in the *Achmea* case.[944] Accordingly, tribunals are not bound to the EIR directly. However,

941. *Nacimiento/Bähr*, NJOZ 2009, 4752, p. 4759.
942. *CJEU*, EuZW 2005, 319, No. 13; Judgment of 1.6.1999 – C-126/97, No. 34; EuR 1982, 334–344, Nos 10–13.
943. *CJEU*, EuR 1982, 334–344, Nos 10–13.
944. *CJEU*, EuZW 2018, 239, No. 49 the Achmea case is, however, more famous for concluding that intra-EU BITs and consequently arbitration based thereon, are in opposition to EU law; *see* for Achmea's consequences for multilateral treaties, specifically the European Energy Charter Treaty (ECT) *Award in ICSID Case No. ARB/14/1* where the tribunal concludes that the Achmea's decision has no consequences for the ECT. The European commission, however, seems to be of a different opinion; Commission provides guidance on protection of cross-border EU investments – Questions and Answers.

private arbitration, as opposed to the bilateral investment treaty (BIT)-based arbitration in the *Achmea* case, can, by way of court aid, gain access to the right to ask the CJEU preliminary questions. This was the crucial point in *Nordsee* and *Achmea* and will at the latest be confronted by the EIR when court set-aside procedures or enforcement proceedings will apply them as *ordre public*, insofar as it is to be considered *ordre public*.[945]

This question has become more relevant in the last few years. Partially due to the famous, or perhaps infamous, *Syska v. Vivendi* cases, the debate on the relationship between community law, national law and *ordre public* has been further highlighted.[946] However, long before these cases, the CJEU, in the *Eco Swiss* case, decided that, based on Article 81 Treaty Establishing the European Community (ECT), European competition law is part of the fundamental *ordre public* of the European Union and the Member States, i.e., *ordre public communautaire*. Furthermore, it decided that violation of these rules should lead to the annulment of an award.[947] In that case, the Court explicitly considers that the correct application of Article 81 ECT falls within the narrow grounds that a court can consider when confronted with a set-aside proceeding.[948] In this manner, rechecking comprehensively if the EU competition law rules have been applied correctly does not constitute *révision au fond* or the full review of the award that is generally prohibited in set-aside and enforcement proceedings.

The reasoning of the court is mainly based on the fact that Article 81 ECT is to be considered a rule that is fundamental to achieving the EU's tasks, in particular, the proper functioning of the internal market.[949] However, applying this test to the EIR does not necessarily lead to a clear answer.

A contra argument to the EIR passing this test is that European competition law constitutes rules of material law, and the EIR does not primarily provide material rules as it is mainly a procedural regulation with many conflict-of-laws rules.[950] However, this is not a disqualifying argument as, first of all, the EIR does have some material norms and second, safeguarding the EU goal of cross-border insolvency coordination

945. *CJEU*, EuR 1982, 334–344, No. 14; *P.K. Wagner*, Abstimmungsfragen zwischen Internationalem Insolvenzrecht und Internationaler Schiedsgerichtsbarkeit, p. 114.
946. *England and Wales Court of Appeal*, IILR 2010, 39–46; *see also Commercial Court*, Judgment of 2.10.2008 - EWHC 2155 (Comm), Nos 18–19.
947. CJEU, Judgment of 1.6.1999 - C-126/97, Nos 35–37 It has been confirmed in several jurisdictions by National courts that EU competition law is considered ordre public; Cour de Cassation, Arrêt of 4.6.2008 - 06-15.320 (Arrêt n° 680); OLG Thüringen, Beschluss of 8.8.2007 - 4 Sch 03/06; Gerechtshof Den Haag, 24.3.2005 - 04/694 and 04/695; Cf. *Baizeau*, Arbitration and Insolvency: Issues of Applicable Law, pp. 97, 108 fn. 48; Gaillard, NYJL 237 (2007), s.l; *P.K. Wagner*, Abstimmungsfragen zwischen Internationalem Insolvenzrecht und Internationaler Schiedsgerichtsbarkeit, p. 62; Award in ICC Case No. 4604, Collection of ICC Awards I, 1990, 546, p. 552; Award in ICC Case No. 2811, Collection of ICC Awards I, 1990, 341, 342–343, 345; The concept has also been applied in arbitration, even before the Eco Swiss judgment, see Award in ICC Case No. 1397, Collection of ICC Awards I, 1990, 179, pp. 180–183.
948. *CJEU*, Judgment of 1.6.1999 - C-126/97, Nos 35–37.
949. *CJEU*, Judgment of 1.6.1999 - C-126/97, No. 36.
950. *Baizeau*, Arbitration and Insolvency: Issues of Applicable Law, pp. 97, 108 fn. 48; *Vorburger*, International Arbitration and Cross-Border Insolvency, p. 56 fn. 155; *P.K. Wagner*, Abstimmungsfragen zwischen Internationalem Insolvenzrecht und Internationaler Schiedsgerichtsbarkeit, p. 118.

requires both material and procedural rules. Thus, the material or procedural nature of the rules is not a consideration under the *Eco Swiss* test.[951]

The *Eco Swiss* test remains primarily that a rule must be vital to achieving the EU's task, especially a functioning internal market. The EIR considers in preamble No. 3 that the EIR is a concretisation of Article 81 TFEU on judicial cooperation and is necessary for the proper functioning of the internal market.[952] The judgment by Justice *Clarke* in *Syska v. Vivendi* shows a similar consideration before applying the EIR wholesale to arbitration: 'Preambles (2) and (4) show that the Regulation is designed to promote the proper functioning of the European internal market by ensuring that cross-border insolvency proceedings operate efficiently [...].'[953]

Such a blanket application of the *ordre public* exception may be considered undesirable by some. However, on the basis of the *Eco Swiss* test and the considerations that the European legislator made in the preambles of the EIR, the conclusion that the EIR constitutes European public policy is legitimated. The only issue that remains under the *Eco Swiss* test that could undermine this conclusion is the question if Article 81 TFEU constitutes an essential rule in the context of accomplishing the tasks of the community and, in particular, the functioning of the European internal market, as the CJEU in *Eco Swiss* stated Article 81 ECT was.[954] Justice *Clarke* considered that all the rules in the EIR are aimed at attaining its objectives, which is the proper functioning of the internal market by ensuring efficient and effective cross-border insolvency.[955] He does not first link these rules to Article 81 TFEU or rather implicitly states that Article 81 TFEU is intrinsically part of the functioning of the internal market, as one can gather from the quote provided above.[956] Even if one would insist on first expressly linking the EIR to Article 81 TFEU and this rule again to the proper functioning of the internal market, the EIR is essential in preventing contradictory decisions within the EU, coordinating insolvency proceedings and the implementation of Article 81 TFEU in general, which is itself again necessary for a functioning internal market.

Before *Syska v. Vivendi*, *Wagner* already concluded that it could not be excluded that the EIR in its entirety must be considered European public policy or that at least the regulation of the recognition mechanism should be considered as such.[957] Although it will be up to the CJEU to finally decide upon this question if and when it is put before it, here it is argued that even beyond the rules of recognition, the EIR, in general, should be considered *ordre public,* as all the rules are indeed necessary to achieve the goals of the EIR.[958]

951. *P.K. Wagner,* Abstimmungsfragen zwischen Internationalem Insolvenzrecht und Internationaler Schiedsgerichtsbarkeit, p. 118.
952. This is Art. 65 ECT as reflected in the old EIR; Council Regulation (EC) No 1346/2000 on insolvency proceedings of 29.5.2000, Official Journal of the European Communities L 160 preamble 2; *Wessels,* International Insolvency Law Part II: European Insolvency Law, p. 16.
953. *Commercial Court,* Judgment of 2.10.2008 - EWHC 2155 (Comm), 1, 18.
954. *CJEU,* Judgment of 1.6.1999 - C-126/97, No. 36 preamble 3.
955. *Commercial Court,* Judgment of 2.10.2008 - EWHC 2155 (Comm), No. 19.
956. *Commercial Court,* Judgment of 2.10.2008 - EWHC 2155 (Comm), No. 19.
957. *P.K. Wagner,* Abstimmungsfragen zwischen Internationalem Insolvenzrecht und Internationaler Schiedsgerichtsbarkeit, pp. 119–120.
958. *Commercial Court,* Judgment of 2.10.2008 - EWHC 2155 (Comm), No. 19.

On the point of arbitrability of the recognition under the EIR, Article 19 EIR, previously 16 EIR, does not create an exclusive authority for a specific court. In fact, recognition is automatic and primarily incidental. As discussed in Chapter 2 §§ 1, 1.5, exclusive jurisdiction is a primary indication of arbitrability. In consequence, a tribunal similar to any court is capable of incidentally recognising insolvencies under this mechanism.[959] Accordingly, EU-seated tribunals can recognise EU insolvencies and will have to follow the rules of the EIR, as set out above.[960]

1.7 Conclusion on the Recognition of Insolvencies in Arbitration

In this section, the recognition of insolvency was discussed in the context of international arbitration. Recognition of insolvency proceedings primarily plays a role in arbitration as a preliminary question to answer other issues in arbitration. Accordingly, applying the rules of recognition in arbitration should primarily be considered necessary insofar as it is necessary to answer legal questions correctly and secure the parties' interest in enforceable and non-annullable awards.

When no exclusive jurisdiction has been provided to courts regarding the question of recognition of foreign insolvency proceedings, this issue can be considered arbitrable. The law applicable to the question of recognition primarily depends on where the potential effects being discussed are localised, i.e., the procedure or assets to be affected by the recognition and associated insolvency. This is because this question necessitates the question of the effects of insolvency in that locale.

Recognition rules become a more prominent part of arbitration insofar as they are to be considered of an *ordre public* nature. Within the context of European legislation, as discussed in this section, the recognition rules of the EIR should be considered to pass the *Eco Swiss* test and, consequently, should be considered as European *ordre public*. In this context, the recognition rules become even more directly relevant to the discussion on annulment and enforcement and should generally be applied by the arbitral tribunal to protect the award from annulment and non-enforcement.

2 CONFLICT-OF-LAWS AND APPLICABLE LAW IN THE COURTS

The second section of Chapter 3 concerns the conflict of laws and applicable law in the courts. This is primarily a preliminary discussion to the discussion of the applicability and application of such rules by arbitral tribunals.

Recognition is only the first issue in discovering the effects of insolvency on arbitration. In the second part of this book, it was discussed the effects of insolvency on arbitration under German domestic law. In an international context, another preliminary question needs to be asked before such effects can be investigated. This is the question of applicable law. Investigation of the applicable law in an international

959. *P.K. Wagner*, Disp. Resol. Int'l 3 (2009), 56, p. 61.
960. *See* Chapter 2 § 1.3.

context typically features the application of conflict-of-laws rules, rules which determine which law applies to specific issues, in case more such laws could theoretically and practically be applicable.

In the context of conflict-of-law rules, courts are bound to apply their *lex fori*. The German courts, for example, are bound to that via Article 20(3) GG. For courts, the question as to which specific conflict-of-laws system applies is one of qualification. This means that they must qualify the issue put before them and find the appropriate conflict-of-laws rules within the body of law they are bound to apply.[961]

The most relevant conflict-of-laws rules in the context of insolvency in arbitration will be those regulating cross-border insolvency. In Germany, these can be found in the EIR (§ 2.1) or for extra-EU insolvencies in the German autonomous international insolvency law as found in the insolvency code (§ 2.2).[962] As is the nature of such rules, they only point towards the law that needs to be applied to the relevant question and will generally not provide substantive rules.[963] They will point out, for example, which law applies to contracts related to immovable assets, *see* Article 11 EIR or § 349 InsO.

2.1 The EIR

The EIR has come up at several points in this book, particularly in the previous section on recognition.[964] Aside from recognition, the second primary function of the EIR is to provide a coherent conflict-of-laws system in intra-EU insolvencies. This system is discussed here and divided into a general examination of the conflict-of-laws rules (§ 2.1.1), a short reference to coordinating and material norms (§ 2.1.2) before discussing the most relevant conflict-of-laws rules in EIR in the context of ascertaining the effects of insolvency on arbitration and the arbitration agreement (§ 2.1.3).

2.1.1 Conflict-of-Laws Rules

The conflict-of-laws system of the EIR replaces that of the autonomous international insolvency laws of the Member States within the scope of the EIR's application, i.e., intra-EU insolvencies.[965] In consequence, the autonomous international insolvency laws of the Member States are limited in their scope of application to what is referred to as third-state insolvencies, meaning insolvencies involving a non-Member State. The German autonomous international insolvency law is discussed in the following subsection.

In general, the recognition discussed in the previous section would lead to the extension of the effects of the insolvency, as postulated in the *lex fori concursus*, to the

961. *Schultze-Moderow*, Schiedsverfahren und Insolvenz, pp. 100–101; *P.K. Wagner*, Abstimmungsfragen zwischen Internationalem Insolvenzrecht und Internationaler Schiedsgerichtsbarkeit, p. 133.
962. Cf. *Mincke*, § 45 Internationales Insolvenzrecht, 1371, No. 10.
963. *Mincke*, § 45 Internationales Insolvenzrecht, 1371, No. 1.
964. *See* §§ 1.2.1, 1.3.
965. Regulation (EU) 2015/848 on insolvency proceedings of 20.5.2015, OJ L 141/19 preamble 66; *Pfeiffer*, Insolvenzeröffnung und internationale Schiedsverfahren, 821, p. 823.

jurisdiction of the recognising state, *see* Article 20 EIR. The conflict-of-laws system of the EIR is found in Articles 7 through 18 EIR. The standard position as found in Article 20 of the EIR is restated in Article 7(1) EIR: the applicability of the *lex fori concursus* to any question regarding the insolvency proceeding or its effects.[966] The rest of the previously mentioned articles provide exceptions to this standard rule. Article 7(1) EIR is a bit broader than Article 20 EIR and provides for the standard position in the secondary proceedings or local proceedings of Article 3(2) EIR as well, which, in Article 20 EIR is merely mentioned as an exception.[967]

The interpretation of this standard rule is not without its issues. The jurisdictions of the EU do not have a uniform interpretation of the 'the insolvency proceedings and its effects' as any jurisdiction in principle is free to determine the reach, goals and nature of insolvency proceedings and their effect. In consequence, the interpretation of the wording Article 7(1) EIR necessarily requires an autonomous interpretation to safeguard the uniform application of the EIR.[968]

In this sense, Article 7(1) EIR presents a qualification problem, where the question is essentially: What is to be defined as an insolvency-related norm?[969] There is currently no conclusive guidance from the CJEU. However, commentators tend to favour a restrictive approach.[970]

The EIR presents a basic framework for what is intended to fall within this qualification and hence the area of application of the *lex fori concursus*. The non-exclusive list in the second subclause of Article 7 EIR is the clearest one. Article 7(2) EIR lists issues to which the *lex fori concursus* will apply. Furthermore, Article 7(2) EIR's main clause states plainly that at least the opening, closing and procedure of the insolvency proceedings are covered by the reference to the *lex fori concursus*. As such, the requirements for the opening of the proceedings are also a matter of *lex fori concursus*,[971] notwithstanding the broad requirements the EIR imposes on the opening of proceedings to be recognised as insolvency proceedings as discussed above in Chapter 3 § 1.3.[972]

The exemptions listed in Articles 8–18 EIR provide for a further negative concretisation of the norm in Article 7 EIR. The exemptions hold a striking similarity to the German autonomous international insolvency law,[973] to be described in the following subsection. Similarly, the general rule of Article 7 EIR is strikingly similar to § 335 InsO.[974] This similarity is far from coincidental as the German legislator

966. BeckOK InsO/*Mock* Art. 7 EuInsVO, No. 4; Paulus/*Paulus* Art. 7 EuInsVO, No. 1; Braun/*Tashiro* Art. 7 EuInsVO, No. 1.
967. Mankowski/Müller/J. Schmidt, EuInsVO 2015/*M. Müller* Art. 7 EuInsVO, No. 7 *see* for a full discussion Rn. 3-48.
968. *CJEU*, Judgment of 20.10.2011 - C-396/09, No. 42; Judgment of 29.10.2009 - C-174/08, No. 24; BeckOK InsO/*Mock* Art. 7 EuInsVO, Nos 5, 7; Paulus/*Paulus* Art. 7 EuInsVO, Nos 3–6.
969. Braun/*Tashiro* Art. 7 EuInsVO, No. 9.
970. BeckOK InsO/*Mock* Art. 7 EuInsVO, No. 20; *Schultze-Moderow*, Schiedsverfahren und Insolvenz, p. 75.
971. Mankowski/Müller/J. Schmidt, EuInsVO 2015/*M. Müller* Art. 7 EuInsVO, No. 8.
972. *See* § 1.3.
973. *Schultze-Moderow*, Schiedsverfahren und Insolvenz, p. 75.
974. Braun/*Tashiro* Art. 7 EuInsVO, No. 5.

deliberately waited for the promulgation of the European regulation on the topic before finalising their own new autonomous international insolvency law.[975] Below, we will discuss these exceptions and the law the EIR applies to the issues incorporated therein.

Article 8 EIR excludes rights in rem from the general rule, i.e., rights associated with a property as opposed to rights in personam, i.e., rights associated with a person or relationship. Property here must be understood broadly, as the article lists tangible, intangible, movable and immovable assets.[976] In consequence, issues such as usufruct, which is covered by Article 8(2)(d) EIR, will be governed by the law of the jurisdiction where the associated property is located, i.e., the *lex rei sitae*.

Article 9 EIR protects rights to set-off insofar as they were permissible under the law applicable to the insolvent's claim. A similar provision is found in § 338 InsO. The relationship of Article 9 EIR to Article 7(2)(4) EIR, which states the applicability of the *lex fori concursus* to set-offs, is from a certain perspective comparable to the principle of *in favorem validitatis*.[977] This is normally a principle of contract law, which provides that the law that validates the contract applies. In this case, Article 7(2)(4) EIR states that the *lex for concursus* applies, and Article 9 EIR provides that if the *lex fori concursus* invalidates the set-off but it remains valid under the law applicable to the relevant claim, it is the former law that applies.[978]

Article 10 EIR enshrines the protection of reservations of titles. In essence, Articles 8 through 18 of the EIR are meant to protect legitimate expectations and reliance in countries other than the opening state.[979] Article 10 EIR is primarily a supplement to Article 8 EIR and provides extra protection for reservations of titles, insofar as Article 8 EIR does not cover such rights.[980]

Article 11 EIR protects not fully performed contracts regarding immovable objects and prescribes for them, in parallel with Article 8 EIR regarding property-related rights in general, the applicability of the *lex rei sitae*. In doing so, Article 11 EIR supplements Article 8 to ensure that all property-related rights, including those stemming from existing contracts relating to immovable objects, are excluded from the standard rule of Article 7(1) EIR.[981] Article 14 EIR, although similar, takes the perspective of the debtor and, in parallel to the above, states that his rights relating to the register-bound property are regulated by the law of the registry-keeping country.[982] Therefore, this can be seen as a reference to the *lex rei sitae*, in the sense that it references the law of the legal domicile of the good, although perhaps not the actual domicile of the goods. For example, ships and planes can and often are naturally factually somewhere else than the country of registry.

975. *Mincke*, § 45 Internationales Insolvenzrecht, 1371, No. 10.
976. BeckOK InsO/*Mock* Art. 8 EuInsVO, No. 8; Paulus/*Paulus* Art. 8 EuInsVO, No. 3.
977. Cf. Paulus/*Paulus* Art. 9 EuInsVO, No. 5.
978. BeckOK InsO/*Mock* Art. 9 EuInsVO, No. 1; *Schultze-Moderow*, Schiedsverfahren und Insolvenz, pp. 76–77.
979. Paulus/*Paulus* Art. 10 EuInsVO, No. 1.
980. Mankowski/Müller/J. Schmidt, EuInsVO 2015/*J. Schmidt* Art. 10 EuInsVO, No. 3; *Wessels*, International Insolvency Law, No. 1067110671.
981. Paulus/*Paulus* Art. 11 EuInsVO, No. 3.
982. Mankowski/Müller/J. Schmidt, EuInsVO 2015/*Mankowski* Art. 14 EuInsVO, No. 13; Paulus/*Paulus* Art. 14 EuInsVO, No. 2.

Article 12 EIR, in recognition of the extreme complexity of financial markets and similar systems,[983] provides an exemption and applies the law that already applies to such markets to the rights and duties related to such markets,[984] also referred to as the *lex systema* or law of the system.[985]

Furthermore, Article 13(1) EIR makes an exception for labour contracts, subjecting them to the governing contract law, i.e., the *lex causae* or *lex contractus*.[986] Often this will be the country where the actual job is situated. *See* Article 8 Rome-I Regulation, i.e., the *lex loci laboris*.[987] Article 15 EIR refers to EU-wide rights, e.g., EU intellectual property rights, to incorporation in the main proceedings. This rule is necessary as it could be debated where these rights should be localised.[988] Article 16 EIR essentially states that insofar as an act to the detriment of the creditors does not lead to a claim or *actio Pauliana* under the *lex causae*, it is excluded from the general application of the *lex fori concursus*.[989] This means that a detrimental act must be challengeable under both the *lex causae* and the *lex fori concursus* if the insolvency administrator aims to challenge the act successfully. Article 17 EIR, providing further good faith protections, subjects the concept of the third-party receiver in good faith of immovable property, registered ships, planes and registered securities to the *lex rei sitae* or country of registry.[990]

2.1.2 Coordination and Material Norms

Aside from the conflict-of-laws norms, the EIR also contains norms that are focused on the coordination between proceedings and some simple material norms, e.g., the establishment of insolvency registers in Article 24 EIR. These norms can mostly be found in Articles 21 et seq. EIR and in particular in Articles 34–52 on secondary insolvency proceedings but also, for example, in Articles 56–77 EIR on the insolvency of multiple group companies. These provisions are not directly relevant to this discussion of insolvency in international commercial arbitration and will not be further discussed here.

2.1.3 The EIR and the Applicable Law to Insolvencies Effects on Arbitration and Related Issues

This subsection discusses the application of the rules of the EIR to arbitration, the arbitration agreement and arbitration-related issues. However, first, a preliminary

983. The text of the articles states payment and settlements systems, the definition of which is referred to in Art. 2(2) EIR and is to be found in two different EU-Directives, 2009/65/EG and 2011/61/EU. In essence it comes to a group of three or more people who have a contract that creates a payment and transfer system, which does not include the normal bodies of a financial market, *see* BeckOK InsO/*Mock* Art. 12 EuInsVO, No. 4.
984. BeckOK InsO/*Mock* Art. 12 EuInsVO, No. 8.
985. MüKoInsO/*Fried* Art. 12 EuInsVU, No. 1.
986. Braun/*Marx* Art. 13 EuInsVO, No. 1.
987. Paulus/*Paulus* Art. 13 EuInsVO, Nos 5–6.
988. Mankowski/Müller/J. Schmidt, EuInsVO 2015/*Mankowski* Art. 15 EuInsVO, No. 2; Paulus/*Paulus* Art. 15 EuInsVO, No. 3.
989. Paulus/*Paulus* Art. 16 EuInsVO, 1, 3.
990. Braun/*Marx* Art. 17 EuInsVO, No. 1.

issue is dealt with. This is the question if the references in the EIR must be understood to refer to the national or international insolvency law of a jurisdiction (i). Second, the preliminary issues concerning Article 18 EIR are discussed (ii). Third, the scope of Article 7(2)(e) EIR and its relation to Article 18 EIR are discussed (iii). As a fourth topic, the issue of objective arbitrability under the EIR is discussed (iv). Finally, some ancillary issues are discussed, i.e., the law applicable to the arbitrator's agreement (v) and the law applicable to an award (vi).

It is primarily Articles 7(2)(e) and 18 EIR that seem to be interesting in the context of insolvency in arbitration. Article 18 EIR refers to the *lex fori* or law of the seat of the proceedings for the regulation of the effects of insolvency on such proceedings and Article 7(2)(e) EIR refers the effect of insolvency on current contracts to the law of the jurisdiction in which insolvency proceedings are opened. Whereas the articles discussed above are relevant in answering factual questions as to the effect of insolvency on individual rights and goods in dispute, both in court and in arbitration, Article 18 EIR is the sole article that speaks to the effect of insolvency on the arbitral proceedings themselves. A discussion that comes up when investigating the effect of the EIR on arbitration, which was also the focus in the previously mentioned *Syska v. Vivendi* case, is to what extent Article 7(2)(e) EIR regulates the arbitration agreement, and Article 18 EIR regulates the arbitral proceedings, c.q. how these articles relate to each other.[991]

The possible tensions are relatively easy to spot: When the arbitration agreement, being the basis for the proceedings, is covered by the *lex fori concursus* of the insolvency but the arbitral proceedings remain governed by the '*lex fori processus*', i.e., the law of the seat, this could lead to contradictions. If, for example, Article 7(2)(e) EIR's application is not somehow limited by Article 18 EIR, it could lead to an arbitral proceeding being theoretically able to continue under the law of the seat as no mandatory suspension applies, e.g., Germany,[992] but the arbitration agreement being annulled, e.g., as was the effect of the polish law in force during the time of *Syska v. Vivendi*.[993] The annulment or invalidation of the arbitration agreement takes away the legitimation of the arbitration and thus renders the arbitration void and the reference of Article 18 EIR useless. This tension and several other questions need an answer if one is to have a coherent functional understanding of the relationship of the EIR and its conflict-of-laws rules to arbitration.

i *Reference to National or International Insolvency Law*

The EIR is understood to supplant the autonomous international law of the individual Member States. However, it is still relevant to consider the scope and nature of this replacement. This is especially relevant in the context of material norms. The EIR does not have material norms, for example, on the suspension of proceedings and refers for

991. *Commercial Court*, Judgment of 2.10.2008 – EWHC 2155 (Comm), 15 et seq.
992. Due to the non-application of § 352 InsO to arbitration, *see* § 2.3.1.
993. *Commercial Court*, Judgment of 2.10.2008 – EWHC 2155 (Comm), 64 et seq.

this to the *lex fori processus* by way of Article 18 EIR. The question then arises: Should the national material norm on international or national insolvency be seized?

The answer to this question can make a material difference. Whereas, for example, § 240 InsO on domestic insolvencies directly provides a material norm, i.e., a suspension of individual proceedings, § 352 InsO on foreign insolvencies does this as well but refers to the *lex fori concursus* for part of the regulation of the same issue in an international context, i.e., the standing to continue the proceedings, *see* § 352(1) InsO.[994] The general opinion here is that the application of the EIR excludes autonomous international insolvency law as a whole.[995] This also seems to be more in line with the *Virgos-Schmit* report, which states that the reference is meant to refer to the internal and domestic law of the state.[996] Accordingly, reference should be had to the rules of domestic insolvency of the *lex fori processus* in the context of Article 18 EIR.

However, some room for interpretation is left. *Müller* argues that the EIR indeed excludes the national conflict-of-law rules but that the national material rules on international insolvency cannot be qualified as such and accordingly are not excluded thereby.[997] *Müller*'s view, however, remains unconvincing. First, regarding *Müller*'s specific argument on § 352 InsO, contrary to what he states, § 352 InsO is not purely a material rule as it refers to the law of the *lex fori concursus* for the capacity to continue proceedings. Second and more important, *Müller*'s view should be disregarded for systematic and teleological reasons. From a systematic point of view, the EIR does not need to put forward material rules on every subject to exclude corresponding material rules in the national law. The EIR replaces the entirety of the Member-State's regulations on international insolvency within the scope of its application, i.e., EU insolvencies.

Consequently, the EIR cannot refer to the rules regarding international insolvencies as it has supplanted these,[998] regardless of if it has provided a material rule on the relevant question. In parallel, the references to other laws in the EIR should be understood as referring to '*Sachnormen*' or substantial norms and not '*Gesamtnormen*' or combined norms, such as § 352 InsO, and certainly not to international private law norms.[999] The application of the domestic material norms is also supported by a teleological approach to the references in the EIR. *Virgos-Schmit* state that the aim of the exceptions to the general rule of the EIR, including specifically Article 15 EIR-old,

994. Although both these norms are non-applicable to arbitration, *see* § 2.3.1.
995. K. Schmidt InsO/*Brinkmann* Vorbemerkungen zur EuInsVO, No. 6; MüKoBGB/*Kindler* Art. 18 EuInsVO, No. 11; BeckOK InsO/*Mock* Art. 1 EuInsVO, p. 4; Paulus/*Paulus* Art. 18 EuInsVO, p. 10; MüKoInsO/*Thole* § 352 insO, No. 2; *BGH*, NZI 2011, 420, No. 11; NZI 2013, 690-692; *OLG München*, NJW-RR 2013, 314-315; although Dutch law is territorial (*see* Arts 203-205 Fw) and does not, without special conventions, recognise and thus regulate foreign international insolvencies arguably making this a non-issue *HR*, JOR 2010, 687-693, 3.2-3.3; *Rechtbank Arnhem*, 31.3.2010 - 177710 / HA ZA 08-1977, 2.3; for Austria *OGH*, IPrax 2007, 235.
996. *Virgós/Schmit*, Report on the Convention on Insolvency Proceedings, No. 8787.
997. Mankowski/Müller/J. Schmidt, EuInsVO 2015/*M. Müller* Art. 18 EuInsVO, No. 18.
998. *BGH*, NZI 2011, 420, No. 11.
999. *Wessels*, International Insolvency Law, p. 555.

i.e., Article 18 EIR, is to provide in those circumstances the effect of domestic insolvency.[1000]

Another goal of the EIR's exceptions, including Article 18 EIR, that of legal certainty and clarity, would also be compromised by the practical consequences of *Müller*'s argument.[1001] The interpretation of references in the EIR as a referral to international insolvency law of the nation would lead to incongruent results in case of the opening of local proceedings. In the understanding that German local insolvency law applies to the suspension of proceedings both before and after the opening of secondary proceedings in Germany, the question of suspension would be dealt with under § 240 ZPO continuously. Whereas in *Müller's* approach, the opening of main proceedings in a different Member State would first lead to the application of § 352 InsO and then, upon the opening of secondary proceedings in Germany, to the application of § 240 ZPO. This applies to every rule for which there are separate local and international insolvency rules and leads to a severe compromisation of legal certainty, predictability and clarity. Arguably, the same shift can occur outside of the EIR's application when autonomous international insolvency law is applied. However, this does not negate the fact that within the application of the EIR, the goals of the EIR should lead to an application that avoids such shifts.

As a consequence of the above, the references in the EIR should be understood to refer to the internal and domestic insolvency rules of the relevant jurisdiction. In light of this conclusion, the Tribunal's misgivings about the arguments for Claimant in ICC Case 12421 are entirely well-founded.[1002] In this case, the claimant argued that insofar as Article 15 EIR-old, now Article 18 EIR, referred to English law for the potential suspension of proceedings, section 130(2) Insolvency Act suspending proceedings in case of domestic insolvency does not apply as the insolvency is foreign. Consequently, the arbitration seated in England should not be suspended due to Italian insolvency.[1003] This approach would defeat the harmonising and coordination effect of the EIR and create a paradoxical situation, as pointed out by the tribunal, in which the Italian insolvency would suspend Italian proceedings, and potential English insolvency would suspend English proceedings, but even with the reference of Article 15 EIR-old there would be no effect across the border.[1004]

ii *Preliminary Issues Regarding Article 18 EIR*

There was discussion about whether the old Article 15 EIR concerning ongoing procedures applied to arbitration. This is the preliminary discussion examined here concerning Article 18 EIR which replaced the old Article 15 EIR.

1000. *Virgós/Schmit,* Report on the Convention on Insolvency Proceedings, 92.2.
1001. Mankowski/Müller/J. Schmidt, EuInsVO 2015/*M. Müller* Art. 18 EuInsVO, No. 3; Cf. *Wessels,* International Insolvency Law, 10712f.
1002. *Final Award in ICC Case No. 12421,* ICC International Court of Arbitration Bulletin 20, 2009, 88, No. 20.
1003. *Final Award in ICC Case No. 12421,* ICC International Court of Arbitration Bulletin 20, 2009, 88, No. 1717.
1004. *Final Award in ICC Case No. 12421,* ICC International Court of Arbitration Bulletin 20, 2009, 88, No. 2020.

The preliminary issue regarding the applicability of Article 18 EIR to arbitration is far less problematic than it was under the current EIR's predecessor's Article 15.[1005] The new wording has squashed any doubt about its application to arbitration. The European legislator has chosen to include arbitration in the wording of the new article, whereas this was absent previously.[1006] However, as is not unusual in this sometimes hydra-like legal field, with the squashing of this one discussion several others rose.

As soon as the term 'arbitration' was included in the EIR, it was questioned what the scope of this term was. As was already discussed regarding the term 'insolvency' in the EIR in Chapter 3 § 1.3.1, the EIR must be interpreted autonomously, c.q. only in the context of EU-wide law.[1007] Whereas the EIR itself does not provide guidance on the term arbitration, it does reference the Rome-I Regulation on contractual relationships in preamble 7. In the context of the Rome-I regulation, the CJEU has provided a broad understanding of arbitration. It states that it means not only those proceedings in which the parties have given a third person final say in a dispute but also every proceeding that is directly related to it, e.g., court proceedings on the validity of the arbitration agreement, the building of the tribunal, the jurisdiction of the tribunal and enforcement and annulment.[1008] Not only because this is an EU-law-specific interpretation of the term arbitration, but also due to the fact that the European legislator directly relates the EIR to the Rome-I Regulation by stating that these together should form a closed regulatory system, this interpretation should be applied in the EIR as well.[1009] This conclusion is crucial in the context of insolvency in arbitration. Due to this wider reach of the term arbitration, Article 18 EIR leads to the continued application of the *lex fori* to any proceedings that concern the arbitration: from the preliminary issues before the courts, e.g., jurisdiction, to the post-award stage, e.g., enforcement and annulment.

Another issue regarding Article 18 EIR is that similar to the situation under the old EIR's Article 15, it is widely stated that Article 18 EIR's reference should be understood as a reference to *lex fori arbitri*, i.e., the law of the arbitration, which need not be that of the seat.[1010] However, this view appears to be at odds with the wording of Article 18 EIR and preamble 73, which clearly and unambiguously refers to the law of the seat of

1005. Council Regulation (EC) No 1346/2000 on insolvency proceedings of 29.5.2000, Official Journal of the European Communities L 160; *Wessels*, International Insolvency Law, 10712g.

1006. *See also* preamble 73 of Regulation (EU) 2015/848 on insolvency proceedings of 20.5.2015, OJ L 141/19; Paulus/*Paulus* Art. 18 EuInsVO, p. 4; *Wessels*, International Insolvency Law Part II: European Insolvency Law, 10712g-h; although even under the old EIR, tribunals concluded that Art. 15 EIR included arbitration *Interim Award in ICC Case No. 10507*, ICC International Court of Arbitration Bulletin 20, 2009, 71, 8.4a-b; *Final Award in ICC Case No. 12421*, ICC International Court of Arbitration Bulletin 20, 2009, 88, No. 2121.

1007. *CJEU*, Judgment of 20.10.2011 – C-396/09, No. 42; Judgment of 29.10.2009 – C-174/08, p. 24.

1008. *CJEU*, EuZW 1999, 413, No. 32; NJW 1993, 189, No. 28; Musielak/Voit/*Stadler* Art. 1 EuGVVO, No. 9.

1009. Paulus/*Paulus* Art. 18 EuInsVO, p. 4; MüKoInsO/*Reinhart* Art. 18 EuInsVO, No. 6.

1010. Braun/*Ehret* Art. 18 EuInsVO, No. 18; MüKoBGB/*Kindler* Art. 18 EuInsVO, No. 24; BeckOK InsO/*Mock* Art. 18 EuInsVO, No. 13; Paulus/*Paulus* Art. 18 EuInsVO, No. 6; Cf. MüKoInsO/*Reinhart* Art. 18 EuInsVO, Nos 3, 6.

arbitration and not the applicable *lex fori arbitri*.[1011] The main argument here seems to be legal certainty, which is the underlying goal of Article 18 EIR,[1012] c.q. the certainty that a different law does not suddenly cover procedural questions upon the opening of insolvency in a different country. In this context, that means that insofar as parties have chosen a different law than that of the seat, this law should be applied.[1013] Whereas most German commentators seem to follow this view, the underlying logic is flawed when examined further. This interpretation leads to the application of a law different than the *lex fori* of the relevant court of annulment to effects of insolvency on the arbitration, e.g., the suspension question, which enlarges the risk of annulment due to a violation of *ordre public*. Furthermore, it requires that one understands the choice by the parties for a certain *lex arbitri* as to include a choice for the rules regarding the effect of insolvency on arbitration proceedings, whereas this is usually part of insolvency law and, as such, should not be seen as included in the choice for a certain *lex arbitri*.[1014] This and the direct contradiction of this view to the text of the regulation should lead to the rejection of this view.[1015]

A final issue regarding the internal workings of Article 18 EIR is the scope of the reference. The reference to the effect of the insolvency on the procedure, as stated in Article 18 EIR, is mostly viewed as a reference primarily to rules on suspension and the related rules on the continuation of the proceedings or rejection thereof.[1016] However, there is a discussion about the 'depth' of the scope of this reference. Primarily it is questioned if the issue of the authority to continue or reject proceedings is also referred to the law of the seat or if this continues to be organised by the *lex fori concursus* of the insolvency.[1017]

Whereas a good deal of German commentators find that this question is not referred to the law of the seat,[1018] the German Federal Supreme Court seems to be of the opinion that Article 18 EIR does cover the authority to continue proceedings.[1019] Internationally, *Wessels* also supports this conclusion with reference to a supporting

1011. Mankowski/Müller/J. Schmidt, EuInsVO 2015/*M. Müller* Art. 18 EuInsVO, No. 25; Some argue that the EIR has left a hole here, in regard to the situation where the law of the seat does not provide the lex arbitri MüKoInsO/*Reinhart* Art. 18 EuInsVO, No. 3 in de 3th edition of the commentary of 2016.
1012. Mankowski/Müller/J. Schmidt, EuInsVO 2015/*M. Müller* Art. 18 EuInsVO, p. 3.
1013. MüKoBGB/*Kindler* Art. 18 EuInsVO, No. 24.
1014. *Born*, International Commercial Arbitration, p. 1599 whereas, there is discussion on the scope of the choice of a procedural law of arbitration, to support the view of the mentioned German commentators a view so wide as to include international insolvency law, if not all conflict-of-laws rules of the relevant law would be necessary.
1015. Cf. *Schmitz*, Schiedsverfahren und Insolvenz, p. 180; *Schultze-Moderow*, Schiedsverfahren und Insolvenz, p. 97.
1016. *BGH*, BeckRS 2017, 136174, No. 12.
1017. Braun/*Ehret* Art. 18 EuInsVO, No. 17; MüKoBGB/*Kindler* Art. 18 EuInsVO; BeckOK InsO/*Mock* Art. 18 EuInsVO, No. 11; Mankowski/Müller/J. Schmidt, EuInsVO 2015/*M. Müller* Art. 18 EuInsVO, No. 18.
1018. Braun/*Ehret* Art. 18 EuInsVO, No. 17; BeckOK InsO/*Mock* Art. 18 EuInsVO, No. 11 and also many commentaries on the old EIR.
1019. *BGH*, NZI 2013, 690, 6 et seq; HambKomm/*Undritz* Art. 15 EuInsVO (old), No. 4; Although some cite this case to support the opposite conclusion without, which, however, finds no support in the text of the decision FK-InsO/*C. Wenner*/*M. Schuster* Art. 18 EuInsVO, No. 12.

Belgian case.[1020] This view is the more convincing one considering that capacity to conduct procedures is intrinsically linked to the *lex fori processus*. This, however, does not hinder the application of the *lex fori concursus* to the question of the substantive authority to conduct procedures in light of Article 7(2)(c) EIR, insofar as this is a requirement under the *lex fori processus.*[1021] It is also important to note that Article 18 EIR does not affect the regulation of the party's capacity in insolvency to stand in legal proceedings in general. This remains directed by the general rule of the EIR, i.e., by the *lex fori processus.*[1022]

iii The Scope of Article 7(2)(e) and Its Relationship to 18 EIR

For an ongoing arbitration, which is by nature based on a current contract, i.e., the arbitration agreement, the relationship between Article 7(2)(e) EIR and 18 EIR is of fundamental importance. These references could result in the arbitration agreement (Article 7(2)(e) EIR) and the arbitration proceedings (Article 18 EIR) being referred to a different law.

Justice Clark in *Syska v. Vivendi* concluded, similar to the conclusion above on the scope of Article 18 EIR, that Article 15 EIR-old in conjunction with Article 4(2)(f) EIR-old, i.e., Article 18 EIR and Article 7(2)(f) EIR applies to arbitration insofar as it was pending when the insolvency was opened.[1023] Consequently, he concluded that the law of the seat applied to these arbitrations. At the same time, he concludes that the application of Article 4(2)(e) EIR-old, now Article 7(2)(e) EIR is limited to arbitration agreements pertaining to arbitrations that have not yet been commenced.[1024] The argument for this is that the application of Article 7(2)(e) EIR, i.e., the application of the *lex fori concursus* to the arbitration agreement after the arbitration has been commenced, would violate the purpose of Article 18 EIR and hollow it out, as the annulment of the arbitration agreement due to the application of the *lex fori concursus* based on Article 7(2)(e) EIR would still lead to cessation of the arbitral proceedings, even if arbitral proceedings could have otherwise continued under the law of the seat.[1025]

This conception of the relationship between Article 7(2)(e) EIR and Article 18 EIR has also found a following in literature.[1026] However, it is also argued that Article 7(2)(e) EIR does not apply to arbitration agreements.[1027] The arguments for such a

1020. *Wessels,* International Insolvency Law, p. 560; *Rechtbank van Koophandel Veurne,* 18.12.2002 – A/01/00410.
1021. Mankowski/Müller/J. Schmidt, EuInsVO 2015/*M. Müller* Art. 18 EuInsVO, Nos 18–19.
1022. Mankowski/Müller/J. Schmidt, EuInsVO 2015/*M. Müller* Art. 18 EuInsVO, No. 19; *Rechtbank van Koophandel Veurne,* 18.12.2002 – A/01/00410 third and second to last paragraphs of the considerations.
1023. *Commercial Court,* Judgment of 2.10.2008 – EWHC 2155 (Comm), No. 100; *see also CJEU,* Judgment of 17.3.2005 – C-294/02, No. 69.
1024. *Commercial Court,* Judgment of 2.10.2008 – EWHC 2155 (Comm), No. 99.
1025. *Commercial Court,* Judgment of 2.10.2008 – EWHC 2155 (Comm), No. 100.
1026. BeckOK InsO/*Mock* Art. 7 EuInsVO, pp. 90–91; differently *Nacimiento/Bähr,* NJOZ 2009, 4752, p. 4759.
1027. *Pfeiffer,* Insolvenzeröffnung und internationale Schiedsverfahren, 821, pp. 824–827.

position are, however, to be dismissed.[1028] *Pfeiffer* argues against this interaction between the articles and primarily the application of Article 7(2)(e) EIR to arbitration agreements. However, he provides only indirect and circumstantial arguments. First, he states that the Rome-I Regulation on contractual relationships excludes arbitration agreements and that this should serve to find that the EIR must also not apply to arbitration agreements. However, this is done explicitly in Article 1(2) Rome-I, which would rather than support the point that the EIR would probably not cover arbitration agreements, support the position that it does cover them as they are not explicitly excluded.[1029] Second, he argues that the CJEU in the *AMI Semiconductor* case did not apply Article 7(2)(e) EIR to the arbitration agreement. However, the argument made in the *Syska v. Vivendi* case that the court, by applying the exemption mentioned Article 4(2)(f) EIR-old (Article 7(2)(f) EIR) to the arbitration agreement, left the scope of Article 7(2)(e) EIR open is more convincing as there was no need for the court to address the potential applicability of Article 7(2)(e) EIR to the arbitration agreement.[1030] Third, he argues that Article 7(2)(e) EIR could conflict with Article 18 EIR.[1031] However, this conflict does not materialise if one follows the view that Article 7(2)(e) EIR only applies to the arbitration agreement insofar as the proceedings have not yet been commenced. Such a view is also not an unfounded tool to safeguard the application of Article 7(2)(e) EIR, as *Pfeiffer* suggests.[1032] Much rather, this view is founded on the correct interpretations of Articles 7(2)(e) and 18 EIR and their goals.

Article 7(2)(e) EIR makes no exception whatsoever to what sort of contracts it covers and should be understood as a general rule.[1033] While *Schultze-Moderow* points out that the CJEU has stated that the EIR's scope should be construed narrowly, referring to the following test:[1034] 'it must be determined whether the right or the obligation which respects the basis of the action finds its source in the common rules of civil and commercial law or in the derogating rules specific to insolvency proceedings',[1035] this certainly cannot lead to a general exclusion of arbitration agreements. Insofar as an arbitration agreement has a functional relationship with the insolvency, as the underlying right or obligation must be considered to have its source in specific rules of insolvency proceedings, it passes this test.[1036] Accordingly, Article 7(2)(e) EIR covers arbitration agreements insofar as they concern claims encompassed by the insolvency, and further rules do not exclude its application in the EIR as the arbitration agreement affects the procedural rights of the estate and the creditors.[1037]

1028. *Schultze-Moderow,* Schiedsverfahren und Insolvenz, 82 et seq.
1029. *Commercial Court,* Judgment of 2.10.2008 – EWHC 2155 (Comm), No. 55; *Pfeiffer,* Insolvenzeröffnung und internationale Schiedsverfahren, 821, p. 824.
1030. *Commercial Court,* Judgment of 2.10.2008 – EWHC 2155 (Comm), No. 89; *CJEU,* Judgment of 17.3.2005 – C-294/02, No. 69.
1031. *Pfeiffer,* Insolvenzeröffnung und internationale Schiedsverfahren, 821, p. 825.
1032. *Pfeiffer,* Insolvenzeröffnung und internationale Schiedsverfahren, 821, p. 826.
1033. *Mankowski,* ZIP 2010, 2478, p. 2483.
1034. *Schultze-Moderow,* Schiedsverfahren und Insolvenz, p. 86.
1035. *CJEU,* Judgment of 4.9.2014 – C-157/13, No. 27; *BGH,* NZI 2015, 1033, No. 18.
1036. *Riedel,* Insolvenz in nationalen und internationalen Schiedsverfahren, pp. 145–146.
1037. *Flecke-Gianmarco/C. Keller,* NZI 2012, 529, p. 533; *Mankowski,* ZIP 2010, 2478, p. 2483; Mankowski/Müller/J. Schmidt, EuInsVO 2015/*M. Müller* Art. 7 EuInsVO, No. 30;

Article 18 EIR makes an exception to these rules when the arbitration has been started.[1038] The reference to pending proceedings and arbitration must be understood to refer to pending proceedings and their related contracts, i.e., the arbitration agreement, as this is necessary to achieve legal certainty and uniform application of a single law, which is the aim of Article 18 EIR.[1039] Another argument in favour of arbitration agreements falling under Article 7(2)(e) EIR is that otherwise, systematically, the exception in Article 18 EIR would be unnecessary and would make little sense. An exception would be unnecessary if Article 7(2)(e) EIR would not be applicable in the first place. One need not make an exception to a rule that would not have covered the excepted circumstances regardless.

In consequence of the above, the conclusion remains that insofar arbitration has been commenced, it is the law of the seat that determines the effect of insolvency on the arbitration agreement, ongoing arbitration and arbitration-related proceedings, including annulment. This broad application is also supported by the broad interpretation that must be given to arbitration in the EIR, as discussed above.[1040]

Article V(1)(a)(2) NYC and § 1059(2)(1)(a) ZPO on the applicable law to the arbitration agreement do not hinder this conclusion. Articles 7(2)(e) and 18 EIR take precedence under the principle of *lex specialis derogat legi generali*, as the EIR contains specialised rules in case of insolvency, unlike the NYC.[1041] A similar conclusion must be reached for the regulation of the procedure as meant under Article V(1)(d) NYC and § 1059(2)(1)(d) ZPO.[1042]

iv *Law Applicable to Objective Arbitrability*

Whereas with the previous discussion, it has become clear which law applies to the effects of the insolvency on the arbitration agreement and the arbitration proceedings, one could still discuss where objective arbitrability fits into this discussion. Arbitrability is generally a question of the law of the seat of arbitration. *See, e.g.*, §§ 1030, 1059(2)(2)(a) ZPO. Second, it is also a question of the law of the place of enforcement as non-arbitrability under the *lex fori* of the enforcing state is a ground for non-recognition.[1043]

However, the EIR should be referred to as specialised rules in case of insolvency and part of *ordre public*. As discussed above, Article 7(2)(e) EIR provides that the *lex*

Nacimiento/Bähr, NJOZ 2009, 4752, p. 4759; *P.K. Wagner*, GWR 2010, 129, p. 131; *P.K. Wagner*, Abstimmungsfragen zwischen Internationalem Insolvenzrecht und Internationaler Schiedsgerichtsbarkeit, p. 147.

1038. *P.K. Wagner*, GWR 2010, 129, p. 131.

1039. Mankowski/Müller/J. Schmidt, EuInsVO 2015/*M. Müller* Art. 18 EuInsVO, No. 22; Paulus/*Paulus* Art. 18 EuInsVO, No. 4.

1040. *See* Chapter 3 § 2.1.3 ii.

1041. *Mankowski*, ZIP 2010, 2478, p. 2483; Cf. *Markert*, Contemp. Asia Arb. J. 2 (2009), 217, p. 235; *P.K. Wagner*, Abstimmungsfragen zwischen Internationalem Insolvenzrecht und Internationaler Schiedsgerichtsbarkeit, p. 114.

1042. Differently *Schultze-Moderow*, Schiedsverfahren und Insolvenz, pp. 94-95.

1043. *See* § 1; *Riedel*, Insolvenz in nationalen und internationalen Schiedsverfahren, p. 148.

fori concursus applies to the arbitration agreement and, based on Article 18 EIR, the law of the seat when the arbitration has started.

Wagner pleads for the application of the other exemptions provided in the EIR to the question of objective arbitrability, e.g., the *lex rei sitae* to the arbitrability of conflict based on the sale of immovable property as in Article 11 EIR.[1044] However, this approach fails to convince, as arbitrability does not flow from the law underlying a contract or property that is the source of the substantive conflict. Due to the earlier discussed concept of separability, the arbitration agreement is a contract on its own, separated from a contract to which it applies. Arbitrability is primarily linked to the arbitration agreement and the law applicable to it. As such, objective arbitrability follows the rules of Articles 7(2)(e) and 18 EIR.[1045] This conclusion is also to be preferred from a teleological point of view as it provides the most legal certainty, as, in case of a pending arbitration proceeding, the law that had previously covered arbitrability, i.e., the law of the seat, will continue to cover arbitrability after the opening of insolvency as per Article 18 EIR.[1046]

v *Law Applicable to the Arbitrator's Agreement*

In the above, much focus has been put on the law applicable to the effect of the insolvency on the arbitration agreement and the arbitration proceedings. However, as discussed in the second part of this book, there are significant potential effects that the insolvency could have on the arbitrator's contract as well. For example, one could ask if the insolvency administrator could dissolve the contract.[1047] Accordingly, it is relevant to investigate the question as to the applicable law to the arbitrator's agreement.

The answer that courts will provide depends on the determination those courts make on the nature of the arbitrator's agreement. As discussed in Chapter 2 § 4.1, the right view is to consider the arbitrator's agreement as an agreement sui generis.[1048] Whereas this would lead to the conclusion that the EIR does not have a specific exemption rule under which the arbitrator's agreement can generally be subsumed, this does not lead to the conclusion that the arbitrator's contract falls under the general rule of Article 7(2)(e) EIR.[1049] Whereas, it is argued above that due to, amongst other

1044. *P.K. Wagner,* Abstimmungsfragen zwischen Internationalem Insolvenzrecht und Internationaler Schiedsgerichtsbarkeit, pp. 142–143.
1045. *Riedel,* Insolvenz in nationalen und internationalen Schiedsverfahren, pp. 149–150; *Schmitz,* Schiedsverfahren und Insolvenz, p. 199.
1046. *Interim Award in ICC Case No. 10507,* ICC International Court of Arbitration Bulletin 20, 2009, 71, 8.4–9.1; Cf. *Schmitz,* Schiedsverfahren und Insolvenz, p. 199.
1047. *See* § 4 particularly 4.2 thereof.
1048. *See* § 4 4.1 and e.g., *Riedel,* Insolvenz in nationalen und internationalen Schiedsverfahren, p. 115; the discussion differs when one finds the agreement has a different nature, *see, e.g.,* Wagner and Schultze-Moderow *P.K. Wagner,* Abstimmungsfragen zwischen Internationalem Insolvenzrecht und Internationaler Schiedsgerichtsbarkeit, p. 171; *Schultze-Moderow,* Schiedsverfahren und Insolvenz, pp. 203–204.
1049. Differently *P.K. Wagner,* Abstimmungsfragen zwischen Internationalem Insolvenzrecht und Internationaler Schiedsgerichtsbarkeit, p. 171.

things, the logic expressed in *Syska v. Vivendi,* the arbitration agreement needs to be included in the scope of Article 18 EIR to safeguard procedural legal certainty, i.e., the arbitration agreement which constitutes the jurisdiction of the tribunal is not governed by another law than the proceedings,[1050] this logic should even more so apply to the arbitrator's contract. Arbitrators' contracts form just as crucial a part of the arbitration proceedings as an arbitration agreement. Without the arbitrator's agreement, there would be no arbitration factually. *See* the discussion in Chapter 2 § 4.2, in particular § 4.2.1. The arbitrator's contract and the arbitration agreement, although separate contracts, are linked.[1051] The arbitrator's agreement also plays a role in questions of jurisdiction; the arbitration agreement determines the scope of the jurisdiction, but the arbitrator's agreement provides the specific arbitrator with the authority to wield this jurisdiction.[1052] Were the arbitrator's agreement to be invalidated, there would be no legitimate tribunal. In conclusion, following the same logic that would place arbitration agreements underlying ongoing arbitrations in the scope of Article 18 EIR would place the arbitrator's agreement there as well.

Whereas, regarding the arbitration agreement, there was an interplay between the application of Article 7(2)(e) EIR and Article 18 EIR, the application of Article 7(2)(e) EIR to arbitrator's contracts is a moot point. Arbitrator's contracts are generally made at the beginning of the arbitration process, with a nomination in the request for arbitration or answer thereto and the contract is formed after the relevant arbitrator has accepted the nomination. Consequently, arbitrators' contracts are generally only present when arbitration is pending, as arbitration is generally considered to be pending at the moment a request for arbitration is filed, c.q. when the request is received, *see, e.g.*, § 1044 ZPO.[1053] In consequence, from the moment they are made, they fall under the auspices of Article 18 EIR.

Some argue that the arbitration agreement is not a necessity for the arbitrator's office, i.e., the arbitrator's role as an arbitrator.[1054] This could potentially be used as an argument against the above conclusions. It is indeed arguable that the termination of the arbitrator's office does not directly mean the termination of the arbitrator's agreement. However, the core of this argument, which presupposes a high degree of abstraction between the office of the arbitrator and the arbitration agreement, should be dismissed. *Born*'s description, in which the arbitrator's agreement forms the basis of the relationship between the parties and the arbitrator, is more persuasive.[1055] Insofar

1050. Mankowski/Müller/J. Schmidt, EuInsVO 2015/*M. Müller* Art. 18 EuInsVO, No. 22; *Wessels,* International Insolvency Law, p. 640.
1051. *Schmitz,* Schiedsverfahren und Insolvenz, p. 98.
1052. *See* for the contractual interplay of the two agreements *Wolff,* Chapter 18, Part XII: Rights and Duties of Arbitrators, 2723, No. 9.
1053. Musielak/Voit/*Voit* § 1044 ZPO, Nos 2-3.
1054. *Wolff,* Chapter 18, Part XII: Rights and Duties of Arbitrators, 2723, No. 11.
1055. *Born,* International Commercial Arbitration, p. 1973; *Trunk,* Internationales Insolvenzrecht, p. 378 who puts the German view down to the high level of abstraction between 'Verfügungshandlungen' or dispostitive acts and the underlying contractual relationships, which is to be viewed critically; *see also Flöther,* Auswirkungen des inländischen Insolvenzverfahrens auf Schiedsverfahren und Schiedsabrede, p. 122; *Schwab,* Schiedsrichterernennung und Schiedsrichtervertrag, p. 509.

as arbitration is described as a process based on the arbitration contract, elevating the office of the arbitrator to something beyond the convenes of the arbitrator's contract seems to contradict this nature and would be more in line with a jurisdictional view of arbitration.

To put it crudely, a judge is a judge even when parties have no case before him, as his office does not depend on the parties. The same cannot be said for the office of an arbitrator, which generally starts and terminates with the arbitration.[1056] It follows that the basis for the arbitrator's office lies with the contracts that underlie the arbitration, primarily the arbitrator's contract, which by reference includes the arbitration agreement.[1057] Any mandatory law or regulation specific to the adjudicatory role of the arbitrator does nothing to change this any more than the regulation of other contractual relationships changes their inherent contractual nature.[1058]

For these reasons, it should be concluded that Article 18 EIR encompasses not only arbitration agreements but also the arbitrator's agreement.

vi *Law Applicable to the Award: Status in Insolvency, Annulment and Enforcement*

Insofar as an award is present in insolvency, one could ask what the role of this award is and, in international insolvency, which law determines that issue. Furthermore, when that award is in enforcement or annulment proceedings, the question arises what the effect of the insolvency is on those proceedings. This was examined in the national context in Chapter 2 § 5.

Within the context of the EIR, the status of an award in insolvency as proof of claim or otherwise is automatically dependent on the *lex fori concursus*, according to Article 7(2)(h) EIR. The question of the status of the award is not a question of the existence of the claim, which is not part of the reference in Article 7(2)(h) EIR and an independent preliminary question, but a question of proof of claim and thus of claim verification covered by Article 7(2)(h) EIR.[1059]

Regarding ongoing enforcement and annulment proceedings, the requirements of Article 18 EIR are merely that the legal dispute was pending during the opening of the insolvency and second that it concerns assets of the insolvent estate.[1060] Therefore, no other conclusion can be supported than the application of Article 18 EIR to enforcement and annulment proceedings where the award concerns a claim encompassed in the

1056. Musielak/Voit/*Voit* § 1035 ZPO, No. 28.
1057. *Schwab*, Schiedsrichterernennung und Schiedsrichtervertrag, 507, 512.
1058. *Born*, International Commercial Arbitration, pp. 1974–1975; differently *Wolff*, Chapter 18, Part XII: Rights and Duties of Arbitrators, 2723, Nos 9–12.
1059. *Cour de Cassation*, Arrêt of 22.6.2010 – Arrêt n° 696 (09-65.481) 3th paragraph of the unnumbered reasoning; *Cour d'Appel de Dijon*, 21.9.2010 – RG no. 09/02080 unnumbered, reference should be had mainly to the first ground for nullication. Mankowski/Müller/J. Schmidt, EuInsVO 2015/*M. Müller* Art. 7 EuInsVO, Nos 52–53; *Wessels*, International Insolvency Law Part II: European Insolvency Law, pp. 289–290.
1060. BeckOK InsO/*Mock* Art. 18 EuInsVO, Nos 3, 8.

insolvency, and the proceeding is pending when the insolvency is opened.[1061] For these proceedings, even the discussion of the inclusion of arbitration proceedings in the reference to ongoing proceedings was already irrelevant before the European legislator decided to include arbitration in Article 18 EIR literally. The enforcement and annulment proceedings are by nature court proceedings and, as such, already fell under Article 15 EIR-old and Article 18 EIR, insofar as insolvency claims are dealt with in the estate. Consequentially, the effect of insolvency on enforcement and annulment awards within the application territory of the EIR is referred to the *lex fori processus*. Whereas Article 18 EIR would apply regardless, it could be stated that annulment and enforcement proceedings would rather fall under the reference to 'arbitration' in Article 18 EIR instead of under 'court proceedings'. This is because the term arbitration in the EIR, as glimpsed from the Rome-I Regulation and discussed above, should be viewed widely and as including proceedings directly related to arbitration.[1062]

The *lex fori processus* will then also be the relevant law for the potential continuation of such proceedings, which may happen if the insolvency administrator disputes the claim or award, *see* Chapter 2 § 2.3.2.[1063]

vii *Interim Conclusion: Arbitration and the EIR*

This subsection examined the applicability and application of the EIR by courts on arbitration and arbitration-related issues. The application of the EIR by courts is not without its hurdles. There are profound discussions on some points of the EIR. However, following the *Syska v. Vivendi* case, the EIR provides a logical and functioning mechanism to handle the contractual nature of the arbitration. It balances the need to protect legitimate interests in the continuous application of a single legal system to ongoing arbitration proceedings and the therewith related autonomy of the parties with the general goal of the EIR to extend the legal consequences of insolvency in one Member State to the others.

It is certain that until the CJEU has provided definitive guidance that discussion will persist on the relationship between Articles 7(2)(e) and 18 EIR. It is even likely that it will persist after such guidance is given until perhaps, as was done to squash the discussion on the inclusion of arbitration in Article 18 EIR's predecessor, a new recast will make further changes to the texts of these articles.

2.2 German Autonomous International Insolvency Law

The German autonomous international insolvency law applies to international insolvencies in Germany insofar as the EIR does not apply. The term refers to the twelfth part of the German Insolvency Code, '*Internationales Insolvenzrecht*', i.e., §§ 335–358 InsO. Its regulation of the issue of recognition, § 343 InsO, was already discussed in the

1061. *S.M. Kröll*, Part IV: Selected Areas and Issues of Arbitration in Germany, Insolvency and Arbitration – Effects of Party Insolvency on Arbitral Proceedings in Germany, 981, p. 1007.
1062. *See* Chapter 3 § 2.1.3 ii.
1063. *See* for Germany, §§ 2.3.1 0, 5.3, 5.4, 5.5.

previous section, Chapter 3 § 1.4. What remains to be discussed are its conflict-of-laws rules and substantive norms. These are discussed here. This subsection mirrors the structure of the previous subsection concerning the EIR to facilitate comparison. First, a general examination of the conflict-of-laws rules in the Insolvency Code is made (§ 2.2.1). Second, the coordinating and material norms will shortly be discussed (§ 2.2.2) before moving on to the law applicable to arbitration and arbitration-related issues (§ 2.2.3).

2.2.1 *Conflict-of-Laws Rules*

The recognition of foreign insolvencies as organised in § 343 InsO extends the effects of the insolvency, according to the jurisdiction in which they were opened, to the German jurisdiction.[1064] That the law of the opening state primarily organises the effect of this recognition in Germany is made explicit by § 335 InsO. § 335 InsO posits a clear conflict-of-laws rule regarding the effect of the foreign insolvency and refers to the *lex fori concursus* as a general rule. The automatic recognition of § 343 InsO and this extension of the effects under the *lex fori concursus* under § 335 InsO show the German system's universalist approach. The mechanism is similar to Article 7 EIR, which contains the general reference to the *lex fori concursus* and Articles 19 and 20 EIR, containing automatic recognition.[1065] The reason that § 335 InsO systemically comes before the regulation on recognising is that, from the German perspective, it applies to every international insolvency, meaning also international insolvencies opened in Germany.[1066] In practice, the effect of international insolvency opened in Germany in foreign jurisdictions depends mainly on the legal system of that respective foreign jurisdiction.

Whereas the reference of § 335 InsO does include both material and procedural norms,[1067] §§ 336–358 InsO do contain a list of exemptions from this general rule, most of which have corresponding rules in Articles 8–18 EIR as the German legislator took guidance from the EIR.[1068] These exemptions also have the same general goal as the exemptions under the EIR, namely to protect legitimate expectations and legal certainty.[1069] For the below, please refer to the discussion in Chapter 3 § 2.1 as many comparisons will be made below.

§ 336 InsO makes the same exemption as Article 11 EIR and refers the effect of insolvency on contracts relating to immovable property to the *lex rei sitae*.[1070] § 337 InsO, like Article 13 EIR, creates a reference to the *lex causae* for the insolvency effects on employment contracts. As stated, this is, in practice, mostly a reference to the *lex*

1064. BeckOK InsO/*Weissinger* § 343 InsO, No. 1.
1065. BeckOK InsO/*Martini* § 335 InsO, Nos 1–3.
1066. MüKoInsO/*Reinhart* § 335 InsO, No. 1.
1067. Entwurf eines Gesetzes zur Neuregelung des Internationalen Insolvenzrechts of 25.10.2002, BT-Drs. 15/16, p. 18 under 'Zu § 335'.
1068. *Mincke*, § 45 Internationales Insolvenzrecht, 1371, No. 10.
1069. BeckOK InsO/*Martini* § 335 InsO, No. 2.
1070. MüKoInsO/*Reinhart* § 336 InsO, No. 3.

loci laboris.[1071] § 338 InsO contains the same system to protect set-offs described above for Article 9 EIR. It essentially protects set-offs from being delegitimised by the *lex fori concursus* insofar as a set-off of the relevant claims would be possible under the *lex causae.*[1072]

The German version of the *actio pauliana* called '*Insolvenzanfechzung*', literally: 'insolvency disputation' and less literally, in the state-provided translation, the '*Contest of Transactions in Insolvency Proceedings*',[1073] is organised in § 339 InsO in keeping with Article 16 EIR.[1074] § 339 InsO primarily restates the general rule, i.e., the *lex fori concursus* applies to detrimental acts. However, it provides the same objection as in Article 16 EIR, i.e., the action is excluded from the operation of the *lex fori concursus* insofar as the one who benefited from the relevant act can prove that another law applies to the act and that, under this law, the act is not challengeable in insolvency. In more explicit terms, the beneficiary of the detrimental act cannot be held liable for that act if the *lex causae* does not provide such liability.[1075]

§ 340 InsO provides by and large the same rules as Article 9 EIR, except that § 340 InsO, unlike Article 9 EIR, also applies to credit institutions and insurances and, in doing so, implements two other European directives: 2001/24/EC on insolvencies of credit institutions and 2001/17/EG on the insolvencies of insurances.[1076] § 340 InsO provides that the effect of insolvency on rights and duties related to financial markets and pensions funds, as defined by the relevant German laws, are excepted from the general rule of § 335 InsO and remain covered by the *lex systema* § 340(1) InsO or § 340(2) InsO the *lex contractus.*[1077]

The next conflict-of-laws rules can be found in the next part of the Insolvency Code, the second section of part eleven thereof, §§ 343–353 InsO containing specific rules concerning foreign international insolvencies. Many relate to the coordination and effects of the foreign proceedings in the German jurisdiction. The first conflict-of-laws rule that can be identified is § 349 InsO, which in keeping with Article 14 EIR, subjects those goods and rights subject to a registry in Germany, specified as ships, boats and security rights attached to planes, to the relevant rules of German law. This is in line with Article 14 EIR as within the scope of the application of § 349 InsO, Germany is by definition the registry-administrating jurisdiction as referred to in Article 14 EIR.[1078]

§ 351(1) InsO organises in rem rights, similar to Article 8 EIR. Although it can be debated if § 351(1) InsO is a conflict-of-laws rule, the German opinion is mainly that it

1071. Braun/*Tashiro* § 337 InsO, 1, 9.
1072. MüKoInsO/*Reinhart* § 338 InsO, Nos 3–4.
1073. *Reusch,* Insolvency Statute, http://www.gesetze-im-internet.de/englisch_inso/print_englisch_inso.html.
1074. Entwurf eines Gesetzes zur Neuregelung des Internationalen Insolvenzrechts of 25.10.2002, BT-Drs. 15/16, p. 19 under 'Zu § 339'.
1075. Braun/*Tashiro* § 339 InsO, 13, 29.
1076. Directive 2001/17/EC on the reorganisation and winding-up of insurance undertaking of 19.3.2001, OJ L 110/28; Directive 2001/24/EC On the reorganisation and winding up of credit institutions of 4.1.2001, OJ L 125/15; Braun/*Tashiro* § 340 InsO, No. 1.
1077. MüKoInsO/*Fried* § 340 InsO, 7, 11.
1078. Uhlenbruck/*Lüer/Knof* § 351 InsO, No. 15; BeckOK InsO/*Weissinger* § 349 InsO, Nos 1–4.

is not,[1079] the effect remains the same. It makes an exemption from §§ 335, 343 InsO and applies German law to security rights attached to a property.[1080] § 351(2) InsO contains a true conflict-of-laws rule, again mirroring Article 14 EIR, referring to the German law for rights related to immovable property and certain registry goods in Germany as identified by § 864 ZPO.[1081]

2.2.2 *Coordination and Material Norms*

Beyond the conflict-of-laws rules, the German autonomous international insolvency law also includes material norms and norms meant to coordinate between a foreign insolvency and the German jurisdiction, particularly secondary proceedings.

Coordination and material norms are primarily organised in conjunction with, and pursuant to, the recognition of foreign insolvencies, as previously discussed and organised in § 343 InsO. However, one rule can be found in § 341 InsO, stating that in German international insolvency, creditors can also register their rights in foreign secondary proceedings. Further rules containing material norms and coordination regulations can be found in §§ 342, 345–348, 350 InsO. However, these do not merit further discussion in the context of this book.

2.2.3 *German Autonomous International Insolvency Law and the Applicable Law to the Effects of the Insolvency*

In this paragraph, the insolvency law applicable to arbitration and arbitration-related issues is discussed as provided for in the German Insolvency Code. Again, the structure and topics mirror those of the discussion under the EIR to facilitate comparison insofar as possible. First, the applicability of § 335 InsO to the arbitration agreement is discussed (i). Second, the applicability of § 352 InsO to the arbitration proceeding is examined (ii). Then it will be discussed if these two articles provide the same tension as seen between Articles 7 and 18 in the EIR (iii). After this, ancillary topics are discussed: the law applicable to objective arbitrability (iv), the law applicable to the arbitrator's agreement (v) and the law applicable to the award (vi).

Similar to the discussion above, concerning Articles 7 and 18 EIR, the rules relevant to the effect of the insolvency on the arbitration agreement and the arbitral proceedings are the most relevant for the regulation of the effects of the insolvency on arbitration. The parallel rules in the German autonomous rules are found in the general rule of § 335 InsO, and the exemption to this general rule in § 352 InsO, for ongoing procedures in Germany.

Due to the relative comparability of §§ 335 and 352 InsO to Articles 7 and 18 EIR, one might expect the same tension between the two articles and the same kind of discussion. However, the current academic discussion seems to belie that expectation.

1079. BeckOK InsO/*Weissinger* § 351 InsO, Nos 3.2–3.3.
1080. BeckOK InsO/*Weissinger* § 351 InsO, Nos 1, 3.4.
1081. BeckOK InsO/*Weissinger* § 351 InsO, Nos 6–7.

i Applicability of § 335 InsO to Arbitration Agreements

There seems to be little discussion on the applicability of § 335 InsO to the arbitration agreement. If it is even mentioned, some authors suggest that insofar as no more specific conflict-of-laws- rules are applicable, § 335 InsO will apply to arbitration agreements.[1082]

Schmitz, however, concludes that the § 335 InsO rule should not apply.[1083] The primary argument again is that arbitration agreements do not fall within the scope of § 335 InsO, similar to the discussion on Article 7(2)(e) EIR in Chapter 3 § 2.1.3 iii. To exclude arbitration agreements, *Schmitz* relies on the scope of § 335 IsnO, stating that this only includes the insolvency-specific norms, c.q. it asks if the relevant norm is meant to ensure or facilitate the equal satisfaction of creditors.[1084] It is unclear how this qualification of norms, c.q. testing if they are specific to insolvency, can lead to the general exclusion of certain types of contract from the effect of such norms, as the type of contract is not the relevant qualification point.[1085] However, *Schmitz* states that as the arbitration agreement is merely a 'choice of forum' in favour of arbitration excluding local courts, c.q. a procedural contract that does not touch upon the insolvency proceedings, it can be excluded from § 335 InsO's reach as it does not affect the insolvency.[1086] Nevertheless, even if the argument is to be understood as stating that contracts that do not affect the insolvency are not affected by § 335 InsO this is to be rejected. Beyond the concept of separability, an arbitration agreement cannot be seen as entirely divorced from its subject matter. Similar to the argument made regarding Article 7 EIR, if the arbitration agreement is meant to decide upon issues that are part of the insolvency proceedings and affects the procedural rights of parties in insolvency, it should be considered within the scope of § 335 InsO.[1087]

Schmitz suggests that deviating from the law of the seat generally thought applicable to the arbitration clause by applying the *lex fori concursus* leads to arbitrary treatment of the arbitration agreements.[1088] However, this ignores the fact that when the seat of arbitration is Germany, this conflict-of-laws rule is part of the law of the seat and if the seat is elsewhere, this rule can only have effect insofar as the local legislation, i.e., the relevant law of the seat, allows it. As such, the application of the *lex fori concursus* follows from the application of the law of the seat. Insofar as this reference

1082. *S.M. Kröll*, Part IV: Selected Areas and Issues of Arbitration in Germany, Insolvency and Arbitration - Effects of Party Insolvency on Arbitral Proceedings in Germany, 981, No. 74; *Poelzig*, ZZPInt. 14 (2009), 393, p. 434; *Riedel*, Insolvenz in nationalen und internationalen Schiedsverfahren, p. 147; *Schmitz*, Schiedsverfahren und Insolvenz, pp. 213–214; *P.K. Wagner*, Abstimmungsfragen zwischen Internationalem Insolvenzrecht und Internationaler Schiedsgerichtsbarkeit, p. 148.
1083. *Schmitz*, Schiedsverfahren und Insolvenz, pp. 221–222.
1084. BeckOK InsO/*Martini* § 335 InsO, No. 33.
1085. As seems to be argued by *Schmitz*, Schiedsverfahren und Insolvenz, pp. 221–222.
1086. *Schmitz*, Schiedsverfahren und Insolvenz, p. 222.
1087. Arguably Martini also links the two tests BeckOK InsO/*Martini* § 335 InsO, No. 30; The German legislator also generally links § 335 InsO to Art. 4 (now 7) EIR Entwurf eines Gesetzes zur Neuregelung des Internationalen Insolvenzrechts of 25.10.2002, BT-Drs. 15/16, p. 18 at 'Zu § 335'.
1088. *Schmitz*, Schiedsverfahren und Insolvenz, p. 223.

to the arbitrary application of law should be understood to mean that it is arbitrary in general to apply foreign insolvency law to an arbitration agreement otherwise governed by the internal law of the seat, that argument clearly cannot succeed. It would invalidate the application of foreign insolvency law on contracts governed by another substantive law in general, i.e., invalidate the basis of any universalist-leaning international insolvency law which recognises the effects of foreign insolvency law as described therein.

In conclusion, § 335 InsO should be deemed applicable to arbitration agreements. In this case, what seems to be the majority opinion is also the correct approach.

ii Applicability of § 352 InsO to Arbitration Proceedings

§ 352 InsO reflects prima facie the same norm as Article 18 EIR, namely the suspension of ongoing proceedings. As such, it is relevant to consider if this applies to arbitration as well. § 352 InsO is a material norm that applies to proceedings in international insolvency in Germany. In line with the conflict-of-laws rules of Article 18 EIR, it refers the regulation of the effects of insolvency on ongoing foreign proceedings to the law of the country where such proceedings are pending.[1089]

Whereas the European legislator in Article 18 EIR has explicitly chosen to apply the suspension of proceedings to arbitration, this remains a debated subject for § 352 InsO as much as it is under § 240 ZPO.[1090] Due to the fundamental similarity between § 240 ZPO and § 352 InsO, it would be systematically incoherent to come to different conclusions regarding their applicability to arbitration. In fact, most authors hardly bother to make an independent argumentation when it comes to § 352 InsO and its application to arbitration.[1091] The fact that § 352 InsO is mainly merely the international version of § 240 ZPO cannot be ignored.[1092] It follows that the same conclusion as was made concerning § 240 ZPO must be supported here in regard to § 352 InsO.[1093]

Consequently, the complete argumentation reference can be read in the above discussion on § 240 ZPO in Chapter 2 § 2.3.1. In short, § 352 InsO is not directly applicable to arbitration.[1094] Mainly because the rules of the ZPO outside of the specific rules on arbitration do not apply to arbitration.[1095] *Paulus* prima facie has a valid point that the fact that the European legislator has actively added the word arbitration to

1089. BeckOK InsO/*Weissinger* § 352 InsO, Nos 1–3.
1090. *See* § 2.3.1 in particular ii; BeckOK InsO/*Weissinger* § 352 InsO, No. 10.
1091. *Nacimiento/Bähr*, NJOZ 2009, 4752, p. 4761; *Schultze-Moderow*, Schiedsverfahren und Insolvenz, p. 50; Although supporting a different conclusion Riedel links the arguments on § 240 InsO directly to § 352 *Riedel*, Insolvenz in nationalen und internationalen Schiedsverfahren, pp. 158–159; MüKoInsO/*Thole* § 352 insO, No. 16.
1092. The German legislator also seems to treat § 352 InsO as the international pendant of § 240 InsO, *see* Entwurf eines Gesetzes zur Neuregelung des Internationalen Insolvenzrechts of 25.10.2002, BT-Drs. 15/16, p. 24 under 'Zu § 352'; *Poelzig*, ZZPInt. 14 (2009), 393, pp. 433–434.
1093. *See* § 2.3.1, in particular ii; *Schmitz*, Schiedsverfahren und Insolvenz, p. 219.
1094. MüKoBGB/*Kindler* § 352 InsO, No. 6; *Nacimiento/Bähr*, NJOZ 2009, 4752, p. 4761; differently *G. Wagner*, KTS 2010, 39, pp. 61–62.
1095. *Schultze-Moderow*, Schiedsverfahren und Insolvenz, p. 50; MüKoInsO/*Schumacher* Vorbemerkungen vor §§ 85 bis 87, No. 53.

Article 18 EIR makes it harder to argue that the wording 'legal disputes' in § 352 InsO would not include arbitration. The German legislator has actively leaned on the EIR while making the German autonomous international insolvency law.[1096] However, the argument is questionable. Whereas the German legislator has leaned on the old EIR for its autonomous international insolvency law, and whereas this supports the position that the interpretation of that piece of EU legislation can be used as an aid to interpret the German law, the argument that the new version of the EIR could also be used is more tenuous. The new EIR cannot directly be used to interpret the legislative intent of the German legislator as it simply did not exist at the time the German autonomous international insolvency law was written into law. Therefore, *Paulus'* argument must rely on several tenuous points: first, that the new EIR simply made explicit what was already implicit in the old EIR, c.q. in the context of Article 15-old and now Article 18 EIR, and second, that the German legislator was either aware of this or incorporated it regardless due to its reference to corresponding rules in the EIR.[1097] There is no proof for this, and consequently, this argument is unpersuasive. Furthermore, as pointed out in the discussion on § 240 ZPO, the discussion on the reach of the word 'proceedings' or 'legal disputes' is relatively futile for the question of its direct application in arbitration. For that application, it is only relevant if the rule belongs to either mandatory law or *ordre public* rules, which courts have not confirmed.[1098] This does not apply to court proceedings that surround arbitration, which will be suspended under § 352 InsO.[1099]

In the above, it has been argued that the EIR, c.q. its conflict-of-laws rules, pass the *Eco Swiss* test and are to be considered *ordre public communautaire* and with that German *ordre public.*[1100] If that conclusion is viewed in conjunction with *Paulus'* argument that the inclusion of 'arbitration' into the new EIR, specifically Article 18 EIR, makes it untenable to argue that it is not included in its equivalent in § 352 InsO, an interesting question arises. If one were to accept the argument that arbitration is technically included in § 352 InsO, and thus most likely also § 240 ZPO, the only hurdle that keeps § 352 InsO from suspending arbitration is that, until now, these rules have not been viewed as *ordre public* rules or rules of mandatory law in Germany that tribunals seated there have to apply to avoid annulment. Arguably the identification of the EIR as EU *ordre public* could speak in favour of identifying the equivalent rules in German law as German *ordre public.* However, as the *Eco-Swiss*-test prescribes, the EIR is to be described as EU *ordre public* as it supports the functioning of the internal market, not due to the specific importance of the suspension rule. Second, insofar as one was to identify the specific suspension rule as particularly important, as some

1096. KPB-InsO/*Paulus* § 352 InsO, No. 4 fn. 12.
1097. Cf. Entwurf eines Gesetzes zur Neuregelung des Internationalen Insolvenzrechts of 25.10.2002, BT-Drs. 15/16.
1098. *BGH*, NJW 2009, 1747–1750, No. 28; *Nacimiento/Bähr*, NJOZ 2009, 4752, p. 4761; the two point; the question if § 352 InsO would technically incorporate arbitrations and its applicability in arbitration, are often not separated by authors, *see* K. Schmidt InsO/*Brinkmann* § 352 InsO, No. 5.
1099. *BGH*, NZI 2017, 774, No. 12.
1100. *See* Chapter 3 § 2.1.

might argue every rule on its own must satisfy the test of EU *ordre public*, this test would only prove its importance in an EU-internal, internal market context. However, it would not directly support the identification of § 352 InsO as *ordre public* in the context of German autonomous international insolvency law.

Application by analogy within the narrow concept thereof used in German law is also to be ruled out.[1101] As *Schmitz* provided concerning the application of § 240 ZPO by analogy, German law and case law have established a narrow understanding of application by analogy, *see* Chapter 2 § 2.3.1 iv. In this case, the primary argument against analogy is that it cannot be proved that there is an unplanned lacuna in the law. The right to be heard as protected by § 240 ZPO and § 352 InsO, is protected in arbitration by §§ 1042(1)(2) and 1059(2)(1)(b) ZPO.[1102]

Based on §§ 1042(1)(2) and 1059(2)(1)(b) ZPO, c.q. the right to be heard an equal treatment, one could, in the non-legal meaning of the term, speak of indirect application, as the application of §§ 1049(1)(2) and 1059(2)(1)(b) ZPO lead to a result analogous to § 352 InsO.[1103]

One could question how far this factual analogy goes, particularly regarding the reference to the rule regarding the continuation of proceedings and the reference made there to the *lex concursus* in the second sentence of § 352(1) InsO. As the suspension only follows from the principles prescribed by the ZPO, the question of the continuation of proceedings is primarily within the discretion of the tribunal, as this rule cannot be directly transferred to arbitration. However, the reference in § 352 InsO to the *lex concursus* regarding the procedural capacity is meant to respect the foreign insolvency proceedings and their effect on this capacity.[1104] This idea is translatable to arbitration under § 1059(2)(1)(a) ZPO, c.q. the right to be heard. Consequently, it is to be respected in the context of the pursuit to protect the award from annulment if not to safeguard enforcement in the state of the foreign insolvency proceedings.[1105]

As such, the same conclusion is reached as in the national context *see* Chapter 2 § 2.3.1, a stay must be provided in ongoing arbitrations but not because of direct or analogous application of § 352(1) InsO to arbitration.

iii §§ 335 and 352 InsO: The Syska v. Vivendi Question or Lack Thereof

As discussed in the previous subsection, practice and academia perceived tension between Article 7(2)(e) and 18 EIR. This leads to the question if this same tension arises between the equivalent, c.q. comparable, sections of the InsO. The superficial answer seems that this is not the case. Taking the point of view that § 335 InsO applies

1101. Differently *Riedel*, Insolvenz in nationalen und internationalen Schiedsverfahren, p. 159.
1102. *See* Chapter 3 § 2.3.1 iv; *Schmitz*, Schiedsverfahren und Insolvenz, p. 72.
1103. *Nacimiento/Bähr*, NJOZ 2009, 4752, p. 4762; *Poelzig*, ZZPInt. 14 (2009), 393, p. 434; MüKoInsO/*Schumacher* Vorbemerkungen vor §§ 85 bis 87, No. 53.
1104. Entwurf eines Gesetzes zur Neuregelung des Internationalen Insolvenzrechts of 25.10.2002, BT-Drs. 15/16, p. 24 under 'Zu § 352'.
1105. *Poelzig*, ZZPInt. 14 (2009), 393, p. 435.

to arbitration agreements but § 352 InsO does not apply in arbitration proceedings more or less seems to nullify the issue discussed in *Syska v. Vivendi* regarding the tension between Articles 7(2)(e) and 18 EIR:[1106] i.e., §§ 335 and 352 InsO are not in competition for applicability, there is no potential overlap.

However, this provides us with another potentially problematic outcome. *Reinhart* provides a neat summary of the potential dogmatic situation: If one applies § 352 InsO to arbitration, one does not have to take into account § 335 InsO for ongoing arbitrations, i.e., the same conclusion reached regarding Articles 7(2)(e) and 18 EIR. However, if one finds – as is argued here – that § 352 InsO does not apply to arbitration, then the rule of § 335 InsO applies, referring the question of suspension of proceedings to the *lex fori processus*, i.e., the law of the insolvency.[1107] In the author's opinion, this is an undesirable outcome as this creates legal uncertainty as a law other than the *lex arbitri* is applied, which might be unforeseeable to a large degree.

An application of the rule of § 352 InsO directly or indirectly depends on the applicable arbitration rules and §§ 1025 et seq. ZPO (Book 10).[1108] Book 10 ZPO provides no mandatory application of § 352 InsO. Neither § 335 InsO nor § 350 InsO constitutes a rule of *ordre public*. However, as provided in the discussion on § 240 ZPO, a factual stay is necessary to effectuate the right to be heard and other *ordre public* principles.[1109]

The application of foreign insolvency law that does not provide the stay provided in § 352 InsO will be restricted by the same *ordre public* principles that support the conclusion that a factual stay must be provided, *see* the previous subparagraph and Chapter 2 § 2.3.1 iii. Moreover, it might even be argued that the need for such a stay is more prominent in the international context as creditors and the administrator are now confronted with a more complex international insolvency.[1110] As such, regardless of § 335 InsO's applicability to arbitration agreements and § 352 InsO's non-applicability to ongoing arbitration, a stay must be provided for arbitration in Germany.

In this context, it is the opinion of the author that the German legislator would do well to make § 352 InsO applicable to arbitration explicitly. This would aid legal certainty and bring the system in §§ 335 and 352 InsO in line with the rules of Articles 7(2)(e) and 18 EIR, a ruleset that the German legislator actively looked at for inspiration.[1111] In doing so, the legislator would essentially be doing what the European legislator did with the EIR-recast in the context of Article 15 EIR-old and Article 18 of the current EIR, *see* Chapter 3 § 2.1.3 ii. Not having to rely on a factual stay and not confronting the parties in arbitration with foreign insolvency law would benefit legal certainty.

1106. *Commercial Court*, Judgment of 2.10.2008 – EWHC 2155 (Comm) *See* Chapter 3 § 2.1.3 iii.
1107. MüKoInsO/*Reinhart* § 335 InsO, No. 81.
1108. *P.K. Wagner*, Abstimmungsfragen zwischen Internationalem Insolvenzrecht und Internationaler Schiedsgerichtsbarkeit, pp. 160–161.
1109. *P.K. Wagner*, Abstimmungsfragen zwischen Internationalem Insolvenzrecht und Internationaler Schiedsgerichtsbarkeit, p. 161.
1110. Cf. Uhlenbruck/*Lüer/Knof* § 352 InsO, No. 1.
1111. *Mincke*, § 45 Internationales Insolvenzrecht, 1371, No. 10.

iv *Law Applicable to Objective Arbitrability*

Whereas § 335 InsO provides that the arbitration agreement will be covered by the *lex fori concursus*. It could be asked if this includes objective arbitrability. There is no more specific conflict-of-laws rule in the German autonomous insolvency law regarding the effect of insolvency on the objective arbitrability of issues. As such, the pertinent question remains if § 335 InsO's reference to the *lex fori concursus* includes the objective arbitrability of issues in insolvency. The majority opinion is that § 335 InsO should be treated as a so-called *Gesamtverweisung* or a general reference as opposed to just a reference to material norms.[1112] This view is correct as in German autonomous law, insofar as the conflict-of-laws rule does not explicitly refer only to the material norms of a law, the conflict-of-laws rules should be understood as a reference to the material and procedural norms, i.e., the complete legal system in the relevant context, a '*Gesamtverweisung*'.[1113] In consequence, the effects of the insolvency on objective arbitrability should be considered within the scope of the reference of § 335 InsO and accordingly be governed by the *lex fori concursus*. However, this does not change the limitations provided by German arbitrability rules in § 1059(2)(2)(a) ZPO.

v *Law Applicable to the Arbitrator's Agreement*

This leaves two ancillary topics for discussion that could profoundly impact the arbitration or effectiveness thereof: the law applicable to the arbitrator's agreement and the law applicable to the award. The first of which is considered here.

Considering the conclusions made before, mainly on the nature of the arbitrator's agreement, i.e., that it is a sui generis contract,[1114] there is hardly any other realistic option than the application of § 335 InsO's reference to the *lex fori concursus* to the arbitrator's agreement.[1115]

The discussion differs when another conclusion is reached regarding the nature of the arbitrator's agreement or if one considers that the arbitrator's contract is not within the scope of insolvency law as it does not concern matters pertaining to the insolvency, as was also discussed regarding the arbitration agreement.[1116] However, the arbitrator's contract and arbitration agreement are in service of resolving a claim, and, as long as that claim is within the scope of the insolvency proceeding, the contracts in service of the resolution of the claim are as well. Furthermore, *Schmitz*'s argument regarding the arbitration agreement, that it is a procedural contract and therefore does not touch upon the insolvency proceedings, is even more untenable in

1112. *R. Geimer/E. Geimer/Geimer*, Internationales Zivilprozessrecht, No. 33753375; BeckOK InsO/*Martini* § 335 InsO, No. 27; MüKoInsO/*Reinhart* § 335 InsO, 9, 11; Braun/*Tashiro* § 335 InsO, No. 8.
1113. *Hay/Rösler*, Internationales Privat- und Zivilverfahrensrecht, p. 118.
1114. *See* § 4 4.1.
1115. *P.K. Wagner*, Abstimmungsfragen zwischen Internationalem Insolvenzrecht und Internationaler Schiedsgerichtsbarkeit, p. 172.
1116. *See* § 2.2.3 i; *Schultze-Moderow*, Schiedsverfahren und Insolvenz, p. 203.

the case of the arbitrator's agreement,[1117] as the arbitrator's agreement contains the substantive rights and duties in the relationship between the parties and the arbitrator as the main stipulations.[1118]

Hence, the arbitrator's agreement is within the scope of the insolvency and, as a contract sui generis, does not fall under any of the exceptions. This leads to the conclusion that § 335 InsO is the only rule that can be applied to the effects of the insolvency on the arbitrator's agreement. Hence, reference should be made to the *lex fori concursus*.

In the above discussion on the EIR, it was argued that the arbitrator's contract should be bundled with the arbitration agreement into the scope of Article 18 EIR. A similar discussion could be had under § 352 InsO. However, since the position is taken here that § 352 InsO finds no direct applicability in arbitration, there is no inherent risk of treating the effects of the insolvency on arbitration contracts, arbitrator's contract and the arbitral proceeding differently. However, were the courts to decide that § 352 InsO should be applied to arbitration, the same view as proposed concerning the EIR should be taken, and § 352 InsO's scope should be considered to encompass both the arbitrator's agreement and the arbitration agreement. However, for that argument to succeed, it would be necessary to argue that § 352 InsO suspension is not merely a material norm but also a conflict-of-laws norm for the effects on lawsuits pending.[1119] However, for the suspension part of § 352 InsO, this cannot be argued, as already follows from the plain text of the article.[1120]

Consequently, the only conclusion remains that § 335 InsO and therewith the *lex fori concursus* applies to the arbitrator's agreement.

vi The Law Applicable to Award: Status in the Insolvency and Annulment and Enforcement

The final question discussed in this subsection is the law applicable to the award. This discussion is relevant as this law will influence or even determine the practical value an award has.

Questions regarding the status of the award are primarily questions for courts to answer after the arbitration proceedings have been closed, except for correction, interpretation and additional proceedings rules such as § 1058 ZPO, which can factually but not legally impact the legal status of an award.

National courts grappling with these questions will automatically apply the *lex fori* as they are bound to do.[1121] Annulment and enforcement proceedings regarding an award on claims covered by the insolvency in Germany will be halted by § 352 InsO. It is commonly accepted that such procedures fall inside the scope of § 240 ZPO, and

1117. *Schmitz*, Schiedsverfahren und Insolvenz, p. 222.
1118. *Born*, International Commercial Arbitration, p. 1975.
1119. *Wessels*, International Insolvency Law, p. 640.
1120. MüKoInsO/*Thole* § 352 insO, No. 1.
1121. *P.K. Wagner*, Abstimmungsfragen zwischen Internationalem Insolvenzrecht und Internationaler Schiedsgerichtsbarkeit, p. 163.

there cannot be a different conclusion on their inclusion in the scope of § 352 InsO that was reached concerning § 240 ZPO.[1122]

Both arbitration and annulment proceedings can be duly continued when the insolvency administrator disputes the claim.[1123] In continued annulment proceedings, especially those stemming from arbitrations wholly or partially conducted by the administrator, the court will have to look at insolvency-specific issues. This can be attributed to specific set-aside grounds. A German court would apply §§ 1059–1061 ZPO for the material norms of enforcement and annulment of awards and § 1062 ZPO for its jurisdiction. The reference in the § 1059(2) ZPO references German law unless otherwise stated, and the court will apply the German concept of *ordre public*, *see also* Article V NYC. Hence, the annulment court must test the award for defects on a case-by-case basis.[1124] For example, they could find a violation of the right to be heard in § 1059(2)(1)(b) ZPO or Article V(1)(b) NYC for failing to provide the administrator with a factual suspension[1125] or violation of insolvency-specific *ordre public* by failing to uphold the German understanding of the equal treatment of the creditors.[1126] The test of *ordre public* in enforcement proceedings for foreign awards is restricted to those concepts of *ordre public* considered international.[1127]

As for the role of the award in the insolvency proceedings, there is only one law that can be referred to, the law governing the insolvency proceedings, the *lex fori concursus*. The claim must be registered with the competent insolvency courts, and those courts will apply their *lex fori*, c.q. the *lex fori concursus*. In Germany, as discussed, the award could, in most circumstances, be registered as proof of a claim,[1128] which can be challenged depending on the time at which they have been rendered, following the relevant procedures.[1129]

1122. *See* § 5.4.1; *BGH*, NZI 2017, 774, No. 11; *Flöther*, Auswirkungen des inländischen Insolvenzverfahrens auf Schiedsverfahren und Schiedsabrede, 52–53, 55; *S.M. Kröll*, Part IV: Selected Areas and Issues of Arbitration in Germany, Insolvency and Arbitration – Effects of Party Insolvency on Arbitral Proceedings in Germany, 981, p. 1007; *Nacimiento/Bähr*, NJOZ 2009, 4752, 4755, 4761; Cf. Entwurf eines Gesetzes zur Neuregelung des Internationalen Insolvenzrechts of 25.10.2002, BT-Drs. 15/16, p. 24 under 'Zu § 352'.

1123. *See, e.g.*, §§ 5.3.2, 5.4.2.

1124. *S.M. Kröll*, Part IV: Selected Areas and Issues of Arbitration in Germany, Insolvency and Arbitration – Effects of Party Insolvency on Arbitral Proceedings in Germany, 981, pp. 1009–1010.

1125. *S.M. Kröll*, Part IV: Selected Areas and Issues of Arbitration in Germany, Insolvency and Arbitration – Effects of Party Insolvency on Arbitral Proceedings in Germany, 981, p. 1009.

1126. Many potential violations have been discussed throughout this book, reference to the discussion on arbitrability, standing and representation and the effect of insolvency on the proceedings, *see* §§ 1.4, 2.2.1, 2.3.1 iii, 2.3.3. *Nacimiento/Bähr*, NJOZ 2009, 4752, pp. 4755–4756.

1127. Musielak/Voit/*Voit* § 1061 ZPO, Nos 23–24.

1128. *S.M. Kröll*, Part IV: Selected Areas and Issues of Arbitration in Germany, Insolvency and Arbitration – Effects of Party Insolvency on Arbitral Proceedings in Germany, 981, pp. 1007–1008.

1129. *See* §§ 5.2, 5.3 et seq.

vii Interim Conclusion: Arbitration and the German Autonomous International Insolvency Law

In this subsection, the conflict-of-laws rules of the German Insolvency Code were discussed, in particular regarding arbitration and arbitration-related issues. Although the German autonomous international insolvency law has much in common with the EIR regarding insolvency in arbitration, the optics might be deceiving. Applying either the EIR or the German autonomous international insolvency law as preliminary questions to, for example, the substantive claim in dispute would not lead to significantly different results. On the contrary, it would lead to the same results in most instances. However, due to the different assessments of their applicability to arbitration and the *ordre public* nature of the Articles 7, 18 EIR versus §§ 335, 352 InsO, the effect on the arbitration proceedings might differ in terms of the rules that are applied. Whereas the next section will speak to what tribunals have to apply as conflict-of-laws rules and applicable law, it is important to note this here as the court in the annulment proceedings will only test this question insofar as rules are mandatory or part of the *ordre public.*

Accordingly, a court in annulment proceedings will not 'apply' § 352 InsO in its assessment of the award. Whereas, insofar as the argument above is followed on the *ordre public* nature of the EIR, it will 'apply' Article 18 EIR. This leads to the conclusion that the system might still throw up different results when applying either the EIR or the German autonomous international insolvency law, despite their optic similarity. Nevertheless, it has to be noted that factually the results are likely still remarkably similar, i.e., a suspension of the procedure. However, the route taken is distinguishable, i.e., the application of Article 18 EIR as *ordre public* or suspension by way of necessity under the right to be heard and the right to equal treatment.

2.3 Conclusion on the Conflicts-of-Rules and Applicable Law in the Court

This section looked at the different relevant sets of conflict-of-laws rules applied to insolvency questions by the German courts, in particular in regard to arbitration and arbitration-related issues. Although clearly there is a discussion on the interpretation and application of the relevant rules, courts have a relatively straightforward framework to rely upon in case they are confronted with insolvency in arbitration. First, they have to qualify the question before them and then look for the appropriate rules and conflict-of-laws system provided by the *lex fori*. Not necessarily in this order, as the qualification of issues is often provided by the conflict-of-laws rules themselves.

The conflict-of-laws rules discussed in the context of an ongoing proceeding should be viewed as aiming to apply a single law to all its procedural aspects. For arbitration, this means not only the procedure but also the necessary agreements therefor. Thus, the arbitration agreement and the arbitrator's agreement should be seen as encompassed by this rule. Arbitration agreements of not initiated proceedings can and are subjected to other laws. Furthermore, the conflict-of-laws rules also generally provide rules that can be used to identify the law that applies to other issues of insolvency in arbitration, such as objective arbitrability and the role of an award. In consequence, the position of the court in their legal order and the related binding to the conflict-of-laws rules and legal framework of this legal order provides them with a way forward to investigate the applicable law to issues of insolvency in arbitration. Whereas, for arbitral tribunals, this might be an entirely different story.

3 CONFLICT-OF-LAWS RULES BEFORE THE TRIBUNAL

In the following section, the discussion of the previous section, i.e., conflict-of-laws rules, will be moved into the context of arbitral tribunals. Before a tribunal can answer any question whatsoever on the effect of international, c.q. foreign, insolvency on an arbitration proceeding, it must look for the right ruleset to apply to find such answers. In this context, this warrants the application of a conflict-of-laws ruleset or doctrine as, in an international context, several different laws could apply.

The question of the applicable law features throughout this part and must be redetermined for every issue. However, the higher-order question of which conflict-of-laws rules apply must be considered first to answer these questions. Similar to the discussion on the relationship between the arbitration proceedings and the seat jurisdiction in the context of in-seat insolvencies, one can ask oneself if the tribunal must apply the seat country's conflict-of-laws rules on international insolvencies. With this also comes the qualification of domestic and foreign insolvencies, as this qualification can only exist from a perspective in which one jurisdiction is considered the 'home' or domestic jurisdiction.[1130]

Some authors step over the question of the applicable conflict-of-laws rules. Due to the non-discussion of the topic, it becomes hard to see if these writers have not identified the issue at all or are merely strongly convinced that the conflict-of-laws rules of the seat should apply or perhaps that no conflict-of-laws rules should apply at all, as the latter is a purported result of the *voie directe* doctrine described below.[1131] Others propose that the arbitration must apply an autonomous conflict-of-laws system. Whatever the case may be, this issue deserves proper attention. The choice of method or doctrine to determine the applicable conflict-of-laws system or its non-application, and with this, the applicable law is entwined with one's view of arbitration. Specifically, it relies on the relationship between arbitration and its seat jurisdiction.[1132]

In the below, the traditional approach of applying the law of the seat will be discussed first (§ 3.1). Then the autonomous approach will be discussed (§ 3.2), and finally, the construction of such an autonomous approach will be attempted and discussed (§ 3.3).

1130. *P.K. Wagner*, Abstimmungsfragen zwischen Internationalem Insolvenzrecht und Internationaler Schiedsgerichtsbarkeit, pp. 86–87.
1131. *Schmitz*, Schiedsverfahren und Insolvenz, 212 et seq.
1132. Chapter 2 § 2.1. contains a discussion on the relation the relationship between the seat jurisdiction and the arbitration.

3.1 The Traditional Approach: Law of the Seat

Historically, it has been the accepted method for the tribunal to apply the conflict-of-laws system of the seat.[1133] Therefore, it is with this approach that this examination is started. Until the start of the seventies, this theory had gone mostly unchallenged, particularly in the European space.[1134] The Institute for International Law (*Institut de Droit International*), an international institute for experts on international law, even ratified a resolution in 1957, which largely shows this to be the international consensus: 'Les règles de rattachement en vigueur dans l'Etat du siège du tribunal doivent être suivies pour déterminer la loi applicable au fond du litige.'[1135] This idea still finds adherence today, albeit not always explicit. Coupling this back to the arbitration theories, this is not surprising. Historically, the jurisdictional view of arbitration has been dominant, i.e., arbitration functioning as part of, and within the boundaries of, a conflict resolution system of national jurisdiction. The application of conflict-of-laws rules of the seat jurisdiction is a logical outcome of the proper application of this theory.[1136]

Arguments in favour of the binding of arbitration to the conflict-of-laws system of the seat primarily centre on the relationship of the arbitration to the seat jurisdiction: i.e., the seat country provides the eventual award with a nationality, c.q. viewing it as domestic or international if not foreign arbitration within the definition of an arbitration law. The seat provides the procedural framework, many of the provided rules can be derogated from but this is still only so by virtue of the relevant law itself. In light of this, it is argued that the *lex loci arbitri* should be considered a true *lex fori* as all this creates a strong link between the seat state and the arbitration. Thus, it is concluded that conflict-of-laws questions should be answered with the rules provided by the law of the seat.[1137]

However, arguing that there is a relationship between the seat country, which provides the legal framework, and the arbitration is simply not sufficient to conclude that the tribunal is bound to apply the conflict-of-laws system of the seat. For the conclusion to be reached that a tribunal is bound to apply the conflict-of-laws rules of the seat state, the tribunal must be considered part of the judiciary to which these rules are addressed. However, following most modern views of arbitration, an arbitral tribunal cannot just reach for the same rules that provide a state court with guidance in relevant cases.[1138] Similar to the discussion on the application of domestic insolvency law, it cannot be said that an arbitral tribunal is bound to these rules per se. The argument in favour of the traditional approach, as described above, relies on a jurisdictional approach to arbitration and directly or indirectly embeds arbitration and

1133. *Ly*, Nw. J. Int'l L. & Bus. 12 (1991), 48, p. 62; *Schlosser*, Das Recht des internationalen privaten Schiedsgerichtsbarkeit, p. 581.
1134. *Sandrock*, RIW 38 (1992), p. 785.
1135. *Százy*, III. L'arbitrage en droit international privé, F. Article 11; as cited by *Sandrock*, RIW 38 (1992), p. 785.
1136. *Schultze-Moderow*, Schiedsverfahren und Insolvenz, p. 120.
1137. *Sandrock*, RIW 38 (1992), 785, p. 786.
1138. *See* Chapter 1, in particular § 4.

the tribunal into the seat's legal order and sovereign adjudication system. However, the arbitral tribunal does not form part of the judicial order of the country and is hence not bound to the same rules as the judiciary. As previously argued in Chapter 2 § 2.1, arbitration is an expression of, and a consequence of, the contractual will of the involved parties. Consequently, the framework in which an arbitral tribunal has to operate is far less clear.[1139]

Due to the contractual nature of arbitration, arbitral tribunals do not have a proper *lex fori*.[1140] The law of the seat as the legal order giving effect to the parties' agreement, the *lex arbitri*, partially takes over this function.[1141] However, whereas most any *lex fori* provides at least a comprehensive if not topic-specific conflict-of-laws rules framework, a *lex arbitri* generally does not. Primarily because *lex arbitri* is understood to only refer to the part of the law specifically applicable to arbitration.[1142] In Germany, only Book 10 ZPO specifically addresses arbitration, as seen in § 1025 ZPO; *see also* § 1043(3) ZPO. The German arbitration code does not provide any guidance on applicable law, except for the law applicable to the substance of the conflict, *see* § 1051 ZPO, which is the only conflict-of-laws rule generally found in arbitration laws. However, even this meagre guidance is disputed. *Voit* argues that the entirety of Book 10 ZPO is only addressed to courts in annulment and enforcement proceedings. From that point of view, even the meagre conflict-of-laws of Book 10 do not directly bind the tribunal but only by virtue of avoiding annulment.[1143] This view is not shared by this author, as the *lex arbitri* contains many rules directed at arbitral tribunals and which are largely irrelevant to the annulment and enforcement proceedings. Furthermore, the legislator states that he wishes to regulate arbitration [seated in Germany], not merely annulment or enforcement proceedings: 'Liegt der Ort des Schiedsverfahrens in Deutschland, soll für das Verfahren künftig zwinged das neue 10. Buch der ZPO gelten, [...]'.[1144] § 1025(1) ZPO, therefore, represents a sovereignty claim

1139. MüKoBGB/*Martiny* Vorbemerkung zu Art. 1 Rom I-VO, 100 et seq; *Schultze-Moderow*, Schiedsverfahren und Insolvenz, p. 101; *Vorburger*, International Arbitration and Cross-Border Insolvency, p. 46; *Eckhardt*, Internationale Handelsschiedsgerichtsbarkeit und Insolvenzverfahren: Die Bestimmung des maßgeblichen Rechts, 934, p. 935.

1140. *Final Award in ICC Case No. 6379*, Collection of ICC Awards III, 1997, No. 2121; *Award in ICC Case No. 2119*, Collection of ICC Awards I, 1990, 355, pp. 356–357 observations Y. Derains; *Final Award in ICC Case No. 1512*, Collection of ICC Awards I, 1990, 3–5, p. 4; *J.D.M. Lew*, Applicable Law in International Commercial Arbitration, p. 535; *P.K. Wagner*, Abstimmungsfragen zwischen Internationalem Insolvenzrecht und Internationaler Schiedsgerichtsbarkeit, p. 136.

1141. *Schultze-Moderow*, Schiedsverfahren und Insolvenz, p. 101; *Vorburger*, International Arbitration and Cross-Border Insolvency, p. 84.

1142. *Blackaby et al.*, Redfern and Hunter on International Arbitration, 3.42–3.47; *Born*, International Commercial Arbitration, p. 1599.

1143. Musielak/Voit/*Voit* § 1025 ZPO, p. 3; Musielak/Voit/*Voit* § 1051 ZPO, No. 9; Cf. Entwurf eines Gesetzes zur Neuregelung des Schiedsverfahrensrechts of 12.7.1996, BT-Drs. 13/5274, 31–32.

1144. Entwurf eines Gesetzes zur Neuregelung des Schiedsverfahrensrechts of 12.7.1996, BT-Drs. 13/5274, pp. 30–31; MüKoZPO/*Münch* § 1051 ZPO, Nos 1–2; *Schultze-Moderow*, Schiedsverfahren und Insolvenz, p. 111; *Schütze*, Armut im internationalen Schiedsverfahren, 867, p. 871.

as to the organisation of arbitration within the jurisdiction.[1145] However, for the conclusions in this book, this discussion is largely irrelevant, as under both premises the sanction for violating the mandatory rules of Book 10 will be annulment, and, more specifically, the *lex arbitri* of Germany does not contain rules relating to insolvency-specific questions.

In line with the above, the traditional approach must be rejected. A tribunal is not directly bound to apply the (entire) conflict-of-laws system of the seat state. However, this does not preclude that specific conflict-of-laws rules of the seat state are applied for other reasons than a direct and inherent binding or because they form part of the *lex arbitri*.

3.2 The Autonomous Approach

The second approach to be discussed in this context is the so-called autonomous approach. As is argued here, this approach is the natural consequence of the conclusion that the tribunal has no true *lex fori*.

With the recognition that an arbitral tribunal has no true *lex fori* comes not only the conclusion that a tribunal is not bound to the conflict-of-law rules of the seat jurisdiction[1146] but also the recognition that it is necessarily not bound to the conflict-of-law rules of any other state.[1147] For example, there is no direct binding to the system of the home jurisdiction of one of the parties or that of prospective enforcement. This conclusion is based on the same reasons why a tribunal is not bound to the conflict-of-laws rules of the seat jurisdiction. If one finds that the nature of arbitration is such as described above in Chapter 2 § 2.1, i.e., based first and foremost on contracts, the conclusion that the tribunal is not bound to such rules and procedures as must be followed and applied by courts extends to the rules of all involved jurisdictions.

Therefore, a new approach is needed to find applicable laws. Several methods and tools have been proposed over the years. To name a few of the more well-known approaches: the cumulative approach, the general principles of the conflict-of-laws approach, and the direct approach. The cumulative approach comes down to checking the conflict-of-laws systems of all involved jurisdictions and looking primarily for a majority therein or, in some circumstances, the most pro-arbitration ruleset out of those systems. Connected to the latter approach is the validation principle, i.e., applying the law that validates the arbitration agreement when determining the applicable law. The general principles approach aims to apply transnational rules based on general principles, i.e., not directly connected to any national system. Finally,

1145. *See* Chapter 2 § 2.1.1; *Handorn*, Das Sonderkollisionsrecht der deutschen internationalen Schiedsgerichtsbarkeit, p. 25; *Schultze-Moderow*, Schiedsverfahren und Insolvenz, p. 111.
1146. *Final Award in ICC Case No. 1512*, Collection of ICC Awards I, 1990, 3–5, p. 4.
1147. *Final Award in ICC Case No. 13954*, Collection of ICC Awards VI, 2013, 519, p. 529; *Partial Award in ICC Case No. 6719*, Collection of ICC Awards III, 1997, 567, 573, 577 note by J.J. Arnaldez; *Final Award in ICC Case No. 6379*, Collection of ICC Awards III, 1997, No. 2323; *Kessedjian*, Chapter 3: Determination and Application of Relevant National and International Law and Rules, 71, p. 81; *J.D.M. Lew/Mistelis/Kröll*, Comparative International Commercial Arbitration, pp. 425–426; *Prioux*, RDCD 1988, 251, p. 267.

a direct approach simply applies a law without taking the conflict-of-laws step, the *voie directe* – primarily based on a 'most-suited-law'-approach.

This book supports the 'autonomous approach', which has been becoming more accepted.[1148] However, it is sometimes hard to clearly delineate between the mentioned approaches, especially in practice where one may be used as an aid in the other and, as such, essentially apply multiple methods at once.

What *Sandrock* describes as the new approach in 1992 is no longer a novelty, as it started to take off in the seventies.[1149] However, his description of the new approach as an approach focused on the tribunal's discretion is an excellent catch-all descriptor of most of the doctrines that have been posited as new and opposite to the above-described traditional approach. More often, these approaches are described as focused on the parties' autonomy.[1150] However, the term 'autonomous' in 'autonomous approach' mainly reflects the fact that the conflict-of-laws system that should be used is to be found autonomously. Autonomously, as used here, means that the conflict-of-laws system should be established independently from the seat jurisdictions' conflict-of-laws system or any other conflict-of-laws systems. It must be established based on the parties' will and subsidiarily the tribunal's discretion when that will is unclear.[1151] To an extent, a discussion about the demarcation between a direct approach and an autonomous approach can be had as both do not, at least directly, follow established state rules and the matter is placed within the tribunal's discretion. This can largely be considered a simple matter of semantics. However, the autonomous approach aims to create an autonomous set of conflict-of-laws rules. The result of these rules, the applicable law, plays into this consideration but is not the consideration itself. Thus, from a semantical perspective, the term autonomous conflict-of-laws ruleset seems a better fit, as, in essence, the goal is to create considerations that operate in a conflict-of-laws analogous way.[1152]

Why the autonomous approach is to be preferred has a lot to do with the nature and principles of arbitration, i.e., the contractual nature and the therewith-entwined supremacy of the parties' will in arbitration. In regard to the applicable law to the dispute itself, the argument is the simplest, as the autonomy of the parties and the discretion of the tribunal are generally clearly stated in the relevant arbitration law. There is a wealth of sources in arbitration laws that provide the parties with the freedom to choose the applicable law, and in case of no choice has been made, the tribunal itself can find and apply a law that it finds reasonable to apply.[1153] This is the only conflict-of-laws rule that is ubiquitous in arbitration laws. Most arbitration laws

1148. MüKoBGB/*Martiny* Vorbemerkung zu Art. 1 Rom I-VO, No. 108; *Ly*, Nw. J. Int'l L. & Bus. 12 (1991), 48, p. 63.
1149. *Sandrock*, RIW 38 (1992), 785, p. 789.
1150. *Schultze-Moderow*, Schiedsverfahren und Insolvenz, pp. 127–128; *P.K. Wagner*, Abstimmungsfragen zwischen Internationalem Insolvenzrecht und Internationaler Schiedsgerichtsbarkeit, p. 137.
1151. *J.D.M. Lew/Mistelis/Kröll*, *J.D.M. Lew/Mistelis/Kröll*, Comparative International Commercial Arbitration, p. 426.
1152. *Schultze-Moderow*, Schiedsverfahren und Insolvenz, p. 128.
1153. *Sandrock*, RIW 38 (1992), 785, p. 790.

contain a rule to determine the law applicable to the dispute.[1154] *See, e.g.*, Article 28 of the Arb.ML. However, the term 'reasonable' [to apply], as used herein, is slightly misleading because the tribunal cannot, unless so empowered, make a decision based on equitability; rather, it has to apply specific rules and considerations to find an applicable law. In this sense, the tribunal cannot choose just any law without reasoning but must 'find' a suitable law and thus apply reasonable conflict-of-laws rules or considerations.[1155] Insofar as the Tribunal is applying Article 28 Arb.ML or other similar articles providing the tribunal with a broad discretion, it is, in the opinion of this author, technically incorrect to speak of a *voie directe* as the tribunal by mentioning such articles is applying the conflict-of-laws rule that this article represents and is per se.[1156]

For questions that cannot be answered by conflict-of-laws rules directly addressed to the tribunal, the search for a conflict-of-law rule persists. As stated above, no *lex arbitri* known to the author contains an exhaustive regulation of conflict-of-laws rules, let alone one specific to insolvency issues. It is understandable that a legal practitioner in such a situation might want to reach back to the clarity of the extensive conflict-of-laws system that a *lex fori* offers. However, this cannot be squared with the current views of arbitration, especially the view propagated above: arbitration as the performance of a special sort of contract within the boundaries created therefor by the law of the seat. In the context of this conclusion, it is important to note that the fact that a tribunal is not bound to the conflict-of-laws rules of the seat is not based on arguments in favour of an absolute autonomous view. Those views argue that the parties' will has some sort of independent constitutive or legislative value separate from any legal order, either intrinsically or based on the application of the *lex mercatoria*.[1157] Instead, the view represented here is based on the lack of guidance provided in the legal framework governing the relevant contract and the fact that beyond this contractual framework, the arbitrator is not obliged to apply the law of the seat as a judge would have to. This lack of specific guidance, c.q. the considerable freedom of the parties can also be seen in the German legal arbitration framework. § 1042 ZPO should also be read like this. No ZPO rules apply beyond the book of arbitration, Book 10.[1158] Aside from § 1051 ZPO, the law applicable to the substance of the dispute Book 10 does not possess any overt conflict-of-laws rules, let alone any rules specific to insolvency issues.

1154. *Ly*, Nw. J. Int'l L. & Bus. 12 (1991), 48, pp. 64–65.
1155. *P.K. Wagner*, Abstimmungsfragen zwischen Internationalem Insolvenzrecht und Internationaler Schiedsgerichtsbarkeit, pp. 136–137; *Kessedjian*, Chapter 3: Determination and Application of Relevant National and International Law and Rules, 71, pp. 81–82.
1156. Although this is often done *Award in ICC Case No. 6840*, Collection of ICC Awards III, 1997, 467, p. 471; *Award in ICC Case No. 6500*, Collection of ICC Awards III, 1997, 452, p. 454.
1157. *Schlosser*, Das Recht des internationalen privaten Schiedsgerichtsbarkeit, p. 582; *Ly*, Nw. J. Int'l L. & Bus. 12 (1991), 48, p. 67; *see* for an application of the lex mercatoria *Final Award in ICC Case No. 8385*, Collection of ICC Awards IV, 2003, 474, pp. 477–480; *Award in ICC Case No. 3540*, Collection of ICC Awards I, 1990, 399, p. 402; in ICC Case 6500 the Tribunal decides to apply the lex mercatoria in a subsidiary role only as a natural connection, i.e., closest connection, to another legal order can be established, *see Award in ICC Case No. 6500*, Collection of ICC Awards III, 1997, 452, pp. 453–455.
1158. *Schultze-Moderow*, Schiedsverfahren und Insolvenz, p. 126.

For lack of guidance, an arbitrator could also decide to bypass the issue of applicable law and answer the relevant questions on an equitable basis. However, this is undoubtedly wrong, insofar as it has not been mandated by the parties,[1159] as it should be beyond question that an arbitrator cannot equitably decide upon the question of the legal personality of a party, c.q. questions of its representation, which become relevant in the context of insolvency administrators.[1160] Legal personality is exclusively provided by and organised by jurisdictions. This is explicitly recognised in arbitration. *See* the annulment ground in § 1059(2)(1)(a) ZPO and Article V(1)(a) NYC, which refers representation issues to the personal law of the party, i.e., the jurisdiction that gave it legal personality.

Insofar as the tribunal is not bound by a choice of the parties, directly or indirectly, by a choice of a set to a conflict-of-laws rule, the tribunal is not directly bound to apply any conflict-of-laws rules. However, considering that it cannot, as stated, just haphazardly apply a particular law, it can apply the so-called direct way or '*voie directe*' and, with the appropriate reasoning, find that a particular substantive law applies. The *voie directe* has become more accepted when it comes to investigating the appropriate law for substantive conflict, c.q. contractual questions, mainly relying on the 'closest relationship'-rule, in which the law with the closest relationship to the contract is deemed applicable to said contract.[1161] The reasoning put forward under the *voie directe*, such as the concept of the 'closest relationship' or 'centre of gravity' test, is a test based on the parties' interests. In the case of the closest-relationship test, this basis is primarily the interest of protecting the parties' legitimate expectations. In the author's opinion, the *voie directe* approach in this way does not so much evade the application of conflict-of-law rules but, in this way, constitutes and creates a conflict-of-laws test in itself.[1162] In this sense, the creation of an autonomous set of conflict-of-laws rules could vice versa also be seen as a set of tests to apply under an application of the *voie directe*.

Thus, for questions not answered in the *lex arbitri*, e.g., the 10th Book of the German ZPO, or mandatory law, the arbitral tribunal must embark on its own mission to find the appropriate conflict-of-laws rules and the relevant qualification of legal issues.[1163] The issue of qualification arises in parallel with the search and creation of autonomous conflict-of-laws rules. Insofar as the tribunal is not referring to a conflict-of-laws ruleset promulgated by a state, it also lacks the qualification of contracts and

1159. *See, e.g., Award in ICC Case No. 3540*, Collection of ICC Awards I, 1990, 399, p. 402; *Award in ICC Case No. 2879*, Collection of ICC Awards I, 1990, 346, p. 347.
1160. *Schultze-Moderow*, Schiedsverfahren und Insolvenz, p. 128.
1161. *Partial Award in ICC Case No. 7710*, Collection of ICC Awards V, 2009, 513, pp. 522–523; *Award in ICC Case No. 6500*, Collection of ICC Awards III, 1997, 452, pp. 453–454; *Award in ICC Case No. 6840*, Collection of ICC Awards III, 1997, 467, pp. 469–471; *Partial Award in ICC Case No. 6719*, Collection of ICC Awards III, 1997, 567, p. 573; *Preliminary Award in ICC Case No. 4132*, Collection of ICC Awards I, 1990, 164–166, 456–458, p. 457; *Kessedjian*, Chapter 3: Determination and Application of Relevant National and International Law and Rules, 71, p. 81.
1162. Cf. *Schultze-Moderow*, Schiedsverfahren und Insolvenz, pp. 134–136.
1163. *Schultze-Moderow*, Schiedsverfahren und Insolvenz, p. 129; Cf. *Derains/Schwartz*, A Guide to the ICC Rules of Arbitration, pp. 240–242a.

issues that come with such a ruleset.[1164] This issue should not be underappreciated. When applying a complete and ready set of conflict-of-laws rules, these usually also come with specific pre-set qualifications, e.g., is a particular issue a question of validity or interpretation of the arbitration agreement. These come either in the form of standing case law, legislation, or other authoritative guidance. A tribunal striking out on its own to find appropriate conflict-of-laws rules for a particular issue will have to answer this question in tandem with the question of qualification. When the tribunal looks at and creates appropriate conflict-of-laws rules for the effect of insolvency on an arbitration agreement, it must simultaneously decide if this is a question of interpretation of the agreement or validity as this qualification excludes or includes specific conflict-of-laws considerations.[1165] Accordingly, qualification is necessary in the context of the scope and application of conflict-of-laws rules.

3.3 Building an Autonomous Conflict-of-Laws Approach

The follow-up question to the conclusion that an autonomous conflict-of-laws approach should be considered for the tribunal is the question of how such an approach is created. This is further explored in this subsection.

Over the years, several authors have come up with rules, guidelines and approaches to find the applicable conflict-of-laws rules, including the previously cited *Sandrock*. In his article on the topic, he described three rules to help find an appropriate conflict-of-laws ruleset.[1166] The first is the convergence rule; if all potentially relevant conflict-of-laws rules, or even the majority, lead to the same results, this should be respected as the parties would have theoretically regarded these rules if they had considered the relevant question. The second rule is the so-called rule of general legal principles. This rule is, in effect, not very different from the first in stating that, insofar as all relevant points of contact in the dispute point towards jurisdictions of a specific legal 'family', the conflict of laws rules of this legal family should be used, e.g., continental law or Anglo-American law. Finally, the third rule is a general 'escape-clause' rule, which posits a check and exemption on the first two rules allowing for other conclusions in light of special circumstances.[1167]

Similarly, the methods mentioned above, the cumulative approach, the general principles of the conflict-of-laws approach and other simplified approaches proposed by other authors can only help guide the search for appropriate rules. These approaches and rules merely attempt to point in a particular direction, often without adequately acknowledging their legitimation and starting point: the contractual nature of arbitration and the parties' autonomy, will, and interests. The usefulness of the above-mentioned rules and any such rule is thus limited to the extent to which they correctly mirror or point towards the parties' intent or, when this is lacking, their best

1164. *Preliminary Award in ICC Case No. 4132*, Collection of ICC Awards I, 1990, 164–166, 456–458, p. 457.
1165. *Schultze-Moderow*, Schiedsverfahren und Insolvenz, pp. 129–130.
1166. *Sandrock*, RIW 38 (1992), 785, p. 794.
1167. *Sandrock*, RIW 38 (1992), 785, pp. 794–795.

interests as an indicator of their implied intent.[1168] Therefore, approaches that are not and cannot be interpreted as an approximation of the parties' will, c.q. interests must be rejected outright.

In the following, the relevant interests that can generally be considered to approximate rules are examined (§ 3.3.1). The second question considered is at what point in time these interests should be measured: *ex nunc* of *ex tunc* (§ 3.3.2). Finally, the problem inherent to an autonomous approach, the lack of a frame of reference for the characterisation and categorisation of legal issues, is considered (§ 3.3.3).

3.3.1 Relevant Interests.

Whereas superficially, a distinction can be made between direct and indirect party interests and abstract and *in causa* party interests, this is unnecessary when one takes an appropriately broad view of the parties' interests.[1169] It is, for example, broadly in the interests of the parties that the answer to certain legal questions, c.q. the question of the applicable law is relatively predictable. Of course, this might run afoul of the interests of one of the parties in the particular case. However, the tribunal must consider the common interest of both parties in a neutral way.[1170] If the parties' common interests are unclear, a more generalised interest of parties in international arbitration can be used as guidance. However, these and other third-party and generalised socioeconomic interests are not applicable per se, but only in the context of 'filling in' the parties' common interests in the particular case.[1171] As such, the *in casu* interests form the framework and thus simultaneously the limits in which general interests can be applied.[1172] The interests selected for examination below are: enforceability and non-annulment (i), legal certainty, predictability and legitimate expectations (ii), uniformity of decisions (iii), neutrality (iv) and efficiency and effectiveness (v).

i Enforceability and Non-annulment

The first generalised interest discussed here concerns enforceability and non-annulment of awards. Although there has long been a back-and-forth in academia regarding the existence, or lack thereof, of a duty for arbitrators to render an enforceable award,[1173] it can be said with certainty that, in general, it is in the interests of parties to have enforceable awards. In this sense, enforceability forms part of the

1168. *Schultze-Moderow,* Schiedsverfahren und Insolvenz, pp. 135–136.
1169. *Kegel/Schurig,* Internationales Privatrecht, p. 137; *Schultze-Moderow,* Schiedsverfahren und Insolvenz, 133 et seq.
1170. Cf. *Marghitola,* Document Production in International Arbitration, pp. 129–130.
1171. *Schultze-Moderow,* Schiedsverfahren und Insolvenz, p. 143.
1172. *See, e.g.,* Belohlávek's considerations on the determination of the seat by the tribunal *Bělohlávek,* ASA Bull. 31 (2013), 262, p. 277.
1173. *Berset/Lévy,* ASA Bull. 16 (1998), 664, p. 671; *Born,* International Commercial Arbitration, p. 1993; *Lozada,* Spain Arbitration Review 2016, 71, p. 73.

arbitrators' mission.[1174] Naturally, the next question is: enforceable where? This is largely case-specific and logically will be the jurisdiction or jurisdictions of intended enforcement. *Derains* notes in a commentary to an ICC award that in this regard, generally, the home jurisdictions of the parties should be considered,[1175] which in case of insolvency often corresponds to the insolvency jurisdiction. Connected to this is often the necessity to make sure that the award is also enforceable in the seat country,[1176] c.q. that it cannot be annulled, as it is still relatively rare that an award will be enforced if it has been annulled in the seat jurisdiction.[1177] Having said all this, it needs to be kept in mind that none of these considerations is absolute. The need for an enforceable award exists only as an expression of the parties' will and interests, and its actual form and shape will depend on the parties in question.[1178] In this line, *Vidal* correctly points out that, for example, the retreat of the Tribunal in the Final Award of ICC Case 12421, where the Tribunal essentially rescinded its own jurisdiction to find a law applicable to the validity of its own previous partial award in favour of the enforcement forum, was unnecessarily excessive.[1179] Certain institutional rules make this interest in enforceable awards explicit, most notably perhaps the ICC Rules in Article 42 (2021). Thereby they turn the need for enforceability from an implicit and general interest of the parties into an explicit and case-specific instruction to the tribunal by the parties by virtue of their choice to apply the ICC rules.[1180]

Whereas 'using such conflict-of-laws rules which are in the parties' interests', prima facie looks like it might provide a significant amount of discretion to the tribunal, this first discussed 'interest' already provides some significant limitations on this perceived discretionary space. In some instances, this might even lead to a downright need to apply a particular set of conflict-of-laws rules. The most relevant example would be if the arbitration is entirely European, meaning all relevant jurisdictions are EU jurisdictions. The conflict-of-laws rules encompassed in the EIR are part of the public policy of the community and, therefore, in the public policy of the Member States.[1181] This conclusion is supported by applying the *Eco Swiss* test, as discussed

1174. *Fouchard*, Rev. Arb. 1998, 471, p. 480.
1175. *Award in ICC Case No. 2879*, Collection of ICC Awards I, 1990, 346, pp. 350–351.
1176. Baizeau even calls it the prime duty of arbitrators to render awards that cannot be set-aside, *see Baizeau*, Arbitration and Insolvency: Issues of Applicable Law, pp. 97, 118.
1177. *Award in ICC Case No. 2879*, Collection of ICC Awards I, 1990, 346, p. 351 note by Y. Derains; However, there are examples of annulled awards being enforced, most notably in France, starting with the *Norsolor* case; *Cour de Cassation*, 9.10.1984 – 83-11355; *Gaillard*, Journal du Droit International 125 (1998), 645, 7 et seq.
1178. *Interim Award in ICC Case No. 10507*, ICC International Court of Arbitration Bulletin 20, 2009, 71, 9.2; *Schultze-Moderow*, Schiedsverfahren und Insolvenz, pp. 148–149; It should, therefore, not be considered 'a mission' of international arbitration by and of itself to 'assure respect for ordre public international', as some would phrase it. *See Partial Award in ICC Case No. 6719*, Collection of ICC Awards III, 1997, 567–577 referring to; *Cour d'Appel de Paris, 1Ch. suppl.*, Revue de L'Arbitrage 1991, 478–486.
1179. *Final Award in ICC Case No. 12421*, ICC International Court of Arbitration Bulletin 20, 2009, 88, No. 2222.
1180. *Award in ICC Case No. 2879*, Collection of ICC Awards I, 1990, 346, p. 350 note by Y. Derains.
1181. *Schmitz*, Schiedsverfahren und Insolvenz, p. 168; Cf. *England and Wales Court of Appeal*, IILR 2010, 39–46; *Commercial Court*, Judgment of 2.10.2008 – EWHC 2155 (Comm).

above.[1182] Consequently, the non-application of the Insolvency Regulation risks violation of the public policy of the EU and its Member States. Courts in several EU Member States have reinforced that this EU public policy translates into their national public policy, which is the only fitting conclusion based on the nature of the EU, representing the common interests of its Member States, their population and its legislation.[1183]

The public policy restriction on enforceability and as a ground for annulment forms arguably the most visible and clear restriction on the tribunal's discretion regarding the applicable law and on considering the appropriate applicable conflict-of-laws rule to apply to specific questions. Aside from this, it can also be considered that many of the other grounds for annulment and non-enforcement could also be considered party interests in their own right, e.g., the right to be heard by both parties as encompassed in the need for a neutral proceeding with an equal and fair opportunity to be heard, *see* Article V(1)(b) NYC.[1184]

ii *Legal Certainty, Predictability and Legitimate Expectations*

The second generalised interest examined here concerns legal principles concerning certainty, predictability and expectations. Legal certainty, predictability and legitimate expectations differ in the aspects of 'trust' they aim to protect, i.e., legal certainty and predictability aim to protect the 'trust' in a legal system in an abstract way, and legitimate expectations aim to protect 'trust' build up in a specific situation.[1185] However, all three principles generally state that the parties should not unreasonably be surprised by applications of law or their outcomes, both in an abstract way and in regard to the facts of the case. Therefore, these principles of 'trust' can be dealt with here as one interest or certainly as one strain of interests.

That legal certainty, predictability and the protection of legitimate expectations are general interests of contractual parties is self-evident. However, how these ideas should help shape the search for an applicable law is debatable.[1186] The legal practice has incorporated the principles in different ways when trying to answer questions of applicable law. In ICC Case 13954, the Tribunal stated that the Tribunal had to at least reason their choice of an applicable law in accordance with the legitimate expectations of the parties.[1187] This can be considered the minimum requirement imposed on the

1182. *See* Chapter 3 § 2.1.3.
1183. *Baizeau*, Arbitration and Insolvency: Issues of Applicable Law, pp. 97, 108; *P.K. Wagner*, Abstimmungsfragen zwischen Internationalem Insolvenzrecht und Internationaler Schiedsgerichtsbarkeit, p. 62 As Baizeau notes, in regard of the European Anti-Trust legislation it was already established at the time of his writing that this was also part of the public order of the Member States; *see*, *OLG Thüringen*, Beschluss of 8.8.2007 – 4 Sch 03/06; *Gerechtshof Den Haag*, 24.3.2005 – 04/694 and 04/695; *CJEU*, Judgment of 1.6.1999 – C-126/97.
1184. *See* § 3.3.1 iv below.
1185. *Ávila*, Certainty in Law, p. 180.
1186. In ICC Case 5103 the Tribunal even concluded that the legitimate expectations of the parties supported a cumulative law application, *see Award in ICC Case No. 5103*, Collection of ICC Awards II, 1997, 361, 363, 368 note by G. Aquilar Alvarez.
1187. *Final Award in ICC Case No. 13954*, Collection of ICC Awards VI, 2013, 519, No. 2929; *Derains/Schwartz*, A Guide to the ICC Rules of Arbitration, p. 242.

choice of law made by the tribunal by the parties' legitimate expectations. In ICC Case 9163, the Tribunal merely stated that in the search for the applicable law and mandatory rules, it should apply those in conformity with the expectations of the parties.[1188] In ICC Case 7710, the Tribunal went so far as to state that the parties' legitimate expectations were a factor in finding an implicit choice of law by the parties.[1189] As a generalisation, legal certainty, as argued by the English courts, describes protection from the application of unforeseeable rules.[1190] This could be considered a classical application of the legal certainty and predictability principle. As such, this is the consideration to be made when looking for a system to determine the applicable law. More in line with this is the formulation of the Tribunal in ICC Case 8385, stating that: 'In any case, the tribunal finds that the conflicts of laws rules that are most predictable and easily verifiable are appropriate in international arbitration.'[1191]

Kröll and *Born* go further and take a more comprehensive view of legal certainty. *Kröll* posits a rule that the appropriate rule is always that rule which gives party autonomy the widest berth.[1192] *Born* applying the validation principle states that as it is the parties' supposed will to solve their conflict as efficiently as possible, the right law is at least that law that validates the arbitration agreement.[1193] In parallel, he states that the parties can expect that law to be applied that best accomplished their agreement, which is, as one would generally conclude that the parties' agreement is best served by the law that gives the most prominent role to party autonomy, similar to the approach proposed by *Kröll*.[1194]

The attractiveness of the logic proposed by *Born* and *Kröll* is evident: As it can generally not be stated that a party operating in good faith wishes for its arbitration agreement or parts thereof to be inoperative, it can be concluded that it wants and expects a law to apply that validates its contractual stipulations.

However, these ideas are bound to some logical limitations. For example, it can hardly be argued that the parties expected a law to be applied that has nothing to do with the arbitration. In fact, both *Kröll* and *Born* seem to operate with this sometimes-implicit limitation that this tool is only used to choose between the law of states 'involved' in the arbitration, i.e., the law of the seat, that of the parties, the law applicable to the contract and that of the prospective place of enforcement. Second, this interest can be deemed partially subsidiary to the framework provided by public order rules discussed above. For example, it cannot be considered in the parties' interest, even if this is provided for based on predictability or legal certainty, that a law would be applied that leads to public order violations in the country of the seat or the intended country of enforcement.

The proposals of *Kröll* and *Born* are based on considerations of the parties' generalised interests and should not be taken as rules written in stone. Factual

1188. *Award in ICC Case No. 9163*, Collection of ICC Awards V, 2009, 703, p. 704.
1189. *Partial Award in ICC Case No. 7710*, Collection of ICC Awards V, 2009, 513, p. 523.
1190. *Nacimiento/Bähr*, NJOZ 2009, 4752, p. 4760.
1191. *Final Award in ICC Case No. 8385*, Collection of ICC Awards IV, 2003, 474, p. 477.
1192. *Ferrari/S. Kröll*, Conflict of laws in international arbitration, p. 250.
1193. *Born*, International Commercial Arbitration, 542 et seq.
1194. *Born*, International Commercial Arbitration, p. 545.

considerations of how the principles of legal certainty and predictability interact with the parties' interests in the case at hand must be made. Legitimate expectations are already a more case-specific and party-specific application of the principle of 'trust' than the other two principles discussed here. In consequence, one can take the consideration by the Tribunal in ICC Case 8385, i.e., the most predictable and easily verifiable conflict-of-law set is appropriate, as a starting point. In a second step, compare this starting point with the parties' interests in the case at hand, including an interest in an expansive interpretation of the parties' autonomy and the parties' interest in not applying a law that invalidates the contract.[1195]

Whereas consideration of *ordre public*, c.q. annulment and enforcement should already bring a tribunal to apply the EIR in the way described above,[1196] legal certainty might provide another argument. The *Syska v. Vivendi* cases, aside from their relevance in the public policy debate, primarily featured a debate over the nature, scope and relationship of Articles 4 and 15 EIR-old (7 and 18 EIR). The Appeal Court provides that the application of Article 15 EIR-old to arbitrations also relies on considerations of legal certainty and the legitimate expectations of the parties. Justice *Longmore* states, with reference to Recitals 23 and 24 of the regulation: 'The phrase "to protect legitimate expectations and certainty of transactions" [quote from Rec. 24 EIR] is, in my view, apt to include the expectation of businessmen that lawsuits (in which considerable amounts of money may have been invested) should come to an appropriate conclusion.'[1197]

iii *Uniformity of Decisions*

Uniformity of decisions is the third generalised interest discussed in this subsection. The concept of uniformity of decisions can be viewed as a more general form or, depending on the perspective, perhaps a more specific form of predictability and legal certainty. It could be considered the party-superseding version of the legal certainty principle.[1198] Society, parties in general and parties in arbitration have an interest in uniform decisions regarding the conflict-of-laws rules used and the applicable law. Although, as stated before, this socioeconomic interest can only be involved in the calculations as an aspect of the parties' interests, it is worth mentioning separately.

Two aspects of uniformity of decision need to be separated in this context: uniformity of decisions between the award and existing state case law and uniformity of decisions between awards *inter se*. Some argue that a tribunal is not obliged to apply case law provided by the courts interpreting relevant articles, i.e., that the tribunal is not bound to the principle of *stare decisis*.[1199] However, *Born* has to be followed in his view that this goes against the role and function of an arbitrator to approximate the

1195. *Award in ICC Case No. 4996*, Collection of ICC Awards II, 1997, 292, p. 297 note by Y. Derains.
1196. That is, Art. 7(2)(e) EIR to arbitration agreements before arbitration and Art. 18 EIR to arbitration and its related agreements when it is pending; *see* Chapter 3 § 2.1.3 in particular iii thereof.
1197. *England and Wales Court of Appeal*, IILR 2010, 39, 17–18, 24.
1198. *Schultze-Moderow*, Schiedsverfahren und Insolvenz, pp. 151–152.
1199. *K. Peter Berger*, Journal of International Arbitration 9 (1992), 5, p. 15.

law. This role and function would be violated if the arbitrator ignored case law which, depending on the jurisdiction, plays a significant role in establishing the law itself. Following case law from the courts of the seat or expected place of enforcement and, as such, respecting the uniformity of decision is partially if not wholly a product of the other interests of the parties discussed above, such as securing the award from annulment, respecting legitimate expectations, providing legal certainty and predictability.[1200] These same considerations should lead to at least a persuasive authority of previous awards on relevant issues.[1201] There is no hierarchy between tribunals and no accompanying binding rule of precedent.[1202] However, based on the interests the concept of precedence serves, which include the interests mentioned above of the parties in arbitration, the tribunal can and should take into account analysis by previous tribunals and, in this way, 'follow precedent'. In doing so, it should consider the frequency of similar analyses, the tribunals in question and the quality of the reasoning.[1203] In this light, the Tribunal in ICC Case 6363 was correct to say that a previous award has no res judicata effect, c.q. It only had res judicata effect between the parties in that previous case, but it could serve as an authoritative ruling on a question of substantive law.[1204]

The differing frameworks provided by the mandatory parts of national law, differing national case law and limits provided by public policy rules make it unrealistic to have true uniformity of decisions between different seats of arbitration, even on the same or similar legislation and treaties. However, uniformity should be strived for, especially in the context of more international arbitration tools like the NYC or the UNCITRAL Model Law.[1205]

iv *Neutrality*

Another general interest that can be considered is that of neutrality. While it is in the parties' individual interest that rules 'in their favour' are adopted, it is in their shared interest that the decision is made based on as neutral a law as possible. As an overarching principle, neutrality has long been a cornerstone of arbitration.[1206] This interest in a neutral position vis-à-vis the interest of the parties individually also translates into a common interest in a ruleset that is itself neutral, i.e., not skewed towards either side of the dispute.

Aside from this, neutrality also features in the interests of the parties as a ground for non-enforcement and annulment, *see* § 1059(2)(1)(b) and (d) ZPO and Article

1200. *Born*, International Commercial Arbitration, p. 3822.
1201. Differently *Kaufmann-Kohler*, Arbitration International 23 (2007), 357, p. 372.
1202. *Decision on Jurisdiction in ICSID Case No. ARB/02/6*, No. 97.
1203. *Born*, International Commercial Arbitration, p. 3827.
1204. *Final Award in ICC Case No. 6363*, Y.B. Com. Arb. XVII, 1992, 186, pp. 200–201; similarly *Final Award in ICC Case No. 7061*, unpublished, *see* Born, Commercial Arbitration, 2014, 3824.
1205. *Lachmann*, Handbuch für die Schiedsgerichtspraxis, p. 56; *Schultze-Moderow*, Schiedsverfahren und Insolvenz, p. 152; Cf. *Schlosser*, Das Recht des internationalen privaten Schiedsgerichtsbarkeit, p. 188.
1206. *Marghitola*, Document Production in International Arbitration, pp. 129–130.

V(1)(b) and (d) NYC. In consequence, beyond an independent interest in neutrality, this interest is also fortified by an interest in non-annullable and enforceable awards. However, neutrality as a ground for annulment and non-enforcement sets a relatively high standard for breach.[1207] However, this high neutrality standard should not serve as the tribunal's sole measure of neutrality, as neutrality should also be considered independently from this high standard posed by the non-enforcement and annulment grounds.

v *Efficiency and Effectiveness*

The final generalised interest considered in this subsection is the interest in efficiency and effectiveness. Efficiency and effectiveness are used here as complementing terms, referring to speed and costs. The effectiveness of an award can also be used to refer to enforceability and non-annulment, which has already been discussed. An efficient and effective conflict resolution process is also a common party interest that tribunals and courts should recognise.[1208] In terms of speed and costs, lack of efficiency has been a core and persistent complaint against arbitration.[1209] In contrast, it used to be and still is advertised as a core benefit of arbitration.[1210] The interest of parties in efficiency is further illustrated by the fact that efficiency is cited as a prime reason for selecting particular arbitral institutions and arbitral seats.[1211] Consequently, tribunals can and should factor this into their applicable law consideration.

vi *Final Remarks on Relevant Interests*

The above-discussed interests are not an exhaustive discussion of common party interests, and others can be found. However, the above represents the common party interests that will be used to discuss the considerations for finding the applicable law in the section below (Chapter 3 § 4). Due to the non-exhaustiveness of the above discussion and the casuistic nature of the actual interests of the parties, the search of the tribunal should always be guided by an investigation of the case-specific common interests of the parties. In this search, and to further substantiate the party interests, the tribunal can take guidance from those interests that support a functioning economic and legal system, specifically a functioning arbitration system.[1212]

1207. *Del Rosal Carmona, Rafael Carlos,* Chapter 9: Lack of Impartiality or Independence as Grounds to Deny Enforcement under the New York Convention, 137, p. 140.
1208. Also in regard to the competence distribution between them, *see Award in ICC Case No. 4156*, Collection of ICC Awards I, 1990, 517, pp. 519–520 note by S. Jarvin.
1209. *Queen Mary School of International Arbitration/White & Case,* 2018 International Arbitration Survey: The Evolution of International Arbitration, 2–3, 8, 11, 14.
1210. *Born,* International Arbitration, No. 2121.
1211. *Queen Mary School of International Arbitration/White & Case,* 2018 International Arbitration Survey: The Evolution of International Arbitration, 11, 14.
1212. *Schultze-Moderow,* Schiedsverfahren und Insolvenz, 150 et seq.

3.3.2 *Ex Nunc* or *Ex Tunc* Interests: Changing Interests

Having discussed several of the most generalised interest of parties in arbitration that could be used to create an autonomous approach, it is necessary to examine when this interest should be fixated. Interests change over time. Two points in time present themselves as options to examine the parties' interests: an *ex tunc* approach, taking the time of contracting as the relevant point in time, and the interests at present, *ex nunc*. Especially if insolvency is opened between these two points in time, the parties' interests will likely have shifted significantly in the interim.[1213]

Due to the opening of insolvency, one party or at least its representative has likely changed, i.e., the insolvent has been replaced by the insolvency administrator. It depends on the insolvency theory and legislation of the relevant jurisdiction how the role of the insolvency administrator is typified, e.g., as a legal successor of the party, as representative thereof or something sui generis. However, it can be argued that the interests of the insolvency administrator will generally become that of the party.[1214]

It need not be doubted that the interests of the 'original' party and the insolvency administrator will differ, as the goal of arbitration and insolvency differ.[1215] However, the investigation of the parties' interests is primarily an investigation of the probable intent of the parties behind the arbitration agreement. This is the contract, as included by reference in the arbitrator's contract, arbitrators are performing in the arbitration, and it is this contract that underpins and legitimises the entire procedure. Consequently, only the will and intent that could have contributed to that contract can be considered. This support the conclusion that only the interests that existed at the time of contracting can be construed as relevant. When a party goes insolvent in arbitration or at any time after the conclusion of the arbitration agreement, the insolvency-specific interests cannot be considered party interests.[1216] In the event that an insolvency administrator concludes an arbitration agreement, c.q. the party is insolvent when the arbitration agreement is concluded, insolvency-specific interests as party interest at the time of contracting will theoretically have to be considered. However, they can only be taken into account to the extent that this does not violate neutrality and the parties' common interest. Nothing stops parties from coming to agreements after the arbitration agreement that alter or fill in the agreement. Parties, for example, commonly agree on terms of reference that can give procedural guidance to the tribunal. This does not change that, in principle, the examination of the interests of the parties is an *ex tunc* exercise.

3.3.3 Characterisation and Categorisation

Having discussed the factor of time and its role in the examination of the parties' interests above, one more ancillary issue created by the nature of an autonomous

1213. *Schultze-Moderow,* Schiedsverfahren und Insolvenz, pp. 149–150.
1214. *Schultze-Moderow,* Schiedsverfahren und Insolvenz, pp. 149–150.
1215. Cf. *Baizeau,* Arbitration and Insolvency: Issues of Applicable Law, pp. 97, 98.
1216. Cf. *Schultze-Moderow,* Schiedsverfahren und Insolvenz, p. 150.

approach will be examined in this section: the issues of characterisation and categorisation. In other words, the bundling of the above interests so that for specific categories of question, the application of a particular law or particular laws is or are suggested.

Schultze-Moderow, who similarly proposes building conflict-of-laws rules based on the interests of the parties in the context of insolvency in arbitration above, proposes as a next step to create categories of questions in which a consistent field of interests points towards a single applicable law.[1217]

Only through the factual analysis of the parties' interests in a case can one identify a unified field of interests that for a category of questions points in one direction. However, opening and closing the discussion on applicable law and appropriate conflict-of-laws rules with this end-all and be-all observation would be less than scientific and would ignore the substantial commonalities found in arbitration cases in the facts and interests of the parties, as also described in the previous subsections. However, it should be clear that this categorisation is still only a tool and should not be taken as dogma per se. One of the main critiques in this book on the established guidelines and rules, as discussed above, is that although most mean to further party interests, they are often taken as rules in and of themselves. In contrast, they should merely be used as tools to investigate and represent the parties' interests. In parallel, this categorisation should always be regarded as merely another approximation and a generalisation that might not suit particular circumstances.

Although the categories and characterisations offered by other conflict-of-laws rulesets can be used as guidance or sometimes become mandatory in the context of public order, the tribunal is not bound to these per se. A categorisation of questions regarding insolvency in arbitration should be made based on their function, goal and effect, as it is in the context of rules that share a function and goal that similar and relatively consistent considerations about the parties' interests can be made.

Schultze-Moderow differentiates six categories, which would, under normal circumstances, be dominated by the same interests. The categories are: norms that aim to halt arbitration in case of insolvency altogether; norms that concern the competence of parties in regard to the arbitration agreement; norms that organise the relationship between the insolvent and the insolvency administrator; norms that have the aim to influence or affect the 'how' of the proceedings; norms that affect arbitrability of specific issues; and finally, norms that regulate which assets belong to the insolvent mass.[1218] Others make different categorisations. *Wagner*, for example, separates between the different areas of effect of the insolvency and the law applicable to them: the law applicable to the effect of the insolvency on the objective arbitrability; the arbitration agreement; the arbitration proceedings; the setting-aside and enforcement proceedings.[1219]

The value of creating a new system of categorisation and characterisation is limited as these are merely tools and not rules themselves. The categories presented by

1217. *Schultze-Moderow*, Schiedsverfahren und Insolvenz, 138, 157 et seq.
1218. *Schultze-Moderow*, Schiedsverfahren und Insolvenz, pp. 165–168.
1219. *P.K. Wagner*, Abstimmungsfragen zwischen Internationalem Insolvenzrecht und Internationaler Schiedsgerichtsbarkeit, C.III.

Schultze-Moderow and *Wagner* can neither be considered 'correct' nor 'incorrect', merely useful or useless depending on the case at hand. As the applicable law for specific questions relevant to insolvency in arbitration is discussed in the next section, no attempt is made to create a different set of categories here.

3.4 Conclusion on the Conflict-of-Laws Rules Before a Tribunal

In this section, the relationship between tribunals and conflict-of-laws rules was examined. Traditionally the question of the conflict-of-laws rules a tribunal had to apply was answered simply and straightforwardly: the rules of the *lex fori*. However, this conclusion was bound to the notion that tribunals have a true *lex fori* and, beyond the law chosen by the parties, were bound to apply the rules of the seat.

This view, although still represented, has been mostly rejected in contemporary literature. This rejection is logical and solidly based on the contractual nature of arbitration. The laws specifically giving effect to the arbitration agreement and the agreement itself are the relevant sources of 'law' for the tribunal. Therefore, it must rely on the *lex arbitri* and the arbitration agreement to find the correct law to apply. Insofar as neither of those directly prescribes the tribunal to apply a particular law or provides a rule that aids in finding the applicable law, the tribunal must rely on other considerations. Due to the contractual nature of arbitration, it has to investigate the parties' intentions and otherwise interpret the contract in line with the parties' interests.

It will be primarily these considerations of interests that will have to guide the tribunal in finding the applicable law to a whole slew of questions that are highly unlikely to have been considered in the arbitration agreement of the applicable arbitration law. Some of these interests are easy to spot and form a point of discussion in many arbitrations, e.g., the interest in an enforceable and non-annullable award. Others might not often be a direct subject of discussion in practice, e.g., uniformity of decisions. Considering these interests holistically and balancing them appropriately can lead to considerations as to which law should apply to a particular question. Whereas these considerations should always be made on a case-by-case basis, generalisations can be made, which will be the point of discussion in the next section.

4 APPLICABLE LAW IN THE ARBITRATION

In this final section of Chapter 3, the examination of the last two sections is brought to its conclusion by examining the applicable law in arbitration in the context of insolvency. As stated, the categories discussed in the previous sections are in no way binding or to be construed as a rule. This also makes a theoretical discussion of the validity of any categorisation largely pointless as one is not more valuable or correct than the other. The generalisations represented by categorisation can make sense as a tool from a practical point of view and could accordingly be valued by measurements of how widely they can be applied in practice. Nevertheless, their application will always require consideration of the question *in causa*, asking if the unique interests of the parties necessitate divergence.

For discussion in this book, guidance has been taken from the categorisations discussed above with amendments and expansions where necessary and where questions remained. For example, a short discussion of the law to apply by a tribunal in an EIR context and a discussion of the applicable law to the arbitrator's agreement were added to the discussed categories, notwithstanding that the discussion of the applicable law to arbitrator's agreements generally falls outside of the purview of the arbitral tribunal. The topics discussed here have all been topics of discussion in Chapter 2, where their relevance in insolvency and arbitration has been substantiated. This leads to the following order of topics in this section: applicable law within the scope of the EIR (§ 4.1), the validity and binding power of the arbitration agreement (§ 4.2), the competence to enter into arbitration agreements (§ 4.3), standing, representation and competencies of the administrator and the insolvent (§ 4.4), the regulation of the proceedings (§ 4.5), objective arbitrability (§ 4.6), the insolvent estate (§ 4.7), the substantive dispute (§ 4.8), and finally the arbitrator's contract (§ 4.9).

4.1 Applicable Law Within the Scope of the EIR

The first topic of this section concerns the entirety of the topics, c.q. all relevant applicable law questions, in this section but within the scope of the EIR. The interest in non-annulment and enforcement of awards is, as discussed, likely the most unambiguous, generalised interests of parties in arbitration. Tribunals, in consequence, must apply those conflict-of-laws rules that are considered *ordre public* or mandatory law, first and most stringently those in the seat jurisdiction and second and arguably to a lesser degree those of the likely place of enforcement, e.g., the insolvency forum.

In the previous sections, it has been stated that the EIR is to be considered *ordre public* of the EU and therewith of the Member States.[1220] Therefore, the only logical subsequent conclusion that can follow from that conclusion concerning the applicable law is the wholesale application of the conflict-of-laws rules in the EIR.[1221]

Consequently, one can apply the conflict-of-laws rules of the EIR to find the applicable law to any of the groups of issues below, as the EIR covers most if not all insolvency-related issues. Important to note is that with the application of the EIR, the qualifications of the EIR must also be respected, e.g., the discussion if an arbitration contract can be considered a running contract under Article 7(2)(e) EIR.[1222] Therefore, national discussions on the nature of the arbitration agreement or the arbitrator's agreement are of little to no consequence in this context, even as it pertains to those in the seat.

4.2 The Validity and Binding Power of the Arbitration Agreement

Outside and aside from the context of the EIR, other considerations could be made. The first topic considered in that context is the validity and binding power of the arbitration agreement.

1220. *See* Chapter 3 §§ 2.1.3, 3.3.1 i.
1221. *Vidal,* ICC International Court of Arbitration Bulletin 20 (2009), 51, p. 61.
1222. *CJEU,* Judgment of 20.10.2011 – C-396/09, No. 42; BeckOK InsO/*Mock* Art. 7 EuInsVO, No. 5.

Many authors treat the effect of insolvency on the arbitration as a singular category, c.q. convoluting the ability to proceed with the proceedings and the effect on the 'how' of the proceedings, i.e., the effect of the insolvency on the arbitration proceedings.[1223] It is certainly, not illogical to attempt a holistic approach to determine the effects of insolvency on an arbitration proceeding. In general, national laws regarding international insolvency tend to see the effects of insolvency on the arbitration proceedings as one category, e.g., § 335 InsO, which generally applies the *lex fori concursus* of the insolvency to such questions. Similar rules can be found in the EIR; *see* Article 4(1) EIR. There are considerations of party interests that could support this categorisation and the related reference to the *lex fori concursus*, i.e., predictability and efficiency.[1224]

However, if one fully follows a categorisation based on a congruence of fields of interest, the argument that parties can have very different interests when it comes to the possibility of continuing the proceedings generally and the 'how' it will proceed cannot be denied. A similar separation can be found in Article V(1)(a) and (d) NYC, where different rejection grounds are found for the validity of the arbitration agreement and the procedure applied. Thus, it is good to discuss the overall question of whether arbitration can be continued separately. The parties can be considered to arguably have the most pronounced interests in relation to this question, namely that a law applies that does not delegitimise the proceedings.[1225] It is not only the direct rules, such as the now infamous and defunct polish rule from the *Vivendi* cases, that invalidate arbitration agreements in case of insolvency but also those rules that otherwise frustrate the arbitration agreement from operating between the parties or a representative of the estate. All such rules seek to take away the effect of the arbitration agreement in case of insolvency. Aside from these 'automatic' effects, this category should also be considered to contain rules that provide the insolvent with special nullification rights regarding the arbitration agreement or arbitration proceedings. The effect of such rules is the same, namely, to create absolute or relative invalidity of the arbitration agreement in case of insolvency, which provides for a similar field of interest.[1226] In the case of the 'how' of the proceedings, the parties' interests are more nuanced and more focused on the neutrality of the proceedings.[1227]

In conclusion, a broad categorisation is not appropriate here and the search for the law applicable to the absolute and relative validity of the arbitration agreement, or what one could call the 'if' of the proceedings, should be separated from the 'how' of the proceedings or the law applicable to the procedure followed in the arbitration.

1223. *Vorburger,* International Arbitration and Cross-Border Insolvency, Ch. 5; *P.K. Wagner,* Abstimmungsfragen zwischen Internationalem Insolvenzrecht und Internationaler Schiedsgerichtsbarkeit, 149 et seq.
1224. *Schultze-Moderow,* Schiedsverfahren und Insolvenz, p. 175.
1225. In his note to ICC Case 4996, Derains states that the parties' legitimate expectations should lead to the application of law which does not invalidate a contract by the parties *Award in ICC Case No. 4996,* Collection of ICC Awards II, 1997, 292, p. 297.
1226. *Schultze-Moderow,* Schiedsverfahren und Insolvenz, p. 166.
1227. *See* Chapter 3 § 4.5.

What remains, however, is to determine which law needs to be applied to the 'if' question.

Beyond the general consideration represented in the well-known validation principle that it is in the parties' interest to not apply a law that delegitimatises the arbitration, several possibilities can be considered for the specific law to be applied: the law of the arbitration; the law controlling the competence of the parties, i.e., the law of incorporation; the law of the seat; the law of the insolvency (*lex fori concursus*); and the law of the arbitration agreement.

The law of the seat cannot be ignored entirely for any of the categories discussed in this section, as it will always feature in setting-aside proceedings in the form of the mandatory law and public policy exception. However, this constitutes only an exception and not a rule and serves as a lever of control for the seat state to protect it from such applications of foreign law that would undermine the most basic rules of the state.[1228] Therefore, other considerations must be made to find a more holistic rule.

There are arguments to be made that consideration of party interests should lead to the same conclusion as proposed by the international private law of the seat state, i.e., generally the *lex fori concursus*. First of all, this delivers predictability and a related legal certainty. Second, it also delivers a uniformity of decisions between arbitral awards and state courts. Third, it insulates, to a certain degree, the award from setting-aside and unenforceability.

The arbitration agreement is the basis for the legitimacy of the arbitration.[1229] Any questions regarding the absolute ability and relative ability to pursue arbitration in case of insolvency should, therefore, be answered based on the law applicable to this agreement.[1230] This rule is also reflected in the NYC (Article V(1)(a) and national *lex arbitri* (§ 1059(2)(1)(a) ZPO). They refer to the law applicable to the arbitration agreement when judging its validity.[1231] The codes also differentiate between the law applicable to the validity of the arbitration agreement and that to the proceedings, compare Articles V(1)(a) and V(1)(d) NYC and §§ 1059(2)(1)(a) and 1059(2)(1)(d) ZPO. This supports the assessment that these two questions should be looked at separately. It is these specific arbitration rules that the courts will have to use when assessing setting aside and enforcement. Although § 1059 ZPO does not directly address the tribunal,[1232] there is a solid case for the arbitral tribunal to find that these rules should be followed as part of the *lex arbitri* and as a practical consequence of the interest of the parties in solid awards, i.e., enforceable and insulated from setting-aside.[1233]

However, the question remains about how one determines the law that applies to the arbitration agreement. It is widely accepted that the parties can choose the law that

1228. *Schultze-Moderow*, Schiedsverfahren und Insolvenz, p. 173.
1229. *Schultze-Moderow*, Schiedsverfahren und Insolvenz, pp. 176–177.
1230. *Berset/Lévy*, ASA Bull. 16 (1998), 664, p. 667.
1231. Musielak/Voit/*Voit* § 1059 ZPO, No. 8; Differently MüKoZPO/*Münch* § 1059 ZPO, No. 19.
1232. *Schultze-Moderow*, Schiedsverfahren und Insolvenz, p. 176.
1233. Cf. *Mankowski*, ZIP 2010, 2478, p. 4783.

applies to the arbitration agreement. However, in practice, this is seldom done.[1234] If such a choice is lacking, academia and practice describe several ways forward. In some cases, the tribunals have applied national rules, general principles or common usages of international law in recognition of the international nature of the arbitration.[1235] Disputed but oft-mentioned, perhaps for its ease of use, is the simple extension of the choice of the law made in the main agreement, i.e., the law applicable to the substantive dispute, to the arbitration agreement.[1236] However, due to the principle of separability, this can only be legitimately based on party autonomy and interests if there are indications that the parties actually meant to apply this choice to the arbitration agreement itself as well.[1237] This link should not be too readily assumed; the choice of law for the substance of the dispute is often based on very different considerations than that of an arbitration agreement and can be subject to different rulesets, e.g., the Rome-II Regulation does not apply to arbitration agreements.[1238] The NYC points towards the law of the seat in Article V(1)(a) NYC, when a choice is lacking. Arbitration might be without a true *lex fori*, but the arbitration agreement is given effect and executed within a specific jurisdiction, i.e., the seat jurisdiction. Consequently, this rule is to be followed, as is done in many arbitrations, and ignoring it could lead to setting aside the award.[1239]

Applying the rule of Article V(1)(a) NYC is, in this case, again a concretisation of the parties' interests, as this rule does not directly apply outside of enforcement and

1234. *Born*, International Commercial Arbitration, pp. 491–560; Musielak/Voit/*Voit* § 1059 ZPO, No. 8.

1235. *Award in ICC Case No. 6840*, Collection of ICC Awards III, 1997, 467, p. 472; *Interim Award in ICC Case No. 5065*, Collection of ICC Awards II, 1994, 330, 330–331, 334–336; *Award in ICC Case No. 4381*, Collection of ICC Awards II, 1994, 263, p. 265; *Interim Award in ICC Case No. 4131*, Collection of ICC Awards I, 1990, 146–153, 464–473, pp. 148–149.

1236. *Award in ICC Case No. 9667*, Collection of ICC Awards IV, 2003, 579, p. 587 note by D. Hascher; *Award in ICC Case No. 6840*, Collection of ICC Awards III, 1997, 467, 469, 472; *Final Award in ICC Case No. 6752*, Collection of ICC Awards III, 1997, 195, No. 33; *Final Award in ICC Case No. 6379*, Collection of ICC Awards III, 1997, No. 8; *Interim Award in ICC Case No. 6149*, Collection of ICC Awards III, 1997, 315, No. 44; *Arbitration Court Attached to the Chamber of Foreign Trade, Berlin*, Y.B. Com. Arb. 1990, 66–69; *Award in ICC Case No. 2626*, Collection of ICC Awards I, 1990, p. 316; *Hof van Beroep Brussel*, Y.B. Com. Arb. 1989, 618, No. 5-10587.

1237. *Preliminary Award in ICC Case No. 5505*, Collection of ICC Awards II, 1994, 142, pp. 148–149; *Born*, International Commercial Arbitration, 439 et seq; For an example of a Tribunal that did extend the choice of law based on such indications; in ICC Case 6752 the Tribunal found that an article containing a blanket reference to Italian Law, necessarily extends to the arbitration agreement contained in the same article as such using a grammatical and systematic interpretation to extend the choice of law to the arbitration agreement, *see Final Award in ICC Case No. 6752*, Collection of ICC Awards III, 1997, 195, No. 33.

1238. *Award in ICC Case No. 9667*, Collection of ICC Awards IV, 2003, 579, p. 587 note by D. Hascher.

1239. *Final Award in ICC Case No. 14046*, Collection of ICC Awards VI, 2013, 543, No. 3; *Final Award in ICC Case No. 6162*, Y.B. Com. Arb. XVII, 1992, 153, pp. 160–162; *Award in ICC Case No. 4504*, Collection of ICC Awards II, 1994, 279, p. 280; *Award in ICC Case No. 4392*, Collection of ICC Awards I, 1990, 473, p. 474; *Award in ICC Case No. 1507*, Collection of ICC Awards I, 1990, 215, p. 216; a rule that has been applied in Switzerland for a long time, *see BGE*, Urt. of 2.10.1931 – BGE 57 I 295, p. 303; *Born*, International Commercial Arbitration, pp. 477–478; *P.K. Wagner*, Abstimmungsfragen zwischen Internationalem Insolvenzrecht und Internationaler Schiedsgerichtsbarkeit, p. 145.

setting-aside proceedings. However, it is in the parties' interests to have the same law applied throughout the proceedings and create enforceable awards and awards insulated from being set aside.[1240] In consequence, either the law chosen explicitly or implicitly to apply to the arbitration agreement or, if no such choice has been made, the law of the seat will apply to the questions concerning the validity and legitimacy of the arbitration agreement and proceedings.[1241] Therefore, this law will form the starting point for questions regarding what is described above as the 'if' questions in insolvency.

4.3 The Competence to Enter into Arbitration Agreements

The second separate question discussed in this section is the competence to enter into arbitration agreements. The question of competence is to be separated from the question of the validity of the arbitration agreement per se. Although the lack of competence on either side of the agreement can lead to an invalid arbitration agreement, this is only an indirect effect. Whereas the result of a non-competent party agreeing to an arbitration agreement will have to be determined by the law applicable to the arbitration agreement, the determination of the competence itself is a separate question.[1242]

This same separation is also visible in the international and national laws, § 1059(2)(1)(a) ZPO and in parallel Article V(1)(a) NYC, which refers to the personal law of the party.[1243] Consequently, for state courts, this is seen as guiding.[1244] Arbitral tribunals also usually apply the personal law of the party to the question of competence.[1245] The view, which is still prevalent in Germany,[1246] that the reference in German law to 'the Law applicable to them' or the German '*persönlich maßgebliche Recht*' does not constitute a conflict-of-laws rule is to be dismissed. Perhaps this discrepancy is due to the German version being arguably grammatically less clear than the English version on this point. The interpretation that 'the law applicable to them' is a direct reference to the applicable law of the country where the company is incorporated - or has its seat - is preferable from a systematic and teleological

1240. *Schmidt-Ahrendts/Höttler*, SchiedsVZ 2011, 267, p. 273; Cf. *Brekoulakis*, Law Applicable to Arbitrability: Revisiting the Revisited Lex Fori, 99, p. 100f.
1241. *Interim Award in ICC Case No. 6149*, Collection of ICC Awards III, 1997, 315, No. 6; *Award in ICC Case No. 5832*, Collection of ICC Awards II, 1994, 533, p. 540; *Award in ICC Case No. 1110*, Collection of ICC Awards IV, 2003, 1, p. 3 although the applicable ICC Rules here provided explicitly for this solution.
1242. *Born*, International Commercial Arbitration, p. 627.
1243. Wolff/*Wilske/Fox* Art. V NYC, pp. 105–107.
1244. *Born*, International Commercial Arbitration, pp. 626–627.
1245. *Final Award in ICC Case No. 10515*, ICC International Court of Arbitration Bulletin 20, 2009, 74, p. 75; *Interim Award in ICC Case No. 7337*, Collection of ICC Awards IV, 2003, 308–320, p. 310; *Award in ICC Case No. 5832*, Collection of ICC Awards II, 1994, 533, p. 541; *Award in ICC Case No. 4381*, Collection of ICC Awards II, 1994, 263, p. 265.
1246. *Lachmann*, Handbuch für die Schiedsgerichtspraxis, No. 286286; *Schmidt-Ahrendts/Höttler*, SchiedsVZ 2011, 267, p. 275; Musielak/Voit/*Voit* § 1059 ZPO, No. 6; *BGH*, NJW 1998, 2452, II(2)(a).

perspective.[1247] If one views the rule regarding the substantive validity of the arbitration agreement under Article V(1)(a) NYC as a conflict-of-law rule, as expanded on above, then it could hardly be argued that the rule regarding competence in that same subclause is not a conflict-of-law rule, using merely a tortured grammatical interpretation of the first sentence of this article without regard for context.

However, this is arguably what the German Federal Supreme Court has done and what is still largely a standing doctrine in German academia.[1248] They have found that 'the law applicable to them' refers to what law applies to them according to the applicable (national) conflict-of-laws set of the *lex fori*. In the case of Germany, however, the factual outcome does not differ as applying German international private law rules as in case law on this point also leads to the law of the state in which a company is incorporated or seated or of which a person is a national, *see* for natural persons Article 7(1) EGBGB.[1249]

Regardless of how one interprets the NYC and national arbitration law on this point, the same arguments made previously should induce the arbitral tribunal to follow these rules. This leads to the conclusion that it will be the personal law of the party that has to be applied, including those of that jurisdiction that are specific to insolvency.[1250] Due to these rules being part of the grounds for non-enforcement and setting aside, the need to apply these rules flows directly from the most unambiguous interests of the parties, i.e., the prevention of those grounds being fulfilled. Aside from this, it has the benefit of being predictable, creating legal certainty and creating uniformity between courts and tribunals.

4.4 Standing, Representation and Competencies of the Administrator and Insolvent

The fourth subject of this section concerns the law applicable to the standing, representation and competencies of the administrator and the insolvent. Aside from the subjective arbitrability, which concerns the ability of the administrator and the insolvent to be a party to the arbitration, the main question to be asked here concerning the insolvency administrator is how he should be involved in the proceedings. The balance of interests in this field of questions is ordinarily different from that of the category in § 4.2 above, which includes absolute subjective arbitrability, and the second category in § 4.3 above. The questions in this category concern 'how' the procedure should be held and not if the procedure should be held at all.[1251] The questions on competence and what could be defined as the standing of the insolvency

1247. *Blackaby et al.*, Redfern and Hunter on International Arbitration, pp. 81–82; *Born*, International Commercial Arbitration, pp. 626–627; differently *Schmidt-Ahrendts/Höttler*, SchiedsVZ 2011, 267, p. 275.
1248. MüKoZPO/*Münch* § 1059 ZPO, No. 15; Musielak/Voit/*Voit* § 1059 ZPO, No. 6; *BGH*, NJW 1998, 2452–2453.
1249. *Böckstiegel/S.M. Kröll/Nacimiento* (eds.), Arbitration in Germany, p. 463; *Schack*, Internationales Zivilverfahrensrecht, No. 598; *Schmidt-Ahrendts/Höttler*, SchiedsVZ 2011, 267, p. 275.
1250. *Schultze-Moderow*, Schiedsverfahren und Insolvenz, p. 194.
1251. *Schultze-Moderow*, Schiedsverfahren und Insolvenz, p. 195.

administrator and his relationship to the insolvent can be considered as a single question or group thereof in the form of the question: Which law defines the role and powers of the insolvency administrator? However, it makes sense to separate the questions of 'if' and 'how', i.e., if the arbitration can be validly held or continued and how to do so. The argument, as made above in § 4.2, that the fields of interest are drastically more pronounced in the case of 'if' questions cannot be denied.[1252]

On the one hand, the determination of who is a party to a contract and, therefore, is the relevant party in an arbitration is determined by the relevant law applicable to that agreement.[1253] On the other hand, powers of attorney and issues as legal representation in the proceeding are organised by the procedural law of the arbitration, c.q. its conflict-of-laws rules on this point.[1254] However, questions regarding the standing of an administrator are questions of the competence to represent a company or, in some jurisdictions, a question of legal succession concerning one of the parties to the arbitration agreement.[1255] Tribunals tend to determine the representative power of officers of a company and other questions of internal competence allocation or succession based on the law applicable to that company, the *lex societatis*.[1256] This is a common rule in international private law. *See, e.g.*, the case law of the German Federal Supreme Court or 154(1) and 155(c) of the Private International Law Act (PILA) in Switzerland.[1257] Mostly that would be the home jurisdictions of the company. However, in, for example, the EU, this does not necessarily have to be the case. *Wagner* writes that the *lex concursus* of the insolvency should be decisive. Nevertheless, he motivates this choice with the fact that this is most often the home jurisdiction of the party.[1258] Overall, there seems to be a consensus that this issue should be governed by the law of the domicile jurisdiction of the party. Although the logic seems apparent and practical, this choice is often not overtly motivated in the awards. For the actual substitution of the insolvent by the administrator, regard should also be had for the law applicable to the arbitration procedure and the arbitration rules, insofar as they have relevant rules on the subject of substitution. *Berset* and *Lévy* even speak of a cumulative test of the *lex societatis* and the law applicable to the arbitral proceedings.[1259]

Schultze-Moderow only considers two laws: the law of incorporation and the law of insolvency. If these laws are not the same and do not provide the same solution, he states a preference for the insolvency law. This conclusion should be followed. In fact, the insolvency code should always be the first solution as a *lex specialis* as it provides

1252. *Schultze-Moderow,* Schiedsverfahren und Insolvenz, p. 195.
1253. *Interim Award in ICC Case No. 5029,* Collection of ICC Awards II, 1994, 69, p. 75.
1254. *Award in ICC Case No. 5832,* Collection of ICC Awards II, 1994, 533, p. 541; *Interim Award in ICC Case No. 5029,* Collection of ICC Awards II, 1994, 69, p. 74.
1255. *Interim Award in ICC Case No. 7337,* Collection of ICC Awards IV, 2003, 308–320, No. 88.
1256. *Final Award in ICC Case No. 16369,* Y.B. Com. Arb. XXXIX, 2014, 169, No. 3131; *Final Award in ICC Case No. 13954,* Collection of ICC Awards VI, 2013, 519, No. 2626; *Interim Award in ICC Case No. 7337,* Collection of ICC Awards IV, 2003, 308–320, No. 88; *Award in ICC Case No. 2694,* Collection of ICC Awards I, 1990, 320, 322, 324 note by Y. Derains; *BCCI,* Y.B. Com. Arb. 1979, p. 191; *Berset/Lévy,* ASA Bull. 16 (1998), 664, p. 666.
1257. *BGH,* NJW 2002, 3539, p. 3540; NJW 2003, pp. 1461–1462; NJW 2009, 289, pp. 290–291; *BGE,* 11.12.2012 - 4A_414/2012, 2.1.
1258. *P. Wagner,* Disp. Resol. Int'l 5 (2011), 189, p. 160.
1259. *Berset/Lévy,* ASA Bull. 16 (1998), 664, p. 678.

a special organisation of legal personality in case of insolvency. It is also the law from which the insolvency administrator draws his powers, and thus it should also provide the limits to his competencies, framing his relation to the insolvent in the process. The insolvency administrator's role is usually considered non-arbitrable and part of public policy. Furthermore, the need to provide the administrator with his role in the proceedings can be considered part of the right to be heard.[1260] These observations lead to the conclusion that the interest in an enforceable award or an award safe from being set aside also points towards the law of the insolvency as the relevant one in this category.

Practice in ICC cases involving insolvency mostly follows the approach described above. In ICC Case 10515, the Tribunal, without much explanation, referred the question of standing to the *lex societatis* of the company.[1261] In ICC Case 7337, the Tribunal took a similar approach. In the context of discussing if the insolvent or its administrator and successor should be a party to the arbitration, it stated that the legal capacity of a party is determined by the law of the domicile of the party and applied the succession law of the party, i.e., Sweden.[1262] The Tribunal in ICC Case 12907 decided to apply the law of the insolvency to the issue of standing in arbitration, in this case, also the law governing the insolvent company.[1263] Here, the Tribunal mentioned that it is essentially free to assess the applicable law due to the applicable ICC Rules. Despite this supposed freedom, the Tribunal takes a relatively rule-following approach. It states that it is agreed that the bankruptcy order is capable of recognition in the seat, England, and continues to interpret the bankruptcy order's scope to include the standing of the insolvent. In consequence, by following the rules of the seat, it lands on an application of the law of the bankruptcy order, i.e., the *lex fori concursus*, to the issue of standing. It is unclear on what grounds the Tribunal came to these conclusions, whether it was based purely on an expression of the contractual agreements by the party, an explicit choice for English law, the general discretion of the tribunal or whether they felt strictly bound to apply the recognition rules of the seat and the effects of this recognition.[1264] In any case, the result was that they applied the same rules as a court in the seat would have done, which is the safest approach in the context of annulment.[1265] However, one should not conclude from this that the tribunal is generally bound to such rules. In the annulment proceedings, the court will only be able to enforce such rules insofar as a violation provides a specific ground for annulment, e.g., interfere with the right to be heard or rules of mandatory nature in the seat or of an *ordre public* nature.

1260. *See* § 1.
1261. *Final Award in ICC Case No. 10515*, ICC International Court of Arbitration Bulletin 20, 2009, 74, 20, 28.
1262. *Interim Award in ICC Case No. 7337*, Collection of ICC Awards IV, 2003, 308–320, p. 310.
1263. *Partial Award in ICC Case No. 12907*, ICC International Court of Arbitration Bulletin 20, 2009, 98, 30, 56.
1264. The Claimant mentions several reasons as to why English conflict-of-laws rules should be applied. However, the Tribunal does not provide a reasoning for its application, *see Partial Award in ICC Case No. 12907*, ICC International Court of Arbitration Bulletin 20, 2009, 98, 30, 56 et seq.
1265. *Partial Award in ICC Case No. 12907*, ICC International Court of Arbitration Bulletin 20, 2009, 98–105.

Furthermore, although the related interests might differ, there is also an interest in finding that the same law applies to the entire question of the role and powers of the administrator. Applying a different law to the administrator's competence and standing might lead to incongruencies damaging efficiency, effectiveness and, to an extent, predictability. The law of the country of insolvency and that of incorporation will regularly and commonly overlap, preventing any further issues. However, this does not necessarily need to be so. Systems such as the EIR create room for local insolvencies of foreign companies.[1266]

Those party interests that can be generally established here only concern one of the parties' interests, the insolvent party. The interests of the non-insolvent party are largely unaffected by the division of competencies between the insolvent and the insolvency administrator. Consequently, neutrality is largely a non-issue in the considerations, and thus, annulment and enforcement of the award and, secondarily, efficiency should be considered.[1267] Enforcement considerations also link the questions of standing, representation and competence to the *lex societatis,* as can be gleaned from the non-enforcement ground of Article V(1)(a) and (b) NYC.[1268] Similar provisions in national laws provide a further link to annulment considerations; *see* § 1059(2)(1)(a) and (b) ZPO. Courts in annulment and enforcement proceedings have to test the competence of the parties to enter into the relevant arbitration agreement in light of § 1059(2)(1)(a) ZPO or Article V(1)(a) NYC, i.e., a reference to the *lex societatis.* Insofar as the relevant arbitration agreement was entered into by the insolvency administrator, reference for his power to do so must also be had to the *lex fori processus* of the insolvency by way of applying German conflict-of-laws rules to this question, which in the case of insolvency are § 335 InsO or Article 7(2)(c) EIR.[1269] These laws remain relevant for the right to be heard, as found in § 1059(2)(1)(b) ZPO and Article V(1)(b) NYC, to test to whom this right should be afforded in the proceedings. As such, for the insolvency administrator, primary reference should be had to *lex fori processus* and secondary the *lex societatis.*

4.5 The Regulation of the Proceedings, Including the Staying of Proceedings

The stay of proceedings is a central part of discussions on insolvency in arbitration. The applicable law for this issue and the broader regulation of the proceedings are discussed in this subsection. This category primarily concerns rules that influence the procedure of arbitration. The most well-known of such rules are those regarding potential stays or suspensions of the arbitration procedure. Therefore, this category concerns what was previously described as the 'how' questions of the proceedings that go beyond the role and relationship between the insolvent and the insolvency administrator. Although one could arguably create an inclusive category of this and the

1266. *See, e.g., Gerechtshof Den Haag,* 12.6.2018 – 200.239.090/01.
1267. *Schultze-Moderow,* Schiedsverfahren und Insolvenz, p. 195.
1268. *See* in the previous section, § 4.3; *Berset/Lévy,* ASA Bull. 16 (1998), 664, p. 666.
1269. Cf. Vorwerk/Wolf/*Wilske/Markert* § 1059 ZPO, No. 31.

previous two categories together as an overall question as to the law applicable to the effects of the insolvency on the arbitration, this would neglect the differing interests that play in these specific aspects and the legal nature of the discussed questions. The questions answered here are restricted to the procedural aspects, not related to the competence and standing of parties and not related to the legal effect and validity of the arbitration agreement.

Although both parties have serious interests at play when it comes to the law that answers the questions as to the effect of the insolvency on the proceedings themselves, this category requires little discussion. As generally provided by the *lex arbitri*, when a choice of law for the arbitral procedure is lacking, it is organised by the rules of the *lex arbitri*, generally the *lex loci arbitri*, commonly amended and further completed by a set of institutional arbitration rules chosen by the parties, *see, e.g.*, § 1042(3)-(4) ZPO.[1270] Similarly, as with the arbitration agreement, a choice of law for the substance of the proceedings should not, without clear indications, be extended to the arbitration procedure.[1271] Not only will not following these rules lead to a violation of public policy, but it will also violate the will of the parties with respect to how the procedure should be held, which is another ground for not recognising and annulling the award, *see* § 1059(2)(1)(d) ZPO.

In practice, the Tribunal in ICC Case 12993, where it had to decide the law applicable to the question of a stay, decided, albeit tentatively, that the *lex arbitri*, specifying this to the *lex loci arbitri*, applies to the potential suspension of proceedings. Furthermore, they separated this from any contractual question regarding the arbitration agreement, which can be organised by a different law than that of the procedure.[1272] Whereas the parties can also choose a procedural law or, more likely, institutional rules, these can only be applied insofar as no mandatory or public policy rules of the *lex loci arbitri* are violated.[1273] This interplay between party autonomy and the interest in enforceable and non-annullable awards is also observable in the ICC Rules in Articles 19 and 42 ICC Rules (2021): the first states the parties' freedom to agree on rules of procedure, and the second states that the tribunal should attempt to make enforceable awards.[1274]

1270. *Award by Consent in ICC Case No. 11443*, Collection of ICC Awards V, 2009, 335, p. 337; *Final Award in ICC Case No. 5294*, Collection of ICC Awards II, 1994, 180, p. 181; *Interim Award in ICC Case No. 5029*, Collection of ICC Awards II, 1994, 69, pp. 60–71; *Award in ICC Case No. 4504*, Collection of ICC Awards II, 1994, 279, p. 280; *Award in ICC Case No. 3540*, Collection of ICC Awards I, 1990, p. 399; *Award in ICC Case No. 2272*, Collection of ICC Awards I, 1990, 11, p. 12; *Final Award in ICC Case No. 1512*, Collection of ICC Awards I, 1990, p. 3; *Blackaby et al.*, Redfern and Hunter on International Arbitration, 3.37–3.39; *Schultze-Moderow*, Schiedsverfahren und Insolvenz, pp. 197–198; *P.K. Wagner*, Abstimmungsfragen zwischen Internationalem Insolvenzrecht und Internationaler Schiedsgerichtsbarkeit, p. 149.

1271. *Interim Award in ICC Case No. 5029*, Collection of ICC Awards II, 1994, 69, pp. 70–71.

1272. *Final Award in ICC Case No. 12993*, ICC International Court of Arbitration Bulletin 20, 2009, 105, No. 103103.

1273. *Award in ICC Case No. 2879*, Collection of ICC Awards I, 1990, 346, pp. 350–352 note by Y. Derains; *Schultze-Moderow*, Schiedsverfahren und Insolvenz, pp. 197–198.

1274. *Award in ICC Case No. 2879*, Collection of ICC Awards I, 1990, 346, pp. 350–351 note by Y. Derains and S. Jarvin.

The question as to applicable law regarding certain issues pertaining or relating to the procedure, the suspension of proceedings, arbitration agreement and the arbitrator's contract being the key examples, can also depend on the status of the insolvency proceedings. As was discussed in the German context above in Chapter 2, the insolvency proceedings might enforce the application of a specific law upon penalty of unenforceability.[1275]

As discussed in the previous part, it is already accepted in Germany that although a stay of proceedings in arbitration is not required by law, it is appropriate and even required under most circumstances by the right to be heard, which should be extended to the insolvency administrator.[1276] Furthermore, the tribunal should consider the rules of other jurisdictions on this aspect and other procedural aspects. Insofar as they are considered, the rules of (international) public order or mandatory parts of insolvency law should be of primary interest. In particular, regard should be had here for the jurisdiction of prospective enforcement, likely the insolvency jurisdiction.[1277] These considerations can only be made on a case-by-case basis, but in general, consideration of the parties' interests will lead to the conclusion that a stay of the arbitral proceeding in some form must be provided.[1278]

Mantilla-Serrano assessed that the dominant trend in 1995 was to deny a request for suspension of the arbitral proceedings if the insolvency was outside of the seat of arbitration.[1279] In general, tribunals tended to ignore the effects of insolvencies outside of the seat jurisdiction.[1280] Such conclusions are often founded on a territorial view of insolvency.[1281] He even goes as far as to say that, in general, arbitrators should continue proceedings.[1282] This view should be considered too radical. A stay of arbitration proceedings in case of insolvency outside of the seat should be considered on a case-by-case basis. Furthermore, the references to territoriality are incorrect or at least incomplete due to the position of the arbitrator. His primary consideration should

1275. *See* Chapter 3 § 4.3 and § 2.3.
1276. *See* Chapter 3 § 2.3.1.
1277. *P.K. Wagner*, Abstimmungsfragen zwischen Internationalem Insolvenzrecht und Internationaler Schiedsgerichtsbarkeit, p. 151.
1278. *See* § 2.3.1 iii.
1279. *Mantilla-Serrano*, Arbitration International 11 (1995), 51, p. 57; and similar decisions can still be found more recently, e.g., procedural order no. 3 as mentioned in *Final Award in ICC Case No. 16369*, Y.B. Com. Arb. XXXIX, 2014, 169, No. 8585; *Final Award in ICC Case No. 13507*, Y.B. Com. Arb. XXXV, 2010, 158, p. 159.
1280. *Ferrari/S. Kröll*, Conflict of laws in international arbitration, p. 373.
1281. *Schiedsgericht des Deutschen Kaffeeverbands an der Handelskammer Hamburg*, Y.B. Com. Arb. 1994, 48–50; *Final Award in ICC Case No. 6057*, ICC International Court of Arbitration Bulletin III, 1994, 487–489, p. 488; *Award in ICC Case No. 5996*, Arbitration International (Article by Mantilla-Serrano) 11, 1995, 58; *Award in ICC Case No. 5954*, Arbitration International (Article by Mantilla-Serrano) II, 1994, 58, p. 59; *IUST*, Y.B. Com. Arb. 1986, 349, p. 352; *BCCI*, Y.B. Com. Arb. 1979, p. 191; *Mantilla-Serrano*, Arbitration International 11 (1995), 51–74.
1282. *Final Award in ICC Case No. 6057*, ICC International Court of Arbitration Bulletin III, 1994, 487–489, pp. 488–489 referring itself to older ICC Cases, numbers 4415, 2139 and 1350, respectively available at; *Final Award in ICC Case No. 4415*, Collection of ICC Awards I, 1990, 530–536; *Award in ICC Case No. 2139*, Collection of ICC Awards I, 1990, 24–25, 237–241; *Final Award in ICC Case No. 1350*, Y.D.I., 1975, 932; *IUST*, Y.B. Com. Arb. 1986, 349, pp. 351–352; *Mantilla-Serrano*, Arbitration International 11 (1995), 51, pp. 57–58.

not be the territorial or international effect of an insolvency but the interests of the parties and how these are affected.[1283] This is achieved by considering several factors. The most important practical considerations would be the assets available in combination with the legal considerations of public policy regarding the right to be heard, due process and equal treatment.[1284] Equal treatment considerations extend not only to both parties in arbitration but also by way of insolvency-related public policy to that of creditors on which some jurisdictions also base their suspension of proceedings. Furthermore, even without a suspension, the tribunal cannot ignore rules regarding communication, service and representation, i.e., the role of the insolvency administrator, which would also lead to factual delays if accounted for properly.[1285]

Considering the above, tribunals should be sensitive to both the legal and practical aspects of the case when deciding upon a stay of proceedings in the case of international commercial arbitration. Besides practical issues, problems with enforceability and setting aside can occur due to issues of due process and violation of *ordre public* and mandatory law both in the seat and the country of enforcement, often the insolvency jurisdiction or the relevant *lex arbitri*.[1286]

4.6 Objective Arbitrability

This sixth subsection concerns the law applicable to the objective arbitrability of insolvency issues. It is widely acknowledged that there is a great deal of discussion and disagreement on the subject of the applicable law to arbitrability. With options ranging from the application of the *lex arbitri*, the *lex fori*, the law of the state of prospective enforcement, the law applicable to the arbitration agreement[1287] and even the law applicable to the merits of the case.[1288] As an explanation for the wide range of options and approaches found in literature, the different settings and stages in which the question of arbitrability can come up are often mentioned. The topic can arise in court

1283. *Berset/Lévy*, ASA Bull. 16 (1998), 664, p. 666.
1284. Cf. *Final Award in ICC Case No. 16369*, Y.B. Com. Arb. XXXIX, 2014, 169, No. 8686.
1285. *Berset/Lévy*, ASA Bull. 16 (1998), 664–680; *Yang*, Insolvency Proceedings and Their Effect on International Commercial Arbitration, p. 33 referring to a case cited by; *Lazić*, Insolvency Proceedings and Commercial Arbitration, p. 301.
1286. *Interim Award in ICC Case No. 10507*, ICC International Court of Arbitration Bulletin 20, 2009, 71, 9.2; Cf. *Yang*, Insolvency Proceedings and Their Effect on International Commercial Arbitration, p. 34.
1287. *Born*, International Commercial Arbitration, p. 597; MüKoInsO/*Reinhart* § 335 InsO, No. 76; applying the law applicable to the arbitration agreement, are e.g., *Final Award in ICC Case No. 6379*, Collection of ICC Awards III, 1997; *Interim Award in ICC Case No. 6149*, Collection of ICC Awards III, 1997, 315, No. 33; Cf. *Award in ICC Case No. 8910*, Collection of ICC Awards IV, 2003, 569, p. 576; applying the law of the arbitration agreement, but stating the law affecting arbitrability depends on the stage of proceedings, i.e., an enforcement forum will apply their lex fori to the question is the Court of Appeal in Brussels, *see Hof van Beroep Brussel*, Y.B. Com. Arb. 1989, 618, Nos 4–8.
1288. *Award in ICC Case No. 1110*, Collection of ICC Awards IV, 2003, 1, No. 1111; Cf. *Partial Award in ICC Case No. 6719*, Collection of ICC Awards III, 1997, 567, p. 568.

and before the tribunal and, in the first case, both before and after the award has been rendered and in enforcement and setting-aside procedures.[1289]

Arbitrability is a subject organised within the *lex arbitri, see, e.g.*, § 1030 ZPO. Although not accepted by all, this law, the law that organises the arbitral proceedings, should, in particular, be followed, especially by the tribunal.[1290] The applicability of the rules of arbitrability of the *lex arbitri* follows directly from the choice of seat,[1291] insofar as no other procedural law has been chosen by the parties and can be seen as an expression of the will of the parties instead of merely a result of an interests analyses. That conclusion is debatable insofar as the choice of seat is not considered a true choice of the *lex arbitri*. However, it can hardly be debated that the paramount interests of the parties to not violate the arbitrability rules of the seat, as doing so would violate their most clear interest that of gaining an award that is insulated from setting aside *see, e.g.*, § 1059(2)(1) ZPO and the related Article 34(2)(b)(i) Arb.ML.[1292] The general approach of courts is to apply their own *lex fori* to the question of arbitrability both in enforcement and in setting-aside proceedings, *see also* Articles II(3) and V(2)(a) NYC. Considering the interest in enforceable awards, the tribunal should also consider the objective arbitrability of the state of prospective enforcement.[1293] This is even more so in case this is also the jurisdiction where the insolvency has been opened.[1294]

If an international piece of insolvency law, such as the EIR, is deemed applicable and of a mandatory or *ordre public* nature, objective arbitrability should be understood as following these rules, particularly the conflict-of-laws rules included in that law.[1295]

It is argued that potentially more restrictive rules from the *lex fori concursus* should not be taken into account. However, as stated, not taking those rules into account endangers enforceability. The arguments in favour of ignoring such rules from

1289. *Hof van Beroep Brussel*, Y.B. Com. Arb. 1989, 618, Nos 4–7; *Born*, International Commercial Arbitration, p. 601; *Fortier*, Arbitrability of Disputes, p. 271.
1290. *See* § 5; *Final Award in ICC Case No. 16369*, Y.B. Com. Arb. XXXIX, 2014, 169, 46; *Final Award in ICC Case No. 8626*, ICC International Court of Arbitration Bulletin 14, 2003, 55, p. 56; *Partial Award in ICC Case No. 8420*, Y.B. Com. Arb. XXV, 2000, 328, No. 1313; *Partial Award in ICC Case No. 6719*, Collection of ICC Awards III, 1997, 567, 568–569, 575 note J.J. Arnaldez; *Final Award in ICC Case No. 6162*, Y.B. Com. Arb. XVII, 1992, 153, p. 158; *Award in ICC Case No. 4604*, Collection of ICC Awards I, 1990, 546, pp. 548–549; *Award in ICC Case No. 1507*, Collection of ICC Awards I, 1990, 215–217; *Brekoulakis*, Law Applicable to Arbitrability: Revisiting the Revisited Lex Fori, 99, p. 100; *Fortier*, Arbitrability of Disputes, p. 275.
1291. *Partial Award in ICC Case No. 8420*, Y.B. Com. Arb. XXV, 2000, 328, No. 9; *Final Award in ICC Case No. 7047*, Collection of ICC Awards IV, 2003, 32, No. 2; *Partial Award in ICC Case No. 6719*, Collection of ICC Awards III, 1997, 567, p. 568.
1292. *Kovacs*, A Transnational Approach to the Arbitrability of Insolvency Proceedings in International Arbitration, p. 44.
1293. *Brekoulakis*, Law Applicable to Arbitrability: Revisiting the Revisited Lex Fori, 99, 103, 107–108 *see* in particular fn. 7 for a description of some alternative views; *Kovacs*, A Transnational Approach to the Arbitrability of Insolvency Proceedings in International Arbitration, pp. 45–46; *J.D.M. Lew/Mistelis/Kröll, J.D.M. Lew/Mistelis/Kröll*, Comparative International Commercial Arbitration, §§ 9–13; *Partial Award in ICC Case No. 6697*, Rev. Arb., 1992, 135–145; Cf. *Gaillard/Savage*, No. 559559.
1294. *Riedel*, Insolvenz in nationalen und internationalen Schiedsverfahren, pp. 149–150; *P.K. Wagner*, Abstimmungsfragen zwischen Internationalem Insolvenzrecht und Internationaler Schiedsgerichtsbarkeit, p. 142.
1295. *P.K. Wagner*, Abstimmungsfragen zwischen Internationalem Insolvenzrecht und Internationaler Schiedsgerichtsbarkeit, p. 143.

the *lex fori concursus* are highly situational; it not being clear where the award will be enforced or an interest in having an award regardless of enforceability, e.g., guarantee or insurance reasons.[1296] Insofar as this rejection of the applicability of the *lex fori concursus* on arbitrability is proposed as a rule in itself, this should be rejected in the light of the fact that the foundation of such a rejection is always a weighing of interests in the case at hand. This weighing will generally point to taking into account the rules of the *lex fori concursus* to preserve enforceability. However, as stated before, there can be situations in which the general 'rule' does not apply due to situational considerations. Therefore, that such circumstances exist does not disprove the general 'rule' but merely reinforces that it is merely a general rule based on general considerations, with situational exceptions based on the consideration of the parties' interests *in casu*.[1297] For example, in ICC Case 6149, the Tribunal decided not to apply the public policy considerations of the home state of one party and the law of the underlying contracts, i.e., Jordanian law, considering that the parties in the case had the intent to remove the issues from Jordanian jurisdictions.[1298] In case of insolvency, a tribunal could make similar considerations and ignore the arbitrability of the *lex fori concursus*. However, it can only do so by sacrificing the enforceability of the award in the jurisdiction of the insolvency, i.e., generally that of one of the parties and thus a likely place of enforcement. There might be situations where this is in the situational interests of the parties. However, generally speaking, it will not be.

The conclusion that the concept of arbitrability of the *lex fori concursus* of the insolvency should be considered is also not in violation of § 1030 ZPO or similar rules found in *lex arbitri* that bind the tribunal to apply the concept of arbitrability of the seat.[1299] This is simply because there need not be exclusivity.[1300] The wording of § 1030 ZPO in no way indicates a prohibition of applying stricter rules taken from the *lex fori concursus*. Since the concept of arbitrability of the *lex arbitri* must be applied if prescribed therein, it provides a minimum standard of non-arbitrability. This means that a topic considered arbitrable by the *lex fori concursus* but not by the *lex arbitri* cannot be arbitrated and, if arbitrated regardless, will lead to annulment. In the reverse scenario, an interest weighing must be made when a topic is considered non-arbitrable by the *lex fori concursus* but arbitrable by the *lex arbitri*. It is foreseeable that this interest weighing will often tip towards taking into account this non-arbitrability as if it will often be the case that the jurisdiction of the insolvency is the jurisdiction in which the party is centred or has the majority of its assets. This jurisdiction will, therefore, also be the likely place of enforcement. As stated, this need not be the case,

1296. *Blackaby et al.*, Redfern and Hunter on International Arbitration, 11.11; *Born*, International Commercial Arbitration, p. 599; *Riedel*, Insolvenz in nationalen und internationalen Schiedsverfahren.
1297. Differently *Schultze-Moderow*, Schiedsverfahren und Insolvenz, pp. 200–201.
1298. *Interim Award in ICC Case No. 6149*, Collection of ICC Awards III, 1997, 315, No. 88.
1299. Differently *Riedel*, Insolvenz in nationalen und internationalen Schiedsverfahren, pp. 148–150; *Schultze-Moderow*, Schiedsverfahren und Insolvenz, p. 201.
1300. *Fortier*, Arbitrability of Disputes, p. 276.

and factual considerations may lead the tribunal to ignore the arbitrability concept of the *lex fori concursus* or, for that matter, that of a place of likely enforcement.[1301]

Trunk proposed an orientation primarily based on the *lex fori concursus*, with only a minimal role for the arbitrability concept of the seat, c.q. intervening where the arbitrability concept of the *lex fori concursus* is considered so strict as to violate the public policy of the seat.[1302] Whereas, on a theoretical level, *Trunk* should be followed. After all, what is the interest of the seat country to consider subjects non-arbitrable that relate to a foreign insolvency?[1303] Suppose arbitrability is considered primarily as rules that determine that certain conflicts are in the sole jurisdiction of a specific court. In that case, there is no valid logic for applying the arbitrability notion of the *lex fori* or seat in cases where a court in the forum jurisdiction would not have had jurisdiction in any case. In practical terms, there would be no valid reasoning to support that an enforcing court should apply its concept of arbitrability when no local court would have had jurisdiction in any case, e.g., in relation to issues falling within the jurisdiction of a foreign insolvency court.[1304] Current legislation, however, does not allow for such an interpretation - both the NYC, Article V(2)(a), and national legislation, § 1061 ZPO, clearly formulate that the objective arbitrability of the forum is at the least a minimum standard for the tribunal and the court in annulment or enforcement proceedings.

Insofar as the *lex arbitri* does not provide the tribunal with a rule on arbitrability, such as § 1030 ZPO or Article 177(1) PILA (Switzerland), it had been argued that Articles II(1) and V(1)(a) NYC provide the tribunal with a reference to the law of the arbitration agreement.[1305] However, there are two issues with this basis. First, Article II(1) NYC makes no reference to applicable law, and Article V(1)(a) refers to non-validity, and non-arbitrability is not a matter of validity. It merely makes the agreement (partially) ineffective. Second, such arguments blatantly ignore the fact that NYC in Article V(2)(a) clearly refers arbitrability to the *lex fori*. In any case, the NYC only directly applies to courts and does not directly affect tribunals but affects arbitration indirectly in the context of the interest of enforceability.

In conclusion, in light of a weighing of interests, the tribunal should mainly take into account the law of the seat's concept of arbitrability and, secondarily, the arbitrability of the law of the state of prospective enforcement.

4.7 The Insolvent Estate

The law applicable to the insolvent estate is of crucial importance in arbitration as it determines the scope of the estate. This subject is examined here. Questions regarding

1301. Cf. *Award in ICC Case No. 4604*, Collection of ICC Awards I, 1990, 546, p. 554 note by Y. Derains.
1302. *Trunk*, Internationales Insolvenzrecht, p. 291.
1303. This is often heard objection to the orientation of objective arbitrability on the arbitrability concept of the seat; *Brekoulakis*, Law Applicable to Arbitrability: Revisiting the Revisited Lex Fori, 99, pp. 107–108; Cf. *Born*, International Commercial Arbitration, 604 et seq.
1304. *Brekoulakis*, Law Applicable to Arbitrability: Revisiting the Revisited Lex Fori, 99, p. 106.
1305. *Hanotiau/A. van den Berg*, SAcLJ 26 (2014), 874, 879 et seq.

the size and scope of the estate, c.q. which assets do and do not belong to it, if found arbitrable, should generally be considered based on the *lex fori concursus*. This, as this law describes and defines the insolvency estate. From the perspective of a weighing of interests, this conclusion also makes sense in the context of enforcement, i.e., not violating principles of the law of the prospective state of enforcement or even of the seat state. If the seat is not also the state in which the insolvency has been opened, potential international rules of public order regarding insolvent estates should also be investigated.

Especially in arguments regarding the scope of the estate, i.e., that an asset is not part of an estate and that, therefore, the relevant insolvency regulation does not apply, another law could be considered. Such arguments can be brought by the insolvent itself as opposed to the insolvency administrator,[1306] as he looks to separate an asset from the insolvency and retain control over it. They can also be made by a creditor attempting to separate an asset from the insolvency. However, suppose the tribunal would consider another law than the *lex fori concursus* in assessing the extent of the estate and, therefore, provide the insolvent over the insolvency administrator with standing in the ensuing arguments. In that case, the court could set aside the award because the insolvency administrator's right to be heard has been violated. In most state courts, this right to be heard is measured based on the *lex fori concursus*.[1307] Second, awards based on an erroneous consideration of the scope could be held to violate the prohibition on individual enforcement. Courts, at least in the insolvency jurisdiction, will refer to the *lex fori concursus*. Court bound by the EIR will do the same as this issue is referred to the *lex for concursus* under Article 7(2)(b) EIR. A similar conclusion, although a more general rule, is reached under § 335 InsO.[1308]

4.8 The Substantive Dispute

The penultimate subject discussed here is the applicable law to the substantive dispute in arbitration. Although often an object of dispute, the law underlying the contract or claim in dispute has more explicit ways of being determined than that used for the applicable law questions above. It is either the law the parties have chosen to apply or the law applicable by applying the conflict-of-laws rule of the *lex arbitri*, c.q. the law found applicable by the tribunal.[1309] In Germany, this rule can be found in § 1051 ZPO. § 1051(1) ZPO states that the parties' choice determines the applicable substantive law of the dispute. § 1051(2) ZPO provides the backup rule, referring to the law with the

1306. Although, this situation can generally only occur in private insolvency.
1307. *Schultze-Moderow*, Schiedsverfahren und Insolvenz, pp. 202–203.
1308. MüKoInsO/*Reinhart* § 335 InsO, No. 44.
1309. *Final Award in ICC Case No. 7205*, Collection of ICC Awards III, 1997, 622–628, p. 623; *Final Award in ICC Case No. 6379*, Collection of ICC Awards III, 1997, 135–126; *Final Award in ICC Case No. 4629*, Collection of ICC Awards III, 1997, 152, p. 157; *Award in ICC Case No. 2119*, Collection of ICC Awards I, 1990, p. 355; *Final Award in ICC Case No. 1512*, Collection of ICC Awards I, 1990, 3–5, pp. 4–5.

closest connection.[1310] Although described as a rule connected to the *voie directe*, this is incorrect. In fact, it constitutes a conflict-of-laws rule.[1311] This is not changed by the fact that the conflict-of-law rule essentially provides the tribunal with a *voie directe*-like discretion.

However, it is clear from the above analyses of the EIR and the German autonomous international insolvency law that the law applicable to the contract is not necessarily the law to be referred to for the effects of the insolvency on this contract. It is debatable if a choice of law of the parties also includes a reference to the conflict-of-laws rules, in this context, the insolvency-specific conflict-of-laws rules. This would depend on an interpretation of the actual choice that the parties made. To make things slightly easier the German arbitration code in § 1051(1) ZPO states in the second sentence that unless explicitly agreed otherwise, the choice must be understood as merely a reference to the substantial rules of the chosen jurisdiction.

Insofar as the question is put forward within the scope of the EIR, the answer is relatively easy again due to the *ordre public* nature thereof, its rules and, in particular, the general rule referring to the *lex fori processus* apply. However, outside of this scope, several laws could be considered: the *lex contractus*, the *lex fori processus*, and the law of the seat. It would be most prudent to refer to the effect under the *lex fori processus* or the law of the insolvency to secure enforcement of the award. Nevertheless, a tribunal should also always consider the rules of the *ordre public* in the seat.[1312]

The effect of the insolvency on the substance of the dispute can also encompass the previously discussed question of the claim's potential encompassment by the insolvent estate. Which, depending on the *lex fori concursus* and the law of the seat, might not be considered arbitrable as a primary question.[1313] However, the encompassment of claims into the insolvency estate is closely related to the '*Prozessführungsbefugnis*', the right to take legal action. In most jurisdictions, only the insolvency administrator will have standing and the right to take action if the claim belongs to the estate. In consequence, the question of whether a claim belongs to the estate becomes a preliminary question for tribunals' consideration of the claim, c.q. in their assessment of the question if the party bringing the claim or defending the claim has the authority to do so. Courts in annulment proceedings in Germany and elsewhere will take this into account when assessing the right to be heard under § 1059(2)(1)(b) ZPO or local equivalents, *see also* Article V(1)(b) NYC for enforcement proceedings. To determine who this right to be heard should be awarded to the court in Germany will be bound to apply § 335 InsO and, in consequence, investigate if the claim is part of the insolvent estate and based on the *lex fori concursus*. Therefore, as was also concluded concerning questions regarding the insolvent estate in general, the consideration of the parties'

1310. A doctrine often used in arbitration, also to fill in, for example, the tribunal's discretion provided by Art. 13(3) ICC Rules, now Art. 21(1) ICC Rules, *see Award in ICC Case No. 6500*, Collection of ICC Awards III, 1997, 452, p. 453.
1311. Compare *Kessedjian*, Chapter 3: Determination and Application of Relevant National and International Law and Rules, 71, p. 81.
1312. *Schultze-Moderow*, Schiedsverfahren und Insolvenz, pp. 202–203.
1313. *Badel*, ASA Bull. 25 (2007), 36, p. 37.

interest surrounding annulment and enforcement also supports reference by and large to the *lex fori concursus*.[1314]

In ICC Case 2114, a Dutch Tribunal applied Belgian insolvency rules to the claim in question as it considered that the Belgian insolvency rule in question was of an *ordre public* nature. Furthermore, it considered that, according to an execution treaty between Belgium and the Netherlands, the effects of insolvency orders rendered in one country extended to the other and that, thus, enforcement in the Netherlands would also be impossible if the relevant Belgian insolvency rule was violated.[1315] However, in most cases, the enforcement of the award in the relevant countries will not be so closely linked, and the tribunal must provide more extensive consideration as to why it takes into account a material rule of an out-of-seat insolvency. This is what, for example, the Tribunal in ICC Case 10687 did. It referred to the *lex fori concursus* to see how it could render the award, c.q. if and how it could condemn a party to pay. It did this based on a perceived need to, as far as possible, deliver awards enforceable at the seat of the insolvent party.[1316] This need is also apparent from the previously discussed interests of the parties. Consequently, not only for the effects of the insolvency on the substantive claims in the arbitration directly[1317] but also for the way in which it handles those claims in the awards, it should refer to the *lex fori concursus*.

4.9 The Arbitrator's Contract

The last subject discussed here is the law applicable to the arbitrator's contract. Whereas, as represented above, there are questions regarding the effect of the insolvency on the arbitrator's contract, it is not the place of the arbitrators to make determinations on the arbitrator's contract, whether it concerns validity in general or the effects of the insolvency thereon. First, this follows from the principle of *nemo judex in re sua* or the principle that one cannot be the judge in its own case, as the arbitrators clearly have an interest in the outcome of such determinations regarding the arbitrator's contract.[1318] Second, most arbitration agreements do not provide the arbitrators with substantive jurisdiction to decide these issues. It is important to note that the view that the arbitrator somehow becomes a third party to the arbitration agreement with the arbitrator's contract also becoming part of this system as proposed by the Court of Appeal in *Hyundai* should be dismissed.[1319] The arbitrator's agreement is a contract connected with the arbitration agreement, but that connection cannot

1314. Cf. *Schultze-Moderow*, Schiedsverfahren und Insolvenz, p. 203.
1315. *Award in ICC Case No. 2114*, Y.B. Com. Arb. V, 1980, p. 193.
1316. *Final Award in ICC Case No. 10687*, ICC International Court of Arbitration Bulletin 20, 2009, 77, p. 78.
1317. Cf. *Final Award on Jurisdiction in ICC Case No. 13085*, Y.B. Com. Arb. XXXIV, 2009, 212, No. 3535.
1318. *Mourre*, Chapter 1. Sed Quis Custodiet Ipsos Custodes? On Jurisdiction Upon Arbitrators, 13, p. 15.
1319. *England and Wales Court of Appeal*, QB 1992, 863–887, p. 885; *Mourre*, Chapter 1. Sed Quis Custodiet Ipsos Custodes? On Jurisdiction Upon Arbitrators, p. 13; Cf. *Wolff*, Chapter 18, Part XII: Rights and Duties of Arbitrators, 2723, No. 9; *see also* § 4 4.1.

change that the arbitrator is a constituent party to the arbitrator's agreement. Considering the arbitrator a third party to a contract that is supposed to embody his or her duties is illogical and goes against the principle that one cannot make a contract to the detriment of third parties. Furthermore, were the logic in *Hyundai* followed, one could argue that arbitrators would have the jurisdiction to decide upon the arbitrator's agreement in violation of the principle of *nemo judex in re sua* due to the doctrine of competence-competence, the principle that they can interpret their own jurisdiction as provided by the arbitration agreement and more broadly due to the fact that they are allowed to interpret the arbitration agreement.

Consequently, courts will have to be seized to determine the effect of the insolvency on the arbitrator's contract. Those courts will apply their own conflict-of-laws rules and qualifications to determine the effect of the insolvency on the arbitrator's agreement. As discussed in Chapter 2 § 4.1, there is a discussion on the nature and qualification of the arbitrator's agreement.

4.10 Conclusion on the Applicable Law in the Arbitration

In this last section of Chapter 3, the examination of the previous two sections culminated in a discussion on the applicable law to several important arbitration issues and topics potentially affected by insolvency. Whereas the primary consideration of the arbitrators on the question of applicable law should always be the interests of the parties in the case, it is clear from the above that in many cases these interests are consistent and support the applicability of a specific law to a particular issue or group of issues. It is quite understandable that practice has come to discuss and apply these common outcomes as rules and has to a significant decree abstracted these rules and discussion on applicable law from the discussion on the parties' interests in the particular case. However understandable, such abstraction should be discouraged. It is vital for tribunals to be aware of the dogmatic basis of these so-called rules. Only when an arbitrator has a clear understanding that these rules hold little value on their own but mostly and merely as an expression of the parties' interests can he make informed considerations as to the application of this rule or the potential need to come to a different conclusion.

ICC Case 6149, as discussed above, although not involving insolvency, serves as an excellent example of arbitrators that at least subconsciously are aware of these considerations.[1320] They rejected the application of Jordanian law and its *ordre public* rules in favour of arbitration as this was considered the implicit will of the parties. Thereby they most likely negated the chance of enforcement in Jordan, which, as described, they should generally try to secure. These are the considerations that a tribunal should make, weighing the parties' interests and letting them point to a particular outcome.

Regardless of all the talk of considerations and weighing of interests, it is hard to ignore that certain considerations are so strong that they will lead to a particular

1320. *See* § 4.6; *Interim Award in ICC Case No. 6149*, Collection of ICC Awards III, 1997, 315–331.

outcome in almost all cases. The primary example is the consideration that the annulment of the award should be avoided. Within the EU, this leads to the application of the EIR in the insolvency context and will rarely allow for any further considerations. Outside of the EU context, it provides the permanent consideration of mandatory law and *ordre public* rules of the seat. Furthermore, any conflict-of-law rule or plain applicable law rule taken from the annulment framework, which are often copies of the enforcement framework of Article V NYC represented in Article 34 Arb.ML, *see* § 1059 ZPO, will be very hard to ignore for a tribunal.

5 CONCLUSORY REMARKS TO CHAPTER 3

In this final substantive part of the book, specific issues introduced by putting insolvency in arbitration in an international context were examined. In this part, it has become clear that the factor of internationality adds a whole new dimension of considerations and uncertainty to the issue of insolvency in commercial arbitration. The tension between insolvency and arbitration within one jurisdiction is provided with another axis of tension, the tension between multiple jurisdictions. Tribunals wishing to solve these issues cannot afford to have a confused understanding of their role and position within the international and national legal order. Neither can they be confused about the nature of arbitration. Only a solid understanding of the fundaments of insolvency and arbitration will be able to guide the tribunal through the issues without damaging the interests of the parties.

In more practical terms, the tribunal will have to struggle with the concept of recognition, which should be used beyond its role as an excuse not to take into account 'foreign' insolvencies, to solve preliminary questions with which the tribunal is confronted. However, the primary issue that internationality adds to this book's discussion is the determination of the applicable law to all the different aspects of insolvency in arbitration. The tension between insolvency and arbitration is on full display here. Furthermore, the understanding of arbitration is critical in the discussion of the applicable law and conflict-of-law rules. Whereas a jurisdictional approach would likely lead to the application of the conflict-of-laws rules of the seat, the contractual approach followed here leaves the tribunal prima facie with little guidance. Consequently, an investigation must be made into the parties' interests and how these can inform the considerations of applicable law. The rules and guidelines that practice has provided on the applicable law to the different aspects of arbitration are not necessarily wrong, e.g., the closest connection consideration, but they can only serve to investigate the parties' interests. This guiding function and value of these rules, as opposed to an intrinsic value, is often ignored in practice.

In practice, tribunals have come to conclusions mostly supportive but also contrary to some of the conclusions in this discussion, as can be seen by the references made throughout. However, the more significant issue is that awards often still lack holistic considerations of the discussions made here.

CHAPTER 4

Conclusion

After having discussed the necessary 'basics' in Chapter 1, providing a broad discussion of topics relevant within the context of insolvency in arbitration in a national setting in Chapter 2, and discussing the complicating factors introduced in the international context in Chapter 3, this Chapter 4 is the conclusion of this work. Aside from giving as holistic a discussion of insolvency in commercial arbitration as possible within the framework of a dissertation, it was always an aim of the research to provide arbitral practice with guidance on the issue of insolvency in international arbitration. From all the considerations above and discussions with practitioners, it has become quite clear that such guidance would be helpful as it is easy to lose sight of where even to start considerations on applicable law, and it is common to leave out essential considerations or jump to, for example, to the applications of specific laws.

To provide this guidance, as part of the final and conclusory part of the book, an attempt will be made to formulate some guiding considerations that can be used to steer the tribunal's considerations through the maze that is insolvency in commercial arbitration. Since the term 'guidelines' has become somewhat of a black sheep amongst many practitioners of international arbitration, the guidance here will be provided in a set of considerations. Considerations are also a more appropriate term as they are the author's interpretation of the generalised interests of the parties that a tribunal should consider and crucially should only consider in that context, i.e., a possible representation of the parties' interests. These considerations mainly represent this book's factual and legal conclusions as they are based on a distillation of the discussion herein. After the proposed considerations (§ 1), a traditional conclusory section will follow (§ 2).

1 PROPOSAL FOR A LIST OF CONSIDERATIONS FOR INSOLVENCY IN INTERNATIONAL ARBITRATION

The list of considerations below is based on generalised party interests in insolvency in arbitration and, as such, does not require any direct adoption or prescription by institutions or incorporation into an arbitration agreement to be relevant. However, this notwithstanding, such prescription is not only possible but is to be encouraged as it would only serve the purpose of these considerations, which is to create clarity and certainty by giving the considerations more visibility.

The considerations proposed below are products of the discussions had and conclusions drawn throughout the book and, therefore, find their place here in the conclusory part of the work. Short substantiations and explanations will accompany the considerations, but in line with their nature as conclusions and reiterations of the considerations throughout this work, there will not be a complete restatement of their reasoning. Instead, reference can be had and will be provided to the respective parts of the book upon which they build.

1.1 Considerations for Insolvency in Arbitration

1.1.1 Relevance and Application

(1) These Considerations are meant to provide guidance to arbitrators and parties confronted with insolvency in arbitration and apply only in those circumstances.
(2) These Considerations primarily serve as guidance for the Tribunal's considerations of the Parties' interests in case of insolvency in arbitration. Their applicability or relevance relies, thus, on the extent to which the Considerations accurately represent the Parties' interests in the case with which the Tribunal is confronted.
(3) Notwithstanding Subconsideration 2, these Considerations are directly applicable if the Parties so agree.
(4) These Considerations are not meant to displace otherwise applicable mandatory laws, including the mandatory rules of the *lex arbitri*.
(5) Insofar as these Considerations are used as guidance, they cannot displace rules and regulations agreed to by the Parties, including as embodied in and incorporated into, the arbitration agreement.

Substantiation: The scope of application presented here is primarily a restatement of the above preamble. Whereas providing the Considerations with the status of a Party agreement can only be encouraged, the basic concept of these Considerations revolves around their ability to restate the interests of parties confronted with insolvency in arbitration. Consequently, they are meant to be used by Tribunals as a list of considerations that they can make, which will generally reflect the interests of the Parties in such a situation. Whereas the Parties agreeing to these Considerations makes explicit that these Considerations represent the Parties' will, this does not diminish their value as generalisations of the Parties' will in case such an agreement is lacking. In those circumstances, however, these considerations should always be disregarded if the Parties' interests in the case before the Tribunal provide a different outcome. Finally, regardless of their status, the Considerations cannot override applicable mandatory law and, unless their application has been agreed upon, can also not override explicit Party agreements.

1.1.2 Definitions

The terms used in these Considerations should be understood to refer to:

> *'Insolvency Practitioner'*: follows the definition thereof in Regulation (EU) 2015/848 and thus, means any person or body whose function, including on an interim basis, is to:
>
> i. verify and admit claims submitted in insolvency proceedings;
> ii. represent the collective interest of the creditors;
> iii. administer, either in full or in part, assets of which the debtor has been divested;
> iv. liquidate the assets referred to in point (iii); or
> v. supervise the administration of the debtor's affairs.
>
> Reference for examples of such persons can be had to Annex B of Regulation (EU) 2015/848;
>
> 'Arbitration': in these Considerations refers to commercial arbitration and, in this context, specifically to commercial arbitration involving a claim involved or arguably involved in an insolvency proceeding.
> 'Arbitrator(s)': the Arbitrator(s) in the particular case.
> 'Arbitrator's Contract': the contract between the Parties and the Arbitrator(s) or the arbitration institute and the Arbitrator(s), otherwise known under names such as: *Schiedsrichtervertrag*, contract of investiture, *contrat d'investiture*, contract of the arbitrator, *contratto di arbitrato.*[1321]
> 'Consideration(s)': a Consideration in this set of Considerations or these Considerations as a whole.
> 'Insolvency': is meant to refer to those proceedings in which the debtor is divested, and the right to dispose of the estate is transferred to the Insolvency Practitioner in a collective proceeding to satisfy the creditors. Reference can be head to Annex A of the Regulation (EU) 2015/848 on insolvency proceedings.
> 'Insolvent': the Party subjected to insolvency proceedings.
> 'Part(y/ies)': a party or the parties in the particular arbitration.
> 'Tribunal': the tribunal in the particular case.
>
> Usages of the terms 'seat (jurisdiction, of the)' and 'insolvency (jurisdiction, of the)' or similar terms are to be given their ordinary meaning, referring to the seat of the particular arbitration and the jurisdiction in which the insolvency was opened respectively.
>
> Terms not defined here should be understood autonomously in an international fashion and in the spirit of these Considerations.

1.1.3 General Principle

The Considerations represent considerations of generalised interests of Parties. Therefore, tribunals should take the Considerations primarily as a checklist of issues

1321. *See* § 4; *Born,* International Commercial Arbitration, p. 1969.

that they need to consider and a proposal for the outcome of considerations of these issues based on the most common interests in arbitration. These Considerations in no way should be understood as hard rules, and tribunals should always deviate from these Considerations if the common will or interests of the Parties so require. To determine the common will and interests of the Parties, the Tribunal should specifically consider the arbitration agreement and subsequent agreements, including but not limited to such documents as the Terms of Reference. The Parties' interests should be interpreted *ex tunc*, referring to the moment of contract conclusion. Unless otherwise provided by the facts of the case, the interests of the Parties that a tribunal should consider include, but are not limited to:

(1) The effectiveness of the award, including primarily the interest in non-annullable awards and, secondarily, the interest in enforceable awards. For considerations of enforceability, the likely places of enforcement should be considered, which, as a rebuttable presumption, include the insolvency jurisdiction and the home jurisdictions of the Parties.
(2) Legal certainty, predictability and legitimate expectations and other concepts of legitimate trust in the application of certain laws or the manner of their application. The Tribunal will consider as an aspect thereof the interest in uniformity of decisions.
(3) The neutrality of the proceedings and applicable laws.
(4) The efficiency of the arbitration proceedings, including both temporal and financial efficiency.

Substantiation: Due to the nature of arbitration, as argued in this book, the root concern of the Tribunal should be performing the arbitration agreement, giving effect to the will of the Parties, and otherwise acting in the interests of the Parties. The interests that are mentioned here are those explored in this book. This list is non-exhaustive as more interests can generally be found in arbitration. Furthermore, the Tribunal should investigate and consider the actual interests in the case.[1322] Some further basic terms are defined here, and a general rule is established that Tribunals should refrain from interpreting these Considerations based on domestic or national definitions. Guidance is taken from the EIR to create a more familiar and more substantiated frame of reference. This also motivates the use of the term Insolvency Practitioner over Insolvency Administrator or other terms.

In the Interests of the Parties, the Tribunal will consider:

i *Consideration No. 1 Concerning the Role of Insolvency in Arbitration*

(1) The Tribunal will consider the insolvency of one of the Parties or that otherwise affects the claims in arbitration and its proper effects in arbitration, regardless of the place of insolvency.

1322. *See* Chapter 3 §§ 3.3.1, 3.3.2.

(2) The Tribunal should not ignore orders made regarding the insolvency in the seat jurisdiction and will also duly consider those made in the jurisdiction of the Insolvent.
(3) The considerations of the Tribunal on the effects of the insolvency in arbitration will be reasoned. This reasoning should primarily refer to the interests of the Parties.

Substantiation: After the discussion in this book, it might seem unnecessary to propose a Consideration as this Consideration No. 1. However, this Consideration is necessary and even crucial. Tribunals have in the past ignored insolvencies, especially those outside of the seat of arbitration, regularly without any or without proper reasoning for doing so. Therefore, the first premise for any further considerations must be that tribunals should consider and acknowledge the insolvency and investigate what it means for the arbitration. This includes potential recognition regimes. The second premise builds on this and states that a tribunal should consider the relevant insolvency orders.[1323] Finally, as a third premise, they must provide proper reasoning for their conclusions on these points, and those reasons must reflect the contractual nature of arbitration, c.q. the will and interests of the Parties. Consequently, the Tribunal must motivate its non-application or application of insolvency rules and, in general, the way it handles the insolvency based on these interests.

ii *Consideration No. 2 Concerning Arbitrability*

(1) The Tribunal will take into account the arbitrability of insolvency-related issues as applicable in the insolvency jurisdiction.
(2) Insofar as the jurisdiction of the insolvency is not the jurisdiction of the seat, the consideration as meant in subclause (1) should still be made. The Tribunal, in such circumstances, should also consider the relevant arbitrability concept of the seat, applying both in concurrence and giving preference to the more restrictive of the two.
(3) In case the insolvency jurisdiction has excessively more restrictive rules on insolvency-related arbitrability than the seat, this can be a consideration to disregard these more restrictive rules. In considering such an outcome, the Tribunal should consider at least its effects on the effectiveness of the award, risks of annulment and non-enforcement and provide a reasoned decision based on the interests of the Parties.

Substantiation: As discussed in Chapter 3 § 4.6, a tribunal should primarily be concerned with the arbitrability concept of the seat. Insofar as the seat jurisdiction is also that of the insolvency, there is little question about which concept of the arbitrability of insolvency issues is relevant. However, insofar as the jurisdiction of the insolvency is not the same as the seat, the Tribunal should take into account both to

1323. *See* Chapter 2 § 2.1 and Chapter 3, § 1.

protect from annulment and ensure enforcement in one of the most likely places of enforcement, i.e., the insolvency jurisdiction. Whereas this Consideration might read as anti-arbitration, it is meant as pro-effectivity. It is true that giving effect to a more restrictive concept of arbitrability will necessarily lead to a conclusion that excludes more issues from arbitration. However, if this is necessary to ensure the enforceability of the award in the jurisdiction where a Party likely has the majority of its assets, it will generally be in the interests of the Parties to consider the more restrictive approach.

The third subclause has a dual purpose in trying to avoid the application of abusively anti-arbitration concepts of arbitrability and comparing the two most relevant concepts of arbitrability. In this comparison, it should not be ignored that applying a highly restrictive approach to arbitrability might, under certain circumstances, be considered in itself a violation of certain specific relevant rules in the seat. Reference can be had to the consideration in ICC Case 6149, although not involving insolvency, the Tribunal did not apply the *ordre public* of the home state of one of the parties, as this would essentially render the arbitration without purpose, as the tribunal would not be able to arbitrate the core of the issue put before it and this could not be considered the will of the parties when agreeing to arbitrate such issues. In the context of insolvency, it could be considered excessively restrictive and against the parties' will to apply a rule that would block the rendering of any kind of useful award on the central claims, be it as an enforceable award or as part of a verification procedure in insolvency.

iii Consideration No. 3 The Arbitration Agreement

(1) The Tribunal should consider the effect of the insolvency on the arbitration agreement based on the law applicable to the arbitration agreement, which is the law of the seat if not otherwise agreed.
(2) The effect on the arbitration agreement proposed by the insolvency jurisdiction can be considered. Effects that invalidate the agreement or the proceedings wholly or substantially should not be applied by the Tribunal unless this would render the arbitration without purpose.
(3) Arbitration agreements made before the opening of the insolvency will generally be considered not to include in their scope claims that are based solely on insolvency law, considering that these issues cannot have been at the disposal of the Parties at the time of contract conclusion.
(4) The Tribunal can generally consider all preliminary questions necessary to answer the questions put before it in arbitration as falling within the scope of the arbitration agreement. This explicitly includes the answering of questions as to the effects of insolvency on different aspects of questions subjected to its jurisdiction.

Substantiation: This Consideration reflects the conclusions reached regarding the effect of insolvency on the arbitration agreement and its scope. The Tribunal will hardly be able to ignore the effects the insolvency has on the arbitration agreement based on the law applicable to it, as doing so would lead to an annullable award. Therefore, the Tribunal should have regard for the effect of the law of the insolvency on the arbitration agreement. However, if this law invalidates the arbitration agreement or process entirely or in such a way that arbitration is without purpose, the Tribunal should consider not applying these effects. If it considers not to apply these effects, it should be aware that there will likely be no successful enforcement in the jurisdiction of the insolvency. In case enforcement in this jurisdiction is a primary or the sole objective of the arbitration, the Tribunal should still consider applying these rules even if they invalidate the arbitration agreement. In that case, the purpose of the arbitration cannot be met by continuing the arbitration and continuing the arbitration would only lead to more costs. This Consideration should be considered to also refer to rules that grant the Insolvency Practitioner the option of dissolving or invalidating the arbitration agreement that are not applied automatically. *See* the considerations in Chapter 3 § 4.2 of this book.

A not uncommon discussion in the context of insolvency in arbitration is if the issues that are being discussed in the arbitration due to insolvency are within the jurisdiction of the Tribunal. The scope of the arbitration agreement is a large part of this consideration. Due to the contractual nature of arbitration, depending on the relevant law, Parties cannot generally resolve issues by arbitration that they could not resolve contractually or otherwise consensually. Insolvency-specific claims did not exist at the time of contract conclusion and were not at the disposal of pre-insolvent parties. In this line, it is possible to discuss the effect of insolvency on a claim flowing from a contract between the Parties, e.g., non-performance. It is, however, not possible for pre-insolvency parties to have subjected, for example, the application of rules regulating insolvency disputation, e.g., *actio pauliana*, to arbitration.[1324] In this example, the Insolvency Practitioner might be able to subject such issues to arbitration insofar as they are considered arbitrable.

However, to provide the answers to certain questions in arbitration, the Tribunal will have to deal with preliminary issues related to the insolvency. It was argued above that tribunals should be considered to have the authority and jurisdiction to answer any preliminary question necessary to answer the questions the Parties have put before it if such questions themselves are arbitrable. This consideration is reflected in subclause (4).[1325]

iv *Consideration No. 4 The Role and Position of the Insolvency Practitioner*

(1) Insofar as the applicable insolvency law does not exclude it, the Insolvency Practitioner should be considered bound to the arbitration agreement, aside from the effects described in Consideration No. 3.
(2) The Insolvency Practitioner will be invited into the proceedings by the Tribunal.

1324. *See* Chapter 2 § 3.6.
1325. *See* Chapter 2 § 2.3.5.

(3) The Insolvency Practitioner will enter the proceedings in the same position as the insolvent Party and should be bound to the procedural position of this Party, including his choice of arbitrator unless the Tribunal considers:
   (a) That previous actions by Insolvent in the Arbitration are challengeable under insolvency-specific regulations, and that finding that the Insolvency Practitioner is bound to these actions is unreasonable or endangers the effectiveness of the award.
   (b) That the factual substitution of the Insolvent by the Insolvency Practitioner leaves the Tribunal imbalanced or otherwise skewed towards one Party.

(4) The Tribunal will refer to the law of the insolvent Party for issues regarding the role, powers and competencies of the Insolvency Practitioner.

(5) Insofar as the Insolvency Practitioner is not bound to the arbitration agreement and does not join the arbitration proceedings upon invitation, the Tribunal will consider the continuation of the proceedings with the Insolvent insofar as this does not harm the effectivity of the award or this can otherwise be considered in the Parties' interests. The Tribunal will otherwise consider the termination of the arbitration proceedings.

Substantiation: This Consideration, especially subclause (1), is formulated in a less nuanced fashion than the previous ones. Insofar as the arbitration is not considered wholly invalidated or this effect can be ignored, arbitration can only continue if the Tribunal finds that it has authority over the Insolvency Practitioner in the sense that the Insolvency Practitioner is bound to the arbitration agreement. Most laws will find that Insolvency Practitioners are generally bound to the contracts of the Insolvent and provide special insolvency-specific rules on how to handle and potentially dissolve or not perform such contracts. This consideration is reflected in subclause (1). Subclause (2) provides that the Tribunal must actively invite the Insolvency Practitioner into the proceedings. This is primarily a reflection of the right to be heard and thus the need to protect the award from annulment and non-enforcement. It is, however, also a consideration of efficiency, as an active approach by the Tribunal can contribute to a faster resolution of the arbitration. Subclause (3) provides that the Insolvency Practitioner must essentially accept the arbitration as is.[1326] The first exception acknowledges the role of insolvency disputation and the concept of the *actio pauliana*: if the Insolvent has knowingly disadvantaged the estate, the Insolvency Practitioner cannot be expected to be bound to such actions. More generally, if an action of the Insolvent is considered challengeable by the relevant insolvency law, binding the Insolvency Practitioner to such actions could lead to annulment and non-enforcement on grounds of *ordre public*.[1327] For example, this could be a violation of the equality of creditors if the Insolvent has admitted specific claims to certain creditors in the arbitration. The second exception to this rule is based on the considerations of the KG Berlin as

1326. *See* Chapter 2 §§ 2.2, 3.3.
1327. *See* Chapter 2 §§ 2.2, 3.5.3.

discussed in Chapter 2 § 2.3.6 above.[1328] If the Tribunal is skewed towards one or the other Party due to the substitution of the Insolvent with the Insolvency Practitioner, the Tribunal should consider finding that the Insolvency Practitioner is not bound to the Insolvent's choice of arbitrator. In the cited case, the arbitrator was linked to both original parties, c.q. their representatives. After the substitution, only the non-insolvent party's link remained, leaving the tribunal skewed. Insofar as the Insolvency Practitioner brings this argument within a reasonable time after having been invited into the proceedings, precluding the Insolvency Practitioner from making the argument, as the time for challenges has passed or for other reasons, would be unreasonable and would ignore that the Insolvency Practitioner is at least factually a new Party, regardless of his position under the applicable law. However, this exception is not purely based on considerations of equitability and fairness. A biased tribunal can lead to annulment and non-enforcement of the award. Subclause (4) refers to the law applicable to the internal competencies of the Insolvent and its Insolvency Practitioner. As discussed, these issues are typically referred to the *lex societatis* of a company and not doing so might lead to annulment and non-enforcement, *see, e.g.*, Article V(1)(a) but also (b) NYC.[1329]

Subclause (5) considers the situation in which the Insolvency Practitioner cannot be considered bound to the arbitration agreement and does not join the arbitration agreement by free will. In many circumstances, this will harm the effectiveness of any subsequent award in such a way as to make arbitration purposeless. If the insolvency jurisdiction is also the seat jurisdiction, continuing the arbitration insofar as it concerns insolvency claims will likely lead to an annullable and non-enforceable award. Insofar as the insolvency jurisdiction is not that of the seat, the award will likely be unenforceable there if not in other jurisdictions that recognise the effects of the insolvency as promulgated by the insolvency jurisdiction. In consequence, the Tribunal must very carefully consider if there is a genuine interest in the continuation of the proceedings in light of these potential issues. Considered can be, for example, likely enforcement in other jurisdictions or not enforcement-related purposes of a potential award.

v *Consideration No. 5 The Suspension of Proceedings*

(1) Upon the opening of the insolvency, the Tribunal will consider the suspension of proceedings based on the law of the arbitration proceedings primarily and secondarily on the law of the insolvency. In doing so, it will consider the effectiveness of the award in light of the identifiable interests of the Parties, including here primarily;
   (a) The risk of annulment of the award if the suspension is denied.

1328. *KG Berlin*, SchiedsVZ 2005, 100–102.
1329. *See* Chapter 3 § 4.4.

   (b) The risk of non-enforcement of the award in the jurisdiction of the insolvency if suspension rules are not applied, including if this non-enforcement violates the interests of the Parties.
(2) In its considerations, the Tribunal should consider at least a temporary suspension based on principles of the right to be heard and equal treatment of the Insolvency Practitioner and the principle of an adversarial proceeding.

Substantiation: The suspension of proceedings is often a core issue in debates about insolvency in arbitration. Whereas other issues should definitively not be ignored, this focus is understandable. The suspension has a direct and tangible effect on the arbitration. This Consideration is meant to provide the Tribunal with the most relevant points of consideration for such a suspension and to provide that, in general, a suspension should be considered to preserve the rights of the insolvent Party, c.q. its Insolvency Practitioner, and the creditors and, in doing so, protect the awards from annulment and non-enforcement.[1330]

vi *Consideration No. 6 Resumption of Proceedings*

(1) The Tribunal should confer with the Parties on their wish to continue the proceedings, considering the cost of the arbitration in the context of the realistic quotient of the claims that might be received in insolvency based on a potential award.
(2) Unless convincing considerations can be made to lift the suspension at another point in time, the suspension should generally last until the Insolvency Practitioner has made a decision regarding the claim;
   (a) In case the Insolvency Practitioner admits the claim, the Tribunal should consider bringing the proceedings to an end unless there is a reasonable and convincing interest in the continuation of the proceedings and the rendering of an award and the other Party is willing to bear the costs therefor.
   (b) In case the Insolvency Practitioner disputes the claim, the Tribunal will continue the proceedings to make a final determination upon the claim.
(3) Insofar as the insolvency regime provides a right to other creditors to dispute the claim and such a creditor exercises this right, the creditor should be considered as exercising a right belonging to the insolvency estate and will as such be invited into the proceedings in parallel or instead of the Insolvency Practitioner depending on the law of the insolvency.
(4) Notwithstanding Consideration No. 5, insofar as the insolvency regime provides a right to the Insolvent to dispute the claim instead of the Insolvency Practitioner, the Insolvent when exercising this right, will be considered as exercising a right belonging to the insolvency estate and will be invited into the proceedings, insofar necessary, respecting the law of the insolvency.

1330. *See* Chapter 2 § 2.3.1.

Substantiation: The first Subclause considers that the calculus behind the proceedings is drastically changed due to insolvency. Considering the coverage percentages in insolvency for non-secured claims can often hover around 2% to 3%, the costs of the arbitration will often be much higher than any money or other value that the non-insolvent party can hope to receive based on the award. This needs to be pointed out to the parties, so they can consider if the continuation of the proceedings is in their interests. Subclause (2) determines that the suspension should generally last until the Insolvency Practitioner has made a decision upon the claim, as continuing the proceedings when the Insolvency Practitioner might accept the claim goes against efficiency considerations. However, those same considerations might lead the Tribunal to decide that the proceedings must be continued, e.g., when for some reason, the Insolvency Practitioner ignores the proceedings entirely or has otherwise used the suspension abusively. Finally, even if a claim is admitted, some Parties might have an interest in having a final award. However, if the Insolvency Practitioner has admitted the claim into the insolvency, costs of continued proceedings usually are not considered debts incumbent on the estate. Therefore, the Party that wishes to continue the proceedings regardless must be willing to bear the costs of continuing the proceedings.[1331]

Subclause (3) provides a Consideration for the special circumstances in which a creditor can dispute a claim of another creditor in insolvency. It depends on the law of the insolvency whether such a creditor is considered bound to the arbitration agreement and if, in consequence, the relevant court will refer the creditor to arbitration. However, this Consideration provides that the Tribunal should at least invite the disputing creditor into the arbitration, either in parallel to or instead of the Insolvency Practitioner as provided by the relevant law, to facilitate the final admission or denial of the claim in the insolvency proceedings.[1332] Subclause (4), like subclause (3), is meant to take into account such regimes that leave the Insolvent room to dispute claims, especially if the Insolvency Practitioner does not dispute them.

vii Consideration No. 7 The Object of the Proceedings

(1) The Tribunal should consider amending the object of the proceedings or informing the Parties that they might wish to do so. It should otherwise consider granting claims only in a declaratory manner and avoid granting monetary relief. In its considerations, the Tribunal will consider the Parties' interests, including: the grounds for annulment in the seat, enforcement in the insolvency jurisdiction and the potential evidentiary role of an award.

(2) In conjunction with the considerations of subclause (1), the Tribunal will generally consider itself free to grant monetary relief concerning claims and debts incumbent on the estate, insofar as these are payable when due under

1331. *See* in particular Chapter 2 § 2.3.4.
1332. *See* in particular Chapter 2 § 2.3.4.

the insolvency law or are otherwise not encompassed by the insolvency's moratorium on individual enforcement.

Substantiation: Due to the common insolvency principle of the prohibition on individual enforcement, providing awards that award monetary relief can endanger the effectiveness of the award and consequently go against the interests of the Parties. Therefore, the Tribunal should consider whether it is necessary to amend the object of the proceedings outrightly or to suggest this to the relevant Party for these reasons. Insofar as the object of the proceedings is not amended, the Tribunal can consider granting the claims partially in the sense that it merely declares the existence of the claim in question but does not award monetary relief.[1333] Subclause (2) constitutes the recognition of the special nature of debts of the estate. In this context, one can think in particular of the costs of the proceedings, which regularly become debts of the estate if the proceedings are resumed.[1334]

viii *Consideration No. 8 Dissolution*

(1) If one of the Parties in arbitration has been finally dissolved, the Tribunal shall consider that this Party can no longer be a Party in the arbitration unless:
   (a) There are indications that an award might still be enforced against the dissolved Party, there is a reasonable chance for it to produce such an award, and the other Party wishes to continue the arbitration and is willing to advance the costs otherwise payable by the dissolved Party.
   (b) The dissolution was fraudulent or otherwise solely aimed at frustrating the arbitration, and the other Party is willing to advance the costs otherwise payable by the dissolved Party and has a reasonable interest in continuing the arbitration.
(2) Insofar as no Party on either claimant's or respondent's side is left due to the consideration in Subconsideration (1), the Tribunal should bring the arbitration proceedings to an end unless the dissolved Party can be substituted by another Party under the arbitration rules and the laws applicable to the Party.

Substantiation: Companies generally cease to exist when they are fully dissolved and, as such, can no longer be a party to proceedings. Some tribunals have continued arbitration after a party has been fully dissolved. This situation must be an exception as it cannot generally be considered in the Parties' interest to continue arbitration when one Party has fundamentally ceased to exist. There are, however, jurisdictions in which, under certain circumstances, litigation can be held against fully dissolved companies, and they can be fictionally brought back into existence for the sole purpose of the proceedings and the enforcement of their outcome.[1335] This is the primary

1333. *See* Chapter 2 § 2.3.3.
1334. *See* Chapter 2 § 2.3.4.
1335. *See* Chapter 2 § 2.4; as discussed in e.g., *Supreme Court of British Columbia*, 7.3.2014 – 2014 BCSC 370.

situation referred to in the exception of subclause (1)(a). The exception in subclause (1)(b) refers to the situation described in ICC Case 2139 and the considerations regarding this case in this book.[1336] It was suspected that the state-run company was dissolved to avoid liability. This behaviour should not be rewarded. However, the other Party must have a legitimate interest in continuing arbitration and, as the Tribunal cannot be expected to attempt to enforce its own costs claims against the non-existent Party, the other Party must be prepared to advance the entirety of the cost in return for a potential claim of said costs against the dissolved Party. Subclause (2) reflects the considerations of several awards discussed above, which consider that the arbitration might be continued against legal successors, parent companies, or even states as owners of the relevant companies.[1337]

ix *Consideration No. 9 Impecuniosity and Costs*

(1) Any Party, including the Insolvent, arguing impecuniosity has the burden to prove factual impecuniosity, for which the state of insolvency will not be considered sufficient proof by itself.
(2) The Tribunal will not accept arguments of incapability or impossibility to perform the arbitration agreement based on impecuniosity if;
  (a) The advance on costs has been paid.
  (b) The other Party advances the cost share of the impecunious Party.
(3) Insofar as security for costs can be ordered, the Tribunal will consider that the state of insolvency itself is not sufficient to order such security for costs. Insofar as not otherwise provided by the Parties and the applicable arbitration rules, the Tribunal should consider the factual risk of non-payment of a potential cost award, which the requesting Party must prove.

Substantiation: In practice, tribunals have to think about the financing of the proceedings. Arbitrators cannot be expected to work for half pay or no pay, in the sense that in case half their costs or all their costs are allocated to a Party that can and will not pay them. As such, the Tribunal must be confident that the proceeding is adequately financed before starting or continuing them. However, the situation in which a Party can just rely on its own impecuniosity to skirt an arbitration agreement must be avoided. As such, the other Party must be extended the opportunity to bear the costs of the proceedings until the final allocation thereof in the award.[1338]

As provided in the discussion on impecuniosity as an argument for the incapability to perform the arbitration agreement, insolvency does not mean impecuniosity. Thus, insolvency does not mean that a party could not pay a potential award for costs. Consequently, a factual assessment must be made to measure the risk of non-payment

1336. *See* Chapter 2 § 2.4; *Award in ICC Case No. 2139*, Collection of ICC Awards I, 1990, 24–25, 237–241.
1337. *See* Chapter 2 § 2.4.
1338. *See* Chapter 2 § 3.4.

of a potential award for costs.[1339] Here, as in the following Consideration No. 10, the burden of proof lies with the Party relying on impecuniosity as an argument.

x *Consideration No. 10 Arbitrator's Contract*

The Tribunal should make no considerations regarding the Arbitrator's contract, including regarding the potential influence of the insolvency on it. However, in case the Tribunal has been provided with proof that the Arbitrator's contract is finally and bindingly dissolved outside of the arbitration or if that dissolution is unchallenged, the Tribunal will bring the proceedings to an end unless this dissolution was evidently fraudulent or it considers that continuation does not harm the effectiveness of the proceedings and is in the interest of the Parties and the Arbitrators are otherwise guaranteed or provided an enforceable right to the payment of their costs and fees.

Substantiation: Discussing the Arbitrators' contracts is outside of the purview of the Tribunal. Any question related to it should be discussed in the relevant forum, being the courts of the seat of arbitration in most circumstances. Whereas it is commonly accepted that the aforementioned is the case, this Consideration serves to reinforce that the Parties need not attempt to make arguments regarding the Arbitrator's contract in arbitration, and the Tribunal need not entertain them.[1340] However, insofar as the arbitrator's contract is dissolved and this is not challenged or has become final and binding, this should, in most circumstances, lead to the end of the arbitration proceedings. The effectiveness of the award will most likely be irreparably harmed, and the basis for the payment of fees and costs to the Arbitrators is at least compromised.

xi *Consideration No. 11 Applicable Law to Insolvency-Related Issues*

(1) The Tribunal will consider that beyond the conflict-of-laws rules in the *lex arbitri* specifically addressed to tribunals, it is not bound to apply any conflict-of-laws rules or applicable law other than those that should be found applicable by reason of the Parties' agreements and the Parties' interests. First of these considerations should be that the Tribunal will apply any conflict-of-laws rules that are of an *ordre public* nature in seat jurisdictions or of which the non-application would otherwise endanger the effectiveness of the award.

(2) Barring the application of rules based on Subconsideration 1, the Tribunal will consider that generally, barring opposing indications, the following outcomes should result from these considerations on the following issues:
   (a) Issues of the validity of the arbitration agreement are to be determined by the law applicable to the arbitration agreement, being, insofar contrary indications are lacking, the law of the seat of arbitration.
   (b) Issues of competence, standing and representation of the Insolvent will be determined by the personal law applicable to the Insolvent.

1339. *See* Chapter 2 § 3.4.
1340. *See* Chapter 2 § 4.

(c) Issues surrounding the regulation of the arbitral proceeding, including but not limited to the potential insolvency-related suspension of proceedings, will be regulated by the law applicable to the arbitration proceedings. The Tribunal will also consider if the applicability of the law of the insolvency is in the interests of the Parties, considering, amongst other considerations, if this jurisdiction is a likely place of enforcement and enforceability there requires its application.

(d) Issues of objective arbitrability will be decided upon by applying the law of the seat of arbitration and, if differing, the law applicable to the arbitration agreement. The Tribunal will consider the application of the arbitrability concept of the insolvency jurisdiction if this is in the interest of the Parties, considering if this jurisdiction is a likely place of enforcement and if enforceability there requires its application. The Tribunal will apply the more restrictive of the here-mentioned concepts of arbitrability insofar as this aids the effectiveness of the award.

(e) Issues concerning the scope and regulation of insolvent estate will be considered based on the law of insolvency, insofar as they are arbitrable based on the considerations of subclause (1)(d). However, the Tribunal will consider differently if the application of the law of the insolvency leads to violations of the law of the seat or otherwise endangers the effectiveness of the arbitration proceedings.

(3) The considerations in this Consideration should not be construed as contrary to the other Considerations. Instead, this Consideration and the specific Considerations above should be understood to complement each other. In the case of perceived contradiction, the specific Consideration regarding the relevant issue has precedence over the considerations in this Consideration.

Substantiation: Due to the nature of arbitration, a contract being effectuated within a specific legal order, and the nature of arbitrators, not administrating state justice or authority, the arbitrators are not bound to apply the conflict-of-laws rules of the seat state beyond what is expressly provided to regulate arbitration. Those rules are, for example, the regulation of the choice of law for the substantive dispute often found in arbitration codes and other rules found there. For every other conflict-of-law question, an autonomous method must be employed based on the parties' interests. The indications of applicable law in this consideration form the results of generalised considerations of the Parties' interests. Particular regard is given to the interest in not having awards annulled and secondarily in the likely interest in having an enforceable award in the insolvency jurisdiction, c.q. can be used in the insolvency proceedings to prove a claim. These considerations are indicative. However, as the main interests considered here are quite universal, failing clear indications otherwise, they will be applicable in most arbitrations.[1341]

1341. *See* Chapter 3 §§ 3, 4.

The first Subconsideration refers to those conflict-of-laws rules that the Tribunal must apply if it does not wish to endanger the awards. As concluded in this book, the EIR should be considered part of the EU communal *ordre public* and should thus be fully applied.[1342] Similar considerations can be made for other instruments; primarily, the Tribunal should consider if conflict-of-laws rules in the seat are of a compelling nature in the sense that their non-application would lead to annulment.

2 CONCLUSORY REMARKS AND REFLECTION

After having provided a list of considerations that hopefully can be of aid to tribunals, parties and insolvency administrators confronted with insolvency in arbitration, it remains for this author to make some concluding remarks. Many works on this subject mention that insolvency in arbitration is becoming and will keep on becoming a more significant problem in international arbitration. Although it is often the more interesting position to disagree with the majority, this observation cannot be denied. For the complexity the issue presents and the predictable connection of extensive legal battles to insolvency, the subject has received decidedly little attention. Several works, primarily written as dissertations and a decent number of articles, deal with the subject more or less extensively. Whereas it is in the nature of those writing a dissertation to overestimate the importance and relevance of their work, it is still surprising that the subject has not received proper or often any attention in the major works on commercial arbitration. The counter-argument that such generalised works cannot deal with such a specific trope does not suffice as the entire point here is that insolvency is not such a unique and niche occurrence that it can be relegated to highly specialised literature.

Specific conclusions and thematic conclusions are already found in the guidelines proposed above and the relevant preliminary conclusions throughout the book. Therefore, a detailed discussion or summary of all the subjects discussed is unnecessary here. However, several overall conclusions can be made, and principal conclusions should be represented here.

Factually it can be concluded that the issue of insolvency in arbitration is not settled and that practice acts accordingly. The field of international arbitration is not a unified field, which is an endemic consequence of its international nature. As such, the difference in approaches to arbitration both in academia and national legislation leads to different answers to many of the questions discussed above. This is why it is so important to have a fixed understanding of the nature of arbitration and the nature of insolvency before one can start discussing the relevant themes. There is not a section in this book in which the conclusions drawn are not linked to the nature of arbitration or the nature of insolvency. If one were to take a jurisdictional view of arbitration, one could rewrite this entire book as different conclusions would have to be drawn, as can be seen in several of the works of colleagues, many of which are cited and discussed.

1342. *See* Chapter 3 § 2.1.

Taking the contractual view of arbitration, as advocated in this book, shapes the entire discussion. The questions the arbitrators have to ask themselves will always start with asking if their approach complies with the agreement that they are performing or if it is otherwise helpful to the performance of the contract or in the interests of the contractual parties. Every other consideration flows from this root consideration. Even in a purely domestic situation, wherein arbitrators usually and often unthinkingly apply the domestic law without incident, insofar as nothing else has been chosen, that choice is not to be dogmatically motivated by some intrinsic duty of the arbitrator to apply this law in the same way a judge would have to. In the domestic situation, there is naturally hardly any other law that could logically be argued to apply, but this does not change that this applicability still dogmatically flows from the contractual nature of the arbitration and hence the performance of the contract in a particular jurisdiction and the choices of the parties therein. In an international context, this nature motivates the choices of tribunals more explicitly, or at least it should.

As stated, in the purely domestic context, i.e., the German context in this book, applicable law questions do not feature in such a problematic fashion. The tribunal will merely, for lack of other valid options, by and large, rely on the domestic framework and hardly ever concerns itself with motivating this choice. Whereas the lack of motivation might be criticised from the standpoint that tribunals must deliver motivated awards, the outcome is hardly disputable. Nevertheless, even in the domestic discussion on German law, German insolvency and German arbitration, the nature of arbitration still plays a significant role. There is an extensive discussion on the application of § 240 ZPO, the suspension of proceedings in case of insolvency, on arbitration. The non-application thereof, as also advocated above, is primarily based on the fact that the tribunal is simply not bound to apply such a rule. In the relatively universalistic and liberal German organisation of insolvency, a good deal of insolvency-related questions remain arbitrable. The arbitrability question depends on the question of whether the parties could have privately agreed on a resolution to the issue. Although this is now no longer the primary rule in German law, that is rather the question as to the property law nature or economic nature or a claim, it still structurally plays a significant role in the question of arbitrability. This is especially true with regard to insolvency-related issues. This test leads to the conclusion that certain rights that are vested solely in the role of the insolvency administrator can only be subjected to arbitration by the administrator and further that if issues can only be resolved or ordered by the court, they are non-arbitrable. In that last category fall such core-insolvency issues as the opening and closing of proceedings.

The broader conclusion on arbitration in insolvency in Germany is primarily that the insolvency should not stop the arbitration permanently. It is right that the administrator should be provided with a suspension of the proceeding to have a reasonable time to enter into the proceedings and decide if he wants to dispute the claim, and similarly, a creditor needs time to register a claim. However, this is based on considerations of the arbitration, i.e., efficiency and the right to be heard. Furthermore, the insolvency-specific rules on non-performance of certain contracts, dissolving certain relationships or otherwise refusing what for the insolvent were binding obligations do not generally apply to the arbitration agreement and do not apply to the arbitration proceedings. Aside from the proceedings and arbitration agreement, arbitrators' agreements represent an entire field of discussion by themselves. For example, their nature is disputed and differs between jurisdictions. In this context, it must be concluded that due to the attracting nature of the arbitration in relation to its associated contracts, they cannot be treated differently than arbitration agreements or arbitration proceedings. The insolvency, however, permeates most of the aspects of arbitration tangibly, as the insolvency will influence everything from the standing in the arbitration to the manner in which an award can be rendered and the role of the award afterwards. All these are effects of insolvency-specific regulations and principles, such as the shift in the rights to dispose of assets to the administrator and the prohibition of individual enforcement.

Most importantly, the effect of the collective process of insolvency shapes the purpose of the proceedings. The claim must be registered with the insolvency administrator, and the arbitration will then primarily operate as a claim verification mechanism insofar as the administrator does not wish to recognise the claim. In this way, it becomes clear that arbitration in insolvency is profoundly shaped and influenced by the insolvency proceedings. Arbitrators who refuse these effects are either ignorant of them or of the results that doing so has on the effectiveness of the award or have made considerations thereupon and decided enough could be said for ignoring certain or all insolvency effects. However, as discussed, the influence of insolvency is often rejected by merely referring to the territorial effect of the insolvency, which in some instances might be a valid outcome but in no instance should be seen as sufficient motivation therefor.

In the discussion on the arbitration agreement, the arbitration proceedings and the award, an underlying discussion features on the timing of both insolvency and the arbitration and how these proceedings interact with each other at their respective different stages. To bring this underlying issue to the fore, a discussion is represented in Chapter 2 § 4, primarily taking the moment an award was made and its status as the point of measurement to discuss the different outcomes. For example, the different treatment of an award that has already been enforced versus one that still needs to go through these proceedings and how this influences the disputation proceedings. This discussion explored that courts in Germany, unlike tribunals, could not but follow the rule of § 240 ZPO in annulment and enforcement proceedings and, hence, suspend these proceedings upon the opening of insolvency. Similarly, it was made explicit that an underlying assumption of much of the discussion in this field is the insolvency of the awards debtor, as this proves the more problematic situation in light of the prohibition of enforcement against the insolvent but not by the insolvent, c.q. the insolvency administrator.

This book's bifurcated discussion on the German domestic and international context allowed a discussion on the European context as well. In consequence, the EIR is thoroughly discussed above. The conclusion was reached that in an application of the *Eco Swiss* test, the EIR must be considered part of the European *ordre public*. In this way, a regulation that does not directly apply to tribunals will have to be applied integrally by tribunals that do not wish to run afoul of the *ordre public* of EU states. No extra Consideration was provided for this above, as this filters into the application of the other Considerations via the parties' interest in effective awards. The conclusion that the EIR should be treated as *ordre public* is probably one of the most controversial conclusions in this book. Whereas the test for *ordre public communautaire* points in the direction of the conclusion presented here, it is clear this will remain disputed until settled by the CJEU.

In practice, the issue of insolvency in international arbitration can be overwhelming. As one practitioner once simply asked this author: 'Where do I start?'; should one start looking at the relevant insolvency laws of the seat or the insolvency jurisdiction, and to what extent must one apply these? This book attempts to represent the considerations that the arbitrator must make, which all start and end with the interest of the parties concerned. As such, to the question, 'must he look at the insolvency law?' and most any question discussed above, the answer is: 'Insofar as is necessary to secure the parties' interests.' This might seem a 'non-rule'-rule or an empty phrase in the sense that it leaves most answers wide open. This is partially true in the sense that, due to the casuistic nature of party interests, rigid rules are difficult to formulate. However, many common considerations can be made regarding the interests that parties will generally have in arbitration. For example, generally, these considerations should lead to at least a temporary stay of arbitral proceedings, as represented in the guidelines above. In the third part of this book, this discussion was extensively represented. Conflict-of-laws rules can be a beacon of the familiar and certain to arbitrators. However, the arbitrator is simply not bound to apply any conflict-of-laws rules not chosen by the parties. The old considerations that the tribunal should apply the conflict-of-laws rules of the seat have been thoroughly and correctly debunked.

Consequently, the entire discussion on applicable law and conflict-of-laws rules must be based on considerations of party interests asking what they expected, what secures their interest in a secure award and other similar considerations. Accordingly, all the tests, rules, approaches, and doctrines provided and prevalent in international arbitration to find the applicable law can only be used to investigate and realise the parties' interests. In line with this conclusion, the book's final sections and several of the above considerations represent the generalisations that can be made regarding applicable law based on common party interests.

As many works on international arbitration state, it would benefit the development of this field and the development of dogmatic answers to the questions discussed in this book to have a systematic publication of international arbitral awards. This book's arbitral case law is primarily focused on ICC cases as ICC cases represent the vast majority of the publicly, but not freely, accessible arbitral case law. Aside from this practical point, it would be interesting to see if national legislators in the future might consider putting forward more conflict-of-laws rules in their arbitration legislation. The author considers this unlikely as it would most likely be considered a limitation of the parties' autonomy and, therefore, an anti-arbitration move to do so. However, it would make many of the issues above far less complicated and provide for much-needed clarity and predictability and, in that sense, help arbitration.

References

Althaus, Christian/Beck, Andreas/Bornheimer, Jörg Münchener Anwalts-Handbuch Insolvenz und Sanierung, hrsg. von Jörg Nerlich, Georg Kreplin, 3. ed., München 2019.

Aufdermauer, Christian Schiedsgerichtsbarkeit und Insolvenz in Deutschland, Europäische Hochschulschriften / European University Studies / Publications Universitaires Européennes 5507, Frankfurt a.M 2013 (cited: *Aufdermauer*).

Ávila, Humberto Certainty in Law, Law and Philosophy Library 114, Basel 2016 (cited: *Ávila*).

Badel, Francoise Faillite et Arbitrage International, ASA Bull. 25 (2007), 36–47 (cited: *Badel*, ASA Bull. 25 2007, 36).

Baizeau, Domitille Arbitration and Insolvency: Issues of Applicable Law, in: Christoph Müller, Antonio Rigozzi (eds), New Developments in International Commercial Arbitration, Zurich/Basel/Geneva 2009, pp. 97–120 (cited: *Baizeau*).

Barraclough, Andrew/Waincymer, Jeff Mandatory Rules of Law in International Commercial Arbitration, MJIL 2005, 205–245 (cited: *Barraclough/Waincymer*, MJIL 2005, 205–245).

Baumbach, Adolf/Lauterbach, Wolfgang/Albers, Jan et al. Zivilprozessordnung, Mit FamFG, GVG und anderen Nebengesetzen, 76. ed., hrsg. von Peter Hartmann, München 2018 (cited: Baumbach/Lauterbach/Albers/Hartmann-*Bearbeiter*).

Becker, Christoph Insolvenzrecht, 3. ed., Academia iuris, Köln 2010 (cited: *Becker*).

BeckOK InsO, mit InsVV und EUInsVO, 25. ed., hrsg. von Alexander Fridgen, Arndt Geiwitz, Burkard Göpfert, München 2021 (cited: BeckOK InsO-*Bearbeiter*).

BeckOK FamFG, 40. ed., hrsg. von Meo-Micaela Hahne, Jürgen Schlögel, Rolf Schlünder, München 2021 (cited: BeckOK FamFG-*Bearbeiter*).

Bell, John Montgomerie Treatise on the Law of Arbitration in Scotland: With an Appendix of Forms, Edinburgh 1861 (cited: *Bell*).

Bělohlávek, Alexander J. Importance of the Seat of Arbitration in International Arbitration Delocalization and Denationalization of Arbitration as an Outdated Myth, 31 ASA Bull. 2013, 262–292 (cited: *Bělohlávek*, ASA Bull. 31 2013, 262).

Bělohlávek, Alexander J. The Impact of Insolvency of a Party on Pending Arbitration Proceedings in Czech Republic, England and Switzerland and Other Countries, in: Marianne Roth, Michael Geistlinger (eds), Yearbook on International Arbitration. Vol. 1, Copenhagen 2010, pp. 145–166 (cited: *Bělohlávek*).

Berends, Arend Jacobus Insolventie in het internationaal privaatrecht, Amsterdam Univ. Diss. 2005, Recht en praktijk 133, Deventer 2005 (cited: *Berends*).

Berger, Christian Schiedsrichtervertrag und Insolvenz der Schiedspartei, in: Herbert Kronke, Karsten Thorn (Hrsg.), Grenzen überwinden – Prinzipien bewahren, Festschrift für Bernd von Hoffmann zum 70. Geburtstag, Bielefeld 2011, pp. 903–913 (cited: *Berger*).

Berger, Klaus Peter 'Sitz des Schiedsgerichts' oder 'Sitz des Schiedsverfahrens', RIW 39 (1993), 8–12 (cited: *Berger*, RIW 39 1993, 8).

Berger, Klaus Peter The International Arbitrators' Application of Precedents, Journal of International Arbitration 9 1992, 5–22 (cited: *Berger*, Journal of International Arbitration 9 1992, 5).

Berset, Dominique/Lévy, Laurent Faillite et arbitrage, ASA Bull. 16 1998, 664–680 (cited: *Berset/Lévy*, ASA Bull. 16 1998, 664).

Blackaby, Nigel/Partasides, Constantine/Hunter, Martin et al. Redfern and Hunter on international arbitration, New York, London 2015 (cited: *Blackaby* et al.).

Böckstiegel, Karl-Heinz/Kröll, Stefan M./Nacimiento, Patricia Part I: Germany as a Place for International and Domestic Arbitrations – General Overview, in: Karl-Heinz Böckstiegel, Stefan M. Kröll, Patricia Nacimiento (eds), Arbitration in Germany: The Model Law in Practice, Second Edition, Alphen aan den Rijn 2015, pp. 1–50 (cited: *Böckstiegel/Kröll/Nacimiento*).

Bogdan, Michael Some Arbitration-Related Problems of Swedish Private International Law, Swedish and International Arbitration 1990, 70–79 (cited: *Bogdan*, Swedish and International Arbitration 1990, 70).

Born, Gary International Arbitration, Law and Practice, Alphen aan den Rijn 2016 (cited: *Born*).

Born, Gary International Commercial Arbitration, Commentary and Materials, Second Edition, New York, Ardsley, NY 2001 (cited: *Born*).

Born, Gary International Commercial Arbitration, Alphen aan den Rijn 2014 (cited: *Born*).

Borris, Christian Die 'Schiedsfähigkeit' von Beschlussmängelstreitigkeiten in der Personengesellschaft, Zum Beschluss des BGH vom 6.4.2017 ('Schiedsfähigkeit III'), NZG 2017, 761–767 (cited: *Borris*, NZG 2017, 761).

Börtinghaus, Ulf Die Unterbrechung des Räumungsprozesses nach Eröffnung des Insolvenzverfahrens, NZM 2010, 326–328 (cited: *Börtinghaus*, NZM 2010, 326).

Breetzke, Ernst Vertrag und Vergütung des Schiedsrichters, NJW 1968, 1113–1117 (cited: *Breetzke*, NJW 1968, 1113).

Brekoulakis, Stavros L. Law Applicable to Arbitrability: Revisiting the Revisited Lex Fori, in: Loukas A. Mistelis, Stavros L. Brekoulakis (eds), Arbitrability: International and Comparative Perspectives, International Arbitration Law Library, Alphen aan den Rijn 2009, pp. 99–120 (cited: *Brekoulakis*).

Buchwitz, Wolfram/Schütt, Phillip Die Durchsetzung von Vorschussansprüchen in Schiedsverfahren, SchiedsVZ 2015, 1–10 (cited: *Buchwitz/Schütt*, SchiedsVZ 2015, 1).

Cole, Tony/Bantekas, Ilias/Ferretti, Federico et al. Legal Instruments and Practice of Arbitration in the EU, Study, European Parliament Policy Department C: Citizens' Rights and Constitutional Affairs, Brussels 2014, http://www.europarl.europa.eu/RegData/etudes/STUD/2015/509988/IPOL_STU(2015)509988_EN.pdf (accessed 11 December 2017).

Commission provides guidance on protection of cross-border EU investments – Questions and Answers, European Commission, Brussels, Pressemitteilung vom 19.07.2018, http://europa.eu/rapid/press-release_MEMO-18-4529_en.htm (accessed 6 February 2019).

Dahl, Michael/Schmitz, Daniel Das neue Insolvenzanfechtungsrecht, NJW 2017, 1505–1511 (cited: *Dahl/Schmitz*, NJW 2017, 1505).

Dahl, Michael/Thomas, Johanna Die Bindungswirkung von Schiedsklauseln im Insolvenzverfahren, NZI 2012, 534–537 (cited: *Dahl/Thomas*, NZI 2012, 534).

Darwazeh, Nadia/Greenberg, Simon No One's Credit is as Good as Cash: Awards and Orders for the Payment of the ICC Advance on Costs, Journal of International Arbitration 31 2014, 557–574 (cited: *Darwazeh/Greenberg*, Journal of International Arbitration 31 2014, 557).

del Rosal Carmona, Rafael Carlos Chapter 9: Lack of Impartiality or Independence as Grounds to Deny Enforcement under the New York Convention, in: Katie Fach Gomez, Ana M. Lopez-Rodriquez(eds), 60 Years of the New York Convention, Key Issues and Future Challenges, Alphen aan den Rijn 2019, pp. 137–152 (cited: del Rosal Carmona, Rafael Carlos).

Derains, Yves/Schwartz, Eric A. A Guide to the ICC Rules of Arbitration, Second Edition, The Hague 2005 (cited: *Derains/Schwartz*).

Dieterich, Thomas/Hanau, Peter/Schaub, Günter Erfurter Kommentar zum Arbeitsrecht, 22. ed., bearb. von Thomas Dieterich, Peter Hanau, Günter Schaub, München 2022 (cited: Dieterich/Hanau/Schaub-*Bearbeiter*).

DIS DIS-Statistics 2016, German Arbitration Institute, s.l. 2017, http://www.disarb.org/upload/statistics/DIS%20Statistics%202016.pdf (accessed 18 October 2018).

Dorda, Christian Arbitration and Insolvency Proceedings, Annals FLB – Belgrade Law Review Year LVII (2009), 83–89 (cited: *Dorda*, Annals FLB – Belgrade Law Review Year LVII 2009, 83).

Draguiev, Deyan The Effect of Insolvency on Pending International Arbitration: What Is and What Should Not Be, Journal of International Arbitration 32 2015, 511–542 (cited: *Draguiev*, Journal of International Arbitration 32 2015, 511).

Duve, Christian/Wimalasena, Philip Part IV: Selected Areas and Issues of Arbitration in Germany, Arbitration of Corporate Law Disputes in Germany, in: Karl-Heinz Böckstiegel, Stefan M. Kröll, Patricia Nacimiento (eds), Arbitration in Germany, The Model Law in Practice, Second Edition, Alphen aan den Rijn 2015, pp. 927–961 (cited: *Duve/Wimalasena*).

Eberl, Walter Das Schiedsverfahren in der Insolvenz, InVO 2002, 393–395 (cited: *Eberl*, InVO 2002, 393).

Eckhardt, Diederich Die Feststellung und Befriedigung des Insolvenzgläubigerrechts, in: Karlhans Fuchs (Hrsg.), Kölner Schrift zur Insolvenzordnung, Das neue Insolvenzrecht in der Praxis, Herne, Berlin 2010, pp. 743–780 (cited: *Eckhardt*).

Eckhardt, Diederich Internationale Handelsschiedsgerichtsbarkeit und Insolvenzverfahren: Die Bestimmung des maßgeblichen Rechts, in: Herbert Kronke, Karsten Thorn (Hrsg.), Grenzen überwinden – Prinzipien bewahren, Festschrift für Bernd von Hoffmann zum 70. Geburtstag, Bielefeld 2011, pp. 934–948 (cited: *Eckhardt*).

Ehricke, Ulrich Die Feststelunng streitiger Insolvenzforderungen durch ein Schiedsgericht, ZIP 2006, 1847–1854 (cited: *Ehricke*, ZIP 2006, 1847–1854).

Emmerson, Frank D. History of Arbitration Practice and Law, 19 Cleveland State Law Review 1970, 155–164, https://engagedscholarship.csuohio.edu/clevstlrev/vol19/iss1/19/ (accessed 2 October 2018) (cited: *Emmerson*, Cleveland State Law Review 19, 1970, 155).

EuInsVo 2015, Europäische Insolvenzordnung 2015: Kommentar, hrsg. von Peter Mankowski, Michael Müller, Jessica Schmidt, München 2016 (cited: Mankowski/Müller/J. Schmidt, EuInsVO 2015-*Bearbeiter*).

Fagbemi, Sunday A. The Doctrine of Party Autonomy in International Commercial Arbitration: Myth or Reality?, JSDLP 6 2016, 202–246 (cited: *Fagbemi*, JSDLP 6 2016, 202).

Fenger, Hermann Insolvenzrecht, Schnell erfasst, Recht – schnell erfasst, Berlin, Heidelberg 2005 (cited: *Fenger*).

Ferrari, Franco/Kröll, Stefan Conflict of Laws in International Arbitration, Munich 2011 (cited: *Ferrari/Kröll*).

Flecke-Gianmarco, Gustav/Keller, Christoph Die Auswirkung der Wahl des Schiedsorts auf den Fortgang des Schiedsverfahrens in der Insolvenz, NZI 2012, 529–534 (cited: *Flecke-Gianmarco/Keller*, NZI 2012, 529).

Fletcher, Ian F. Effect on Arbitration Proceedings of the EU Regulation, 22 Insolvency Intelligence 2009, 60–62 (cited: *Fletcher*, Insolvency Intelligence 22, 2009, 60).

Fletcher, Ian F. The Law of Insolvency, Fourth Edition, London 2009 (cited: *Fletcher*).

Flöther, Lucas F. Auswirkungen des inländischen Insolvenzverfahrens auf Schiedsverfahren und Schiedsabrede, KTS-Schriften zum Insolvenzrecht 10, Köln, München 2001 (cited: *Flöther*).

Flöther, Lucas F. Schiedsverfahren und Schiedsabrede unter den Bedingungen der Insolvenz, DZWIR 2001, 89–95 (cited: *Flöther*, DZWIR 2001, 89–95).

Fortier, L. Yves Arbitrability of Disputes, in: Gerald Aksen, Karl-Heinz Böckstiegel, Michael J. Mustill et al. (eds), Global Reflections on International Law, Commerce and Dispute Resolution, Liber Amicorum in Honour of Robert Briner, ICC Publication No. 693, Paris 2005 (cited: *Fortier*).

Fouchard, Philippe Arbitrage et faillite, Rev. Arb. 1998, 471–494 (cited: *Fouchard*, Rev. Arb. 1998, 471).

Frankfurter Kommentar zur Insolvenzordnung, Mit EuInsVO, InsVV und weiteren Nebengesetzen, 9. ed., hrsg. von Klaus Wimmer, Köln 2018 (cited: FK-InsO-*Bearbeiter*).

Gaillard, Emmanuel Extent of Court Review of Public Policy, 237 NYJL 2007, s.l. (cited: *Gaillard*, NYJL 237 2007, s.l.).

Gaillard, Emmanuel L'exécution des sentences annulées dans leur pays d'origine, Journal du Droit International 125 1998, 645–674 (cited: *Gaillard*, Journal du Droit International 125 1998, 645).

Gaillard, Emmanuel/Savage, John Fouchard, Gaillard, Goldman on International Commercial Arbitration, The Hague 1999 (cited: *Gaillard/Savage*).

Gaul, Hans Friedhelm Die Rechtskraft und Aufhebbarkeit des Schiedsspruchs im Verhältnis zu Verbindlickkeit des staatlichen Richterspruchs, in: Klaus Peter Berger, Werner F. Ebke, Siegfried Elsing et al. (Hrsg.), Festschrift für Otto Sandrock zum 70. Geburtstag, Heidelberg 2000, pp. 285–328 (cited: *Gaul*).

Geimer, Reinhold/Geimer, Ewald/Geimer, Gregor Internationales Zivilprozessrecht, 7. ed., Juris, Köln 2015 (cited: *Geimer/Geimer/Geimer*).

Gesellschaftsrecht, BGB, PartGG, HGB, GmbHG, AktG, DCGK, GenG, UmwG, InsO, AnfG, IntGesR, 5. ed., hrsg. von Martin Henssler, Lutz Strohn, München 2021 (cited: Henssler/Strohn GesR-*Bearbeiter*).

Goode, Royston Miles Principles of Corporate Insolvency Law, Fourth Edition, London 2011 (cited: *Goode*).

Gottwald, Peter Internationales Zivilprozessrecht, 7. ed., Juris, Köln 2013 (cited: *Gottwald*).

Graf, Ulrike Die Anerkennung ausländischer Insolvenzentscheidungen, Zugl.: Mannheim, Univ., Diss., 2002–2003, Studien zum ausländischen und internationalen Privatrecht 113, Tübingen 2003 (cited: *Graf*).

Günter, Michael Internationale Schiedsgerichtsbarkeit und Insolvenz, Zur Berücksichtigung von Insolvenzverfahren und ihren Auswirkungen vor internationalen Schiedsgerichten mit Sitz in der Schweiz, Zugl.: Luzern, Univ., Diss., 2011, Luzerner Beiträge zur Rechtswissenschaft 61, Zürich, Basel, Genf 2011 (cited: *Günter*).

Hamburger Kommentar zum Insolvenzrecht, InsO - EuInsVO - EGInsO (Auszug) - InsVV - VbrInsVV - InsOBekV -Insolvenzstrafrecht, 6. ed., hrsg. von Andreas Schmidt, Köln 2017 (cited: HambKomm-*Bearbeiter*).

Hammer, Gottfried Überprüfung von Schiedsverfahren durch staatliche Gerichte in Deutschland, München 2018 (cited: *Hammer*).

Handorn, Boris Das Sonderkollisionsrecht der deutschen internationalen Schiedsgerichtsbarkeit, Zur Bestimmung des anwendbaren materiellen Rechts gemäß § 1051 Abs. 1 und 2 Zivilprozessordnung, Zugl.: Berlin, Freie Univ., Diss., 2004, Studien zum ausländischen und internationalen Privatrecht 141, Tübingen 2005 (cited: *Handorn*).

Hanefeld, Inka/Trittman, Rolf Part II: Commentary on the German Arbitration Law (10th Book of the German Code of Civil Procedure), Chapter II: Arbitration Agreement, § 1029 - Definition, in: Karl-Heinz Böckstiegel, Stefan M. Kröll, Patricia Nacimiento (eds), Arbitration in Germany, The Model Law in Practice, Second Edition, Alphen aan den Rijn 2015 (cited: *Hanefeld/Trittman*).

Hanotiau, Bernard/van den Berg, Albert The Law Applicable to Arbitrability, 26 SAcLJ 2014, 874–885 (cited: *Hanotiau/van den Berg*, SAcLJ 26, 2014, 874).

Häsemeyer, Ludwig Insolvenzrecht, 4. ed., Berlin 2010 (cited: *Häsemeyer*).

Hay, Peter/Rösler, Hannes Internationales Privat- und Zivilverfahrensrecht, 5. ed., Prüfe dein Wissen Rechtsfälle in Frage und Antwort, München 2016 (cited: *Hay/Rösler*).

Heidbrink, Alfried/Groeben, Marie-Christine von der Insolvenz und Schiedsverfahren, ZIP 2006, 265–272 (cited: *Heidbrink/Groeben*, ZIP 2006, 265–272).

Hoffman, Bernd von Der Internationale Schiedsrichtervertrag – eine kollisionsrechtliche Skizze, in: Alain Plantey (Hrsg.), Festschrift für Ottoarndt Glossner zum 70. Geburtstag, Heidelberg 1994, pp. 143–153 (cited: *Hoffman*).

Hölters, Wolfgang (ed.) Aktiengesetz, Kommentar, 3. ed., München 2017 (cited: Hölters-*Bearbeiter*).

Hombeck, Jörn/Schneider, Viktoria K. Das Schiedsverfahren in der Insolvenz, Überblick zu besonders praxisrelevanten Themen angesichts der aktuellen Corona-Pandemie, NZI 2020, 449–455 (cited: *Hombeck/Schneider*, NZI 2020, 449).

ICC – International Chamber of Commerce 2017 ICC Dispute Resolution Statistics, ICC Dispute Resolution Bulletin 2018, 51–65 (cited: ICC – International Chamber of Commerce, ICC Dispute Resolution Bulletin 2018, 51).

Icks, Annette/Peter, Kranzusch Sanierungen in Insolvenzverfahren, übertragende Sanierungen und insolvenzplanbasierte Eigensanierungen in NRW, IfM Bonn, Bonn April 2010, https://www.ifm-bonn.org//uploads/tx_ifmstudies/IfM-Materialien-195_2010.pdf (accessed 10 January 2018).

InsO – Kommentar zur Insolvenzordnung, KPB, hrsg. von Bruno M. Kübler, Hanns Prütting, Reinhard Bork, Köln 2018 (cited: KPB-InsO-*Bearbeiter*).

Insolvenzordnung, Kommentar, 13. ed., hrsg. von Wilhelm Uhlenbruck, Heribert Hirte, Heinz Vallender, München 2010 (cited: Uhlenbruck-*Bearbeiter*).

Insolvenzordnung, 8. ed., hrsg. von Godehard Kayser, Christoph Thole, Heidelberg 2016 (cited: HK-InsO-*Bearbeiter*).

Insolvenzordnung, InsO mit EuInsVO, 19. ed., hrsg. von Karsten Schmidt, München 2016 (cited: K. Schmidt InsO-*Bearbeiter*).

Insolvenzordnung, Kommentar, hrsg. von Jörg Nerlich, Volker Römermann, München 2018 (cited: Nerlich/Römermann-*Bearbeiter*).

Insolvenzordnung (InsO), InsO mit EuInsVO (Neufassung): Kommentar, 7. ed., hrsg. von Eberhard Braun, München 2017 (cited: Braun-*Bearbeiter*).

Jaeger, Ernst Insolvenzordnung, Grosskommentar, Band 1 §§ 1–55, hrsg. von Walter Gerhardt, Wolfram Henckel, Berlin 2004 (cited: Jaeger-*Bearbeiter*).

Jaeger, Ernst Insolvenzordnung, Grosskommentar, Band 2 §§ 56–102, hrsg. von Walter Gerhardt, Wolfram Henckel, Berlin 2007 (cited: Jaeger-*Bearbeiter*).

Jaeger, Ernst Insolvenzordnung, Grosskommentar, Band 4 §§ 129–147, hrsg. von Walter Gerhardt, Wolfram Henckel, Berlin 2008 (cited: Jaeger-*Bearbeiter*).

Jaeger, Ernst Insolvenzordnung, Grosskommentar, Band 6 §§ 174–216, hrsg. von Walter Gerhardt, Wolfram Henckel, Berlin 2010 (cited: Jaeger-*Bearbeiter*).

Jahn, Uwe/Brian, Ilka § 27 Geschäftsverkehr mit ausländischen Kunden, in: Herbert Schimansky, Hermann-Josef Bunte, H. Jürgen Lwowski (Hrsg.), Bankrechts-Handbuch, 5. Auflage, München 2017 (cited: *Jahn/Brian*).

Jestaedt, Thomas Schiedsverfahren und Konkurs, Schriften zum Prozessrecht 83, Berlin 1985 (cited: *Jestaedt*).

Jones, Doug Insolvency and Arbitration: An Arbitral Tribunal's Perspective, Arbitration 78 2012, 123–139 (cited: *Jones*, Arbitration 78 2012, 123).

Kamalnath, Akshaya Cross-Border Insolvency Protocols: A Succes Story?, International Journal of Legal Studies and Research (IJLSR) 2 2013, 172–190 (cited: *Kamalnath*, International Journal of Legal Studies and Research (IJLSR) 2 2013, 172).

Kaufmann-Kohler, Gabrielle Arbitral Precedent: Dream, Necessity or Excuse?, Arbitration International 23 2007, 357–378 (cited: *Kaufmann-Kohler*, Arbitration International 23 2007, 357).

Kaufmann-Kohler, Gabrielle/Lévy, Laurent Insolvency and International Arbitration, in: Henry Peter, Nicolas Jeandin, Jason J. Kilborn (eds), The Challenges of Insolvency Law Reform in the 21st Century, Facilitating Investment and Recovery to Enhance Economic Growth, Zürich 2006, pp. 257–284 (cited: *Kaufmann-Kohler/Lévy*).

Kegel, Gerhard/Schurig, Klaus Internationales Privatrecht, 9. ed., München 2004 (cited: *Kegel/Schurig*).

Keller, Ulrich Insolvenzrecht, München 2006 (cited: *Keller*).

Kessedjian, Catherine Chapter 3: Determination and Application of Relevant National and International Law and Rules, in: Julian D.M. Lew, Loukas A. Mistelis (eds), Pervasive Problems in International Arbitration, International Arbitration Law Library vol. 15, Alphen aan den Rijn 2006, pp. 71–88 (cited: *Kessedjian*).

Kindler, Peter § 1. Grundlagen, in: Peter Kindler, Josef Nachmann (Hrsg.), Handbuch Insolvenzrecht in Europa, 4. Ergänzungslieferung, München 2014 (cited: *Kindler*).

Klein, Frédéric-Edouard Considérations sur l'arbitrage en droit international privé, précédées d'une étude de législation, de doctrine et de jurisprudence comparées en la matière, Basel 1955 (cited: *Klein*).

Kovacs, R.obert B. A Transnational Approach to the Arbitrability of Insolvency Proceedings in International Arbitration 2012, https://www.iiiglobal.org/sites/default/files/transnationalapproachtothearbitrabilityofinsolvencyproceedingsininternationalarbitration.pdf (accessed 2 November 2016).

Kramer, Ralph/Peter, Frank K. Insolvenzrecht, Grundkurs für Wirtschaftswissenschaftler, 3. ed., SpringerLink: Bücher, Wiesbaden 2014 (cited: *Kramer/Peter*).

Kraus, Maximilian Das Schicksal internationaler Schiedsverfahren in der Insolvenz des Schiedsbeklagten, Schriften zum Insolvenzrecht v.79, Baden-Baden 2020 (cited: *Kraus*).

Krause, Christophe von/*Filhol, Gaelle* International Arbitration and French Insolvency Proceedings: French Supreme Court Reiterates Importance of Public Policy, White & Case 2009, http://kluwerarbitrationblog.com/2009/10/28/international-arbitration-and-french-insolvency-proceedings-french-supreme-court-reiterates-importance-of-public-policy/ (accessed 02/11/16).

Kreindler, Richard H./Schäfer, Jan K./Wolff, Reinmar Schiedsgerichtsbarkeit, Kompendium für die Praxis, BB Handbuch, Frankfurt am Main 2006 (cited: *Kreindler/Schäfer/Wolff*).

Kröll, Stefan M. Chapter 18: Arbitration and Insolvency Proceedings - Selected Problems, in: Julian D.M. Lew, Loukas A. Mistelis (eds), Pervasive Problems in International Arbitration, International Arbitration Law Library vol. 15, Alphen aan den Rijn 2006, pp. 357–376 (cited: *Kröll*).

Kröll, Stefan M. Part IV: Selected Areas and Issues of Arbitration in Germany, Insolvency and Arbitration - Effects of Party Insolvency on Arbitral Proceedings in Germany, in: Karl-Heinz Böckstiegel, Stefan M. Kröll, Patricia Nacimiento (Hrsg.), Arbitration in Germany, The model law in practice, Second edition, Alphen aan den Rijn 2015, pp. 981–1012 (cited: *Kröll*).

Kröll, Stefan M. The 'Incapable of Being Performed' Exception in Article II(3) of the New York Convention, in: Emmanuel Gaillard, Domenico Di Pietro (eds), Enforcement of Arbitration Agreements and International Arbitral Awards, The New York Convention in Practice, London 2008, pp. 323–353 (cited: *Kröll*).

Kühn, Wolfgang Arbitration and Insolvency, Disp. Resol. Int'l 5 2011, 203–211 (cited: *Kühn*, Disp. Resol. Int'l 5 2011, 203).

Lachmann, Jens-Peter Handbuch für die Schiedsgerichtspraxis, 3. ed., Köln 2008 (cited: *Lachmann*).

Law, Jonathan Oxford Dictionary of Law 2018 (cited: *Law*).

Lazić, Vesna Insolvency Proceedings and Commercial Arbitration, International Arbitration Law Library vol. 5, The Hague, London 1998 (cited: *Lazić*).

Leboulanger, Phillipe The Arbitration Agreement: Still Autonomous?, in: A.J. van den Berg (ed.), International Arbitration 2006, Back to Basics?; [International Arbitration Congress, Montréal, 31 May–3 June 2006; 18th ICCA Congress], ICCA Congress Series vol. 13, Alphen aan den Rijn 2007, pp. 3–31 (cited: *Leboulanger*).

Leibner, Wolfgang OLG Düsseldorf EWiR § 1032 ZPO, Kurzkommentar zu OLG Düsseldorf, Urt. 14.11.2003 - I-16 U 95/98, EWiR 2004, 623–624 (cited: *Leibner*, EWiR 2004, 623).

Lenzen, Elmar Unterbrechung von Beweisverfahren und/oder Schiedsverfahren durch Insolvenzeröffnung?, NZBau 2003, 428–430 (cited: *Lenzen*, NZBau 2003, 428).

Lévy, Laurent Insolvency in Arbitration: Swiss Law, in: Deutsche Institution für Schiedsgerichtsbarkeit (ed.), Financial Capacity of the Parties, A Condition for the Validity of Arbitration Agreements?; Based on a Conference Organised by the German Institution of Arbitration (DIS) on 29th November 2002 in Berlin, Schriftenreihe der August-Maria-Berges-Stiftung für Arbitrales Recht vol. 16, Frankfurt am Main 2004, 87–106 (cited: *Lévy*).

Lew, Julian D.M. Applicable Law in International Commercial Arbitration: A Study in Commercial Arbitration Awards, Dobbs Ferry 1978 (cited: *Lew*).

Lew, Julian D.M. The Law Applicable to the Form and Substance of the Arbitration Clause, in: A.J. van den Berg (ed.), Improving the Efficiency of Arbitration Agreements and Awards, 40 Years of Application of the New York Convention [International Arbitration Congress, Paris, 3–6 May 1998], ICCA Congress Series, The Hague, London 1999, pp. 114–145 (cited: *Lew*).

Lew, Julian D. M./Mistelis, Loukas A./Kröll, Stefan Comparative International Commercial Arbitration, The Hague, London 2003 (cited: *Lew/Mistelis/Kröll*).

Longrée, Sebastian J.M./Gantenbrink, Matthias Insolvenz des Beklagten im Schiedsverfahren, SchiedsVZ 2014, 21–26 (cited: *Longrée/Gantenbrink*, SchiedsVZ 2014, 21).

LoPucki, Lynn M. Universalism Unravels, The American Bankruptcy Law Journal 79 2005, 143–170 (cited: *LoPucki*, The American Bankruptcy Law Journal 79 2005, 143).

Lord, Samantha J. When Two Polar Extremes Collide: An Exploration into the Effects of Insolvency on International Arbitration, Int'l Trade&Bus. L. Rev. 15 2012, 316–359 (cited: *Lord*, Int'l Trade&Bus. L. Rev. 15 2012, 316).

Lozada, Fernando Pérez Duty to Render Enforceable Awards: The Specific Case of Impartiality, Spain Arbitration Review 2016, 71–94 (cited: *Lozada*, Spain Arbitration Review 2016, 71).

Ly, Filip de The Place of Arbitration in the Conflict of Laws of International Commercial Arbitration: An Exercise in Arbitration Planning, Nw. J. Int'l L. & Bus. 12 1991, 48–85 (cited: *Ly*, Nw. J. Int'l L. & Bus. 12 1991, 48).

Ly, Filip de/*Sheppard, Audley* ILA Final Report on Res Judicata and Arbitration, Arbitration International 25 2009, 67–82 (cited: *Ly/Sheppard*, Arbitration International 25 2009, 67).

Ly, Filip de/*Sheppard, Audley* ILA Interim Report on Res Judicata and Arbitration, Arbitration International 25 2009, 35–66 (cited: *Ly/Sheppard*, Arbitration International 25 2009, 35).

Mankowski, Peter EuInsVO und Schiedsverfahren, ZIP 2010, 2478–2486 (cited: *Mankowski*, ZIP 2010, 2478).

Mankowski, Peter EuInsVO und Schiedsverfahren, Zugliech Beschrepchung Court of Appeal England v. 9.7.2009 [2009] EWCA Civ 677 (C.A.), ZIP 2010, 2528 – Syska and Elektrim SA v. Vivendi Universial SA, ZIP 2010, 2478–2486 (cited: *Mankowski*, ZIP 2010, 2478).

Mann, Frederick Alexander Lex Facit Arbitrum, in: Pieter Sanders (ed.), International Arbitration, Liber Amicorum for Martin Domke, The Hague 1967, pp. 157–183 (cited: *Mann*).

Mantilla-Serrano, Fernando International Arbitration and Insolvency Proceedings, Arbitration International 11 1995, 51–74 (cited: *Mantilla-Serrano*, Arbitration International 11 1995, 51).

Marghitola, Reto Document Production in International Arbitration, Teilweise Zugl; Zurich, Univ., Diss., 2014, International Arbitration Law Library vol. 33, Alphen aan den Rijn 2015 (cited: *Marghitola*).

Markert, Lars Arbitrating in the Financial Crisis: Insolvency and Public Policy versus Arbitration and Party Autonomy – Which Law Governs, Contemp. Asia Arb. J. 2 2009, 217–245 (cited: *Markert*, Contemp. Asia Arb. J. 2 2009, 217).

Martiny, Dieter Anerkennung ausländischer Entscheidungen nach autonomem Recht, Handbuch des internationalen Zivilverfahrensrechts/Max-Planck-Institut für Ausländisches und Internationales Privatrecht; Bd. 3,1, Tübingen 1984 (cited: *Martiny*).

Mentzel, Franz/Kuhn, Georg/Uhlenbruck, Wilhelm Insolvenzordnung, Kommentar, Band 1, 15. ed., hrsg. von Heribert Hirte, Heinz Vallender, München 2019 (cited: Mentzel/Kuhn/Uhlenbruck-*Bearbeiter*).

Mincke, Wolfgang § 45 Internationales Insolvenzrecht, in: Jörg Nerlich, Georg Kreplin (Hrsg.), Münchener Anwalts-Handbuch Insolvenz und Sanierung, 3. ed., München 2019, pp. 1371–1396 (cited: *Mincke*).

Moss, Giuditta Cordero Legal Capacity, Arbitration and Private International Law, in: Katharina Boele-Woelki, Talie Einhorn, Daniel Girsberger et al. (eds), Convergence and Divergence in Private International Law, Liber Amicorum Kurt Siehr, Zürich 2010, pp. 619–633 (cited: *Moss*).

Mourre, Alexis Arbitrage et droit de la faillite – Réflexions sur l'office du juge et de l'arbitre, in: Georges Affaki (Hrsg.), Faillite internationale et conflit de juridictions, Regards croisés transatlantiques = Cross-border insolvency and conflict of jurisdictions; a US-EU Experience, Bruxelles 2007, pp. 153–170 (cited: *Mourre*).

Mourre, Alexis Chapter 1. Sed Quis Custodiet Ipsos Custodes? On Jurisdiction upon Arbitrators, in: Laurent Lévy, Yves Derains (eds), Is Arbitration Only as Good as the Arbitrator?, Status, Powers and Role of the Arbitrator, Dossiers / ICC Institute of World Business Law vol. 8, Paris, France 2011, pp. 13–24 (cited: *Mourre*).

Münchener Kommentar zum Aktiengesetz, Band 4 §§ 179–277 AktG, 5. ed., hrsg. von Wulf Goette, Mathias Habersack, München 2021 (cited: MünchKomm-AktG-*Bearbeiter*).

Münchener Kommentar zum Bürgerlichen Gesetzbuch, Internationales Privatrecht II, Internationales Wirtschaftsrecht, Einführungsgesetz zum Bürgerlichen Gesetzbuche (Art. 50–253), 8. ed., hrsg. von Jan von Hein, München 2021 (cited: MüKoBGB-*Bearbeiter*).

Münchener Kommentar zum Bürgerlichen Gezetzbuch, Band 3: Schuldrecht –Allgemeiner Teil II, 8. ed., hrsg. von Wolfgang Krüger, München 2019 (cited: MüKoBGB-*Bearbeiter*).

Münchener Kommentar zum Bürgerlichen Gezetzbuch, Band 6, Schuldrecht –Besonderer Teil III. 2, 8. ed., hrsg. von Martin Henssler, München 2020 (cited: MüKoBGB-*Bearbeiter*).

Münchener Kommentar zum Bürgerlichen Gezetzbuch, Band 5, Schuldrecht –Besonderer Teil II, 8. ed., hrsg. von Martin Henssler, Wolfgang Krüger, München 2020 (cited: MüKoBGB-*Bearbeiter*).

Münchener Kommentar zum Gesetz betreffend die Gesellschaften mit beschränkter Haftung, 3. ed., hrsg. von Holger Fleischer, Wulf Goette, München 2018 (cited: MükoGmbhG-*Bearbeiter*).

Münchener Kommentar zur Insolvenzordnung, Band 2 – §§ 80–216 InsO, 4. ed., hrsg. von Rolf Stürner, Horst Eidenmüller, Heinrich Schoppmeyer, München 2019 (cited: MüKoInsO-*Bearbeiter*).

Münchener Kommentar zur Insolvenzordnung, Band 1 –§§ 1–79 InsO, InsVV, 4. ed., hrsg. von Rolf Stürner, Horst Eidenmüller, Heinrich Schoppmeyer, München 2019 (cited: MüKoInsO-*Bearbeiter*).

Münchener Kommentar zur Insolvenzordnung, Band 3 - §§ 217–359 InsO, 4. ed., hrsg. von Rolf Stürner, Horst Eidenmüller, Heinrich Schoppmeyer, München 2020 (cited: MüKoInsO-*Bearbeiter*).

Münchener Kommentar zur Insolvenzordnung, Band 4 - EGInsO, EUInsVO, Länderberichte, 4. ed., hrsg. von Rolf Stürner, Horst Eidenmüller, Heinrich Schoppmeyer, München 2021 (cited: MüKoInsO-*Bearbeiter*).

Münchener Kommentar zur Zivilprozessordnung, Mit Gerichtsverfassungsgesetz und Nebengesetzen, Band 1 -§§ 1–354, 6. ed., hrsg. von Thomas Rauscher, Wolfgang Krüger, München 2020 (cited: MüKoZPO-*Bearbeiter*).

Münchener Kommentar zur Zivilprozessordnung, Mit Gerichtsverfassungsgesetz und Nebengesetzen, Band 3 - §§ 946–1117, 6. ed., hrsg. von Thomas Rauscher, Wolfgang Krüger, München 2022 (cited: MüKoZPO-*Bearbeiter*).

Mustill, Michael J./Boyd, Stewart C. Commercial Arbitration, Including 2001 Companion Volume, 2d ed. London 2001 (cited: *Mustill/Boyd*).

Nacimiento, Patricia/Bähr, Biner Insolvenz in nationalen und internationalen Schiedsverfahren, NJOZ 2009, 4752–4762 (cited: *Nacimiento/Bähr*, NJOZ 2009, 4752).

Nadeau-Séguin, Sara When Bankruptcy and Arbitration Meet: A Look at Recent ICC Practice, Disp. Resol. Int'l 5 2011, 79–102 (cited: *Nadeau-Séguin*, Disp. Resol. Int'l 5 2011, 79).

Paulus, Christoph G. Der EuGH und das moderne Insolvenzrecht, NZG 16 2006, 609–613 (cited: *Paulus*, NZG 16 2006, 609).

Paulus, Christoph G. Insolvenzrecht, 2. ed., München 2012 (cited: *Paulus*).

Paulus, Christoph G. (ed.) Europäische Insolvenzverordnung, 5. ed., Frankfurt am Main 2017 (cited: Paulus-*Bearbeiter*).

Pérez Lozada, Fernando Duty to Render Enforceable Awards: The Specific Case of Impartiality, Spain Arbitration Review 2016, 71–94 (cited: *Pérez Lozada*, Spain Arbitration Review 2016, 71).

Pfeiffer, Thomas Insolvenzeröffnung und internationale Schiedsverfahren, in: Michael Flitsch (Hrsg.), Festschrift für Jobst Wellensiek zum 80. Geburtstag, München 2011, pp. 821–832 (cited: *Pfeiffer*).

Pielorz, Michael Auslandskonkurs und Disposition über das Inlandsvermögen, Zugl; Bonn, Univ., Diss., 1977, Schriften zum Prozeßrecht 55, Berlin 1977 (cited: *Pielorz*).

Poelzig, Dörte Parteieninsolvenz in der Internationalen Schiedsgerichtsbarkeit, ZZPInt. 14 2009, 393–441 (cited: *Poelzig*, ZZPInt. 14 2009, 393).

Poudret, J. F./Besson, S. Comparative Law of International Arbitration, Translated by Berti, S.V. and Ponti, A, 2d ed. 2007 (cited: *Poudret/Besson*).

Prioux, R. Le juge et l'arbitre face aux lois étrangères d'application immédiate dans les contrats internationaux: les nouvelles possibilités offertes par la loi du 14 juillet 1987, RDCD 1988, 251–295 (cited: *Prioux*, RDCD 1988, 251).

Prütting, Hans Die rechtliche Stellung des Schiedsrichters, SchiedsVZ 2011, 233–239 (cited: *Prütting*, SchiedsVZ 2011, 233).

Queen Mary School of International Arbitration/White & Case 2018 International Arbitration Survey: The Evolution of International Arbitration, Queen Mary School of International Arbitration; White & Case, London 2018.

Raykin, Alla./Wouters, Nora Corporate Group Cross-Border Insolvencies Between the United States & European Union: Legal & Economics Developments, Emory Bankruptcy Developments Journal 29 2013, 387–423 (cited: *Raykin/Wouters*, Emory Bankruptcy Developments Journal 29 2013, 387).

Redfern, Alan/Hunter, Martin Law and Practice of International Commercial Arbitration, 2d ed., London 1991 (cited: *Redfern/Hunter*).

Redfern, Alan/Hunter, Martin, Blackaby, Nigel/Partasides, Constantine Law and Practice of International Commercial Arbitration, 4th ed., London 2004 (cited: *Redfern/Hunter, Martin, Blackaby, Nigel/Partasides*).

Reusch, Ute Insolvency Statute, Insolvency Statute of 5 October 1994 (Federal Law Gazette I page 2866), as last amended by Article 19 of the Act of 20 December 2011 (Federal Law Gazette I page 2854), Bundesministerium für Justiz und Verbraucherschutz o.J. [2011], http://www.gesetze-im-internet.de/englisch_inso/print_englisch_inso.html (accessed 28 September 2018).

Riedel, Maximilian Insolvenz in nationalen und internationalen Schiedsverfahren, Schriften zum Verfahrensrecht Band 54 2015 (cited: *Riedel*).

Ristelhuber, Johannes Der Schiedsspruch im Insolvenzverfahren, ZinsO 2004, 427–431 (cited: *Ristelhuber*, ZinsO 2004, 427).

Rubellin-Devichi, Jacqueline L'Arbitrage: Nature juridique, droit interne et droit international privé, Paris 1965 (cited: *Rubellin-Devichi*).

Sachs, Klaus Insolvency Proceedings and International Arbitration, Collected Courses of the International Academy for Arbitration Law, 2011 1 2013, 1–48 (cited: *Sachs*, Collected Courses of the International Academy for Arbitration Law, 2011 1 2013, 1–48).

Sachs, Klaus/Lörcher, Torsten Part II: Commentary on the German Arbitration Law (10th Book of the German Code of Civil Procedure), Chapter V: Conduct of the Arbitral Proceeding, in: Karl-Heinz Böckstiegel, Stefan M. Kröll, Patricia Nacimiento (eds), Arbitration in Germany: The Model Law in Practice, 2d. ed., Alphen aan den Rijn 2015 (cited: *Sachs/Lörcher*).

Samuel, Adam/Currat, Marie-Françoise Jurisdictional Problems in International Commercial Arbitration: A Study of Belgian, Dutch, English, French, Swedish, Swiss, U.S., and West German law, Publications of the Swiss Institute of Comparative Law 11, Zürich 1989 (cited: *Samuel/Currat*).

Sandrock, Otto Welches Kollisionsrecht hat ein Internationales Schiedsgericht anzuwenden?, RIW 38 1992, 785–795 (cited: *Sandrock*, RIW 38 1992, 785).

Schack, Haimo Internationales Zivilverfahrensrecht, Mit internationalem Insolvenz- und Schiedsverfahrensrecht ein Studienbuch, 7. ed., Juristische Kurz-Lehrbücher, München 2017 (cited: *Schack*).

Schäfer, Erik Part IV: Selected Areas and Issues of Arbitration in Germany, Arbitration of Intellectual Property Related Disputes in Germany, in: Karl-Heinz Böckstiegel, Stefan M. Kröll, Patricia Nacimiento (eds), Arbitration in Germany: The Model Law in Practice, 2d ed., Alphen aan den Rijn 2015, pp. 907–926 (cited: *Schäfer*).

Schlosser, Peter Das Recht des internationalen privaten Schiedsgerichtsbarkeit, 2. ed., Tübingen 1989 (cited: *Schlosser*).

Schlosser, Peter Der Schiedsgerichtsobmann als Vertragspartner, SchiedsVZ 2004, 21–26 (cited: *Schlosser*, SchiedsVZ 2004, 21).

Schmidt, Karsten Prozessunterbrechung und Prozessaufnahme in der Gesellschtsinsolvenz – Ungelöste Probleme im Umgang mit § 240 ZPO, §§ 85 ff. InsO, in: Hans Haarmeyer, Heribert Hirte, Hans-Peter Kirchhof et al. (Hrsg.), Verschuldung, Haftung, Vollstreckung, Insolvenz, Festschrift für Gerhard Kreft zum 65. Geburtstag, Recklinghausen 2004, pp. 503–524 (cited: *Schmidt*).

Schmidt-Ahrendts, Nils/Höttler, Philipp Anwendbares Recht bei Schiedsverfahren mit Sitz in Deutschland, SchiedsVZ 2011, 267–276 (cited: *Schmidt-Ahrendts/Höttler*, SchiedsVZ 2011, 267).

Schmitz, Daniel Schiedsverfahren und Insolvenz, Deutsches, Europäisches und Vergleichendes Wirtschaftsrecht Band 99 2015 (cited: *Schmitz*).

Schöldström, Patrik The Arbitrator's Mandate: A Comparative Study of Relationships in Commercial Arbitration under the Laws of England, Germany, Sweden and Switzerland, Rättsvetenskapliga biblioteket 6, Stockholm 1998 (cited: *Schöldström*).

Scholz, Franz GmbHG, Band 3 §§ 53–85, hrsg. von Georg Bitter, Köln 2015 (cited: Scholz-*Bearbeiter*).

Schönau, Vanessa Die Anerkennung von Urt.en aus Mehrrechtsstaaten nach § 328 Abs. 1 ZPO am Beispiel der USA und Kanadas, Studien zum internationalen Privat- und Verfahrensrecht 23, Jena 2009 (cited: *Schönau*).

Schultze-Moderow, Lukas Schiedsverfahren und Insolvenz, Eine autonome Kollisions-Lösung für Schiedsgerichte mit Sitz in Deutschland, GLEISS LUTZ Schriftenreihe zum deutschen und internationalen Wirtschaftsrecht v. 59, Baden-Baden 2017 (cited: *Schultze-Moderow*).

Schütze, Rolf A. Armut im internationalen Schiedsverfahren, in: Birgit Bachmann, Stephan Breidenbach, Dagmar Coester-Waltjen et al. (Hrsg.), Grenzüberschreitungen, Beiträge zum internationalen Verfahrensrecht und zur Schiedsgerichtsbarkeit, Festschrift für Peter Schlosser zum 70. Geburtstag, Tübingen 2005, pp. 867–876 (cited: *Schütze*).

Schütze, Rolf A. Schiedsgericht und Schiedsverfahren, 6. ed., NJW Praxis 54, München 2016 (cited: *Schütze*).

Schwab, Karl Heinz Schiedsrichterernennung und Schiedsrichtervertrag, in: Gerhard Lüke, Othmar Jauernig (Hrsg.), Festschrift für Gerhard Schiedermair zum 70. Geburtstag, München 1976 (cited: *Schwab*).

Schwab, Karl Heinz/Walter, Gerhard Schiedsgerichtsbarkeit, 7. ed., München 2005 (cited: *Schwab/Walter*).

Schwander, Ivo Entscheid des Bezirksgerichts Zürich 4. August 1999, bestätigt durch das Obergericht des Kantons Zürich, 11. Oktober 1999, Anerkennung eines ausländischen Konkursdekrets. Fehlende Gegenseitigkeit im Verhältnis zu Österreich, ZIER 10 2000, 382–390 (cited: *Schwander*, ZIER 10 2000, 382).

Schwartz, Alan A Contract Theory Approach to Business Bankruptcy, Yale L.J. 71 1998, 1807–1851 (cited: *Schwartz*, Yale L.J. 71 1998, 1807).

Schwarz, Franz T./Ortner, Helmut 'Chapter III: The Arbitration Procedure – Procedural Ordre Public and the Internationalization of Public Policy in Arbitration', in:

Christian Klausegger, Peter Klein, Florian Kremslehner et al. (eds), Austrian Yearbook on International Arbitration 2008, Munich, Vienna 2008, pp. 133–220 (cited: *Schwarz/Ortner*).

Seehawer, Dominik Das Verfahren zur Vollstreckbarerklärung von Schiedssprüchen, Eine Untersuchung der verfahrensrechtlichen Probleme unter besonderer Berücksichtigung von materiellen Einwendungen und ihrer Präklusion, Schriften zum Zivilprozessrecht 45, Hamburg 2016 (cited: *Seehawer*).

Siehr, Kurt Das internationale Privatrecht der Schweiz, Zürich 2002 (cited: *Siehr*).

Solomon, Dennis Die Verbindlichkeit von Schiedssprüchen in der internationalen privaten Schiedsgerichtsbarkeit, München 2007 (cited: *Solomon*).

Staehelin, Daniel Die Anerkennung ausländischer Konkurse und Nachlassverträge in der Schweiz, (Art. 166 ff. IPRG), Basel, Univ., Diss, Schriftenreihe des Instituts für Internationales Recht und Internationale Beziehungen 45, Basel 1989 (cited: *Staehelin*).

Statistisches Bundesamt Bis 2015 beendete Insolvenz-verfahren: Gläubiger erhielten durch-schnittlich 2.2% ihrer Forderungen zurück, Pressemitteilung vom 17.05.2017, https://www.destatis.de/DE/PresseService/Presse/Pressemitteilungen/2017/05/PD17_162_52431.html;jsessionid=884E41BDBDBA38FDB7694C9E51AA433C.InternetLive2 (accessed 1 October 2018).

Statistisches Bundesamt Bis 2017 beendete Insolvenzverfahren: Gläubiger müssen auf 96.1% ihrer Forderungen verzichten, Statistisches Bundesamt, Pressemitteilung vom 27.03.2019, https://www.destatis.de/DE/Presse/Pressemitteilungen/2019/03/PD19_115_52411.html (accessed 18 November 2020).

Statistisches Bundesamt Insolvenzverfahren, Fachserie 2 Reihe 4.1, Statistisches Bundesamt, Wiesbaden, Bonn, Berlin 11.01.2019, https://www.destatis.de/DE/Publikationen/Thematisch/UnternehmenHandwerk/Insolvenzen/Insolvenzen2020410181104.pdf;jsessionid=19DDA1EB03A45FD3DD3BDB4EC3056A9F.InternetLive1?__blob=publicationFile (accessed 8 March 2019).

Statistisches Bundesamt Juli 2020: 16.7% weniger Unternehmensinsolvenzen als im Juli 2019 durch ausgesetzte Antragspflicht, Vorläufige Angaben für eröffnete Regelinsolvenzverfahren im September 2020: -34.5%, Statistisches Bundesamt, Pressemitteilung vom 08.10.2020, https://www.destatis.de/DE/Presse/Pressemitteilungen/2020/10/PD20_394_52411.html (accessed 18 November 2020).

Statistisches Bundesamt Oktober 2018: 3.5% mehr Unternehmensinsolvenzen als im Oktober 2017, Statistisches Bundesamt, Wiesbaden, Pressemitteilung vom 11.01.2019, https://www.destatis.de/DE/PresseService/Presse/Pressemitteilungen/2019/01/PD19_011_52411.html;jsessionid=19DDA1EB03A45FD3DD3BDB4EC3056A9F.InternetLive1 (accessed 18 March 2019).

Stein, Friedrich/Jonas, Martin Kommentar zur Zivilprozessordnung, Band 3 §§ 148–279, 23. ed., bearb. von Friedrich Stein, Martin Jonas, Tübingen 2016 (cited: Stein/Jonas-*Bearbeiter*).

Strauch, Martin Schutz von Schiedsvereinbarung und vereinbarter Vertraulichkeit bei Insolvenzeröffnung, Eine rechtsvergleichende Untersuchung zur Bindungswirkung, zur Insolvenzanfechtung sowie zum Schutz von Vetraulichkeit und

Geschäftsgeheimnissen, Zugl.: Leipzig, Univ., Diss., 2018, Schriften zum Zivilrecht 31, Berlin 2019 (cited: *Strauch*).

Stuber, Walter/Stuber, Adriana M.G. Brazil: Insolvency: Arbitration, JIBLR 23 2008, 116–117 (cited: *Stuber/Stuber*, JIBLR 23 2008, 116–117).

Sutcliffe, Jonathan/Rogers, James Effect of Party Insolvency on Arbitration Proceedings: Pause for Though in Testing Times, Arbitration 76 2010, 277–290 (cited: *Sutcliffe/Rogers*, Arbitration 76 2010, 277).

Százy, M. Entienne III. L'arbitrage en droit international privé, L'Institut de Droit international, Amsterdam 1957, http://www.idi-iil.org/app/uploads/2017/06/1957_amst_03_fr.pdf (accessed 16 November 2018).

Trunk, Alexander Internationales Insolvenzrecht, Tübingen 1998 (cited: *Trunk*).

Tsvengrosh, Marta Arbitration and Insolvency: Conflict of Laws Issues, Conflict of Laws in International Arbitration: Cross-Border Insolvency Cases, Saarbrücken 2011 (cited: *Tsvengrosh*).

UNCITRAL Report of the United Nations Commission on International Trade Law, Fifty-First session, United Nations, New York 2018.

UNCITRAL Status, UNCITRAL Model Law on Cross-Border Insolvency (1997), United Nations Commission for International Trade Law 2017, http://www.uncitral.org/uncitral/en/uncitral_texts/insolvency/1997Model_status.html (accessed 1 November 2017).

UNCITRAL UNCITRAL Model Law on Cross-Border Insolvency (1997), United Nations Commission for International Trade Law 2017, http://www.uncitral.org/uncitral/en/uncitral_texts/insolvency/1997Model.html (accessed 1 November 2017).

UNCITRAL UNCITRAL Model Law on Cross-Border Insolvency with Guide to Enactment and Interpretation, United Nations Commission for International Trade Law, New York 2014, http://www.uncitral.org/pdf/english/texts/insolven/1997-Model-Law-Insol-2013-Guide-Enactment-e.pdf (accessed 1 November 2017).

UNCITRAL Working Group V Recognition and Enforcement of Insolvency-Related Judgments: Draft Guide to Enactment of the Model Law, Note by the Secretariat, United Nations General Assembly, New York 23.02.2018, https://documents-dds-ny.un.org/doc/UNDOC/LTD/V18/009/44/PDF/V1800944.pdf?OpenElement (accessed 1 October 2018).

Uttamchandani, Mahesh/Muro, Sergio/Bertens, Erin The Calm Before the Storm: Early Evidence on Business Insolvency Amid COVID-19, World Bank, 2021 06/19/2021 15:49:35, https://blogs.worldbank.org/psd/calm-storm-early-evidence-business-insolvency-amid-covid-19 (accessed 19 June 2021).

van Buchem-Spapens, Anne-Marie J./Pouw, Th.A. Faillissement, surseance van betaling en schuldsanering, 8. ed., Monografieën Privaatrecht nr. 2, Deventer 2008 (cited: *van Buchem-Spapens/Pouw*).

van de Ven, F.A. The Cross-Border Insolvency Protocol: What Is It and What Is in It?: From a European Union Perspective, Master Thesis, Leiden, Leiden University, 2015.

van Genugten, M.C. Faillissement en lopende procedures (art. 27 t/m 30 Fw): Een drietal draden uit de kluwen, Een onderzoek naar de gevolgen van faillietverklaring op arbitrage- en bindend adviesprocedures, op procedures met samen hangende vorderingen en op het instellen van rechtsmiddelen, Tijdschrift voor Curatoren 2015, 192–198 (cited: *van Genugten*, Tijdschrift voor Curatoren 2015, 192).

van Mierlo, A.I.M./van de Hel-Koedoot, M. Faillissement en Arbitrage, Ondernemingsrecht 2010, 39–43 (cited: *van Mierlo/van de Hel-Koedoot*, Ondernemingsrecht 2010, 39).

Vidal, Dominique Arbitration and Insolvency Proceedings: Comments on ICC Awards and Other Recent Decisions, ICC International Court of Arbitration Bulletin 20 2009, 51–69 (cited: *Vidal*, ICC International Court of Arbitration Bulletin 20 2009, 51).

Virgós, Miguel/Garcimartín, Francisco The European Insolvency Regulation, Law and Practice, The Hague 2004 (cited: *Virgós/Garcimartín*).

Virgós, Miguel/Schmit, Etienne Report on the Convention on Insolvency Proceedings, European Union, Brussels 03.05.1996, https://globalinsolvency.com/resource-article/virgos-schmit-report-convention-insolvency-proceedings-now-regulation-insolvency (accessed 5 February 2019).

Vizepräsidentin Prof. Dr. Claudia Buch Finanzstabilitätsbericht 2020 der Deutschen Bundesbank, Rede anlässlich der Pressekonferenz zur Vorstellung des Finanzstabilitätsberichts, Deutsche Bundesbank, Frankfurt am Main, Pressemitteilung vom 13.10.2020, https://www.bundesbank.de/de/presse/reden/finanzstabilitaetsbericht-2020-der-deutschen-bundesbank-847064 (accessed 18 November 2020).

Vorburger, Simon International Arbitration and Cross-Border Insolvency: Comparative Perspectives, International Arbitration Law Library vol. 31, Alphen aan den Rijn 2014 (cited: *Vorburger*).

Vorwerk, Volkert/Wolf, Christian (eds) BeckOK ZPO, 42. ed., München 2021 (cited: Vorwerk/Wolf-*Bearbeiter*).

Vranes, Erich Lex Superior, Lex Specialis, Lex Posterior – Zur Rechtsnatur der 'Konfliktlösungsregeln', ZaöRV 2005, 391–405 (cited: *Vranes*, ZaöRV 2005, 391).

Wagner, Gerhard Impecunious Parties and Arbitration Agreements, SchiedsVZ 2003, 206–218 (cited: *Wagner*, SchiedsVZ 2003206).

Wagner, Gerhard Insolvenz und Schiedsgerichtverfahren, KTS 2010, 39–67 (cited: *Wagner*, KTS 2010, 39).

Wagner, Philipp Insolvency and Arbitration: A Pleading for International Insolvency Law, Disp. Resol. Int'l 5 2011, 189–201 (cited: *Wagner*, Disp. Resol. Int'l 5 2011, 189).

Wagner, Philipp K. Abstimmungsfragen zwischen Internationalem Insolvenzrecht und Internationaler Schiedsgerichtsbarkeit, Unter besonderer Berücksichtigung der Anerkennung grenzüberschreitender Insolvenzen durch Schiedsgerichte, Zugl.: Rostock, Univ., Diss., 2007, Schriftenreihe der August Maria Berges Stiftung für Arbitrales Recht 21, Frankfurt, M. 2008 (cited: *Wagner*).

Wagner, Philipp K. Die insolvente Partei im Schiedsverfahren – eine Herausforderung für alle Beteiligten, GWR 2010, 129–132 (cited: *Wagner*, GWR 2010, 129).

Wagner, Philipp K. Feststellung der Insolvenzforderung im Zahlungsschiedsspruch, GWR 2009, 44–45 (cited: *Wagner*, GWR 2009, 44).

Wagner, Philipp K. Feststellung der Insolvenzforderung im Zahlungsschiedsspruch, GWR 2010, 129–132 (cited: *Wagner*, GWR 2010, 129).

Wellensiek, Tobias § 13 Der Bauvertrag in der Insolvenz, in: Gerd Motzke, Günter Bauer, Thomas M.A. Seewald et al. (Hrsg.), Prozesse in Bausachen, Privates Baurecht, Architektenrecht, 3. Auflage, NomosProzessHandbuch, Baden-Baden 2018 (cited: *Wellensiek*).

Wessels, Bob International insolvency law, 3. ed., Insolvency law 10, Deventer 2012 (cited: *Wessels*).

Wessels, Bob International Insolvency Law Part II: European Insolvency Law, 4th ed., Insolventierecht X, Deventer 2017 (cited: *Wessels*).

Wessels, Bob/Boon, Gert-Jan Cross-Border Insolvency Law, International Instruments and Commentary, Alphen aan den Rijn 2015 (cited: *Wessels/Boon*).

Westbrook, Jay L. Choice of Avoidance Law in Global Insolvencies, Brook. J.Int'l L 17 1991, 499–538 (cited: *Westbrook*, Brook. J.Int'l L 17 1991, 499–538).

Wieczorek, Bernhard Zivilprozessordnung und Nebengesetze, Großkommentar, Elfter Band §§ 916–1066, 4. ed., hrsg. von Rolf A. Schütze, Berlin 2014 (cited: Wieczorek-*Bearbeiter*).

Wilmowsky, Peter von Choice of Law in International Insolvencies: A Proposal for Reform, in: Jürgen Basedow, Toshiyuki Kono (eds), Legal Aspects of Globalization, The Hague, London 2000, pp. 197–212 (cited: *Wilmowsky*).

Wolaver, Earl S. The Historical Background of Commercial Arbitration, University of Pennsylvania Law Review 1934, 132–146 (cited: *Wolaver*, University of Pennsylvania Law Review 1934, 132).

Wolff, Reinmar Chapter 18, Part XII: Rights and Duties of Arbitrators, in: Manuel Arroyo (ed.), Arbitration in Switzerland: The Practitioner's Guide, 2d ed., Alphen aan den Rijn 2018, pp. 2723–2741 (cited: *Wolff*).

Wolff, Reinmar Party Autonomy to Agree on Non-final Arbitration?, ASA Bull. 26 2008, 626–641 (cited: *Wolff*, ASA Bull. 26 2008, 626).

Wolff, Reinmar (ed.) New York Convention, Convention on the Recognition and Enforcement of Foreign Arbitral Awards of 10 June 1958: Commentary, München, Oxford, Baden-Baden 2012 (cited: Wolff-*Bearbeiter*).

Wong, Venus, Valentina/Siwy, Alfred Recalcitrant Parties and the Tribunal's Power to Order Cost Advance Payments, in: Christian Klausegger, Peter Klein, Florian Kremslehner et al. (eds), Austrian Yearbook on International Arbitration 2014, Munich, Vienna 2014, pp. 201–221 (cited: *Wong, Venus, Valentina/Siwy*).

Yang, Ge Insolvency Proceedings and Their Effect on International Commercial Arbitration, LLM Thesis, Ghent, University of Ghent, 2012.

Yu, Hong-lin A Theoretical Overview of the Foundations of International Commercial Arbitration, Contemp. Asia Arb. J. 1 2008, 255–286 (cited: *Yu*, Contemp. Asia Arb. J. 2008, 255).

Zivilprozessordnung, Mit FamFG (Paragraphen 1–185, 200–270, 433–484) und Gerichtsverfassungsgesetz, den Einführungsgesetzen, mit Internationalem Zivilprozessrecht, EU-Verordnungen, Kostenanmerkungen: Kommentar, 31. ed., hrsg. von Richard Zöller 2016 (cited: Zöller-*Bearbeiter*).

Zivilprozessordnung, Familienverfahren, Gerichtsverfassung, Europäisches Verfahrensrecht: Handkommentar, 9. ed., hrsg. von Ingo Saenger, Baden-Baden 2021 (cited: Hk-ZPO-*Bearbeiter*).

Zivilprozessordnung, Mit Gerichtsverfassungsgesetz: Kommentar, 18. ed., hrsg. von Hans-Joachim Musielak, Wolfgang Voit, München 2021 (cited: Musielak/Voit-*Bearbeiter*).

Zöller, Richard Zivilprozessordnung, 32. ed., hrsg. von Richard Zöller, Christoph Althammer, Christian Feskorn u.a., Köln, Saarbrücken 2018 (cited: Zöller-*Bearbeiter*).

Zumbro, Paul H. Cross-Border Insolvencies and International Protocols: An Imperfect but Effective Tool, Business Law International 11 2010, 157–169 (cited: *Zumbro*, Business Law International 11 2010, 157).

Index

A

Administrator, the insolvency
  power to enter into arbitration agreements, 57–58
  standing in arbitration proceedings, 53–57
Annulment
  awards in, 136–138
  Conflict-of-Laws
    EIR, 197
    German Autonomous international insolvency law, 208
Applicable Law
  arbitration agreement
    competence to enter into, 233–234
    validity and binding power, 229–233
  arbitration proceedings, 237–240
  Arbitrator's contract, 246–247
  competence, 234–237
  dispute, the, 244–246
  EIR, 229
  estate, the, 243–244
  objective arbitrability, 240–243
  standing, 234–237
Arbitrability
  in Germany, 38–40
    of Insolvency Disputes, 40–42
  of Insolvency Disputes, 42–45
  objective and subjective, 38
  and Public Policy, 37–38
Arbitration
  in Germany
    arbitration agreement, 26–28
    New York Convention, 24–26
    UNCITRAL Model Law, 24
  nature of, 28–29
Arbitration Agreement
  binding power of, 89–91
  dissolve, possibility to, 94–101
    expiration of mandates, 96
    pre-insolvency transactions, 96–99
    right to choose, 94–96
  incapability to perform, 91–94
  nature of, 86–88
  objecting creditors, 108–109
  rights of separation and separate satisfaction, 103
  scope of, 101–109
  termination for compelling reason, 99
  validity of, 88–89
Arbitration theory
  autonomous theory, 32
  contractual theory and delocalisation, 30–31
  hybrid theory, 31
  jurisdictional theory, 29–30
Arbitrator's agreement, 114–119
Arbitrator's Contract
  dissolve, possibility to, 114–120
  nature of, 111–113
Autonomous theory, 32
Award
  effect of insolvency on

additional award proceedings, 138–141
annulment proceedings, 136–138
correction proceedings, 138–141
enforced, 141–142
enforcement proceedings, 130–136
executed awards, 142
execution proceedings, 142
in favour of insolvency debtor, 144–145
Insolvency Proceedings, 123–124
Interpretation proceedings, 138–141
Non-enforced Pre-insolvency, 125–130
Non-enforcement in, 137–138
Post-insolvency, 121–122
status of, 125–127

B

Background, theoretical, 7–8, 32–33
Binding Power of Insolvency
localised/delocalised arbitration, 50–51
performance of contract/part of judicial order, 51–53
seat jurisdiction and arbitration, 47–50

C

Characterisation and Categorisation of insolvency-related issues, 226–228
Choice of Arbitrator, 77–78
Claim Registration, 72–74
Conflict-of-Laws
arbitral tribunal
autonomous approach, 214–219
efficiency and effectiveness, 225
enforceability and non-annulment, 219–221
legal certainty, 221–223
legitimate expectations, 221–223
neutrality, 224–225
predictability, 221–223
traditional approach, 212–214
uniformity of decisions, 223–224
in court, 182–183
EIR
applicable law to, 186–198
coordination and material norms, 186
rules, 183–186
German autonomous international insolvency law
applicable law to, 201–210
coordination and material norms, 201
rules, 199–201
Considerations
definitions of, 252
general principle
applicable law to, 262–264
arbitrability of, 253–254
arbitration agreement, 254–255
dissolution, 260–261
impecuniosity and costs, 261–262
object of proceedings, 259–260
resumption of proceedings, 258–259
role and position of insolvency practitioner, 255–257
role of insolvency in arbitration, 252–253
suspension of proceedings, 257–258
relevance and application, 250–251
Contesting
Claims in insolvency, 106–107, 117–119
Pre-insolvency transactions, 96–99
Contractual theory, 30–31

D

Delocalisation, 30–31
Delocalised arbitration, 30–31
Dissolution
of employment contracts, 115–116
of the insolvent, 78–84
of mandates, 116–117

of service contracts, 115–116

I

Impecuniosity, 91–94
Inability to perform the arbitration agreement, 91–94
Insolvency
  in Germany
    European insolvencies, 10–13
    international insolvencies, 15
    national insolvency framework, 8–10
  UNCITRAL Model Law
    Cross-Border Insolvency, 13–14
    Insolvency-Related Judgments, 14–15
  verification, 107–108
International Insolvency Theory
  German approach, 19–20
  legal order, 15–16
  practical middle ground, 18–19
  territorialism, 17
  universalism, 17–18

L

Liabilities of the estate, 74–75

O

Object of the proceedings, 72–75
Objecting creditor, 108–109
Ordre public, *see public policy*

P

Public policy, 37–38

R

Recognition
  in arbitration, 166–176
  concepts of, 151–156
  European Insolvency Regulation (EIR), 157–161
  German arbitral tribunals, 176–182
  German insolvency code, 161–166
  UNCITRAL Model Law on Cross-Border Insolvency, 156–157
Resumption of Proceedings
  § 180(1) and 180(2)
    application of § 180(2) InsO to Arbitration, 65–66
    functioning of, 67–69
    InsO and arbitration, 69–72

S

Scope of the arbitration proceedings
  Preliminary questions, 75–77
Stay of Proceedings
  analogous application, 63–65
  applicability to arbitration, 60–61
  factual stay of proceedings, 61–63
  ZPO, 60

www.ingramcontent.com/pod-product-compliance
Lightning Source LLC
LaVergne TN
LVHW020643300926
849161LV00004B/787